Essentials of Elementary Social Studies

Essentials of Elementary Social Studies is a teacher friendly text that provides comprehensive treatment of classroom planning, instruction, and strategies. Praised for its dynamic approach and its writing style that is conversational, personal, and professional, this text enables and encourages teachers to effectively teach elementary social studies using creative and active learning strategies.

This sixth edition has been refined with new and relevant topics and strategies needed for effectively teaching elementary social studies. A few of the new features include:

- An expanded chapter on the decision-making process in elementary social studies. This chapter provides additional discussion about the importance of helping young learners better understand the decision-making process and offers strategies for helping teachers make connections between choices, values, character development, and social justice.
- An updated chapter on technology designed to better prepare elementary teachers to effectively incorporate technology into social studies instruction. Attention is given to virtual teaching and learning, media literacy, teaching with film, and numerous other ways to improve teaching and learning in the digital age.
- Updated further readings and helpful resources for all chapters to include supplemental digital and video sources related to various topics throughout the chapter.
- New "Checking for Understanding" section at the end of each chapter that focuses on comprehension, application, and reflection on key concepts throughout the chapters.
- An updated chapter on lesson plans, in keeping with the book's emphasis on planning and teaching. This chapter is designed to provide elementary social studies teachers with new classroom-tested lesson plans and includes two classroom-tested lessons for each grade level (K–6).

William B. Russell III is Professor of Social Science Education at the University of Central Florida, Orlando.

Stewart Waters is Associate Professor of Social Science Education at the University of Tennessee, Knoxville.

Essentials of Elementary Social Studies

6th Edition

William B. Russell III
and Stewart Waters

Routledge
Taylor & Francis Group

NEW YORK AND LONDON

Sixth edition published 2022
by Routledge
605 Third Avenue, New York, NY 10158

and by Routledge
2 Park Square, Milton Park, Abingdon, Oxon, OX14 4RN

Routledge is an imprint of the Taylor & Francis Group, an informa business

First edition published by Pearson Education, Inc 1994
Fifth edition published by Routledge 2018

Library of Congress Cataloging-in-Publication Data
Names: Russell, William B., author. | Waters, Stewart, author.
Title: Essentials of elementary social studies / William B. Russell III,
    Stewart Waters.
Description: Sixth edition. | New York, NY : Routledge, 2022. |
    Includes bibliographical references and index.
Identifiers: LCCN 2021007946 (print) | LCCN 2021007947
    (ebook) | ISBN 9780367643300 (hardback) | ISBN
    9780367643317 (paperback) | ISBN 9781003123934 (ebook)
Subjects: LCSH: Social sciences—Study and teaching
    (Elementary)—United States.
Classification: LCC LB1584 .T87 2022 (print) | LCC LB1584
    (ebook) | DDC 372.83—dc23
LC record available at https://lccn.loc.gov/2021007946
LC ebook record available at https://lccn.loc.gov/2021007947

ISBN: 978-0-367-64330-0 (hbk)
ISBN: 978-0-367-64331-7 (pbk)
ISBN: 978-1-003-12393-4 (ebk)

Typeset in Bembo
by Apex CoVantage, LLC

Contents

Figures

Tables

Preface to the Sixth Edition

Welcome to the sixth edition of *Essentials of Elementary Social Studies*. This book is intended for pre-service and in-service social studies teachers and for social studies teacher educators. The book is designed to accomplish one primary goal. We seek to help elementary teachers develop the knowledge and skills necessary to effectively teach elementary students to become effective problem-solving citizens. This text offers a problem-solving approach to elementary social studies. Included in the text are various examples of lesson plans and effective teaching methodologies.

The text includes 12 chapters, and each chapter includes a focus activity to prepare readers for the chapter content; questions for checking understanding, which can be used to assess the reader's understanding of the chapter content; an extension activity for extending the learning experience beyond the reading of the text; and "helpful resources" and "further readings" at the end of each chapter to provide readers with additional readings and information for individuals interested in furthering their knowledge base.

This sixth edition has been refined with new and relevant topics and strategies needed for effectively teaching elementary social studies. A few of the new features include:

- An expanded chapter on the decision-making process in elementary social studies. This chapter provides additional discussion about the importance of helping young learners better understand the decision-making process and offers strategies for helping teachers make connections between choices, values, character development, and social justice.
- An updated chapter on technology designed to better prepare elementary teachers to effectively incorporate technology into social studies instruction. Attention is given to virtual teaching and learning, media literacy, teaching with film, and numerous other ways to improve teaching and learning in the digital age.
- Updated further readings and helpful resources for all chapters to include supplemental digital and video sources related to various topics throughout the chapter.
- Added a "Checking for Understanding" section at the end of each chapter that focuses on comprehension, application, and reflection on key concepts throughout the chapters.
- An updated chapter on lesson plans, in keeping with the book's emphasis on planning and teaching. This chapter is designed to provide elementary social studies teachers with new classroom-tested lesson plans and includes two classroom-tested lessons for each grade level (K–6).

Many thanks to the countless students, teachers, and professors who have used the previous editions and who have provided valuable feedback, which has allowed us to improve the text. Additionally, the authors would like to thank our respective families and friends for support and encouragement.

William B. Russell III
University of Central Florida
Stewart Waters
University of Tennessee

Contemporary Elementary Social Studies

Chapter 1

▶ LOOKING AHEAD

The aim of this chapter is twofold: (1) to help you see why social studies is needed in the elementary school and (2) to suggest an overall approach to elementary social studies curriculum and teaching of the curriculum. To achieve these goals, you need to understand what social studies is and how it springs out of a need in society.

To understand social studies, you must first understand the purpose that it serves in the total school curriculum. That purpose, stated in simple form, is to develop good citizens for the democratic society in which we live. Becoming a good citizen is sometimes referred to as developing civic virtue, and there is, of course, a wide interpretation of exactly what either term really means. Even so, we can say that we want students to feel positive about themselves and have a desire to be positively contributing members of the various communities of which they are a part. It also means that students will develop the desire and the ability to be economically independent, to be informed about and involved in the decision making that goes on in their communities, and to be aware of and knowledgeable about the world around them. We want students to be free from prejudice and to be fair minded in dealing with others, to believe in a system of justice and law, to take leadership roles, and to give reasoned and fair support for legitimately appointed or elected leaders.

Because society is changing rapidly, teaching social studies is even more of a challenge today than it was in the past. Teachers really need to think about different approaches to teaching social studies. They need to work more effectively with students who have different cultural backgrounds. They need to teach in ways that involve active learning and to find approaches that focus on solving problems. The final section of this chapter addresses the goals of social studies as perceived by different groups. Social studies itself is a product of the changing society, prevailing approaches to its teaching, and the varying conceptions that social studies teachers have of its goals.

1

CAN YOU? DO YOU?

Can you . . .

- Describe how the field of social studies has changed since you were in elementary school?
- Explain how social studies has remained the same?
- Explain the goals of social studies?

Do you . . .

- Have an understanding of a problems approach to teaching social studies?
- Have an idea of what a teacher needs to know about social studies?
- Think of social studies simply as history and/or geography?

FOCUS ACTIVITY

Before reading this chapter, try the following focus activity.

Take a scrap piece of paper and draw a picture of social studies. Be sure to use images and not words. Share your drawings with others. Discuss the details of the drawings. Compare drawings for substance with others. Does your drawing share common themes/elements with others'? If so, what are the themes/elements?

▶ THE GOALS OF SOCIAL STUDIES

What do you need to know about social studies? The answer probably seems to be more than you do know or can learn. It is certainly more than you will be able to get from any textbook. As a teacher, you owe it to the generations of students that you teach to become mindfully, curiously, purposefully alive to them, to their world, to social studies as a thick endless blanket of stories about people and events, and to the values and rules needed for people to live together.

Social studies in the elementary school has most often been regarded as a subject that should be taught – but only if time allows. Priority time in the school day, of course, is given to the basic skill areas of reading, mathematics, and language. It has not been that social studies is considered unimportant, but that the basic skill areas are seen by society, by administrators, and by elementary teachers as "fundamentals" that have to be learned first. Important as language and mathematics skills may be, they are taught only because the students will need them to live in the social world.

The "back to basics" years of the 1970s and early 1980s had a strong adverse influence on elementary social studies. Separate studies by Gross (1977) and Hahn (1977) affirmed that social studies was disappearing in the early grades. According to research, this trend continues in today's twenty-first-century classrooms (Barton, 2011; Bisland, 2011; Heafner & Fitchett, 2012; Russell, 2009). Some researchers suggest that social studies is embedded in curriculum and is taught as frequently now as in the past (Anderson, 2009; Holloway & Chiodo, 2009). This curriculum involves an emphasis on reading stories, poems, and plays, all of which have extensive social studies content. Then, too, the school day itself consists of a rich and complex series of social situations and problems, ranging from recess to lunch to the school bus.

Educators and politicians may soon have to wake up to the fact that effective social studies curriculum is basic and fundamental in the earliest schooling. Educational reform has not had any real impact on achievement in the basic skills areas, and schools have about run out of time to take from other content areas or activities during the school day. There simply should be more attention given to help students learn about themselves and their place in and responsibility to society. The National Council for the Social Studies Task Force on Early Childhood/Elementary Social Studies (2009) stated:

> The purpose of elementary school social studies is to enable students to understand, participate in, and make informed decisions about their world. Social studies content allows young learners to explain relationships with other people, to institutions, and to the environment, and equips them with knowledge and understanding of the past. It provides them with skills for productive problem solving and decision making as well as for assessing issues and making thoughtful value judgments. Above all, it integrates these skills and understandings into a framework for responsible citizen participation locally, nationally, and globally. The teaching and learning processes within social studies are uniquely organized to develop these capacities, beginning with the youngest learners in our schools.

The Task Force goes on to say that the teaching and learning of social studies "in the elementary classroom should be meaningful, integrative, value-based, challenging, and active. These qualities of powerful social studies learning are foundational to the development of students' knowledge, skills, and dispositions as participating citizens."

FYI: "Decision making is the heart of social studies instruction" (Shirley Engle, 1960).

Barth (1993) has said that one of our most basic beliefs is that "Social Studies is citizenship education." Hartoonan (1993) adds that "our work should be to illuminate the essential connection between social studies learning and democratic values" and thus be a "liberating force in the lives of citizens" (p. 59). Put another way, the two primary jobs of schools are to help society by producing effective, contributing citizens and to help the students lead happy lives in which they are enabled to achieve their potential. That is what social studies is all about and why social studies is so needed in the elementary school.

Though social studies educators disagree as to priorities, the following list identifies those aims that are most often associated with social studies programs:

- Preparing responsible citizens for the nation, the state, and the local area.
- Preparing students who have the knowledge and skills in social studies needed for college.
- Developing awareness and understanding of contemporary social issues.
- Developing healthy self-concepts.
- Teaching the methods of social scientists.
- Motivating students to want to learn about the social studies.

FYI: Democratic decision making is considered a foundation of the C3 framework.

- Developing the ability to solve problems and make decisions.
- Developing culturally responsive "global" citizens.

Whatever we do as teachers is certainly done for the present, but it has to be done with an eye to the future.

In trying to help you become good elementary social studies teachers, or good teachers of anything for that matter, it is important to get you to look at what happens if you succeed as teachers. The students you teach will, in due course, become adults themselves. They will obviously be living in a different kind of society, one that teachers must try to anticipate and prepare them for. However, beyond that, the kind of impact that teachers will have on students and the kind of people they become are critical outcomes of education. The following are just a few of the areas in which teachers of elementary social studies will have had an impact when their students become adults:

- The jobs they have and the way they do their jobs.
- The way they feel about themselves.
- The way they handle responsibility.
- The way they treat other people.
- How they meet and resolve problems and difficulties.
- Their motivation and overall attitudes.
- What they value and how they treat the things they value.
- How they relate to their heritage.
- How they relate to their environment.
- How they relate to and deal with people of other cultures, nationalities, and ethnic groups.

In each of these and in other areas in which teachers influence students, it is safe to say that most of us would happily accept a broad variety of outcomes and still feel that we had made a positive impact in a student's life. The question is, "Just how much in each area can we expect of ourselves?"

That is not a question that can be left unanswered. A good analogy is putting together a jigsaw puzzle. It is always easier to do a puzzle with a picture of what it is going to look like when complete. The same holds true for teaching. From an attitudinal standpoint, it is useful to envision students ten or fifteen years into the future and imagine them in the most positive light.

Goals and objectives should be the first and most important concerns of any teacher, especially any elementary social studies teacher. They complement one another. Goals are distant, immeasurable, and even unattainable. They give direction to our efforts, and, if we are goal oriented and goal driven, we constantly work toward them yet never reach a point when they are achieved. How can one reach the goal of becoming an effective problem solver, for example, or the even broader goal of being a good citizen? The essence of goals is that they describe the person we are constantly in the process of becoming (Moore et al., 1989).

Objectives, on the other hand, are short term, attainable, often measurable, and very specific. We can know when we achieve them, so they become for us milestones and markers of our progress. Goals determine the directions we want to go, but the accomplishment of objectives lets us know that we are getting there.

In education, we generally begin planning by defining our goals. Once goals are set, we try to describe the specific teaching and learning outcomes (objectives) for short periods of instruction that will move students toward the goals. Goals without objectives remain as only dreams. Objectives without relationship to goals are purposeless. Objectives for social studies tend to be decided based on the specific content being taught and the group to which it is being taught. The broadest goals for the field have been centrally determined and defined in the United States by various groups, given authority by still-larger organizations. Regardless of the group, throughout this century and the next, social studies has and will be invariably linked to goals of citizenship education. The frameworks developed in the reports of the various commissions, task forces, and committees have served as models for textbook curricula and for those developed for state and local school districts. Reports impacting elementary school social studies in the twenty-first century include the NCSS Task Force on Creating Effective Citizens (2001), the National Council for the Social Studies Task Force on Early Childhood/Elementary Social Studies (2009), and the NCSS Task Force on Early Childhood/Elementary Social Studies (2001).

The introductory statement of the goals section of the report of the National Council for the Social Studies (NCSS) Task Force on Creating Effective Citizens (2001) set a problem-solving focus for the social studies and emphasized thinking skills. The Task Force stated the students should have the skills necessary to "solve real problems in their school, the community, our nation, and the world." Additionally, effective citizens should use "effective decision-making and problem-solving skills in public and private life." The responsibility of social studies is to prepare young people to identify, understand, and work to solve the problems of an interdependent world.

The NCSS Task Force on Early Childhood/Elementary Social Studies (2009) echoed that teaching and learning elementary social studies should be "meaningful, integrative, value-based, challenging, and active." Additionally, critical thinking, problem solving, and the development of learning skills and positive attitudes toward self and others were given priority.

The Task Force of the National Commission on the Social Studies was funded by the Carnegie Foundation, the Rockefeller Foundation, the MacArthur Foundation, and the National Geographic Society. It enjoyed the sponsorship of the National Council for the Social Studies and the American Historical Association. Over two years in preparation, the Task Force's report, titled *Charting a Course: Social Studies for the 21st Century* (1989), formulated the following goals that the social studies curriculum should enable students to develop:

1. Civic responsibility and active civic participation.
2. Perspectives on their own life experiences so they see themselves as part of the larger human adventure in time and place.
3. A critical understanding of the history, geography, economic, political, social institutions, traditions, and values of the United States, as expressed in both their unity and diversity.
4. An understanding of other peoples and of the unity and diversity of world history, geography, traditions, and values.
5. Critical attitudes and analytical perspectives appropriate to the analysis of the human condition.

▶ A PROBLEMS APPROACH TO SOCIAL STUDIES

There is no doubt about it: elementary social studies must be different in today's society from what it was before. Society has changed. Schools have changed. Students' lives keep changing. Even the problems that students face are different. For example, there has been a constant increase in the number of students involved in child abuse, divorce, domestic violence, cyberbullying, gangs, substance abuse, single-parent homes, and crime. Schools are preparing students for an ever and rapidly changing world with new and unique demands for citizens. There have also been changes that influence students' present and future lives in other ways. There has been a dynamic, complex revolution in technology, information, and communication. There have been major shifts in society, including sweeping changes related to gender roles and ethnic and cultural relationships. There have also been major changes in the governmental and economic make-up of the United States and the world.

In a world in which change has become the norm and we have to constantly face dilemmas for which there are no precedents, social studies is needed more than ever to help students learn to deal with problems. Teachers need to take a problems approach. Though the word "problem" may be defined in many ways, we are going to define it as "any task or situation for which a solution is required or desired and for which a method of solution is not provided or immediately apparent." Problem solving is more than the situation itself. Often, problems involve moral dilemmas; persisting issues; and/or difficulties, dangers, or curiosities for which there are no verifiable solutions. Problems require that existing knowledge be retrieved and used to resolve new or different difficulties. Most importantly, intrinsic to problem solving is the ability to deal with failure and with the inability to identify easy or quick solutions in constructive ways.

Problem solving is the most pervasive of skills from a curricular standpoint. It is the one skill that is most needed throughout life. Almost all the situations we face as a society and nearly all the personal events demanding decisions may be best described as problems. If students (and teachers) can develop the requisite mindset, attitudes, and skills of problem solvers, they will be equipped to meet the needs of the future. If they do not, their education becomes obsolete almost before it is complete. Problem solving is the essential skill for each of the disciplines. That is, a person with a problem-solving mindset will be a more successful student. This is an ability that teachers need to emphasize if every student is to become an independent learner. Problem solving is also the essential survival skill for school. Each teacher, each class, each student, each school day, each assignment presents a unique intricacy of circumstances and demands. It would not be an overstatement to say that the essential life role is problem solving.

▶ PROBLEMS APPROACH: K–THIRD GRADE CLASSROOM

A teacher who uses the problems approach is going to be constantly asking questions, trying to arouse curiosity, and having the students make decisions. The teacher will be encouraging students' questions and helping them find ways of seeking answers. The entire environment of the classroom becomes fixed on learning how to learn. Students' awareness of problems and their ability to generate alternative solutions are heightened in this kind of environment. Perhaps the best way to look at how the problems approach works is to look at how one teacher used this approach as she entered a study of community.

▶ CLASSROOM EPISODE #1

The teacher started her first graders on their study of the community by reading Dr. Seuss's *Horton Hears a Who* (Geisel, 1954). She soon had them thinking and talking about the perils and dangers faced by the people of the tiny world in the story. The point of the story, of course, is that everybody in a community needs to work together to solve the problems, and these students thought themselves very clever when they figured it out.

The teacher would not let them rest on that, though. Soon she had them talking about how to recognize problems and different ways that the "Whos" could have solved their problem. One of the questions that she asked was how different television characters might have solved the problem. (Both cartoon characters and prime-time heroes were suggested.) She also got them thinking about how important they were in their own community and how they could not help unless they knew more about their community and its own particular dangers and problems.

The next day, the teacher took the students on a walking field trip of their community. They went only a few blocks, but as they went, they began looking for different problems in their own community. Sometimes the teacher had to make suggestions and probe with questions, but always, she let the students decide if something was a problem. When they got back to the classroom, they began making a list of the problems they had seen. The list included some things that were dangers and some others that just seemed to give people difficulties. Different types of garbage and litter were among the most common things that the students noticed, but the teacher tried to shift their attention to other kinds of problems. This all started to sound somewhat negative, so they also started making a list of the good things they knew about or had seen in their community.

That day the students went home with the assignment of asking their parents and others about problems in their community as well as what the adults liked about the community. The next day, in school, the students added to their lists, taking a little time to talk about the ideas that had been brought in. The teacher put all the ideas on large pieces of paper, but she left lots of room. When the list was finished, she passed out scissors and old magazines and newspapers. The students worked in pairs, each pair trying to find a picture that showed one of the ideas. If they could not find a magazine picture that they thought was appropriate, the teacher encouraged the students to draw a picture. The pictures later helped serve as reminders to these mostly non-reading students of what each sentence said.

Later, the students built a box community on a large table. They got to decide what went into a community and to design their own buildings. The teacher and a parent volunteer helped them label buildings. One of the questions they had been asking was, "Why is there so much litter in the community?" To help them understand, the teacher covered the completed scene with a tablecloth. Each day for a week, every child put a single small piece of scrap paper under the tablecloth. When they removed the cover, everyone was surprised at how much trash had accumulated on the streets of their community.

The box community was used to study other community problems as well. The students had tried to follow the layout of their own community in designing it. Therefore, they were able to look at such problems as traffic congestion and sidewalk hazards through their own model.

Soon the students decided that they needed a map of the community, and they began making one. The teacher started them thinking about the problems of making a map: for example, things like accuracy, relative size, symbols, and orientation.

There was a natural flow in every transition. Each situation led to a new set of questions and curiosities. Though there were some places where some students seemed to be lost for a few minutes, most often due to a lack of verbal memory, the presence of the problems was so pervasive that attention was never lost for long.

▶ PROBLEMS APPROACH: FOURTH–SIXTH GRADE CLASSROOM

In grades four through six, the focus is shifting toward independence. Students can deal with problems and content that are much more distant and removed from their own experience. These students need to be more involved in the systematic development of questions and problems. Since fourth-through-sixth-grade students have more skills, knowledge, and experience, they can be involved in a greater variety of research activities. They are more peer oriented and less teacher oriented, so group problem solving can be structured into the activities. The emphasis remains on an environment where curiosity is encouraged and stimulated. The teacher in such an environment is going to be constantly leading students to events and ideas that will set them thinking. The students in this setting are going to be "on the learn."

▶ CLASSROOM EPISODE #2

Looking again at a particular classroom, this time we will focus on a fifth-grade teacher who has launched into a study of the medieval period in European history. The teacher began by trying to get the students to systematically examine their existing concepts of the period. They talked about movies and television programs that they had seen as well as some things that had been picked up from cartoons, comic books, and games. Some of the students also had some knowledge that came from children's literature. There was as much, if not more, fantasy as reality in what they thought they knew about the period.

At about this time, the class was surprised by a visit from two people in medieval clothing. One of these men told the students that he was an architect and that he was involved in designing and building castles. The other man said that he was a knight. The men described a situation they were involved in on the coast of England near the Welsh border. King Edward had sent them there to build a castle. Now they had to decide exactly where to build it, but it was not very easy. While the men were in the classroom, they talked with the students about the reasons for castle building, about all the problems that might be involved, and about the rudiments of castle defense.

By the time the men left, an idea had evolved. Soon the students had developed a hypothetical map of what the region would be like. At the teacher's insistence, the map was quite large. In addition, the students were urged to orient their map to some real area on the English coast. The map itself was not altogether fiction because the students did some reading about the geography of the area. The completed map showed a seacoast, the Welsh border, three villages for which the students made up names, and a monastery. It also showed a river, some fens or swampy land, a forest area, and a few roads. Other features were added as the students continued to read and discuss. They learned something about feudal land division and tried to reflect it in the map. Other landmarks, including a ruined castle and some churches, were added. The villages themselves began to take on detail and show differences in size and complexity. As the students researched, they decided that there had to be a feudal manor or two in the area with fortifications; these were added.

The people came last. The students' research began to reveal the different roles and social statuses that the various people at the monastery and in the villages would have had in all likelihood. The class developed a set of characters, each of whom they tried to describe in some detail. They gave them names and described where they lived, what they did and how they did it, how they dressed, and what their lives were like. They were particularly fascinated by the diet of the common people during this period. The study of daily life, clothing, and customs evolved through group work over about a week.

The students then drew names so that each could "become" one of the characters. Once more in groups, this time according to where they "lived," they continued researching their characters. The groups also began talking about where they wanted the king's castle to be built. They considered the dangers and fears that faced the lives of the people of this period.

Nearly three weeks after their first visit, the two medieval men returned. For this visit, the students had planned and worn costumes of their own, and the questions were almost unstoppable. The students eagerly told the visitors what they had been doing. Then each group made a presentation in which they introduced themselves in their medieval roles. The groups each made a case for one site for the king's castle. Some of the groups, especially the one representing the monastery, did not want the castle built right in their area. Others had noticed not only the protection that the castle offered, but also the commercial possibilities that a garrison of soldiers would have for the nearest town. When the groups were finished, the architect and the knight explained where they thought the king's castle should be built. Most importantly, they showed that they had listened to the students' reasoning as they presented their case.

This was the beginning rather than the end. The study went on into the actual building of the castle and to several follow-up activities. However, this beginning had laid a foundation of interest and reason for research, on which the teacher could continue to build. The students were exploring nearly every major theme and concept of medieval life as they created scenarios and solved problems as they arose.

► LOOKING BACK

Social studies throughout the last half of the twentieth century was reformist in nature and will continue to be throughout the twenty-first century; that is, the curriculum has been and will be in flux. This is due, in part, to the constant changes in the social world.

The one educational need that remains constant in a world of change is that students need to learn how to solve problems. When teachers take a problems approach in social studies, they work at enabling students to deal with situations in which their experience and knowledge offer no ready answers. Problem solving is, perhaps, the most pervasive of all skills.

Despite growing concern that social studies may be disappearing from elementary classrooms, two main jobs of the school continue. Those jobs are producing effective, contributing citizens and helping students lead fulfilling lives. Social studies has a variety of purposes that relate to these two jobs, which include preparing students to be responsible, to be aware of contemporary issues, and to have a world vision. In some cases, elementary social studies teachers should be concerned about preparing students for college and even for careers in the social sciences. If students are to be successful, teachers must help them develop both the love of learning and the ability to solve problems.

Goals and objectives should be major concerns of teachers of social studies. Goals are distant and unattainable, but they give direction to teaching. Objectives, on the other hand, are short term and obtainable. Objectives are the building blocks toward goals.

The National Council for the Social Studies, as the organization of teachers most concerned with social education, has constantly examined and reexamined the goals of the social studies. Recent task forces of that organization have particularly emphasized problem solving and thinking skills.

EXTENSION ACTIVITY

SCENARIO

You are searching for an elementary teaching position in your hometown school district, which is a very difficult district to "get your foot in the door." Just as you are losing hope, you receive a phone call from Dr. Russell, the principal of Yourtown Elementary School (YES). Dr. Russell invites you for an interview. During your interview, an enthusiastic committee member asks you, "What do you believe to be the goals and purpose of social studies?" Your response could be the difference between being offered the elementary teaching position and not being offered it.

TASK

For this activity, write down how you would answer the enthusiastic committee member. Be sure to clearly discuss the goals and purpose of social studies.

CHECKING FOR UNDERSTANDING

1. How would you characterize the problems approach to social studies?
2. Why was the map-creation exercise so critical in the class where they were studying medieval history?
3. In what areas are elementary social studies teachers going to have an impact?
4. In what ways did the NCSS task force groups referred to in the chapter stress the role of thinking skills in social studies?

▶ HELPFUL RESOURCES

Watch the first half of this video to see an overview of why social studies is important in elementary schools:
www.teachingchannel.org/videos/tch-presents-social-studies-essentials
Watch this video of NCSS executive director Susan Griffin defining social studies and the connection with the C3 Framework:
https://youtu.be/3HD9apVNq0I
With limited time to teach social studies in elementary schools, teachers must consider collaborative planning and integrative learning. See the next video on the importance of collaborative teaching and integrative learning:
www.teachingchannel.org/videos/collaborative-teaching-ntn
Many teachers struggle with ideas for how to cover or discuss difficult social issues. This video is an example of a way to share content about 9/11 with elementary students:
www.flocabulary.com/unit/week-in-rap-extra-9-11/
Watch the next video for an example of a kindergarten teacher engaging students in an "antiques roadshow" to help them better understand time and place:
www.teachingchannel.org/videos/show-and-tell-themes
Visit the next website (Video #5: Leaders, Community, and Citizens) to see an example of a first-grade teacher engaging students in problem solving about community issues:
https://www.learner.org/series/social-studies-in-action-a-teaching-practices-library-k-12/leaders-community-and-citizens/
Visit this website (Video #13: Making a Difference Through Giving) to see an example of a fourth-grade classroom engaged in a service learning project to help solve an issue important to their local community and the world:
https://www.learner.org/series/social-studies-in-action-a-teaching-practices-library-k-12/making-a-difference-through-giving/

▶ FURTHER READING

Engle, S. (1960). Decision making: The heart of social studies instruction. *Social Education*, *24*(7), 301–306.

This article discusses the role of decision making in the social studies and emphasizes its purposes as the central and vital aspect of social studies instruction. This seminal article outlines decision making as an approach to social studies and played a significant role in the way social studies was viewed.

Russell, W. (Ed.). (2011). *Contemporary social studies: An essential reader*. Charlotte, NC: Information Age Publishing.

The field of social studies is unique and complex. It is challenged by the differing perspectives related to the definition, goals, content, and purpose of social studies. This book discusses the contemporary issues surrounding social studies education today. This book encourages and inspires readers to think. The 28 chapters included in this volume are written by prominent scholars in the field of social studies. The collection inspires and provokes readers to reconsider and reexamine social studies and its contemporary state. Readers will explore the various critical topics that encompass contemporary social studies.

Barr, R., Barth, J., & Shermis, S. (1977). *Defining social studies*. Silver Spring, MD: National Council for the Social Studies.

This book discusses the various perspectives and issues surrounding social studies and its identity. This book includes five chapters analyzing the nature of social studies, its goals and objectives, and the issues surrounding the lack of a consistent definition.

Ochoa-Becker, A. (2006). *Democratic education for social studies: An issues-centered decision making curriculum*. Charlotte, NC: Information Age Publishing.

This influential book was originally published in 1988 and written by the iconic social studies educator Shirley Engle. This volume includes a rationale for an issues–centered, decision-making curriculum for the social studies classroom.

▶ REFERENCES

Anderson, L. W. (2009). Upper elementary grades bear the brunt of accountability. *Phi Kappa Delta*, *90*(6), 414–418.

Barth, J. L. (1993). Social studies: There is a history, there is a body, but is it worth saving? *Social Education*, *57*(2), 56–57.

Barton, K. C. (2011). Wars and rumors of war: Making sense of history education in the United States. In T. Taylor & R. Guyver (Eds.), *History wars and the classroom: Global perspective* (pp. 189–204). Charlotte, NC: Information Age Publishing.

Bisland, B. L. (2011). The marginalization of social studies in the elementary grades: An Overview. In W. Russell (Ed.), *Contemporary social studies: An essential reader* (pp. 173–191). Charlotte, NC: Information Age Publishing.

Engle, S. (1960). Decision-making: The heart of social studies instruction. *Social Education*, *27*(4), November, 301–304.

Geisel, T. (1954). *Horton hears a who*. New York: Putnam.

Gross, R. E. (1977). The status of the social studies in the public schools of the United States. *Social Education*, *41*(November/December), 194–200, 205.

Hahn, C. W. (1977). Research in the diffusion of social studies innovations. In F. P. Hunkins (Ed.), *Review of research in social studies education: 1970–75* (pp. 137–177). Washington, DC: National Council for the Social Studies and Boulder, CO: ERIC Clearing House for Social Studies/Social Science Education Consortium.

Hartoonan, M. (1993). A guide for redefining the social studies. *Social Education*, *57*(2), 59–60.

Heafner, T., & Fitchett, P. (2012). Tipping the scales: National trends of declining social studies instructional time in elementary schools. *The Journal of Social Studies Research*, *36*(2), 188–213.

Holloway, J., & Chiodo, J. (2009). Social studies IS being taught in the elementary school: A contrarian view. *The Journal of Social Studies Research*, *33*(2), 235–261.

Moore, C. et al. (1989). Mental terms and the development of certainty. *Child Development*, *60*, 167–171.

National Council for the Social Studies (NCSS). (2001). *Creating effective citizens*. Available at: https://www.socialstudies.org/sites/default/files/publications/se/6505/650511.html.

National Council for the Social Studies (NCSS). (2001). *Powerful and purposeful teaching and learning in elementary school social studies*. Available at: https://www.socialstudies.org/social-studies-and-young-learner/22/1/powerful-and-purposeful-teaching-and-learning-elementary.

National Council for the Social Studies (NCSS).. (2009). *Powerful, purposeful pedagogy in elementary school social studies*. Available at: www.ncss.org/positions/powerfulandpurposeful.

Russell, W. B. III. (2009). Social studies, the lost curriculum: A research study of elementary teachers and the forces impacting the teaching of social studies. *Curriculum and Teaching*, *24*(2), 75–86.

Task Force of the National Commission on the Social Studies in the Schools. (1989). *Charting a course: Social studies for the 21st century*. Washington, DC: The National Commission on the Social Studies in the Schools.

Chapter 2

Social Studies Curriculum

▶ LOOKING AHEAD

What social studies topics and themes are to be taught in elementary schools? What is to be taught about these topics and themes? Questions such as these are constant and troubling for social studies educators. Though there is little disagreement that the selection ought to be related to carefully selected goals and that the teaching itself should be done in a purposeful way, what is taught and what materials are used continue to be ongoing problems in the social studies. In this chapter, we will look at some of the forces influencing social studies and how these forces have changed the field. You need to be aware of how these developments affect how and what you will teach. This awareness will help you understand that social studies curriculum is evolving.

Recognizing that social studies has a strong knowledge base, we will also want to look at the social science disciplines. These disciplines all examine the world from a different perspective, with different emphases and foci and, often, using different scholarly tools. The social scientists working in these disciplines provide the scholarship, methods, concepts, and information that are the basis for social studies curriculum in the elementary schools. The better we understand them and their relationships to one another, the better we can utilize and select from what they have to offer.

CAN YOU? DO YOU?

Can you . . .

- Identify reasons why there is controversy in social studies?
- Describe the Expanding Environments curriculum?
- Identify and explain the various social science disciplines?
- Explain how the social sciences relate to what students learn in social studies?

Do you . . .

- Know all the social science fields that are included in social studies?
- Know how the social studies curriculum is organized?
- Know what an instructional theme is?
- Know the history of the term "social studies"?

FOCUS ACTIVITY

Before reading this chapter, try the following focus activity.

Think back on your elementary experience. What did social studies mean to you as an elementary student? What curriculum was included in social studies? Share experiences with classmates. Discuss the details of experiences and compare. Do your elementary social studies experiences share common attributes with others? If so, what attributes? What does social studies mean to you now?

▶ WHY IS THERE CONTROVERSY IN SOCIAL STUDIES?

Social studies has been, and will continue to be, constantly under attack by critics. The content taught in social studies is constantly being examined. The root reason for this is that learning social studies is a lot more complex than developing an ability or skill such as reading and mathematics. It is almost without boundary or borders.

There are, arguably, five overlapping social studies curricula existing in most elementary schools. First, there is the formal curriculum that is the basis of social studies classes. It usually is prescribed for, or determined by, the teachers and has clearly defined goals and parameters and is embodied in a course of study, standards, or a required textbook. Second, there is a curriculum that is very pronounced in the primary grades and has to do with events and with the calendar itself. Holidays, birthdays, seasons, weather, and current events all conspire to form this curriculum which is, by its very nature, more fluid and flexible than the formal curriculum. This second curriculum may be reasoned out by the teacher to relate to the formal curriculum and have corresponding goals. The third curriculum is really embedded in the materials used to teach other subjects, especially reading and language arts. The stories in readers and the literature program deal with people, places, and events, and readers have traditionally paralleled social studies content. Through fictional and nonfictional literature, students are made aware of how people live, think, and get along with others. Science and arithmetic similarly present social studies content, particularly regarding the stories behind discoveries, inventions, and theories. The fourth curriculum has to do with the organizational functions of the school and the classroom and is embodied in what is taught about the ways to work together and independently, the development and following of class and school rules, and the way that students are taught to act throughout the school day. This curriculum is very closely tied to the fifth curriculum, which is becoming increasingly more manifest in schools: the program specifically to develop values and/or character.

With this richly varied array of curricula, which may at times be contradictory, there are factors that contribute to the controversial nature of social studies. Those factors include:

- Anything that human effort produces is, by definition, imperfect. Before we even get a curriculum together, we and others begin to see the flaws and problems. When we put something into use, those flaws become glaringly apparent to us.
- Cultural change is constant. We live in an era of immense societal complexity and rapid change. As rapidly as we develop a program, changes occur that require adjustments. Social studies curricula are responsive to changes in the social climate. Changes in emphasis are likely to reflect the times. Wars, depressions,

periods of prosperity, international relationships, and a host of other things that influence the public climate can impact what and how things are taught in social studies classrooms.

- People have differing values, priorities, and viewpoints. Social studies is not just a skills subject. In a democratic society, there is little likelihood of long-term consensus and none of universal agreement on what ought to be taught and from what viewpoint.
- Special-interest groups influence curriculum. In our society, there are pressure groups with their own agendas and expectations. They want to influence or even control what is being taught in the schools.
- Social studies represents an enormous changing body of knowledge. Social studies curriculum simply defies coverage or even adequate sampling. We can never have enough depth or breadth.

The term "social studies" is a product of the twentieth century. It was officially adopted as the name for the curricular area in 1916 by the Committee on Social Studies, a sub-group of the Commission to Reorganize Secondary Education, which had been set up by the National Education Association. The committee reported the conclusions in the *1916 Report*, which outlined the good citizenship concept and also recommended the curricula for grades five through eight (see Table 2.1), which were traditionally considered part of elementary or grammar school.

In the late 1930s, Paul Hanna proposed a sequence of instructional topics that was to revolutionize elementary school social studies. This framework, known as the Expanding Communities Model or Expanding Environments curriculum, was based on a theory that students' ability to understand their world progresses through a series of developmental stages and that social studies programs should be structured to coincide with those stages (Hanna, 1957, 1963). The progression was from a study of the students themselves and their homes and families through increasingly larger communities that were more remote and abstract to students' thinking.

Despite all the pressure for change, the Expanding Environments concept has been the major influence on social studies curriculum for over 50 years. The first eight grades of the twelve-grade Hanna model are shown in Table 2.2. Alongside it, the dominant pattern of curriculum organization currently used in textbook and school curricula is shown.

The beauty of the Expanding Environments model was its logic. It made sense to a lot of people both from the standpoint of its reflection of a reasonable pattern of child development and as a logical way to organize social studies curriculum. Hanna's model was developed at a fortunate time in many ways. The social climate of the nation was ideal, with America coming through a depression and a world war from which it

Table 2.1 Curricula for Grades Five Through Eight

Grade	Subject
Fifth Grade	American History
Sixth Grade	World History (Western Civilization)
Seventh Grade	Geography
Eighth Grade	American History

Table 2.2 Expanding Environments Model and Contemporary Curricula

Grade	Expanding Environments Model	Contemporary Curricula
Kindergarten	Kindergartens were not mandatory at this time.	Self, School, Home, Families, Community
First	The Child, the Home, the Family, the School	Families Community
Second	The Neighborhood Neighborhood Helpers	Neighborhoods
Third	The Larger Community Cities	Communities
Fourth	The State The Region	State History Geographic Regions
Fifth	The United States and its Neighbors	American History
Sixth	The World (Western Civilization)	World Cultures The Western Hemisphere
Seventh	World Geography	World Geography
Eighth	History of the United States	American History

emerged as the leading power in the free world. Technology and communication as well as the economic conditions were also right. Hanna's model was soon adopted by many school systems and by textbook publishers. It is, to this day, the most common model used in elementary schools in the United States.

From the 1960s to the 1970s, a spirit of reform gripped the social studies that was known as the New Social Studies (Byford & Russell, 2007; Fitchett & Russell, 2011). It manifested itself in a series of well-warranted criticisms of the Expanding Environment curriculum as it was by then represented in textbook series and school curricula across the country and in the development of new curricula, many of which were closely tied to the various social science disciplines. Critics pointed out that social studies teachers relied too heavily on textbooks and that there was too much memorization of facts. But there was major curricular criticism as well. Critics charged that social studies lacked sufficient substantive content; that African Americans, Hispanic Americans, women, and other groups were insufficiently represented, stereotypically represented, or misrepresented; and that significant issues and content topics of controversy were avoided. The New Social Studies movement was spurred in part by federal funding and in part by the social consciousness and concern of the period. The lasting changes injected into social studies by these reform efforts during this era included:

- A greater sensitivity to the representation of various ethnic groups and women in social studies material.
- Focus on inquiry and values.
- Greater global consciousness.
- Focus on social sciences other than history and geography as sources of insight and methods of inquiry about the world.
- Greater awareness of and ability to deal with controversy in the social studies classroom.
- An emphasis on learning concepts and generalizations rather than isolated facts.

More recent efforts to set the direction for social studies have reaffirmed the importance of history and geography while at the same time accepting a less structured and more incidental social studies content for elementary grades. Perhaps the most prestigious of the recent groups to examine the future of social studies have been two curriculum task forces. The first of these was the Curriculum Task Force of the National Commission on the Social Studies in the Schools, which published a report, *Charting a Course: Social Studies for the 21st Century* (1989). In it, the Task Force advocated a curriculum of stories about people accompanied by holiday study and following up time and location information in reading stories, mathematics, and other materials. The Task Force suggested that such a program was sufficient to ensure elementary understanding of world geography, the civic and political traditions of the United States, and human life on different continents and at different times in the past (1989, p. 9). The Task Force envisioned three courses being taught in grades four, five, and six, which would include (in no specified order) (1) United States History, (2) World History, and (3) Geography.

The second group, set up by the National Council for the Social Studies, was called the Task Force on Standards for the Social Studies. It worked over a period of three years before coming out with its original report in 1994, *Expectations of Excellence: Curriculum Standards for Social Studies*. This report established ten themes for social studies and was intended to influence and guide curriculum design and overall student expectations for grades K–12. In 2010, the Task Force released a revised and updated report *National Curriculum Standards for Social Studies: A Framework for Teaching, Learning, and Assessment*. The updated report provides a description of the ten basic themes for social studies (see Table 2.3).

▶ INCORPORATING THEMES FROM THE STANDARDS

The focus themes identified by the Standards Task Force are, to some extent, taken from the social science disciplines and represent their essential lines of inquiry. Following a kind of candlewick principle, these themes can run through topics of study and across grade levels, drawing essential content and skill development to themselves.

> **FYI:** Inquiry is considered a foundation of the C3 Framework.

Thematic units represent one approach to implementing the standards. Such units are integrally related to literature-based programs and unify the content of social studies with other curricular areas. In non–graded settings, thematic units can be part of an internal structure.

Examples of thematic unit topics at each grade level are detailed in Table 2.4. The list is not presented as a sequential model curriculum and certainly will not reflect precisely any particular school or textbook curricular program. These unit topics are presented to give an idea of topics that might be taught, suggest connections to the Standards and to a specific discipline, and to illustrate the notion of thematic threads.

▶ SOCIAL STUDIES AND COMMON CORE STANDARDS

When discussing standards in education during the era of accountability, certainly one of the most popular and emerging topics revolves around the Common Core Standards (Common Core Standards, 2012a). These standards represent a state-led effort coordinated by the National Governors Association Center for Best Practices (NGA Center)

Table 2.3 Descriptions of NCSS's Ten Themes for Social Studies

Theme	Definition
Culture	Social studies programs should include experiences that provide for the study of culture and cultural diversity.
Time, Continuity, and Change	Social studies programs should include experiences that provide for the study of the past and its legacy.
People, Places, and Environment	Social studies programs should include experiences that provide for the study of people, places, and environments.
Individual Development and Identity	Social studies programs should include experiences that provide for the study of individual development and identity.
Individuals, Groups, and Institutions	Social studies programs should include experiences that provide for the study of interactions among individuals, groups, and institutions.
Power, Authority, and Governance	Social studies programs should include experiences that provide for the study of how people create, interact with, and change structures of power, authority, and governance.
Production, Distribution, and Consumption	Social studies programs should include experiences that provide for the study of how people organize for the production, distribution, and consumption of goods and services.
Science, Technology, and Society	Social studies programs should include experiences that provide for the study of relationships among science, technology, and society.
Global Connections	Social studies programs should include experiences that provide for the study of global connections and interdependence.
Civic Ideals and Practices	Social studies programs should include experiences that provide for the study of the ideals, principles, and practices of citizenship in a democratic republic.

and the Council of Chief State School Officers (CCSSO) to provide a list of standards for K–12 schools to help students prepare for college and the workforce (Kenna & Russell, 2014). A variety of contributors developed the standards, including teachers, administrators, and other content specialists, and were informed by all the current state standards of education as well as standards from other top-performing countries around the world. One of the primary purposes behind the Common Core Standards is to help provide a clearer and more consistent set of expectations for student learning at each grade level across the United States. Attempting to clarify and identify high-achieving expectations for student learning across the states has become increasingly important because not all states go through the same process of adopting state standards; thus, what states deem important for academic and personal growth can vary greatly.

For elementary teachers, the Common Core Standards emphasize English language arts (reading/writing) and mathematics. The Common Core Standards for other specific content areas have not been developed, and according to Common Core Initiative (http://www.corestandards.org/about-the-standards/frequently-asked-questions/) (Common Core Standards, 2012b), there is no plan to develop standards specific for

Table 2.4 Examples of Thematic Units for Each Grade Level

Unit Topic	Possible Theme(s)	Themes	Social Science Discipline(s)
Kindergarten			
Social studies typically begins with topics related to home, family, and school. Emphasis is on the immediate environment, but there needs to be plenty of opportunity to look at the world beyond.			
Who am I?	Identity Personality	4	Psychology
Our Families	Interdependence	5	Sociology
Friends Away from Home	Socialization	4	Sociology
Rules We Need	Responsibility	6	Political Science Psychology
Who Makes the School Work?	Authority Authority Careers	4, 6	Sociology
Being Careful Going Shopping	Authority Society	5, 7	Economics
The World, the Continents, and the Oceans	Location	3, 10	Geography
First Grade			
Social studies units at this level typically begin with the local area and associate it with the larger world. Often comparisons are made. Emphasis is on individuals.			
The Shopping Mall	Consumption/Exchange	7	Economics
People We Need	Interdependence	3, 4, 7	Economics
Friends Away from Home	Socialization	4	Sociology
What Happens in the Factory	Production	7	Economics
Great Men and Women	Leadership Individual Differences	2, 3	History
Families in India	Cultural Diversity	1, 9	Anthropology Geography

(Continued)

Table 2.4 (Continued)

Unit Topic	Possible Theme(s)	Themes	Social Science Discipline(s)
Second Grade			
Social studies units often emphasize contact, travel, and relationships among neighborhoods.			
Moving Around and Telling Others	Transportation Communication	3	Geography History
Neighborhoods Changing	Cause and Effect Local Pride	2, 3	History Geography
Farms and Cities	Resources Culture	1, 2, 3	Culture Geography
Fast Foods	Exchange	7	Economics
Suburbs	Adaptation Location	2, 3	Geography
Money and Banks	Exchange	7	Economics
Third Grade			
Social studies units at this level are generally focused on the larger community. The intent is to have students develop an understanding of the conceptual characteristics of a community, community differences, and community changes.			
How the City Changes	Adaptation Change	1, 2, 3	Political Science Geography History
Special Cities	Physical Differences	3, 8	Geography
Towns and Cities in Early America	Historical Change	3, 6, 10	History
Feeding the People	Production Transportation Exchange	7, 8	Economics Geography
People Who Made Change	Historical Judgment	2, 5, 9	History

Fourth Grade

Environmental features of the Earth are emphasized, and regions of the United States are studied. How to go about adopting and adapting to the environment and the home state are sometimes part of the focus.

Unit	Standards	Discipline	Themes
Living in the Deserts of the World	1, 3, 9	Geography	Region; Adaptation
History All Around Us	2	History	Change
Rain Forests	1, 3, 8	Geography	Location; Physical Features
The Midwest	1, 3	Geography	Regions
Regions of the United States	3, 7, 9	Geography	Regions

Fifth Grade

Social studies units at this level often emphasize the history of the United States. Units also include the United States and Canada or the United States and South America.

Unit	Standards	Discipline	Themes
New Lands New Promises	2, 3, 10	History; Geography	Cause and Effect; Location
Forging the Nation	2, 3, 6	History; Political Science	Historical Judgment; Authority/Responsibility
African Americans	2, 3, 4	History	Identification Equality
The American West	2, 3, 4	History; Geography	Historical Progression; Location
The American Civil War	2, 6, 10	History	Causation; Historical Judgment
American Labor and Industry	3, 6, 8	History; Economics	Change; Adaptation

(Continued)

Table 2.4 (Continued)

Unit Topic	Possible Theme(s)	Themes	Social Science Discipline(s)
Sixth Grade Social studies at this level may include a study of Latin America and Canada or may emphasize Western civilization or the history of Europe and Asia.			
Models of Ancient Governments	Citizenship Authority	2, 6, 9	Political Science History
Castles and Moats	Adaptation Cause and Effect	2, 5, 6	History
Renaissance and Reformation	Cause and Effect Individual Impact	6, 9, 10	Sociology

other content areas. Nonetheless, the current language arts standards include standards for literacy in history/social studies, science, and technical subjects. For elementary teachers, this may prove to be a welcomed site, since a large portion of the elementary curriculum is dedicated to literacy development, and content areas are often integrated in the classroom setting. Since most states have dedicated standards or strands for each content area at every grade level, elementary teachers might indeed find the Common Core Standards to be a more manageable and practical resource than current state standards.

▶ COLLEGE, CAREER, AND CIVIC LIFE FRAMEWORK AND SOCIAL STUDIES

In 2013, the National Council for the Social Studies developed the College, Career, and Civic Life Framework for Social Studies Standards (C3 Framework). The C3 Framework was designed "for states to upgrade their state social studies standards and for practitioners – local school districts, schools, teachers and curriculum writers – to strengthen their social studies programs" (www.ncss.org/c3).

The C3 Framework has three primary objectives:

a. enhance the rigor of the social studies disciplines;
b. build critical thinking, problem solving, and participatory skills to become engaged citizens;
c. align academic programs to the Common Core State Standards for English Language Arts and Literacy in History/Social Studies.

(www.ncss.org/c3)

The C3 Framework foundation is inquiry learning, and the framework hopes to better strengthen social studies instruction. According to the NCSS website:

> The C3 Framework, like the Common Core State Standards, emphasizes the acquisition and application of knowledge to prepare students for college, career, and civic life. It intentionally envisions social studies instruction as an inquiry arc of interlocking and mutually reinforcing elements that speak to the intersection of ideas and learners.

Furthermore, the C3 Framework is organized into four dimensions. The four dimensions (see Table 2.5) center on the use of questions to spark curiosity, guide instruction, deepen investigations, acquire rigorous content, and apply knowledge and ideas in real-world settings to become active and engaged citizens in the twenty-first century (www.ncss.org/c3).

▶ CONSTRUCTIVISM AND SOCIAL STUDIES

Social studies educators have given a great deal of attention to theories and research about how students learn. A teacher's concept of the way in which students acquire and retain knowledge should influence teaching methodology. The last generation of teachers has largely rejected the notion that they could simply present information, and it would, somehow, be absorbed and learned. They have also pretty much cast aside behaviorism, with its view that learning occurs through systematic stimulus and

Table 2.5 C3 Framework Organization

Dimension 1: Developing Questions and Planning Inquiries	Dimension 2: Applying Disciplinary Tools and Concepts	Dimension 3: EvaluatingSources and Using Evidence	Dimension 4: Communicating Conclusions and Taking Informed Action
Developing Questions and Planning Inquiries	Civics Economics Geography History	Gathering and Evaluating Sources Developing Claims and Using Evidence	Communicating and Critiquing Conclusions Taking Informed Action

(**Source**: NCSS, 2013, p. 12)

response, punishment, and reward. These explanations of learning have simply been inadequate descriptions of how knowledge is acquired and understood.

The learning theory that most social studies educators subscribe to is called constructivism. Constructivist thought dominates the thinking of most scholars and writers in social studies. This means that constructivist beliefs influence the development of curriculum materials and ideas about how best teaching can be achieved.

The basic concepts of constructivism were expressed by John Dewey and later by psychologists Jean Piaget and Jerome Bruner. The major article of belief of constructivists is that knowledge is something that learners build or construct for themselves. They do this individually and socially. Learning is an active process in which sensory input is used. Knowledge is the result of assimilating any new information, ideas, and experiences in order to give them meaning. The new information has to make sense with and tie into what a learner already knows for it to have any meaning. That is why the term "constructivism" is used; the learner literally constructs his or her own knowledge by combining new impressions and information with existing perceptions and conceptions.

Von Glasersfeld (1987) has suggested that constructivism has two major principles, which are paraphrased next:

1. Knowledge is actively constructed by the learner, not passively received from the environment.
2. What the learner knows is constantly adapting and being modified by experience.

To put it another way, we make sense of the world by fitting new information and new ideas with what we already know. We construct meaning or explain what we encounter. An oversimplified example is found in our love of the use of analogy in explanation and definition. We try to find a basis of comparison for something novel in what our audience already does understand.

▶ WHAT IS THE PLACE OF THE SOCIAL SCIENCE DISCIPLINES?

Social studies is the name given to a broad curricular area taught in elementary schools. The focus of social studies is on the student learning to understand, interpret, and live in his or her world. "Social studies" is also an inclusive term for that broad field of study that includes courses that focus specifically on history, geography, sociology, economics, psychology, government, anthropology, and related subjects. Some people use the phrase "the seamless web" to describe the relationships among all these subjects. They like to see social studies as an interdisciplinary curricular area that draws its content from what scholars in a variety of disciplines know about the social world.

The disciplines themselves would more correctly be called social sciences, and each of them offers different content emphases and different methods of inquiry from the others. When social scientists start counting off the social sciences, different numbers are likely to be given. That is partly because there are some disciplines, such as philosophy and religion, that some people accept as social sciences and that other people see as humanities or even natural sciences. An additional factor is that each social science keeps dividing as specializations develop. As a specialization gathers more scholars and knowledge, its perspective and methods of scholarship change too. Over time, it becomes as different from its parent discipline as that discipline is from every other one. Some see archeology as a part of anthropology and others as a branch of sociology.

For our purpose, let us admit to eight social sciences, while recognizing that someone else might have a longer or shorter list. The eight we will look at are, in alphabetical order: anthropology, economics, geography, history, political science, psychology, religious studies, and sociology. We will look at each of them in turn, basically to refresh our memories and clarify our thinking about the chief concerns of these disciplines and the essential roles each plays in elementary social studies. The descriptions of each discipline will be in alphabetical order. While we need to keep in mind that each of the social sciences utilizes concepts from all the other disciplines, we also need to recognize that each discipline has unique contributions.

Anthropology

Anthropology is the study of culture, especially human culture. "Culture" may be defined as a system of beliefs and values, behavior patterns, and customs that is shared by a society of people. A sense of sharing and oneness with others in this society is often part of what defines and distinguishes cultures. Scholars in the field generally like to think of their approach as holistic because they are interested in everything there is to know about a culture. Anthropologists study everything from ancient ruins and human remains to existing cultures. There are numerous and varied specializations within the field, including archeology and ethnography. Because cultural change is a major concern of anthropologists, technological development within a culture has immense importance in many of these specializations.

Anthropologists look for cultural generalizations. They want to know what defines a culture and what makes it fit together. Anthropologists look carefully at a process they call enculturation, which has to do with how young people learn about their own culture and the influences that cultures have on one another, especially those that result in acculturation or the cultural exchange that occurs when there is long-term contact. Like geographers, they are concerned with the natural environment. However, anthropologists have a different perspective, their concerns being mostly with how culture is influenced by environment and what part culture plays in how humans adapt.

Anthropologists attempt to immerse themselves thoroughly within a culture, often becoming very personally involved. From this experience, they expect to gather immense amounts of data about that culture for further study. There is, of course, concern about how much anthropologists influence a less technologically advanced culture as they study it.

The concept of culture is an essential one for elementary school social studies. Students need to become less ethnocentric and learn more about other cultures. Anthropological focus can be an important part of interdisciplinary programs, but the focus of many primary units is on comparing cultures. Social studies has also found that some of the investigative techniques of anthropologists, chiefly archeological site excavation and interviewing and observation, are highly adaptable for use with elementary school students.

Economics

Economics deals with resources and with the production, exchange, and consumption of goods and services. Economics is perhaps the most problem centered of the social sciences since its basic concept is scarcity. The resources are scarce and are always likely to be exceeded by human needs and wants.

Economists try to analyze the use of and demand for various resources in order to make recommendations about the problems that relate to scarcity. Economics is often mathematical and quantitative. Economists continually try to predict the future and to recommend courses of action that will create a more fortunate situation in the future. Therefore, they are continually trying to find ways to look at quantities produced, exchanged, and consumed. Because in societies where there is specialization, some medium of exchange (money) is going to exist, economics is also concerned with money and other forms of capital and with related areas such as banking, taxation, and investment.

The real importance of economics to elementary students is that throughout life, students will be playing the roles of worker (producer of goods or services), consumer (user of goods and services), and citizen (part of a society that operates under some economic system). They need to learn several economic consumer skills and develop economic values that can be embedded in social studies. These should have to do with such diverse areas of their lives as handling money, banking, budgeting, buying and selling goods and services, and choosing a way of making a living. They also will need to learn to deal with how scarcity relates to and impacts their own lives. There is also some important economic content for students both as future citizens and as students studying other countries. In both roles, students need at least some understanding of how the economy operates and how this affects people's lives.

Geography

Though maps and globes are among the major tools of geographers, and a branch of geography, cartography, is devoted to the science of mapping, the field of geography is far broader, encompassing the study of the Earth's surface and how that relates to human beings. Geographers are interested in how humans adapt to various living conditions and how humans alter the geography. Physical geographers tend to focus on the Earth's natural features (topography, landforms, climate, bodies of water, vegetation, animal life, etc.). Cultural geographers are concerned with people and with the factors that influence their location as well as how humans use and impact resources.

Basic to geographic understanding is some knowledge of where places are in the world. Many students and teachers lack very basic information about their world. With the great variety of colorful, interesting, interactive, and/or electronic maps available to use with students today, there is little excuse for not drawing students into map study. In a world where people have become much more mobile and where people are drawn closer by communication and transportation revolutions, it seems clear that students need more place location knowledge than ever before.

Geographic knowledge is basic to understanding and knowing about the world and its people, and geography-related problems are among the most important ones facing the world today. Elementary students are aware of many of these problems and need to be informed and knowledgeable about their impact on their world. Students often have only heard enough to frighten them about geography-related problems, ranging from overpopulation to pollution, from the depletion of the ozone to the destruction of the rainforests, from the rapid consumption of fossil fuels to world famines and droughts.

As defined by the National Council for Geographic Education and the Association of American Geographers in 1984, geographic education is focused on five themes.

1. *Location*: Position on the Earth's surface.
2. *Place*: The characteristics that distinguish and define each place.
3. *Relationships within places*: Advantages and disadvantages for human settlement.
4. *Movement*: Interactions of humans.
5. *Regions*: Areas that display unity in terms of selected criteria.

The questions that geographers ask deal with where people live and why. They are interested in the factors that make the Earth habitable. They are also concerned with how variations in geographic factors influence economic development, culture, and sociopolitical organization.

Students can easily be drawn into a study of other settings and other people. Everything has a geographic setting, and the realization that we understand events and people's actions better when we know more about that geographic setting makes the study of geography important for every subject students study throughout life. Flora and fauna or minerals and rocks they study in the sciences, stories and poems they read in literature, and the people and events they study in the past all relate to numerous geographic factors.

History

History is the study of the past, or at least the surviving record of the past. Generally, we limit our study to the human past, but that is very broad. There is a history of scholarship, of military events, and of economic, cultural, and social phenomena. History examines, in fact, the whole spectrum of humans in interaction with one another and with the Earth.

The problem of history is that the record of the past is always incomplete, full of bias, and distorted. This problem has produced two schools of thought regarding historical inquiry. On the one hand, narrative historians, sometimes called humanist historians, suggest that the inadequacies of the record and the complexity of the past defy any attempt to generalize. They conceive the historian's job as one of basically describing the past more accurately, insightfully, and fully. Scientific historians, on the other hand, attempt to use scientific methods, often with quantitative data.

Historians study documents, records, personal letters, diaries, business inventories, legal papers, wills, bills of sale, newspapers, and government papers. Historians also study and compare the physical remains of the past from buildings, roads, and walls to the smallest of objects – either preserved through time in someone's safekeeping or found in such places as ruins and tombs. Historians also look at such things as paintings, recordings, photographs, and, for most recent times, video recordings. Finally, historians use people as a resource through approaches such as interviews and observations.

Elementary social studies usually include the learning of historical facts. Involving students in the narrative or the story and drama of history and in the quest for historical knowledge is essential if history is to be learned effectively. Historical fascination is the key to historical learning.

History deals with questions through which a picture is reconstructed of how events occurred, why they occurred, and whether/how they impacted subsequent events. Teachers can stimulate a genuine interest in what life was like in the past. When students are led to examine history as a series of mysteries and problems, they can be naturally led to look at some of the primary resources that historians use. It is really exciting to watch when a student experiences an "Aha!" moment (a moment when a student discovers and understands something new). Once they begin seeking new knowledge, concepts like historical change, cultural bias, civilization, colonization, and cause and effect begin to be perfectly logical to them and to come with the learning.

Political Science

Political science is the study of government and all that is associated with the governing process. It deals with human behavior throughout the entire political system and includes the study of the legislative, the judicial, and the executive processes. Political scientists study governmental organizations, political parties, pressure groups, voting and elections, and other related parts of the process. They also study different types of government and different types of performance by those involved in governing.

Political science attempts to give an accurate and complete picture of the way that the political process works, both generally and at particular points in time. Certainly, the basic tools of the political scientists are analyses of documents, court cases and governmental acts, and media coverage of political events. However, political scientists also attempt to predict, based on the notion that when conditions are similar, it is likely that outcomes and results will tend to repeat.

In elementary school, students are in the process of becoming aware of the forms and functions of government. Their political awareness is often closely linked to their geographical and historical understanding. Students are typically politicized by the age of 12. Throughout the elementary grades, they are developing numerous political concepts, including right and wrong, justice, authority, power, security, and politics. They become aware of their own exposure to vast barrages of propaganda.

Political science is the source of a great deal of useful information and many concepts in the process of learning about government. Since political science is largely based on questioning the process, in looking analytically at every event, the methods of the discipline are useful at the elementary level.

Psychology

Psychology is the study of the behavior and thinking of individuals, especially humans. One branch of psychology, social psychology, is even devoted to behavior in groups.

Psychologists study development across the entire life span. They are interested in a number of factors that relate to the social studies, including individuality and self-concept, motivation and attitudes, learning and cognition, human personalities, and behavior of individuals in groups.

Psychology provides insight into social behavior in the classroom and into several elements related to learning. As elementary students learn about other people and other times, they need to understand why people behave as they do. They also need to understand something about the kinds of action taken by different types of leaders.

Religious Studies

Religious studies examine the systems of beliefs and the various practices associated with the various faiths of the world. It is an extremely broad field. Scholarship in religious studies reaches from large formal religions, such as Buddhism, Islam, Christianity, Hinduism, and Judaism, to small, relatively obscure cults. Likewise, the spectrum goes from ancient religions that have not been practiced for centuries to modern religions with both ancient and recent origins. Religious study scholars also have great interest in political philosophies that contain substantively religious ideas and have important ramifications that impact religious practices. Confucianism and communism are examples of such.

The importance of religious studies to elementary social studies relates to the importance of religious beliefs in people's lives. As students study other times and other places, they need some understanding of the religious context. Geography and history are at least partly attributable to religious factors. Religious studies does not teach a religion; it teaches about various religions.

It may also become important for students to understand that religious views sometimes impact some of the activities of the classroom as well. They need to understand the difference between studying religious views and advocating them. There may be families represented in the class with religious beliefs that will not allow the students to participate in some school activities. In the last half century, a related issue has been the place of religious beliefs in the schools. Several questions have been raised about traditional school practices that are related to religious beliefs. These questions have brought about many constitutional controversies involving infringement on freedom of religion and the concept of separation of church and state.

Sociology

Sociology is the study of how people act in groups. Sociologists are interested in different kinds of groups, both formal and informal, and how these groups operate and interact with other groups. They are interested in individuals only with regard to the roles they have within groups. They are very much aware of the influence that societal values and norms have on individuals. An essential assumption of sociology is that individuals need groups to survive.

Sociologists study many groups that are very important to elementary students. They examine the family, the classroom, the school, the community, and numerous types of organizations within the community. Sociology's important contributions to elementary social studies should have to do with what the discipline tells us about group behavior. Sociologists offer perspectives about how people act in different institutional and community settings. Sociologists also examine how changes in the institutions occur. They look at social order and influence and authority within groups. They examine the different roles people play and social relationships, as well as the impact of technological change on social institutions.

▶ LOOKING BACK

Social studies is constantly changing because of the variety of influences and pressures for change. The elementary curriculum for over half a century has in some way related to the concept of expanding the world of the child. In the era of accountability, understanding the importance of NCSS standards, Common Core Standards, and the C3 Framework is vital.

Social science disciplines have had a continued and important role as the source of the content of the social sciences. Each of the social sciences – history, geography, anthropology, sociology, economics, political science, psychology, and religious studies – offers a body of knowledge, a unique perspective about the world, and a method of inquiry from which students can learn.

EXTENSION ACTIVITY

You have just accepted a job at Yourtown Elementary School (YES). It is orientation night, and you are meeting all your new students and parents. As you are sharing your daily schedule with the group, you mention that you will be teaching social studies from 1:05 to 2:25 p.m. A parent perplexed by your schedule raises her hand and asks, "What is social studies?"

TASK

The field of social studies is unique and complex. It is challenged by the differing perspectives related to the definition, goals, content, and purpose of social studies. For this activity, write down how you would answer the perplexed parent.

CHECKING FOR UNDERSTANDING

1. What is the C3 Framework?
2. How does the Expanding Environments curriculum relate to the curriculum of contemporary social studies programs?
3. What is the difference between the terms *the social sciences* and *the social studies*?
4. How would you define constructivism?
5. Why does social studies curriculum often focus on history and geography?
6. How does anthropology relate to and differ from geography?
7. What are the Common Core Standards?

▶ HELPFUL RESOURCES

Visit this website (Video #2: A Standards Overview: K–5) to see a short video regarding the K–5 social studies curriculum as it relates to NCSS themes:
https://www.learner.org/series/social-studies-in-action-a-teaching-practices-library-k-12/a-standards-overview-k-5/

See the next video as an example of a way to share content about Thanksgiving with elementary school students:

www.flocabulary.com/unit/thanksgiving/

See the following video as an example of a way to share content about women's rights with elementary school students:

https://www.flocabulary.com/lesson/womens-history/

Watch this video to see Sarah Brown Wessling discuss the integration of Common Core Standards into the classroom curriculum:

www.teachingchannel.org/videos/how-to-read-common-core

(Visit www.corestandards.org to explore the Common Core state Standards.)

This video provides an overview of the Common Core Standards, including what it is and what it is not:

https://youtu.be/NxRg__r9HLg

This video provides an overview of Common Core Standards:

https://youtu.be/5s0rRk9sER0

This video is hosted by Michelle Herczog. She interviews and discusses the C3 framework with an array of social studies scholars from across the country. Includes discussion with C3 project director, Kathy Swan:

https://youtu.be/AESqr-vGgLE

Watch this video from NCSS that details how the C3 Framework aligns with the Common Core Standards:

https://youtu.be/kb0QW6GwNbg

For a full-text copy of the C3 Framework, visit:

www.ncss.org/c3

The Council for Economic Education (CEE) is an organization for economic education. CEE publishes numerous books and resource materials for the economics classroom:

www.councilforeconed.org

Visit the website here (Video #6: Making Bread Together) to see how a first-grade teacher introduces the economic concepts of supply and demand and needs versus wants:

https://www.learner.org/series/social-studies-in-action-a-teaching-practices-library-k-12/making-bread-together/

Watch the following Flocabulary video on the Five Themes of Geography. Also, feel free to share this video directly with your elementary students:

www.flocabulary.com/unit/five-themes-of-geography/

Watch the following Flocabulary video on George Washington Carver as an example of how to get students excited about historical figures. Also, feel free to share this video directly with your elementary students:

www.flocabulary.com/unit/george-washington-carver/

Watch the following Flocabulary video on the three branches of government as an example of creative ways to share political science content with students. Also, feel free to share this video directly with your elementary students:

www.flocabulary.com/unit/3-branches-of-government/

Watch the following Flocabulary video on the major world religions. Also, feel free to share this video directly with your elementary students:

www.flocabulary.com/unit/major-world-religions/

Watch this video of an elementary school teacher engaging students in understanding democracy and the community through art:

www.teachingchannel.org/videos/teaching-democracy-through-art

▶ FURTHER READING

Thornton, S. (2003). From content to subject matter. *The Social Studies*, 92(6), 237–242.

This article discusses the purpose and goals of social studies. It also examines the relationship of verbiage and terms between social studies and the various social science disciplines.

Loewen, J. (2018). *Lies my teacher told me: Everything your American history textbook got wrong*. New York: The New Press.

This book is a fascinating and entertaining look at many of the historical myths perpetuated by U.S. History textbooks over the years.

National Council for the Social Studies. (2010). *National curriculum standards for social studies: A framework for teaching, learning, and assessment*. Silver Spring, MD: National Council for the Social Studies.

This book is the framework for social studies educators. The book outlines the goals and purpose of social studies. In addition, the book outlines the themes and national standards and presents readers with possible products students will produce and the process by which the students work to obtain the knowledge.

Kenna, J., & Russell, W. (2014). Implications of Common Core state standards on the social studies. *The Clearing House: A Journal of Educational Strategies, Issues, and Ideas*, 87(2), 75–82.

This article discusses the Common Core standards and the impact they have on social studies instruction.

National Council for Geographic Education. (1994). *Geography for life: The national geography standards*. Washington, DC: National Geographic Society Committee on Research and Exploration.

This book is the framework for geography education. The book outlines the goals and purpose of geography education. In addition, the book outlines the themes and national standards and presents readers with possible products students will produce and the process by which the students work to obtain the knowledge.

► REFERENCES

Byford, J., & Russell, W. (2007). The new social studies: A historical examination of curriculum reform. *Social Studies Research and Practice*, 2(1), 38–48.

Common Core Initiative. (2012a). *Common core standards*. Available at: www.corestandards.org.

Common Core Initiative. (2012b). *Common core FAQ's*. Available at: http://www.corestandards. org/about-the-standards/frequently-asked-questions/.

Fitchett, P., & Russell, W. (2011). Reflecting on MACOS: Why it failed and what we can learn from its demise. *Paedagogica Historica: International Journal of the History of Education*, 47(1), 1–16.

Hanna, P. R. (1957). Generalizations and universal values: Their implications for the social studies program. In *Social studies in the elementary school: Fifty-sixth yearbook of the national society for the study of education* (pp. 27–47). Chicago: University of Chicago Press.

Hanna, P. R. (1963). The social studies program in the elementary school in the twentieth century. In G. W. Sowards (Ed.), *The social studies*. Glenview, IL: Scott Foresman.

Kenna, J., & Russell, W. (2014). Implications of Common Core state standards on the social studies. *The Clearing House: A Journal of Educational Strategies, Issues, and Ideas*, 87(2), 75–82.

National Council for Geographic Education. (1984). *Guidelines for geographic education: Elementary and secondary schools*. Washington, DC: Association of American Geographers/ National Council for the Geographic Education.

National Council for the Social Studies. (2013). *The College, Career, and Civic Life (C3) framework for social studies state standards: Guidance for enhancing the rigor of K-12 civics, economics, geography, and history*. Silver Spring, MD: NCSS. (www.ncss.org/c3).

Task Force of the National Commission on the Social Studies in the Schools. (1989). *Charting a course: Social studies for the 21st century*. Washington, DC: The National Commission on the Social Studies in the Schools.

Task Force on Standards for the Social Studies. (1994). *Expectations of excellence: Curriculum standards for social studies*. Washington, DC: The National Council for the Social Studies.

Task Force on Standards for the Social Studies. (2010). *National curriculum standards for social studies: A framework for teaching, learning, and assessment*. Washington, DC: The National Council for the Social Studies.

Von Glasersfeld, E. (1987). Learning as a constructive activity. In C. Janvier (Ed.), *Problems of representation in the teaching and learning of mathematics*. Hillsdale, NJ: Lawrence Erlbaum.

Chapter 3

Decision Making in Social Studies

▶ LOOKING AHEAD

Social studies has traditionally been charged with helping students develop into effective citizens who better understand the world and the various people in it. With this in mind, a focus of social studies has to be on the decision-making process. This chapter focuses on a variety of ways that elementary teachers can focus on the decision-making process in the social studies curriculum. While topics dealing with the decision-making process and formation of values will always be controversial, the necessity of this work in the field of social studies cannot be denied. Teachers want students to develop high moral character and grow to exemplify civic virtue, which is the central element of civic engagement. Both high moral character and civic virtue require an understanding of the decision-making process. Civic virtue focuses on a commitment to democratic principles and values that manifests itself in the everyday lives of citizens, which directly correlates to the importance of social justice issues (NCSS Task Force on Character Education, 1997; NCSS, 2013).

FYI: The NCSS (2013, p. 33) states that civics "teaches the virtues – such as honesty, mutual respect, cooperation, and attentiveness to multiple perspectives – that citizens should use when they interact with each other on public matters."

Character education and values education are not quite the same. Character education is a broad, overreaching phenomenon aimed at developing a personal code of behavior based on doing what is right rather than serving one's own self-interests. That code predisposes how an individual will act in any situation.

Value, on the other hand, may be defined in various ways. Value can be used to refer to the relative worth of a person, material goods, services, or ideas. Value education refers to what is important in life. Our values are the principles or standards of quality we use in making decisions. Our values shape our attitudes toward actions, people, and things. They also direct our aspirations and ambitions. As elementary teachers, we need an understanding of the ways that personal values are shaped during the elementary school years. It is equally important that we think about our own roles and responsibilities in this process.

Character, values, decision making, and attitudes are critical attributes of school success or failure (Berkowitz & Bier, 2005). They influence whether students do their work and how well they do it, how students behave in any setting, and interpersonal relationships. Teachers deal with these values constantly. They want students to feel positive toward school; to strive to do their best work; to have certain kinds of ambitions for themselves; to be fair and friendly in dealing with other students; and to be honest, industrious, loyal, and so on. On the other hand, there is a delicate balance between values and ways of teaching and dealing with values that are acceptable and appropriate and those that are not. In American public schools, for example, it is inappropriate to teach religious values or to advocate a religion, but religious values are not the only ones that are inappropriate. There is a point at which dealing with political situations or teaching about loving one's country becomes indoctrination. There is even a point when teaching what are thought of as family values may conflict with what is taught at home.

This chapter focuses on the decision-making process and how it relates to the formation of values and the ways that teachers can address this topic in elementary schools. A problems approach offers an effective way of dealing with the decision-making process, values, and social justice issues because this approach enables students to make their own decisions, but to do so with a solid basis.

CAN YOU? DO YOU?

Can you . . .

- Explain why decision making and character education is important for today's schools?
- Describe your own values and tell how they were formed?
- Identify or describe some specific decision-making skills?
- Think of some activities in which students could have experiences in determining alternatives?

Do you . . .

- Know and understand the meaning of decision making and character education?
- Know which values to teach?
- Understand why it may be necessary to deal with values related to living in a pluralistic society in school?
- Understand different ways of teaching about values?

FOCUS ACTIVITY

Before reading this chapter, try the following focus activity.

Think back on your educational experiences as an elementary school student. Did your school have a character education program? Should elementary schools have character education programs or initiatives? What are the goals of character education? What are the pros and cons of character education programs? Do character education programs relate to social justice issues? How do the objectives of character education align with social studies and the overall objectives of public schools? Share your experiences and thoughts with classmates. Discuss how and why you might incorporate character education into your classroom instruction.

▶ CHARACTER EDUCATION AND CITIZENSHIP

Over the last few decades there has been increasing support for programs and approaches in schools that will help develop a child's character traits early on during their academic training (Foster & Daly, 2016). The National Council for the Social Studies' report, *Fostering Civic Virtue: Character Education in the Social Studies* (NCSS Task Force on Character Education, 1997), explains that social studies teachers have a "clear responsibility and duty to refocus their classrooms on the teaching of character and civic virtue." The report made strong statements about fostering moral and civic virtue in school environments, which are themselves models of the core values and principles being taught to young people. Teachers are reminded that they have a responsibility to be role models. The report also points out the need for schools to have dialogue with community members over the values that schools will teach. Similar statements have been issued by state organizations like the California Council for the Social Studies (CS4, 2000), the National Organization of Secondary School Principals (Harned, 1999), and the National Association of Elementary School Principals (www.naesp.org). Given the events of the 2020 presidential election and contemporary social and political unrest in the United States, it is reasonable to assume that there will only be increased pressure and emphasis on civic education, social justice, values, and decision making in public schools.

▶ CHARACTER EDUCATION, VALUES, AND DECISION MAKING

The goals of character education include establishing life patterns and personal codes of behavior that include qualities such as integrity, belief in self and others, responsibility, and honor. Character itself has a strong relationship to how individuals view the world and their values. What individuals feel to be important or even worthwhile has an impact upon character, as does how they view the importance of themselves and others.

Particularly during childhood, an individual's values and worldview are developing and changing. The family and school, as well as other formal and informal social structures, help shape and form the individual's worldview and his/her interwoven values and attitudes. In a democratic society, we want children to grow in their reasoned commitment to such democratic principles as majority rule, equal opportunity, individual rights, the rule of law, freedom of speech, and religious freedom.

Every society tries to shape the values of the young. Those who personally care about an individual child, and this includes parents, teachers, and others, want the child to grow up with the very best set of values possible. However, not everyone agrees about what that set is or about how it needs to be developed.

Parents and other family members present their child with their perspective, often a complex one. Various social groups attempt to exert pressure as well, having what is termed a conserving influence. Conserving influences in any culture are those that transmit, maintain, and preserve that culture as it is. Religious, political, and social groups pressure a child to accept and believe in the values upon which the groups themselves are based. Schools also exert their own conserving influence. It should go almost without saying that the influence of any of these forces is not always unified (nor is it always positive).

▶ DECISION MAKING AND VALUES

One goal of social studies education is to develop students' abilities to make decisions based on democratic principles and sound moral values. There is nothing new about this. It was implicit in the education of young Roman citizens in the ancient Roman republic. In modern times, generations of social studies teachers have praised and quoted Shirley Engle's eloquent advocacy of the belief that decision making is the heart of the social studies (Engle, 1960). Making decisions involves value judgment calls. Engle pointed out that evaluation skills are needed throughout life. People constantly decide not only what is the right thing to do, but also what is the best thing to do, what they want to do, and what they have to do. Evaluation skills are always difficult because of dilemmas and conflicts and because there is often doubt about evaluative criteria and questions such as relevance, truth and accuracy, suitability, importance, utility, greatness, potential, goodness, beauty, quality, effort, or even quantity.

We make judgments and decisions based on what we hold to be important, sensible, good, and worthwhile. However, the essential evaluation skills that teachers need to develop in students build from awareness and reasoning. To develop this awareness, students need to be given frequent and significant opportunities to make decisions. They need to learn how and when to question what they see and hear. Teachers need to model how such decisions are made.

Students need to learn to determine when and how they should make decisions. They need to be able to distinguish between different kinds of situations requiring decisions. Here are some situations a student may encounter that require decision making:

- Sometimes decisions must be made based on some single criterion, and sometimes it is necessary to weigh and consider several criteria.
- Sometimes the difference between right and wrong is clear-cut, but more often, the decision is not so clear.
- Some decisions should be made with only partial information.
- Some judgment calls are easy, and some are difficult because of conflicts in how we feel.
- Often we have to make holistic judgments based on experience.
- Some decisions are made on purely personal bases, solely on what serves one's own ends, personal ambitions, or feelings and emotions.
- Some decisions should be made altruistically with the good of one's self sacrificed for the good of others or of the group.
- Values are involved in determining what alternatives are available (what the options are) in a given decision-making situation. Values also are the basis for making choices among the available alternatives:
    - What course of action should be pursued?
    - What solution is the best "fit" to existing conditions?
    - What alternative offers the most advantages or fewest disadvantages?
    - Which choice is most dangerous or most safe?

Values even influence how we deal with evidence (distinguishing fact from speculation, conclusion from opinion, fantasy from reality, truth from falsehood, etc.), determining relevance, determining adequacy of evidence, projecting a trend, and making personal decisions or determination of ultimate courses to take (e.g., defining justice or morality in a situation). Helping students become more responsible as well as more effective problem solvers requires providing experience and practice that help develop evaluation skills. The following are evaluation skills and examples of each.

Determining Alternatives

- On a map, have students determine alternative routes to a single location or alternative destinations that will fill a particular need for the crew of a ship (political safety during a war, water before the crew dies of thirst, etc.).
- Have students hold class contests over topics such as a favorite historical character, favorite book, ideal vacation spot, best place to live, and so on. Have a nomination process and then choose advocates.
- Have students nominate possible sites for real and hypothetical projects, field trips, and so on.
- Have students suggest menus, ingredients, activities, etc., for social events and cultural celebrations.
- Do brainstorming activities in which students have a specific number of responses to something (e.g., ten best reasons for, ways to interpret music through movement, etc.).
- Include nominating (favorite, best, etc.) as a regular part of daily activities.
- As students read about people's actions, stop and ask what else these people could have done that would have demonstrated honesty, honor, caring, etc.

Choosing Among Alternatives

- Give students alternatives from which to choose as a regular activity. These can be very real decisions that have impact on them and what they do. Help them to understand the consequence and the implications of particular choices.
- Talk about the reasonableness of different explanations and theories. Include the alternatives available to different people in history, the school, the home, and their possible reasoning in making the decision.
- Give three or four alternative titles for stories and let students choose among them and explain their reasoning.
- Have students vote for favorites among short series of stories, television shows, movies, and so on.
- In studying history and geography, give students real or made-up biographies of several different people. Then have them choose the best person for such things as an Arctic expedition, a safari, a rescue mission, a delegation to take a particular message to the president, and so on.

Distinguishing Fact From Speculation, Conclusion From Opinion, Fantasy From Reality, and Truth From Falsehood

- Give students a series of statements and let them try to identify which statements are fact and which are opinion.
- Give students a series of untrue statements about some topic they have been studying and have them explain why the statements are untrue.

- Have students identify fantastic elements in stories, television shows, movies, and so on.
- Show a picture and let the children make a series of statements about the picture. As each statement is made, have the other students determine if the statement is actually true or if it is speculation, conclusion, or opinion.

Determining Relevance

- Give students a statement that makes an assertion or hypothesis. Then present them with a series of other statements of fact and opinion. With each of these, have the children decide if the statement is relevant.
- Write a question on the board. Have students scan a paragraph and volunteer to read any statements that are relevant to the question.
- Give students a proverb, truism, or superstition. Follow it with a collection of action statements and facts. Let them classify the actions and facts as relevant or not. They should be able to reach the conclusion that a fact may be relevant and supportive without proving the original statement to be true.

Determining the Adequacy of Evidence

- Give students a series of arguments or reasons and then ask them to judge if a case has been made.
- Give students a series of "If A and B, then C" statements. Have them determine which ones they accept and which ones they do not.
- Give students a series of assertions. Ask them to tell what it would take by way of evidence for them to accept the truth of each one.
- Tell students a preposterous story about a well-known historical person. Make it so far-fetched that they cannot believe it. When they start expressing their disbelief, have them try to tell why they do not believe. An example of a preposterous story could include the teacher explaining to students that it was not George Washington but an exact look-alike who turned up at Mount Vernon, and the look-alike became the first president.

Projecting a Trend

- Give students a series of events and have them predict the event(s) that will follow.
- Describe a series of events and have students give the trend a name.
- Have students do a relevance web showing the connections among events that make the series of events a trend.

Defining Justice for Particular Instances

- Read stories with a moral purpose and let them verbalize their own views of "the moral of the story."
- Provide a series of open-ended scenarios and problems and ask students to tell what they think would be the right thing to do in these situations.
- Read some examples of actions of courts and governments and ask students to decide if the action taken was fair.

> **FYI:** The NCSS (2013, p. 103) defines "personal values" as "ethical and moral commitments that guide individuals' actions and interpersonal relationships. Examples: Personal values include empathy, integrity, self-reliance, generosity, trustworthiness, and creativity."

 ## WHAT VALUES DO YOU TEACH?

The place of values in the classroom is controversial. Whether teachers should teach values is not really the point. Every teacher has and will always teach values either directly or indirectly. Opinions differ, though, about what values should be taught and how we should teach them. Teaching a particular religious or political viewpoint, how to vote in an election, or what constitutes acceptable reading or entertainment is certainly problematic. There are, however, at least three areas in which it seems important that the schools take an active and effective role in developing students' beliefs. These are:

- Values related to living in a democracy.
- Values implicit within a multicultural society.
- Values that relate to school success and to the functional classroom.

The main purpose of social studies is to help students develop as good citizens. Character education is at least implied in the goal of civic virtue. While few would take issue with the importance of good citizenship or the development of character, there is controversy over what these terms mean and about the methods that can and should be used (Waters & Russell, 2012).

Emotional charges of indoctrination can be levied easily, and words such as "nationalism" can be intoned with either positive or negative meanings. Though a broad spectrum of viewpoints exists, there seem to be at least six areas of values in which teachers need to work for the democracy to continue to exist:

- The need for participation.
- The worth of and rights of the individual.
- The rule of the majority and the rights of the minority.
- Personal responsibility.
- Respect for law and authority and for other people.
- Equality and justice.

The goals of character education in relation to these values can be developed in many ways. Teachers should develop classrooms that are moral communities, where fairness, trust, caring, and taking responsibility are both expectations and norms.

History is an important part of the development of these values and intrinsic to character development and the decision-making process. Classrooms that are themselves moral communities should promote greater awareness in students of what has happened in the past and what is happening now related to their own country and others. Knowledge of the reasons that governments exist, the principles and purposes upon which they were founded, and the events leading up to their present state is essential for understanding the present and preparing for the future. Simply looking at the founding of this country and others and studying history in general, of course, are part of an established educational tradition. However, to build democratic values, an active learning approach is needed. Students can be given responsibility, can make decisions, and can develop their own views in relation to what has happened in the past and present. Teachers can hold mock elections and mock trials, and they can use opinionnaires and polls in the classroom. They can set up classroom governments and look at questions of equality, justice, human rights, and individual and corporate responsibility in current events. Even playing games and sports can become occasions to talk about the importance of decision making, rules, personal responsibility, and concern for the rights of others. Things that teachers do to help individuals gain acceptance, success, and confidence are all an important part of citizenship education in a democracy.

Multicultural Education, Decision Making, and Values

Multicultural education is a definitive attempt to make students more aware of the distinguishing differences and unifying similarities among various cultures and ethnic groups in the world. It is not simply education of a particular nature designed for minority groups. Part of its outcome should be helping students value themselves and others. Multicultural education is directly tied to our democratic values, the principle of equality, the pluralistic nature of our society, and the concept of the global village. Multicultural education is aimed at the eradication of racism, classism, discrimination, sexism, prejudice, and ethnocentrism.

There are many reasons for moving to greater emphasis on multicultural education in social studies. Among them are the following ideas:

- We live in a pluralistic society, a global village.
- Almost without exception, cultural groups have a history of prejudice and discrimination.
- There is a natural tendency among human beings to distrust people who are different and to hold them at arm's length.
- It is generally believed that the more people know about another culture, the more positive they will feel about it.
- Women, ethnic groups, racial groups, and numerous cultures have been largely ignored or misrepresented in curriculum materials in the past and present.

Multicultural education works on several basic assumptions and beliefs. For example, there are some generally held beliefs about the nature of various cultural, ethnic, and racial groups in the world. One of them is that members of every cultural and ethnic group have been and are productive and resourceful and, therefore, have made substantial contributions to world civilization. Another is that no sex and no race or cultural or ethnic group is innately superior or inferior to any other. Such assumptions become important teachings in multicultural education, as do assumptions about people. The latter include the belief that historic injustices and discrimination are not reasons for present personal guilt or retribution and neither are they cause for the continuation of prejudice into the future. An important realization that is part of this assumption system is that everyone has prejudices and biases.

Finally, multicultural education is based on some major educational assumptions. The chief among these is that ethnocentrism, racism, and provincialism are going to continue to thrive without the kind of strong positive effort of multicultural education. These assumptions have led to the development of a variety of goals for multicultural education. Typical of such goals is the following set.

Students will develop . . .

- An understanding of cultural diversity within our society and diversity within culture groups.
- The ability to communicate with other culture groups both to resolve conflict and to improve relationships.
- Attitudes, values, and behavior that are supportive of ethnic and cultural diversity.
- Pride in their cultural heritage.
- Knowledge, appreciation, and understanding of other cultures, both in this country and throughout the world.
- A sense of the history of both their own culture and those of others.

The most significant tool of multicultural education is knowledge. Knowing about one's own and other cultures and viewing others through undistorted pictures of their strengths and accomplishments are essential to appreciation. Naturally, it follows that increased positive, mutually beneficial contact with people of other groups (e.g., other cultures, races, religions, sexes) is going to promote mutual understanding and appreciation.

Values That Relate to School Success and to the Functional Classroom

Values relating to being good students have implications for both the present and future lives of students. The success of the school experience is based on a student doing his/her own work, giving effort, staying on task, completing work on time, getting along with others, participating, not bothering others, obeying the rules, doing what the teacher says, and other related behaviors. These, in turn, are based on values such as (work) integrity and honesty; the work ethic (the view that success ought to come from work and indeed will result if you work hard); the high value of achievement; the importance of honest effort; the importance of (and belief in) the essential code of fairness, justice, and equality governing individuals and (to an acceptable extent) societal behavior; concern for others; and complying with and having respect for authority.

The fact is that schools function on such values. The classroom can only "work" if most of these values are, at least in some measure, broadly accepted. The same is true of most workplaces and of the entire society. A teacher should have control and be the authority.

Essentially, these values are taught in several ways, not the least of which are traditional expectations that students bring to the first day of school. Students come to school expecting to have to behave in certain ways and with a set of pre-formed notions about what teachers are and how they are supposed to be treated. Schools continue this development through the classroom expectations of teachers, through the development of patterns and habits of behavior, through constant and consistent practice, and through setting and making clear sets of school and classroom rules.

▶ DEVELOPING VALUES

Those who attempt to develop and/or alter values and beliefs, including character educators, use several different approaches. Some of these approaches utilize questionable propaganda techniques, even to the point that they appear to be nothing less than types of indoctrination. A teacher should have ethical concerns about such approaches even when motivated by unselfish caring and concern. Other approaches, at first glance, seem unlikely to have any influence at all. However, the teacher should realize that any single approach could be used ineffectively as well as effectively. Ryan (2000) explained that talk about character education is easier than doing it. He outlines six methods that he calls the six "Es" of character education: *e*xample, *e*xplanation, *e*xhortation (praise and pep talks), *e*thos (ethical environment), *e*xperience, and *e*xpectation of excellence. The six "Es" are one way of conceptualizing how we go about teaching value-laden material. However, we have found the following five basic categories of methodology to be more useful.

Teaching About Decision Making and Values Through Pronouncements, Rules, and Warnings

Many times, adults simply tell young people what to believe. This may occur very openly, or it may be much subtler. In school, for example, it is common to begin by giving students a set of classroom rules. There may or may not be discussion of these rules, but the fact is that students are told that these rules must be obeyed. The rules tell them what is right, what is wrong, what is good, what to admire, and so on. Values are also taught very directly when certain behaviors are expected in students. Teachers, parents, and other adults imply what is good and bad by the behaviors that they demand or expect. Values are taught directly through home and school rules, requirements, and individual and group orders and statements. The teacher says, "Stand up straight! Do your homework! Write carefully and neatly!" The teacher wants and expects work to be on time and complete. The headings should all be alike. Paper and writing utensils should meet certain standards. Students are to be quiet except when the teacher wants them to talk. These actions imply compliance with authority, responsibility, taking pride in work, and other attributes that constitute at least part of being good. The pronouncements are often supported with consequences.

Elementary students vary in the extent to which they may be influenced by this way of teaching. They are not as likely to believe something that contradicts values they have learned earlier, especially strongly entrenched beliefs. Nonetheless, a constant and unvarying repetition of the same message or of the same expectations has a conditioning effect. For instance, when students are quieted whenever they speak out in class, when they are required to sit in the same seat every day, or when at the same hour and on the same cue they are required to get out a book and turn to a prearranged page, they grow to believe that this is the way things are supposed to be. When behavioral expectations are accompanied by a consistently applied punishment and reward system, over time, behavior and beliefs fall into line. Some systems of classroom management are based on this approach.

Teaching About Decision Making and Values Through Examples and Models

Elementary students have idols, heroes, and role models whom they strive to be like. These include people they know, people they see on television and in movies, and people they read about or hear about. Characters in nearly every story serve as models for students. Even toys such as Mickey Mouse, Dora the Explorer, Superman, and Spider-Man, which are advertised for children, become models of ideals. When used in school, the modeling approach involves getting students to look at figures in stories and history as the kind of people that they should aspire to be like. As a way of teaching values, modeling involves making students more aware of people and of accomplishments and principles and makes children feel more positively toward these people.

Teachers often model values unconsciously. They show who and what they think highly of or, conversely, do not think highly of by their emotional reactions. They share personal role models, preferences among activities, approval and disapproval of the actions of people, and other qualities with emotional signals that communicate in infectious ways to students. We also should not ignore the fact that the teachers become models themselves. Over the course of a school year, students grow to like and admire different qualities that they see in their teachers. Teachers are often models of fairness, caring, intelligence, dress, and so on for students. Teachers also unconsciously or consciously begin using a modeling approach when they hold students up for praise or when they display students' work. They are saying to students, "This is the way I want you to be."

The most obvious use of modeling in social studies involves identifying role models in history, present-day real life, fiction, radio, motion pictures, or television. Elementary teachers do this by telling stories, encouraging discussion, and having children read. Teachers who use this approach most effectively present desirable role models in exciting ways and bring out the most admirable qualities of these individuals.

This approach can make school more interesting and positive and may even make the teacher seem more aware of the real world in which the students live. Schools tend to ignore the many positive characters in television shows and in movies, and this is one place where this set of experiences can be brought to good use. Folk tales are rich in heroes and can provide a way of helping students see qualities that are admirable while examining cultural values and beliefs. Most children's books involve protagonists who represent the good versus the antagonists who are perceived as bad.

A major issue with the modeling approach with real-life role models is that real people have weaknesses, shortcomings, and even vices. Whenever we deal with real role models, we risk later disillusionment. Students find out that some of the stories that they learned as "truth," stories that even their teachers thought were true, are merely legends and are probably not true at all. The story of George Washington chopping down the cherry tree is a prime example. Even worse, students may discover that the role models they thought were perfect have made bad mistakes, shown prejudice or other very negative emotions, or been unfair or even dishonest. It is often difficult to maintain admiration for what role models have stood for when their imperfections and humanity are revealed. Disillusionment with a hero or role model may also mean rejection of the positive values she or he represents.

The problem is that there are no infallible role models. This may be an argument for reliance on mythical and fictional heroes. These kinds of models have a distinct advantage. Their lives are limited to the stories in which they appear. Hidden flaws cannot be discovered outside that context. But the advantage is also a limitation. Most story heroes lack depth, and because of this they do not always seem real enough to serve as models. The best solution seems to be to continue with a combination of historical and fictional heroes, teaching students to admire the positive aspects of their role models while recognizing shortcomings and weaknesses.

Teaching About Decision Making and Values Through Stories With Morals or Lessons

Another way of approaching decision making, values, and worldviews is through stories and examples that speak directly to values. A story is told with a lesson embedded in it. Typically, the stories show how to behave or act in situations in which a decision has to be made. Often in these stories, acceptable behaviors and actions are rewarded, and, of course, unacceptable behaviors bring undesirable consequences.

Fables and parables have been used to teach right and wrong for thousands of years. This approach is most effective when the listener or reader is provoked to think and discuss the story, leading to the discovery of the embedded moral or lesson. This approach is not very successful if a lesson runs contrary to the existing worldview of the audience or when the story seems to be an attempt to force a belief that they do not want to accept. The story approach offers a lot of possibilities for the teacher. Most importantly, stories have plots, characters, and settings, which are all factors that make them both interesting and memorable.

Nonfiction and fiction stories provide a way to look at different cultures, different times, and different beliefs. Every folk story tells a great deal about the culture from which it came. It shows what those people believed and, more importantly, what they thought was worth teaching or passing along to the younger generation.

Stories offer opportunity for discussion and thinking, for questions, for focusing on alternatives, and for comparison with other stories and with personal experiences. Students can learn through dramatizing experiences with stories, through looking at character motivation, through examining alternative outcomes and beginnings, and through looking at the author's viewpoint, for example.

Teaching About Decision Making and Values by Examining Personal Actions

Elementary teachers can help students develop their values by giving them experiences in which they can become more reflective and analytical about what they do and what they see. Teachers need to have students examine the occurrences of everyday life, how they have acted and felt in situations, and the reasons behind these feelings. This kind of values analysis involves looking carefully and sequentially at the details of what happened, making special note of behavior, then looking at the causes or reasons contributing to that behavior as well as the outcomes of it. The analysis does not end there. The next step is to speculate about alternative possible behaviors and consider what might have been more reasonable, moral, acceptable, and effective in the situation. There must be constant reminders of what the principal people involved did and did not know at the time.

One of the outcomes of this approach is that it makes students look at their own lives instead of just two-dimensional characters in media, storybooks, and history. The teacher may begin with autobiographical anecdotes or descriptions of events in the classroom that students have experienced. The autobiographical stories serve as models to provoke examples from students and as one way of communicating the real humanity of the teacher. Often the stories point out times when the teacher did not act in the best way. If the teacher can share an embarrassing moment, it may have a releasing effect on students. The shared class experiences need to be carefully selected, however, and developed as a group effort. The teacher should not be using the approach as a way of criticizing or scolding students. Rather, it should be an honest joint exploration of an event that was not exactly satisfactory in its outcome. Used well, the approach also has a bonding effect for the class.

Usually the approach goes through a series of definitive steps, beginning with a narrative description of the situation, which is then discussed from the standpoint of identifying the central issue, concern, or problem. This method may require considerable time because it is critical to get a clear vision of the heart of the matter. The next step is to look at all sides of the matter, examining minute details and looking for things that may appear trivial but, upon examination, are critical. This is essentially an information-gathering stage. That information is then examined and sifted to remove the clutter of irrelevant or unimportant observations that are not needed for judgment. The final stages take the students through tentative judgments that are evaluated and appraised before final assessments are made.

Teaching About Decision Making and Values Through Problem Solving

Many of the approaches to effective teaching that have been developed involve problem solving. They begin with dilemmas or conflicts in which decisions are demanded and ask the learner to make a judgment and then explain it. Both the moral reasoning approach, which involves moral dilemmas, and clarification approach are essentially of this type. Moral reasoning approaches, popularized by Lawrence Kohlberg (1984, 1985), involve the development of a sense of justice through a series of progressive stages. The basis of Kohlberg's approach is that individuals can be guided and accelerated in these stages, developing their reasoning ability by thinking about a series of dilemmas in which there are no clear-cut right and good actions to take. The individual has to choose between alternatives where it is a matter of determining "the lesser of two evils." An example of such a dilemma can be seen in Figure 3.1.

If they are shown dilemmas such as the one described here, students can soon develop the ability to create their own in a guided discussion format. The dilemmas themselves, which can be designed to fit the age level and the content being studied, should involve creating points of departure for discussions of moral values. The essential position of the Kohlbergian research is that the development of moral reasoning occurs through exposure to such dilemmas and that growth is both irreversible and important in influencing moral behavior.

Values analysis approaches are designed to help students become clearer about why they act and think as they do. The essential view is that people should reflect their

In the 1840s, a boy who was traveling by wagon train to Oregon becomes the head of his family when his parents sicken and die. Other families in the wagon train are occupied with their own survival problems to try to take all these children under their wings, so the boy is pretty much on his own. Soon, the boy and his brothers and sisters are the last wagon in the train, struggling just to keep up. Because the wagon train has been slowed by a series of difficulties, the food supply for the boy's family soon begins to run out. One day, the boy sights a herd of deer crossing the trail in back of the wagon train. If he stops to hunt, the wagon train will move on without his family and the winter may close down on them in the mountains. If he does not hunt, he and his brothers and sisters may starve. Should he have his own family make camp while he goes after the deer or simply try to keep up with the rest of the wagons?

Figure 3.1 Moral Dilemma Example

values in the way they act, but they do not always do so. The reason they do not is that they do not see what implications their belief systems have for their lives. The approach confronts students with decisions that simply have to be reasoned out or clarified. Teacher questions that probe the reasons for feelings and decisions are at the heart of this technique. The student is often confronted with open-ended situations in which the question of what the meaning is becomes most important. Students may be asked to set priorities, choose from among alternatives, and examine choices.

Problem-related approaches could be adapted for use with practically any topic or theme under study. They allow the student to examine questions of right and wrong as well as other values in the past, in other cultures, in hypothetical and fictional settings, in current events, and in their own lives.

▶ SOCIAL JUSTICE ISSUES, DECISION MAKING, AND VALUES

If one of the main goals of social studies is civic engagement and being a good citizen, then certainly social justice issues will need to be addressed in the elementary school curriculum. While topics such as racism, discrimination, poverty, etc. can be controversial, that does not mean teachers can simply ignore these topics to preserve their own comfort. Teachers have a responsibility to engage students in these important discussions from historical and contemporary perspectives. Given the current social and political climate in the United States, it is evident that teachers need to spend more time guiding students to a more nuanced understanding of the complexities in the world. Obviously, elementary teachers have a major responsibility in regards to curricular and instructional choice regarding social issues. What issues can/should you discuss with elementary students? What is age appropriate? How much detail do you provide? How should you introduce or frame discussions surrounding social justice issues?

We believe decision making, values, and character education can be used as catalysts for meaningful instruction surrounding social issues. For that reason, all the aforementioned examples and instructional approaches in this chapter could be used to develop social justice lessons by focusing on controversial topics. Moral dilemma discussions, for example, could easily be geared to focus on important social justice issues like gender equality, rights of the LGBTQ community, racial discrimination, and climate change. (Just to name a few!) We present these topics as intertwined because we have found this to be an effective method to introduce social issues to young learners in a systematic way that is less threatening to parents who might have strong values, opinions, and viewpoints. Anyone who has taught in public schools will likely tell you that parents (and even some administrators) are not always keen on teachers discussing social issues in the elementary setting. Whether they think the topic is inappropriate, the kids are too young, or they do not trust the teacher to responsibly and objectively handle such important topics, parents certainly do have rights and legitimate concerns that should not be overlooked. However, when these social issues are introduced and framed within the decision making, values, and character education context, there is always a solid foundation of standards and instructional precedent to introduce controversial topics in scaffolded ways. Children's literature is an excellent resource for elementary teachers who want to tackle social issues through the decision-making process. For a list of appropriate and relevant children's literature, we strongly recommend the National Council for the Social Studies (NCSS) Notable Trade Books for Young People annual list found at www.socialstudies.org/notable-social-studies-trade-books. These lists are updated yearly and organized by grade levels, themes, topics, and reading levels. While obviously not exhaustive, these lists do provide elementary teachers with a good starting point of appropriate children's books that could be used to address social issues and the decision-making process.

▶ LOOKING BACK

Decision making and character education involve the development of moral and civic virtue (Diggs & Akos, 2016). This means that teachers are involved in developing the value systems of their students. Values have a close relationship to our personal worldview and decision-making process. They have an impact on decision-making ability and especially on every aspect of evaluation. Elementary teachers should expose students to many types of values-based decision-making activities, including those in which students determine alternatives, choose alternatives, distinguish fact from speculation, determine relevance or adequacy of evidence, and project trends.

In social studies, elementary teachers need to be most concerned with values related to living in a democracy, values implicit within a multicultural society, and those values related to school success and issues of social justice. Teachers can help students develop values through a variety of approaches, including direct teaching, modeling, moral stories and lessons, and examination of personal actions and the actions of others.

EXTENSION ACTIVITY

You are at the end of the first nine weeks at Yourtown Elementary School (YES). Your first nine weeks of your teaching career have flown by. It is Friday afternoon, and the weekend is almost here. You have one final parent conference meeting of the nine weeks. The parent conference is moving along smoothly, when a concerned mother asks you, "Do you teach about racism and discrimination? If so, how? If not, why?" Unprepared for the answer, you pause and think.

TASK

For this activity, write down how you would answer the concerned mother. Think of all the direct and indirect ways decision making and values intersect to discuss important social justice issues like racism and discrimination. Share your response with peers/instructor.

CHECKING FOR UNDERSTANDING

1. What does character education mean?
2. Why is there a need for multicultural education?
3. How are values taught indirectly?
4. What are some different ways of modeling values?
5. What are some stories that you know that focus on social justice issues?

▶ HELPFUL RESOURCES

This video workshop for K–5 teachers provides a framework for teaching social studies, with a focus on creating effective citizens:

http://learner.org/resources/series176.html

A school principal shares how character education is implemented in her school and the role students play:

https://youtu.be/zofsiFm8Eto

Watch this panel discussion to learn more about racial justice and equity in education:

www.youtube.com/watch?v=y4qd5fUlq0M

Watch this Boston University TED talk about the importance and need for character education in a multicultural society:

https://youtu.be/AWtK0oUNsls

Watch this video about Character Counts and the importance of developing life skills in students with character education programs:

https://youtu.be/cmHf7qTxtR0

Watch this lesson of a kindergarten class exploring American symbols and what they mean to diverse students:

https://learn.teachingchannel.com/video/just-the-facts-complete-lesson

▶ FURTHER READING

Berkowitz, M., & Bier, M. (2005). *What works in character education: A research-driven guide for educators*. Washington, DC: Report from the Character Education Partnership.

This comprehensive report contains a detailed synthesis and analysis of research on many character education programs being implemented in U.S. schools. The purpose of the report is to examine more closely and critically the effects that character education programs have on student achievement to determine what is, or is not, working in schools.

Raths, L., Harmin, M., & Simon, S. (1966). *Values and teaching: Working with values in the classroom*. Columbus, OH: Charles E. Merrill.

This book outlined the foundation of the controversial "values clarification" approach to moral development during the turbulent 1960s. The book explains how teachers should approach the task of values education in the classroom.

McClellan, B. E. (1999). *Moral education in America: Schools and the shaping of character from colonial times to the present*. New York: Teachers College Press.

This book provides an extensive and complete history of moral education in America. The author provides excellent documentation and evidence explaining how the practice of educating students in the moral domain has changed and evolved throughout the history of the United States.

Martell, C. (2017). Approaches to teaching race in elementary social studies: A case study of pre-service teachers. *The Journal of Social Studies Research*, *41*(1), 75–87.

This article is a must-read for elementary educators interested in learning more about teaching race. The case study research highlights the importance of and need for increased attention to explicitly discussing race in teacher preparation programs.

▶ REFERENCES

Berkowitz, M., & Bier, M. (2005). *What works in character education: A research-driven guide for educators*. Washington, DC: The Character Education Partnership.

CS4. (2000). *Character education and the social studies: A position statement for the council for state social studies specialists*. Available at: https://cs4.socialstudies.org/about/aboutus.

Diggs, C., & Akos, P. (2016). The promise of character education in middle school: A meta-analysis. *Middle Grades Review*, *2*(2), Article 4.

Engle, S. H. (1960). Decision making: The heart of the social studies. *Social Education*, *24*(November), 301.

Foster, A., & Daly, K. (2016). Focus on elementary: Creating global citizens: Using attitudes and action to teach character education. *Childhood Education*, *92*(1), 80–85.

Harned, P. (1999). Leading the effort to teach character in the schools. *NAASP Bulletin*, *83*(October), 25–32.

Kohlberg, L. (1984). *Essays on moral development: Vol. 2: The psychology of moral development*. New York: Harper and Row.

Kohlberg, L. (1985). *The meaning and measurement of moral development*. Worcester, MA: Clark University.

National Council for the Social Studies (NCSS). (2013). *The College, Career, and Civic Life (C3) Framework for social studies state standards: Guidance for enhancing the rigor of K-12 civics, economics, geography, and history*. Silver Spring, MD: NCSS. (www.ncss.org/c3).

NCSS Task Force on Character Education. (1997). Fostering civic virtue: Character education in the social studies. *Social Education*, *61*(April/May), 225–227.

Ryan, K. (2000). *The six E's of character education: Practical ways to bring moral instruction to life for your students*. Available at: https://www.scu.edu/character/resources/the-six-es-of-character-education/.

Waters, S., & Russell, W. (2012). Character, moral, and values education: The foundation of effective citizenship. In W. Russell (Ed.), *Contemporary social studies: An essential reader* (pp. 97–116). Charlotte, NC: Information Age Publishing.

Planning Social Studies Instruction

▶ LOOKING AHEAD

The aim of this chapter is to help you become a better planner. To do this, we begin with the problems that teachers have in planning. We then move to the structures of different teaching plans. As you read the chapter, you need to consider these questions:

- What are your strengths and weaknesses as a planner?
- What do you need to be able to do to plan a teaching unit?
- Are you likely to rely heavily on a textbook?
- How can you effectively plan long term?
- Are you planning to meet the needs of all your students, including those with special learning needs and those whose cultural backgrounds are different from your own?

everytime you are planning, you want to ask these questions.

Effective planning is a necessary and essential ingredient of effective teaching. Obviously, there is more to teaching than planning, but imagine a teacher who does not plan. Such a teacher has no sense of what is to go on in the classroom and quickly loses efficacy and impact. Fortunately, many teachers do at least some planning, but many do far too little. Too often, teaching plans consist of cryptic notes in lesson–plan books referring to pages in the textbook. These kinds of plans can hardly lead to exciting, creative classrooms.

CAN YOU? DO YOU?

asking yourself if you are able to do these tasks

Can you . . .

- Plan an instructional social studies unit?
- Identify and describe different types of units?
- Write instructional objectives?
- Establish a "set" in a lesson?
- Identify the basic components in a lesson plan?

Do you . . .

ask if you already do these tasks

- Have experience in collaborative planning?
- Know how to go about choosing a unit topic?
- Know how to create a curriculum map/guide?
- Know what is meant by the term *webbing* when referring to planning?
- Understand instructional objectives?

FOCUS ACTIVITY

Before reading this chapter, try the following focus activity.

Think back on your educational experience. What was the most memorable lesson/unit you experienced as a student? What made the lesson/unit memorable? Share experiences with others. Discuss the details of experiences and compare. Do your educational experiences share common attributes with others'? If so, what attributes? Do you think these experiences will have an impact on how you plan for instruction? If so, how?

▶ WHY IS PLANNING IMPORTANT?

Planning has special importance in broad content areas like social studies in which there is so much information. Because of the breadth of the field, even the best and most experienced teachers will not have comprehensive knowledge. All teachers need to use numerous resources. The resource possibilities are constantly growing. The internet and a growing variety of computer software packages alone have increased the possibilities astronomically. One of the major elements in good planning is finding and collecting the best resources and organizing them in a purposeful way. Except for those working at kindergarten and perhaps first-grade levels, most teachers are likely to start their planning with a textbook because many schools/districts set a guideline or require a specific curriculum. Teachers may also get help from mentor teachers in some schools or from a team leader, a lead teacher, a department chair, or an entire group of grade-level colleagues. Since state governments are legally responsible for the public schools, there are state guidelines containing frameworks, rules, standards, and/or regulations regarding what is taught. National teacher organizations also provide input about what should go on in the social studies. (NCSS, the Association for Supervision and Curriculum Development, and the National Education Association are among the largest of these organizations. The NCSS alone publishes two useful journals for elementary social studies teachers, *Social Education* and *Social Studies and the Young Learner*.)

For kinder & 1st grade, most lessons will come from district guidelines.

One problem with having all these resources – and, remember, these are only the beginning points for planning – is that they end up as mountains of pages of print telling the teacher what to do – more than he or she can cope with. By its very size, the accumulation of resource guides, instead of helping, intimidates and confuses new teachers. Teachers feel they can only retreat to the safety of that first resource, the textbook. Staying strictly with that safe resource soon becomes a comfortable and safe pattern. It is a natural thing to do. It reduces uncertainty and confusion and leaves the difficult decisions of planning to the so-called experts. However, it prevents these teachers from reaching their own potential.

There are some good reasons why long-term total reliance on textbooks is not the best course:

1. Following this route means that the teacher, the social studies curriculum, and the classroom are not likely to be very exciting, interesting, or enjoyable for students. If the whole point of schooling is to produce involved, independent learners, then this is surely the last kind of environment one would want to foster.
2. "Read and answer the question" social studies, which is the type of teaching the textbook approach is likely to produce, is not likely to be very meaningful or seem very purposeful to students. Though it is almost a corollary to reason #1, not only are students not going to enjoy this kind of approach; they are also not going to learn from it or understand why they are doing it.
3. There is little teacher satisfaction gained from such an approach. What makes teaching exciting is seeing what you have planned come alive in the classroom and seeing student learning result from your plans. When you repeatedly use a "canned" plan, teaching soon becomes boring and unrewarding.

▶ SETTING THE STAGE: CREATING THE ENVIRONMENT

If you are the kind of teacher who wants to avoid the textbook pitfall, how do you begin to plan? Curiously, both the planning process and the actual planning product that flows out of this process involve a good deal of scene setting. Doing social studies in the classroom is almost like doing theater. We are trying to create a dramatic climate, one with just the right kind of tension and sufficient excitement for learning to occur. With effective planning in social studies, that climate is there, and it can be identified by some predictable hallmarks.

These hallmarks include:

- *A sense of anticipation or expectancy on the part of the student audience*: They know that something special is going to happen, and they have a fairly good idea of what it is, with just enough uncertainty for the sake of anticipation and suspense.
- *A feeling of purpose and direction*: Students know why they are there and what the class is all about.
- *An awareness that is more than knowledge of continuity*: What is done today relates to yesterday as well as to tomorrow.
- *An atmosphere of involvement or participation in the planning process itself and how the plans flow into the doing*: There is a sense of community or even family that acknowledges that "we are in this together."
- *An awareness of leadership*: To a degree, this seals off or at least pulls the reins to control conflict. It keeps a sense of urgency, allowing flexibility, but keeps at the job.

▶ WHY DON'T TEACHERS PLAN?

It may seem negative to approach planning from a "Why don't teachers plan (even the experienced ones)?" perspective, but if we look at some of the reasons teachers do not plan or at least do not

> **FYI:** "Failing to plan is planning to fail" (Alan Lakein).

plan well, you may see why planning is so difficult yet so important. This may be helpful when we examine some of the planning tools that are used in social studies. First, we must recognize that we must deal with teachers' perceptions of their reasons as the reasons themselves. How teachers feel about what they do and do not do and how they look at themselves are very important. There is a growing belief that time management is an area in which simply understanding the problems and deterrents may help the teacher in overcoming them. Here are a few reasonable conclusions about the factors involved in teachers' failure to plan.

a. *Not enough time*: Teachers have crowded days often filled with unavoidable trivialities, both planned and unplanned. Clerical tasks, students demanding attention, classroom accidents, discipline situations, paper grading, and many others compete to more than fill every minute.

b. *Failure to set time priorities or give priority to planning*: Because teaching is time intensive, teachers must be very careful to choose what they do and give priority to planning.

c. *Dependence on previous material*: Once teachers have taught a topic a few times, they begin to accumulate a quantity of "stuff that works." There are obvious advantages to this, and the old adage "If it ain't broke, don't fix it" comes to mind. But there are also dangers, including staleness and a tendency to get behind the times.

d. *Procrastination*: For some of us, the whole problem is reduced to being slow about getting around to things.

e. *Failure to communicate*: There is a cooperative element even in teacher planning. Good planning means letting involved people (parents, resource people, school officials, other teachers, etc.) know what they need to know and what they need to do in advance.

f. *Experience*: Experience itself may stand in the way of effective planning. Teachers can develop patterns and habits very quickly that are counterproductive, and these may persist and transfer.

g. *Lack of interest or enthusiasm for the content*: Some teachers will say that they do not like social studies.

h. *Fear of the content*: Some teachers do not have the content knowledge to teach social studies effectively and comfortably.

i. *Low energy*: Many teachers say that they just do not have the energy, psychological or physical, to plan.

j. *Inability to deal with peer pressure*: Teachers want to be approved and liked by other teachers. They model their behavior on that of experienced teachers.

There are no easy ways to deal with all these forces that work against planning. Obviously, self-discipline, resolve to plan well, and a firm sense of purpose are qualities that teachers need. However, beyond these difficult and elusive acts of will, there are some concrete strategies that teachers can use to improve planning habits and skills. Not all of the following suggestions will work for everybody, but they are worth a try.

a. Schedule your time to include specifically designated planning time, and stick to the schedule as though a planning time were a meeting with the president.

b. Make lists of planning jobs and prioritize the lists.

c. Examine and change your patterns of behavior to avoid distractions.

d. Do the worst first, meaning complete that which you most dread and want to put off before you do the easier or more satisfying things.

e. Learn to "say no" without feeling guilt, turning off and away those who would interrupt your planning time.

f. Record and celebrate your planning successes in ways that you can remember and then repeat. (If it works, make sure you can do it again.)

▶ LONG-RANGE PLANNING

Long-range planning starts well before the school year begins, at which point the teacher creates a curriculum map/guide for a specific subject for the upcoming school year/semester. In some cases, curriculum maps are centrally created at the district or state level. In other cases, your school's adopted textbook may include a prescribed curriculum map. However, in some cases, it is the responsibility of the teacher or grade-level team to prepare a curriculum map. A basic curriculum map will include curriculum content and standards and a timeframe for which the material will be covered. An example of a social studies curriculum map for the first nine weeks of kindergarten can be seen in Figure 4.1.

> **FYI:** A curriculum map or guide can sometimes be called a scope and sequence or a pacing guide.

Long-range unit planning is more detailed than a curriculum map. The word *unit* is used with a lot of different meanings. Basically, a unit includes everything a group of learners do to explore a particular topic. What unifies the study or makes it a unit is the topic itself. This is true whether that topic is a general category type (such as Transportation), a concept (such as Democracy), a time period or event (such as the Age of Exploration), or a question (such as "What can be done to reduce pollution?"). When we talk about units in teaching, we are usually talking about the teaching plan for that topic. Such plans vary in length, in amount of detail, and even in their source of creation. A unit may attempt to plan for a week or for six weeks of work. Some people think that students need to learn more about each topic while others are convinced that more topics need to be covered. For most teachers, a unit plan will include two to three weeks of instruction. A minimalist unit plan includes the unit objectives, curriculum standards, assessments, and daily lesson plan sequence. A more advanced unit plan will include a detailed curriculum calendar along with detailed daily lesson plans.

▶ TEXTBOOK-CENTERED UNITS

Textbook programs dominate elementary classrooms (Educational Market Research, 2012; Ball & Feiman-Nemser, 1988). Using textbooks does not eliminate the need for preparation but does reduce the amount of preparation and does, to some extent, take the responsibility for making decisions about what students need to learn out of the teacher's hands.

Textbook units offer some important instructional advantages. For teachers who use textbook-centered units, there is common reading material containing the same information for all students. This is of tremendous advantage, for it makes it possible to give single assignments and to unify instruction. Another important positive about this type of teaching is the security of knowing that those who have prepared the material

- Unit 1: Our Classroom/ School   Time Frame: 3 Weeks

Essential Questions: What does it mean to be part of a community? How do my decisions affect those around me? Why is it important to work together?

Standards	Resources/Technology	Key Concepts	Vocabulary	Activities	Assessment
K.6.O1a K.6.O1b K.6.O.2a K.6.O.2b K.6.O.2c K.5.O.2	Smart Board, iPad, Trade Books, Globe, Artifacts from around the world, Encyclopedia, Maps *Miss Bindergarten Gets Ready for Kindergarten* by Joseph Slate Houghton Mifflin Social Studies K Kindergarten GREET THE WORLD Teacher's Book *The Pledge of Allegiance* by Lloyd G. Douglas **Social Studies Games:** http://www.primarygames.com/social_studies.php **Community Building Interactive Site:** http://www.sfsocialstudies.com/k/u2/index.html **Community Helpers Listening & Reading Activities:** http://teacher.scholastic.com/comm club/index.htm	- Who am I? - Character Counts - My role/jobs in daily routine at school - School helpers - Taking care of my School - Money concepts with Math - Cooperation and team building activities - Recite Daily Pledge, Recognize features of Flag	Rules Self Routine Pledge Flag Responsibility Currency Home School Friends Cooperation	- Rules and Expectations at school-Students help Create - Safety at School - Star of the Day or "All about Me" - School Jobs - Class Pet Care - Interview a School Staff Member - School Store - Good Citizenship Cat take home and journal - Gideon Dog-take home and journal	Assess student's journals using writing rubric. Assess vocabulary concepts through student-created definitions at end of unit. Student presentation of "Star of the Day" About me Posters

Notes for Strategies and Accommodations: Edmark Community Signs and Functional Words program. Have student draw a picture for pet care take home journal. Have students create pictures of verbally describe concepts. Alternate school jobs and add peer buddies as needed. Create task analysis to help student complete school job. Create a PowerPoint for the "All about Me" presentation. Provide cue cards of AAC device to conduct school staff member interview. Rubrics and assessments will have varying levels and adaptations based on need.

Figure 4.1 Example of a Social Studies Curriculum Map for Kindergarten (First Nine Weeks)

- Unit 2: Our Community   Time Frame: 3 weeks

Essential Questions: Why do people need to work? How do we read a map? What do safety signs mean?

Standards	Resources/Technology	Key Concepts	Vocabulary	Activities	Special Events	Assessment
K.2.O.2a K.2.O.2b K.2.O.3.a K.2.O.3c K.3.O.1b K.3.O.1c K.3.O.2a K.4.O.3a K.5.O.2 a K.5.O.2b	*Busy People All Around Town* By R.W. Alley *Rosie's Walk* By Pat Hutchins *What Will I Be?* by James Levin *Me on the Map* by Joan Sweeney Online Game for Safety Signs: http://interactives.mped.org/preview_mg.aspx?id=584&title=	- Discuss why people work - Different types of jobs - Look at structure of places in community and purpose - Recognize goods and services - Identify safety signs in school, traffic, and community	Same Different Career Community Helpers Bank Store Post Office Fire Department Hospital Map Roads Transportation Safety Signs Safety	- Share a picture and story about a family member - Research a place in the Community and make a map - Send Letters within classroom mail service	- Career Day - Field trip to Fire Department - Community Monopoly Game	Assess map, story, and letter using appropriate rubrics. Save map, story, and letters as permanent products Assess vocabulary concepts by having students match words with pictures.

Notes for Strategies and Accommodations: Create a map using paint on the computer. Send email instead of a letter.

Figure 4.1 (*Continued*)

- Unit 3: Our Land

Time Frame: 3 weeks

Essential Questions: Where does food come from? What can you learn from a map? What can help you locate items on a map?

Standards	Resources/Technology	Key Concepts	Vocabulary	Activities	Special Events	Assessment
K.3.0.3a K.3.0.3b K.3.0.2c	Me on the Map By Joan Sweeney Mapping Penny's World By Loreen Leedy Geography Games: http://www.kidsgeo.com/geography-games/	- Identify major geographic landscapes - Learn about where food comes from and agriculture - Learn more map symbols and map key	Agriculture Farm Map Ocean Land Lake River Mountains Hills Seasons Directional Terms	- Make a map - Follow a food activity - Graphic Organizer comparing/contrasting geographic features - Sensory Art - Dissect pumpkins vegetables and fruits and breads	- Field Trip to Berry Farm and Pumpkin Patch - Field Trip to Ijams Nature Center or the TN Valley Fair	Assess venn diagram of geographic features Assess vocabulary concepts using maps and globes Students will complete KWL chart for field trip to Ijam's

Notes for Strategies and Accommodations: Use tactile representation of various geographic features. Show photographs.

Figure 4.1 (Continued)

have knowledge and expertise in the field, have done a good deal of research into content, and have given thorough professional attention to the preparation of the text. There is added teacher peace of mind in knowing that modern technology has made it possible to keep the reading level of textual material more precisely at the intended grade level than at any point in educational history.

Textbook-centered units emphasize, usually above all else, getting information from print, most specifically from the textbook. Assignments involving reading pages, portions of chapters, and entire chapters to answer sets of questions or do other types of written exercises are most common.

▶ TYPES OF PLANNING FOR SOCIAL STUDIES UNITS

Textbook teaching is an easy pattern to set and a difficult routine to break. One reason it is so prevalent is that nearly all teachers have to do it. However, there are some positive ways a teacher can make use of this pattern to take control of their own teaching. The simplest of these is to use the textbook as a base but expand from that textbook. In this section, we will look at using and adapting different planning units, beginning with expanded textbook units.

Expanded Textbook Units

Social studies textbooks are structured into units that consist of single chapters or, in many cases, a series of two or more chapters. Teacher editions provide such material as vocabulary lists, activity ideas, day-by-day lesson plans, questions, and even lists of additional resources. Publishers may also provide numerous supplementary materials, including student handouts, project planning procedures, posters, maps, charts, Power-Point presentations, videos, and so on.

Teachers who rely heavily on textbooks need to be especially concerned about purposeful teaching. A regimen of careful planning with a focus on how to use the textbook creatively can help reduce, if not totally avoid, the pitfalls usually associated with textbook teaching. The following steps should be considered by teachers:

1. Try to get the "big picture." Be sure that you understand what the goals of the textbook are and how each book is organized and fits into the entire series.
2. Create a scope and sequence or curriculum map (what you teach and when you teach it) for the school year. As you do this, be sure to consider unequal treatment (giving more time to some topics than others) and omission of some topics.
3. For each unit, use the teacher edition judiciously to plan activities to introduce the topic and to help students achieve the objectives and reach a holistic understanding of the topic.
4. Maintain a high level of sensitivity to reading difficulties students may encounter and be ready to accommodate the individual learning needs of students.
5. Remember, the textbooks and their provided materials are only one of a variety of resources available for effective instruction. Try to think of alternatives to the textbook's suggested activities that address the goals and objectives of each unit in a student-centered way. Try to establish a balance of new versus repeated instructional activities from chapter to chapter. This gives students both the security of being able to learn a set of expectations about how to do things and the motivational freshness of activity variety.

6. Examine evaluation materials provided with the textbook carefully, and use them only after seeing their relationship to the teaching objectives. This usually means that you see what information, concepts, and basic skills are being assessed.

Collaborative Units

In many schools, elementary teachers work in teams to prepare units. The arrangements for doing this vary. In some cases, there are structured formal efforts across entire school districts by appointed groups of teachers. Other formal arrangements may involve grade-level teaming or subject area/discipline-teaming.

> **FYI:** Depending on the organization of your school, you most likely will organize in grade-level teams. Occasionally a school could have additional teams or committees organized by subject matter.

The kind of social studies units produced and the ways that teachers are expected to use them are almost as varied. In most instances, the aim is to combine talents and save individual teachers' planning time while producing some consistency throughout the school or system in the content that is taught. The units may in some instances even be developed to ensure that all teachers will be following the same sequence of activities. It is more common, though, for team planning to produce resource units that can be shared among teachers. Resource units systematically delineate common objectives, identify the most appropriate and useful available resources for teacher and student use, and create and share plans for teaching strategies and activities. Resource units may also include common tests and other evaluation procedures.

Some units that are planned by collaborative effort may be regarded as teaching units. These will not offer the same number and variety of activities as resource units, but they will have specific activities or lesson plans. Only a few, if any, alternative activities will be provided. Teachers may be expected to follow such units entirely, or they may have the option of doing the prescribed lessons or developing their own plans.

Teachers who are making a move into a grade level and school where such collaborative units are used may want to consider the following as guidelines:

1. Find out what degree of conformity and collaboration is expected from you as well as the extent to which you are expected to use units already prepared. At this step and all others, it is good to establish an advice-seeking relationship with a mentor teacher or the lead teacher if possible. (At the same time, you can find out how much creativity is encouraged.)
2. Become familiar with available units, paying attention to the goals and objectives. (Make sure that you understand and follow the pattern of intent.)
3. See how the collaborative units relate to the textbooks that are in the classroom (if there are any).
4. Browse through the activities looking for the overall motivational and teaching quality as well as particularly outstanding ideas and plans.
5. Look for ways that you can put your own creativity into existing activities. Simply by adding details, embellishing, and improving the focus of activities and lessons in existing collaborative plans, you may enliven your own teaching.
6. If the school allows, plan alternative activities and lessons to substitute for those that you see to be weaker.
7. Work through and implement the plans provided. Keep an open mind, but review effectiveness and possible alternatives.

Teacher-Developed Units

When and how should teachers develop their own teaching units? The prevailing pattern for many elementary teachers is to stick to the textbook, partly because teachers have the feeling that this is what they are supposed to do and partly because it is easy and safe. We have already said that textbook teaching is an easy pattern to set and be stuck with. Nearly all teachers, pressured with too much to do and too little time, find it necessary to use textbook-centered units or some other prepared instructional plans.

Teachers should, however, develop new units whenever possible. Teaching is a creative profession, and creative teachers will want to be constantly developing new ideas themselves. However, given the amount of time required to find, adapt, and develop resources, developing new units is an ongoing task.

Teacher-made units may take any form, but whatever form they take is almost certainly going to mean more work for the teacher than simply following a prepared unit plan. The major purpose of developing unit plans is that planning such units will mean more effective and impactful teaching. Teacher-made units are worth the effort because they can be made to fit the specific needs and abilities of your students. Teacher-made units can consider resources that are the teacher's personal possessions as well as those that may be part of a school and/or classroom collection. Such units can also reflect a teacher's individual abilities, talents, personality, and teaching style. Most important, perhaps, is the argument that planning a teaching unit can be creatively and personally satisfying. It can provide teachers with that sense of accomplishment that is so important for retaining a positive attitude and avoiding burnout in any profession, especially one like teaching.

Individual teaching units have the tailor-made quality of being uniquely suited to achieving what the teacher thinks to be most important in the very ways that seem most suitable for the people most directly involved.

▶ DECIDING ON UNIT TOPICS

Teachers do not usually have total freedom in choosing unit topics. The teacher may be expected to follow a set of curriculum guidelines, scope and sequence, or a curriculum map on which a course of study is outlined. In some instances, teachers are required to stick to the topics described in these systems or state guides, but sometimes they have the freedom to develop their own interests as well. A second option that teachers may have is to plan in conjunction with other teachers on their team (either grade level or some other configuration) so that all students are exposed to similar topics or themes. In a few cases, teachers have the initiative of doing teacher-guided group planning through which interests, needs, and problems identified by the students are explored.

Whether the teacher is planning the unit or helping students plan, a similar process occurs. Sometimes a wonderful, exciting idea seems to almost jump out. The teacher or the class experiences some stimulating, motivating event that generates enthusiasm and curiosity. For example, something in the news, an event on the calendar, a happening in the neighborhood, or something someone reads or sees on television grabs your attention and makes some topic seem like the perfect study for the class. More often, the teacher may be searching for a topic. For such searches, thinking goes through four stages:

1. Coming up with a menu of possible topics.
2. Narrowing the field and finding a broad focus.

3. Identifying a topic and refining that selection into a title that adds zest and unique-ness (takes it out of the boring and mundane class).
4. Deciding on the direction and structure that studying that topic ought to take.

The teacher first needs to have an idea of which topics are appropriate for a unit in social studies. It would be true, but not very helpful, to say that the range of topics almost defies description. Looking at one or several textbooks may give some idea of the types of topics that might be appropriate. This is going to provide a limited notion at best and probably an unimaginative one. To get a broad picture, it might be suggested that, among the possible unit topics, the following are typical: countries or groups of coun-tries, regions, civilizations, specific places or types of places, eras, specific time periods, events or series of related events, processes, phenomena, problems, historical figures, historical developments, and issues.

To show how the evolution of selection can take place, it might be useful to exam-ine an example of a fourth-grade teacher who has already gone through the process of selecting a unit topic.

▶ PLANNING EPISODE #1

Mrs. Conner, a fourth-grade teacher at Hart Elementary School, has selected the topic of the Middle East for her next unit. The topic is timely, but greater focus is needed.

At this point, Mrs. Conner uses a few resources and discusses her ideas with colleagues. Eventually, this produces a list of possibilities that vary in quality, focus, usefulness, appropri-ateness, and appeal. The list is:

Middle Eastern Folk Tales
Islam and the Middle East
Leaders of the Middle East Today
From Mohammad to Saladin to Suleiman: People of Influence in Middle Eastern History
European Colonies in the Middle East
The Countries of the Middle East Today
What It Is Like to Live in the Middle East
The Riches and Resources of the Middle East
Cities of the Middle East

Once a satisfactory list has been formed, the narrowing process begins. The individual topics are weighed in the balance of questions such as:

- How does this fit in with the other units that are being taught?
- How does this relate to the overall goals and purposes for the class?
- Is this something that this class might really get excited about?
- Is this broad enough (or narrow enough)? Is it too general (or too specific) in the focus it allows?
- Are the resources available?
- How does this approach fit in with the way we are handling other topics in the class?
- How exciting is this topic for students? For me?

After deliberation, the list is reduced to two or three possible titles, and at last, she decides on "What It Is Like to Live in the Middle East" as the focus. It seems provocative, creates curios-ity, and yet leaves room for some of the geographic focus she wanted. It is precisely because of that openness that more thought is necessary.

Mrs. Conner then starts to flesh out some sense of direction. For example, she considers areas in which students lack accurate knowledge about the Middle East. She also identifies a series of problems related to the topic:

- The belief that the people in the Middle East all have the same culture.
- The belief that all the Middle East is a desert.
- The idea that all Middle Easterners support terrorism.
- Ignorance about how modern Middle Eastern people live.

▶ DEVELOPING THE UNIT PLAN

Once a focus has been found, effort can be directed at developing one of three types of units. Teachers may decide to develop a resource unit. The kind of work that this involves is mainly creating, collecting, gathering, and ordering materials, teaching ideas, and activities, much as a team of teachers would do in developing a collaborative resource unit. One major difference is that the teacher can include personal resources that would not be available to everyone in a collaborative unit. The other two options, sketch units and teaching units, differ from one another most in the extent of development and in the amount of attention that is given to detail. Sketch units are of greatest use to teachers who are trying to form a broad overview of the teaching content, sequence, and activities and who then use the sketch unit as a basis to gather resources and do more specific planning later. These outline plans are also useful to teachers who find it convenient to rely heavily on textual materials but who want to have the control of doing their own basic planning.

Teaching units are more thorough and fleshed out in greater detail. They offer teachers the advantage of a plan of study that needs only calendar and success/failure adjustments. That is, the teacher does very little planning, other than making adaptations when teaching sequences utilize a different amount of time than originally allotted or where careful monitoring indicates a need for additional activities.

Whether the teacher is doing a sketch unit or a teaching unit, the next step in planning is to get a clear and specific picture of the desired learning outcomes. This is going to help in two ways: It will give directional focus, and it will help limit the scope. This targeting tells us what to teach while, at the same time, it keeps us from the pointless and sometimes frustrating activity of trying to teach everything about often broad unit topics.

There are several ways to attack the problem. The teacher may choose to begin by developing a set of instructional objectives. Another starting place is the content itself. Some teachers prefer to start with a content outline or a content organizational chart in which a list of generalizations serves as headings. Another idea is a kind of visual representation called a web, which shows the interrelationships of the different concepts and/or elements to be covered in the unit. Planning webs allow teachers to examine objectives, content outlines, and webs.

▶ INSTRUCTIONAL OBJECTIVES

At some point in planning, a teacher needs to be concerned with the learning outcomes that he or she wants to occur as a result of the instruction. Educators usually refer to these outcomes that are given special focus as objectives. A social studies–centered unit will have multiple objectives. In fact, most social studies activities have several objectives in addition to much incidental learning.

Objectives are targeted gains in knowledge or skills or desired changes in affective areas like aspirations, attitudes, values, and feelings. Since they are targets, objectives need to be identified as specifically as possible. A well-stated set of objectives should give clear direction to the teacher and be of help in planning activities. Specific objectives are also helpful to teachers and students in evaluating learning. By clearly identifying what the outcomes should be, everyone can tell when they are achieved.

For this reason, many school systems insist that teachers use what are referred to as behavioral objectives. Behavioral objectives are even more precise. They identify specific acts that students can perform that will demonstrate that the desired learning or change has occurred. Such objectives are observable, and the standard of successful achievement is identified.

Language is very important in writing behavioral objectives. Words and terms that suggest that the teacher would have to know what was going on inside a student's mind are simply unacceptable. A properly stated behavioral objective would never suggest that the student would "know" or "understand" something. Parallel examples of behavioral and non-behavioral objectives are detailed in Table 4.1. In each set, the first objective

Table 4.1 Examples of Behavioral and Non-Behavioral Objectives

Example Set #1	
Behavioral	Given a cup of multiple-colored candies, students will be able to correctly make a graph showing the distribution by color.
Non-Behavioral	Kindergarten students will learn to graph using one criterion.
Example Set #2	
Behavioral	After studying the community and the people who work in it, the students will be able to match pictures of ten community helpers they have studied with their place of work on a pictographic map of the community.
Non-Behavioral	Students will become aware of the workplaces of community helpers.
Example Set #3	
Behavioral	After a study of the Middle Ages in Europe, students will be able to list three provisions of the Magna Carta.
Non-Behavioral	Students will realize the significance of the Magna Carta.
Example Set #4	
Behavioral	Students will be able to correctly identify areas of high population density on a population map.
Non-Behavioral	Students will understand how to use a population map.
Example Set #5	
Behavioral	After a study of the maps of Africa, the student will be able to name five countries in Africa.
Non-Behavioral	Students will know that Africa is a continent made up of over 40 nations.

uses acceptable behavioral objective language while the second does not. It should be noted that behavioral objectives cannot be written simply by referring to some word list of strong, specific action verbs. Teachers who do this may fall into the trap of focusing on trivialities or identifying activities rather than desired learning outcomes. Words and phrases in isolation may be deceptive. It is the specific identification of an observable action that shows learning that defines an objective as behavioral. It should also be noted that an objective can be very specific, important, and valuable for teaching, yet not be behavioral.

▶ CONTENT OUTLINES AND FLOWCHARTS

Content outlines help the teacher determine what is most important to teach. They help teachers and students discover the structure of the topic being studied. An outline may be a simple content flowchart, as detailed in Figure 4.2, which identifies the key subtopics in a unit on Egypt and the order in which they will be taught. A flowchart not only identifies the areas of study but also begins to suggest the order of the teaching itself.

▶ CONCEPT WEBS

A visual device that teachers can use to frame the big picture of a unit is called a web because its appearance bears a strong resemblance to a spider's work. Basically, a web shows how the various concepts covered in a unit are linked or interrelated. Near the center of the web are the broad topics and most important ideas. Peripheral layers show the subordinate and less important ideas. Unit webs are better evolved in two stages.

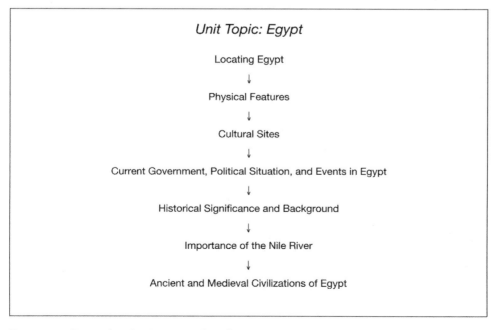

Figure 4.2 Example of a Content Flowchart

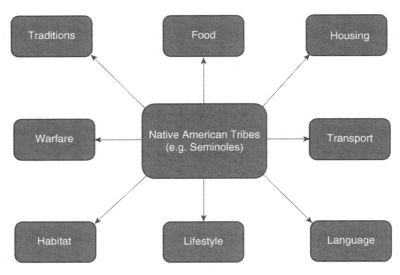

Figure 4.3 Concept Web for a Unit on Native Americans

The first stage is simply brainstorming and choosing topics to study. The second stage arranges these topics according to priorities (importance) and relationships. Webbing is a better tool when the teacher has a comfortable familiarity with the unit topic and therefore knows the content. Figure 4.3 details a concept web for a unit on Native Americans.

▶ MOVING TOWARD THE DEVELOPMENT OF ACTIVITIES

As the teacher is building toward this mental picture of the unit, a lot of other work and thinking needs to be going on simultaneously. One thing that is very important is that the teacher needs to be constantly on the lookout for resources. The possibilities can be overwhelming. Among the available resources are books and magazines with good teaching activities, fiction and nonfiction books and stories that students will want to and be able to read, and other resources such as films, streaming video, digital resources, computer programs, music, and artifacts.

The possible tools of teaching often accumulate until there is a problem of selecting the best, most appropriate, and most useful. The resources, along with the overview of the content and the development of the objectives, begin to shape the kind of learning activities that will form the unit itself.

The dramatic element of the classroom was alluded to earlier. The sequencing of the teaching-learning activities in a unit is very much like structuring the drama itself. Much like a play or a movie, if you can imagine a very long drama, the unit unfolds over several days or weeks. As in a drama, the earliest stages of the unit must grab the students' attention (set); provide a sense of direction and purpose (objectives); create excitement, interest, and suspense; and give a great deal of background information. This is often referred to as the initiation stage of the unit, and teachers usually have just one or, at best, two days to accomplish everything described.

Once the unit is launched, the body of the unit can be built of activities that are aimed at developing the objectives and maintaining and extending interest. These activities, which form the greatest part of the unit, are sometimes referred to collectively as the developmental phase of the unit. Most of the research, information gathering and sharing, problem solving, and extension and enrichment of the unit goes on during this developmental period.

The final phase of a unit, called the culmination phase, serves multiple functional purposes. At this point, it is obvious that closure is needed: some activity or activities that will give students a sense that they are finished with this particular study. A unit needs a climax, and the culminating activities need to provide this. It may be that students will show what they have learned by sharing their knowledge with someone else: parents, the principal, other classes, or even each other. So one type of culmination activity might be a program, a festival or cultural celebration, the making of a movie by the class, or some similar activity. The culmination of the unit also serves as a summative overview and a drawing together of all that has been learned. It should be, in fact, the time when the teacher helps students comprehend the significance of what they have been studying. If students have been working on a problem or a group of problems, this is the point at which solutions are offered and findings and conclusions are reached. Not surprisingly, the culmination of a unit is also the place where the teacher needs to take stock or make the final evaluation of what has been learned. Of course, evaluation should be ongoing and present in every activity, but it is again at this culmination level that the teacher needs to make the final assessment. One last set of functions that the culmination of a unit may serve is that of maintaining or even stimulating interest in the topic that has been studied while providing a transition to some new area of study. While it may seem strange to try to create interest just as you are leaving an area of study, this is the very point at which we want to be saying to students, "We've spent all the time we can, but there are a lot more interesting and exciting things for you to learn if you want to go on your own. Now, here are some other ideas for you to consider, and here are some great resources you can use." The transitional function is equally logical when you think about how students learn. Basically, they understand new experiences by comparing them to things they already know about. So the transitional aspect of the culmination is simply the beginning of showing relationships, similarities, and dissimilarities with the new area of study.

The format of a unit may be developed in many ways, no single one being *the* correct method. To mention a few of the alternatives, units may be organized as sequenced daily lesson plans with lessons of varying duration each structured around one or more specific objectives; as a set of lessons, each teaching specific concepts, generalizations, or subtopics; or as subsets of activities reflecting the various curricular areas from which the activities are drawn (art, music, language arts, etc.). Regardless of the format that shapes the unit, all unit plans need to show reflection on certain necessary elements. These are shown in the format that follows. A brief (one week) unit follows, illustrating how this format may be used.

Unit Elements Format

1. Descriptive and identifying information:
    a. A title. (This may be in the form of a statement, a problem statement, an issue description, or a descriptive and appealing title.)
    b. Grade level(s) of students toward whom the unit is directed.

      c. Estimated or allotted duration (the time in weeks with some description of how much time is to be spent each week).

2. Rationale:
   a. Overview statement of the importance of the area of study regarding both content and the approaches used.
   b. Arguments and assertions regarding the significance and the appropriateness of the topic of study.

3. Unit objectives:
   a. A list of the most important targeted learning outcomes of the entire unit. (These may be categorized in some way, the most common classification being cognitive or knowledge objectives to include facts to be remembered, concepts and generalizations to be understood, etc.; affective objectives to include values and attitudes to be developed, beliefs and aspirations to be gained, appreciations to be cultivated, etc.; and psychomotor or skills objectives.)

4. Content description: This may be embodied in the objectives and not needed as a separate entity. Content description may be presented in several ways, including the following:
   a. A list of generalizations.
   b. A sequenced content outline.
   c. A concept web of the unit.
   d. A list of concept definitions.

5. Activity sequence: There is more than one way to present this area, including the following:
   a. An ordered set of lesson plans with initiating, development, and culminating activities in order.
   b. Parties arranged according to the subject area with which the social studies is being integrated (art, music, language arts, etc.).
   c. Unit activities organized into subunits, each representing a subtopic, a generalization, a key concept, or some other content heading.
   d. Unit organized around key activities with contingency alternatives stemming from each of these.
   e. Units organized into key activities with enrichment activities and skill and background activities plans on a needs basis (often this will be done in the form of Learning Centers).

6. Description of the unit evaluation process: Development of the evaluation or assessment design as it is built into individual lessons and activities. Ways of assessing to what extent learning outcomes have been achieved, detailing evaluation strategies, including any unit test(s).

7. Accommodations: Be sure to plan various accommodating activities and strategies for students with different learning needs.

8. Resources: This cataloging effort may take the form of a simple bibliographic listing or a more useful but more time-consuming series of annotated bibliographic entries. One convenient organization pattern for resources is division into teacher-resource and student-resource sections. It is also useful to create subcategories based on resource type (e.g., audiovisual materials, games and computer resources, reference materials, enrichment trade books, etc.).

▶ PLANNING EPISODE #2

Unit Title: Why Do We Have a President, and What Does a President Do?
Grade Level: Second grade
Allotted Time: One to two weeks, with follow-up sessions throughout the year

Rationale

It is very important for students to begin learning about the office of the president in the government of the United States. Students constantly hear and see presidential references from parents and other adults, on television and in movies, and even as they look at money and stamps. The president is considered the single most important figure in the government, and presidential decisions and policies influence everyone's life. This unit is an introduction to the presidency that will be an aid to understanding in future years. The focus in the initial unit will be on the office itself and the current president. The follow-up to the unit will involve an introduction to the presidents of the past.

> **FYI:** This section provides justification for teaching the content in narrative form – real-life applications or other reasons for covering the material in the manner that you are planning (e.g., Is it mandated by state law? Is the topic relevant in local news?).

CONCEPTUAL AREAS AND CONCERNS

The concept of the president
The current president
The president's jobs
The White House as the home of the president

Unit Objectives

The students will be able to:

- Identify the current president of the United States.
- Explain where the president lives and how the president travels.
- Describe the different jobs and the work of the president.
- Discuss some of the past presidents.

> **FYI:** To write objectives, answer the following question: What skills will the students acquire from this unit/lesson?

Initiating Activity

Begin by showing students a series of pictures of the president. In many classes, some students will be able to make an identification at least by title. Make sure that the word *president* and the president's name are mentioned several times as you talk about the president and what the president does. If possible, find a recording of "Hail to the Chief." Talk about why the bands play that song sometimes when the president arrives. Play any available streaming videos/ movies of the president in the news (avoid recordings that will be boring for elementary students). Videos or pictures showing the president signing bills or making official visits will be useful. Talk with students about what they know about the White House. Again, show pictures. If you think they are ready to learn about location and to do U.S. map work, ask if students know where the White House is and show them Washington, DC, on a map of the United States.

Create four different hats, one for each job of the president:

1. Uncle Sam hat: Chief of State.
2. Army hat: Commander in Chief.
3. Top hat: Director of Foreign Policy.
4. Hard hat: Guardian of the Economy.

Have students color each hat and then practice saying the role. End the activity by having students identify the president by name and title, identify the White House from pictures, and rename the four jobs of the president.

Developmental Activities

1. Make a presidential library in the classroom. This will include a bulletin board and a scrapbook of newspaper and magazine clippings (especially those with pictures). It will also have a browsing table of activities and books about presidents.
2. Look at presidents' pictures on money, stamps, and so on.
3. Show pictures of the First Lady (or First Gentleman, if appropriate) and talk about that role.
4. Have each student tell what he or she would do if he or she were president.
5. Have students share what they would like to say to the president if the president should come to visit their class.
6. Have each student suggest something they would like to show the president about the school.
7. Let the class try to come up with the following information about the president:
   a. How tall is the president?
   b. What is the president's favorite food?
   c. What food does the president not like?
   d. What are the president's hobbies?
   e. Where does the president go to vacation or rest?
   f. What are the president's favorite sports?
   g. Does the president have a favorite movie or television show?
8. Choose two popular cartoon or television characters and have an election for president in the class. Have children try to tell why they think that each would be a good president. Then go through the exercise with written ballots and a voting booth.
9. Show pictures of the Oval Office and talk about it as the president's office. Present a trash can and ask the children to imagine that it is the trash can from that office. Ask them to think about what items might be found in it at the end of a work day for the president.
10. Keep a map showing where the president travels. If possible, present clips from television news showing the president's visits to different places.

> **FYI:** When you are planning a unit, this section is a summary of what you hope students will learn by the end of the unit. You have yet to create daily lesson plans. The daily lesson plans will provide much more detail.

Culminating Activity

Assign students one sentence each about the presidency and have them draw a picture depicting their sentence. After all the pictures are drawn, video students explaining and showing their pictures. Edit the video (using Moviemaker or iMovie) and share the video with students, administration, and parents (if possible).

- _____ is the __ (number) president of the United States.
- The president has many jobs.
- Some of the people who help the president are called the cabinet members.
- The president lives in the White House.
- The White House is in the city of Washington, DC.
- _____, the president's wife (or husband), is called the First Lady (or First Gentleman).
- If the president should die, the vice-president would take over the job.
- The Secret Service guards the president.
- The president is commander in chief of the Armed Forces.
- The president is the head of the government.
- The president is the chief ambassador to other countries.
- The president likes _____ (favorite food).
- The president sometimes travels in a plane called Air Force One.
- I like the president because _____.
- One of the things that the president likes to do is _____.
- When the president signs bills, they turn into laws.
- The president tries to decide what is best for the country.
- George Washington was the first president.

Follow the unit by presenting and talking about one president every week. Keep a cumulative bulletin board with pictures of each president as they are discussed. Each week, have students try to rename all the presidents who have been previously covered as a group choral exercise.

▶ PLANNING EPISODE #3

Unit Title: The Acquisition of the Louisiana Territory
Grade Level: Sixth grade
Allotted Time: Five 50-minute class periods

Rationale

This unit deals with the acquisition of the Louisiana Territory by the United States and the subsequent exploration of that territory. Since the class is studying the history of the United States throughout the year, the study of a particular historic episode in more detail is especially useful to show the human side of history. The Lewis and Clark expedition shows the hazards and some of the difficulties faced by pioneers, without violence or sensationalism. The journal of the expedition is a complete and detailed primary resource that students can read with understanding. The members of the expedition exemplify courage, resourcefulness, a sense of responsibility and duty, and other desirable character traits. The purchase and the exploration of the Louisiana Territory nearly doubled the territorial size of the United States, thus having tremendous impact on the young nation.

Objectives

The students will be able to:

- Identify the importance of the Louisiana Purchase.
- Explain the major details of the Purchase.
- Identify the purposes for the Lewis and Clark expedition.
- Name several of the difficulties that the expedition encountered.
- Trace the approximate route of the expedition on a map and explain how long Lewis and Clark spent on the trip.
- Make comparisons to other explorations.

Content Outline

1. Events leading to the purchase:
   a. The need of Americans on the western frontier to use the port of New Orleans.
   b. The acquisition of Spanish territories by France and the closing of the port of New Orleans.
   c. Monroe and Livingston appointed by President Jefferson to go to France.
   d. The personality and motivations of Napoleon:
      i. Need for money to finance his military efforts.
      ii. Lack of desire to defend large distant territories against a powerful British navy.
   e. The vision and opportunism of Monroe and Livingston to exceed their authorization.

> **FYI:** When planning a unit, you are outlining the objectives you hope students will meet by the end of the unit.

2. The Lewis and Clark expedition:
   a. Purposes of the expedition:
      i. Gathering of scientific information.
      ii. Contact with the natives.
      iii. Proving the feasibility of travel.
      iv. Exploring and mapping.
   b. Difficulties and dangers:
      i. Environment and weather.
      ii. Travel hardships and problems (including the danger of being lost).
      iii. Possible encounters with hostile natives and wild animals.
   c. Impact of the expedition.

Initiating Activity

Procedure

Present the background to the Louisiana Purchase as a series of problems in a storytelling context, getting students to respond.

> **FYI:** When planning a unit, this section is a summary of what you hope students will learn by the end of the unit. You have yet to create daily lesson plans. The daily lesson plans will provide much more detail.

Problems

If you are in a business, what do you have to do? (Sell the goods or services.)

Now, if you have something to sell, and you and your product are in one place, and the people who want it are hundreds of miles away, what is your problem? (To get your product to market as quickly and cheaply as you can. Give the background on the furs and other goods Americans had to take down river to New Orleans.)

Well, what happens when the officials in New Orleans will not let you bring your goods through any longer? (Guide discussion to the eventual involvement of President Jefferson.) What do you think the president will do?

The next step leads into a role-play activity in which two students, portraying James Monroe and Robert Livingston, are given their commission by the president and Congress to buy New Orleans and Florida from France for $2 million. They meet the Emperor Napoleon, who was, so the story goes, in his bath at the time of the interview. (Napoleon should be portrayed by the teacher, another adult, or a very well-coached student.) At the point when Napoleon makes his offer, interrupt the role-play to discuss with the class the implications and the reasoning of all parties. Explain to the students that the final terms were worked out not by Napoleon himself, but by the French Foreign Minister, whose name was Talleyrand Perigord, and by the Treasury Minister, Barbe-Marbois. Tell them that these two ministers got more money out of the Americans than Napoleon expected. Have students guess how much more money. (It was $15 million.) Ask the students about who they think got the better deal. Then bring closure.

Tell the students that Jefferson and the United States had bought "a pig in a poke" (a deal that is foolishly accepted without being fully examined). Hold up a cloth or leather bag and explain the expression. Tell them that Jefferson knew there was a big river involved (pull a long, crooked strip of blue paper out of the bag) and an important port city (pull out many Monopoly-type houses and tiny toy ships). But all Jefferson or anyone else knew about the rest of that purchase was that there was a lot of it. (At this point, empty the bag, which is filled with the jigsaw puzzle pieces representing the current states that were eventually carved from the Louisiana Territory.) Tell the students that Jefferson was not the kind of man who would leave something like this alone. Lead into the commissioning of the Lewis and Clark expedition and its purposes. Close by announcing the objectives of the rest of the unit and then reviewing the details of the purchase, using a large wall map and tracing the expedition's route very quickly.

Developmental Activities

Review the Louisiana Purchase. Tell the children that this amounted to a cost of about two cents per acre. Have them figure the number of acres and square miles. Possibly have them figure cost using inflation.

Explain the purposes of the Lewis and Clark expedition by reading or having students read portions of the Lewis and Clark journals. Discuss the importance of the expedition.

Using journals and maps, have students make a carefully measured timeline of the 28-month journey. Also have them use string measures (pieces of string cut and marked to fit map scale) to measure various segments of the journey. Discuss the reasons some distances would take longer.

Discuss the hardships, dangers, problems, and difficulties that students imagine the expedition might have encountered. Then have students do the following in-basket activity, which is based on actual incidents during the expedition.

In-Basket Activity: Up the River With Lewis and Clark

Students will be able to:

- Explain the dangers and difficulties faced by Lewis and Clark.

- Recognize differences in significance and urgency among frontier situations, where outside help could not be available.

Have students work in pairs playing the roles of Lewis and Clark. The role-play activity should be done in the following steps:

1. Let students examine a map showing the route of the Lewis and Clark expedition. Explain the reasons for and purposes of the expedition.
2. Have students work through fifteen situations prioritizing the need for action and finding solutions. You may want them to write down their solutions. Some will be obvious; others will require some creativity.
3. Discuss the various ways students have ordered the situations and compare solutions.
4. Have students compare their solutions with what Lewis and Clark actually did.
5. Have students discuss how their priorities differ and compare with a historian's views. (Note: You may prefer to use only a teacher copy and present them orally.)
6. Have students discuss what they learned from the activity. You might discuss why most Native Americans were so friendly (this is very different from the picture painted by movies and television), other dangers that might have come up, the length of the journey, and the time it took. Tell students there is, of course, no correct order for the problems to be solved. Then discuss with them the logic that they used in their own sequencing of the tasks.

As a follow-up activity, give students a list of other explorations that they might like to read about and study:

- The voyages of Columbus.
- LaSalle's trip down the Mississippi River.
- NASA space explorations, including Neil Armstrong's moon landing.
- Leif Eriksson's voyages.

Have children discuss how these were like and how they were different from the Lewis and Clark expedition.

Culminating Activity

Have students put on a program consisting of:

1. A reenactment of Jefferson's decision to send emissaries to France and the meeting between Napoleon and Monroe and Livingston.
2. A living timeline in which students costume themselves as events in the Purchase and Lewis and Clark expedition, each describing his or her own event.
3. A floor-map activity in which guides lead guests along a large floor map representation, showing guests the route of the expedition.

Evaluation

Evaluation is built into every activity in some way. A final unit test might consist of the following questions:

- From what country did the United States purchase the Louisiana Territory, and what was the price?
- Name two dangers faced by the Lewis and Clark expedition.

- Give one reason the Louisiana Purchase was important.
- Give one aim of the Lewis and Clark expedition.
- On an unlabeled map, trace the route of the Lewis and Clark expedition, naming the rivers they traveled.

▶ FINDING AND USING PREPARED UNITS

Teachers may feel that they do not have the time, energy, or ingenuity to prepare elaborate and extensive units of their own for the entire school year. At the same time, they may not want to fall into the pattern of teaching directly from the textbook.

There is an alternative available to teachers even if there is no established district or school curriculum guide complete with authorized, already prepared units and even if there is no easy collaborative planning or sharing going on in the school in which they teach. That alternative is to "borrow" premade units from some source outside the school.

The maxim of unit "borrowing" ought to be, "If you are going to 'borrow,' then take the best!" How does a teacher with little time to search (if you had the time, you would have planned your own unit in the first place) find the best?

The first and most prominent of resources is the internet. Searching Google or Yahoo for lesson plans will ensure a plethora of options. However, you need to ensure that the lesson plans are adapted to meet the needs of your students and instructional objectives. Second, you should search professionally, even commercially prepared materials that have already undergone the scrutiny of selection and the polishing of rewrite and editing. A starting place among these are the commercial teaching magazines such as *Instructor, Teacher, Learning,* or *Mailbox.* Professional journals such as *Social Education, Social Studies and the Young Learner, The Social Studies, The History Teacher, The Clearing House, Childhood Education,* and *Social Studies Research and Practice* will be worth a look through, too. A trip to a university library or a search of a library electronic full text will be very fruitful. You can also examine other textbook series' teacher editions. The teacher editions may hold some pleasant surprises. Certainly, any gems found in these outside textbooks will require some adaptation, but that will be true of almost any "borrowed" material. One other resource worth a look through in a university library will be other methods texts in social studies. Some of these contain provocative unit ideas.

Third, you should "always be on the lookout for materials for teaching." At conferences, in the rooms of other teachers, at the teacher center (if your system is lucky enough to have one), browsing online, or even in the dentist's office, the very thing needed may be waiting for the alert person who takes the initiative and the time to nose through the available material. One of the resources for teacher-prepared units is the Association for Supervision and Curriculum Development, which publishes a list of available units and curriculum materials available for school systems.

To use prepared units effectively, the key concern is adaptation. The focus in adaptation must be on the intended learning outcomes and students' needs. If the teacher begins with concern for how a unit plan can bring significant learning, then all other kinds of needed change fall into place. A second and related focus should be on the vitality and motivational appeal of the activities for students. Will students be excited, interested, and stimulated by these activities? A third related concern for the teacher is whether the resources are available. This may have as much to do with a realistic self-assessment of time, energy, and initiative as with material resources, but both are needed.

▶ **PLANNING FOR SHORTER INSTRUCTIONAL SEQUENCES**

The most useful and important among shorter instructional sequences is the lesson plan or daily lesson plan. A lesson plan is in many ways a unit in miniature, and lessons contain similar key elements such as objectives, procedural descriptions of activities, and identification of resources. A lesson plan is a detailed outline of what and how you plan to teach a given topic on a day and/or over several days.

Any lesson plan design that is going to be particularly useful will be one that is structured to help students better retain what they are taught. Where a unit is examining a broad topic, a lesson plan is examining a specific sub-topic of the unit. The format of a lesson plan will depend on your school/district. In the standards and accountability era we live in, a basic lesson plan often includes the information shown in Figure 4.4.

Teachers should consider answering the following questions at the start of planning a lesson. These questions can help organize and "kick-start" the lesson-planning process.

1. What do you want the students to learn from the lesson? (Goal, Rationale)
2. What skills will the students acquire from my lesson? (Objectives)
3. What is the best way to get the information across to the students? (Procedures)
4. Do I have the materials needed to effectively teach this lesson? (Materials)
5. How can I make sure they understand what I am teaching? (Evaluation)

Besides Russell's Basic Components of a Lesson Plan format given in Figure 4.4, there are variations of lesson planning. The Hunter (1990–1991) lesson sequence has been

---

1. Lesson Topic
2. Objectives
3. Rationale

    A. Standards
    B. Real-Life Application
    C. Other

4. Content
5. Materials/Resources (books, maps, tests, rubrics, etc.)
6. Procedures

    A. "Hook"/Involvement Strategies
    B. Sequential Lesson Steps with Time Allotment
    C. Remediation/Enrichment Strategies
    D. Closure/Preview
    E. Assessment and Evaluation (e.g. observation, test, project, etc.)

7. Accommodations

    A. ESOL Accommodations
    B. Special Education Accommodations
    C. Other (Learning Styles, etc.)

Figure 4.4 Russell's Basic Components of a Lesson Plan

a helpful model, especially for teachers, because it is structured in a series of distinctive, easily constructed steps. A lesson design developed from the elements in Hunter's sequence follows.

1. Get the learners' attention and prepare them for what they are going to learn. The teacher needs to think of ways of capturing and focusing interest on the topic of study. This part of the lesson may also review previously studied related material, making a transition and aiding understanding by relating new material to the old. The major purpose is to develop readiness for learning the new topic.

2. Explain the objective(s) or purpose(s). A key element in the Hunter approach is that the students have a good idea of the ends the teacher has in mind. This step includes a clear communication of what the teacher intends to accomplish. In a sense, though, it is something more than that; if possible, the teacher and the students need to reach a consensus so that there can be shared goals that are understood by both.

3. Do direct teaching. In this step, the teacher is communicating the new information of the lesson, teaching concepts, and so on, using a variety of techniques.

4. If it is appropriate, model what you want the learners to do. Though not all lessons require this step, in many it is essential. Basically, it involves demonstration or the completing of examples by the teacher. The teacher shows students how each step in a process is completed (e.g., finding a location using map coordinates).

5. Check for understanding. This is sometimes referred to as the monitor and adjust stage. It is a point at which the teacher determines if the students understand what the lesson is all about. It requires some activity in which students give and receive feedback. This may involve a signaling device in which all students participate, a questioning technique using selected students, or individual responses from every student.

6. Provide guided practice. The teacher gives students a chance to use new skills or concepts. Again, the emphasis is on monitored practice with feedback from the teacher.

7. Provide opportunity for independent practice.

Though this lesson-planning model will not and should not be suited to every lesson, it can provide a useful pattern for many. As a model, the seven steps in the lesson plan show very clearly the importance of developing detail, specificity, and sequence in the procedure of a lesson plan. The following is an example of a plan developed along the lines of the Hunter model.

▶ **PLANNING EPISODE #4**

Teacher: Joshua Kenna
Grade: Fifth grade
Unit Topic: Japanese American Internment Camps
Lesson Topic: Justice Prevails?

Objectives

- Students will be able to identify the prejudice that occurred against Japanese Americans during WWII.
- Students will be able to explain how the internment of Japanese Americans was wrong.
- Students will be able to express empathy toward internees by writing a letter of apology on behalf of the American government.

> **FYI:** Ideally a lesson plan will include two or three objectives.

Standards

- NCSS Standard 2: Time, Continuity, and Change: *Social studies programs should include experiences that provide for the study of the past and its legacy.*
- NCSS Standard 3: People, Places, and Environment: *Social studies programs should include experiences that provide for the study of people, places, and environments.*
- Common Core CCSS.ELA-LITERACY.CCRA.SL.1: Prepare for and participate effectively in a range of conversations and collaborations with diverse partners, building on others' ideas and expressing their own clearly and persuasively.
- Common Core CCSS.ELA-LITERACY.CCRA.SL.2: Integrate and evaluate information presented in diverse media and formats, including visually, quantitatively, and orally.

> **FYI:** This lesson plan aligns with the national standards. Your lesson plan should also align with your state standards.

Daily Planner

- Spectrum Vocabulary: 5–10 minutes.
- Read *Japanese American Internment Camps* by Gail Sakurai: 20–30 minutes.
- Brainstorm activity: 5–10 minutes.
- Rank Injustices and Accomplishments: 10–15 minutes.
- Example Letter of Apology: 5–10 minutes.
- Letter of Apology: Homework.

> **FYI:** This section should list activities and provide the estimated time needed.

Activating Strategy

Whole Group Instruction

The teacher will ask students to look at the white board and recite the two written words, "Injustice" and "Prejudice" as a group (Visual, Auditory).

Then the teacher will complete a "Spectrum Vocabulary" activity.

> **FYI: The activating strategy should engage students and "hook" them into the lesson.**

- Spectrum Vocabulary: Students will be asked to stand along a spectrum based on their knowledge of a given vocabulary word (i.e., they will stand either at the "I know" or "I don't know" spot or anywhere in between, which means they have heard of the word but don't know it well enough to define it). This is a great activity as it requires students to move; also, the teacher can gain a visual of who does or does not know a vocabulary word. The teacher will also ask every student standing in the "I know" section to define the word for the class (Kinesthetic, Auditory, and Visual).

Once the students have completed the activity for both words, the teacher will ask the following essential questions, which should also be written either on the white board or in a PowerPoint: "Was it right to place Japanese Americans in internment camps during WWII? Explain" and "What relationship exists between injustice and prejudice?" (Auditory).

Small Group Instruction/Collaboration

- The teacher will have students read the book *Japanese Americans Internment Camp*, by Gail Sakurai, in small groups, meaning students will take turns reading short passages until the book is completed in its entirety. However, a teacher could read the book with the students or have students sit in small groups but read silently and periodically discuss what they read (Visual, Auditory, Intrapersonal, and Interpersonal).

> **FYI:** This section will detail the instructional procedures.

- Upon completing the book, the teacher will ask the students how they felt about the treatment of Japanese Americans (Auditory).

Guided and Independent Practice

Small Group Instruction/Collaboration

The teacher will have students start a "Brainstorming" activity, and students will not have the aid of the book (Visual, Auditory, and Interpersonal).

- Brainstorming: Students, as a small cooperative group, will try to list all the injustices and accomplishments that Japanese Americans received during the internment camp time period (Visual, Auditory, Kinesthetic, Interpersonal).

Once students have finished compiling the list of injustices and accomplishments, they will have a small group discussion. Each group must rank the injustices and accomplishments from highest degree to lowest degree. Groups will then share their ranked list to the whole class, and they must justify their rankings (Visual, Auditory, Kinesthetic, and Interpersonal).

> **FYI:** In this section, the teacher is detailing how he or she will guide students and how he or she will allow them to work independently.

Closure

Whole Group Instruction

Following the presentations of the ranked lists, the teacher will ask students, "What can one do after an injustice has been committed?" There are various answers, but one answer that the teacher should be looking for is an apology (Auditory).

The teacher will ask students for some necessary components for writing a letter of apology. The students should list the following:

- Name of recipient.
- An apology.
- Acknowledgement of wrongful actions with supporting details.
- Name of offender.

FYI: Here the teacher is wrapping up the lesson and bringing everything together, thus providing closure to the students' learning experience.

Visual

Once students have listed all the necessary components of a letter of apology, the teacher will show an example of an apology letter and go over the homework, in which students will have to write an apology letter on behalf of the U.S. government (Intrapersonal).

Assessment/Evaluation

Individual Assessment

Students are to write a letter to Japanese American internees apologizing on behalf of the U.S. government. Students are expected to include at least two specific injustices and two accomplishments of Japanese Americans. They must also express why they feel the actions taken by the U.S. government in fact were unjust. Students could complete this as homework if desired (Intrapersonal).

FYI: This section details the assessment procedures that will be utilized.

Materials/Technology

- White/chalk board and markers/chalk.
- Projector and PowerPoint or document camera.
- Book: *Japanese American Internment Camps* by Gail Sakurai.
- Butcher paper and markers/crayons.

FYI: All teachers want to make sure all required materials are obtained prior to the lesson. You don't want to start baking a cake only to find out halfway through you have no flour.

Cross-Curricular Connections

- *Reading/Literacy*: Students will read a nonfiction book titled *Japanese American Internment Camps*, by Gail Sakurai.
- *Writing*: Students will write an apology letter to Japanese American internees on behalf of the U.S. government.

FYI: Cross-curricular connections are more common in today's classroom than ever before and form a major theme of the Common Core standards.

Meeting Individual Needs of Diverse Learners

- *Multiple Intelligences*: This lesson fosters auditory, visual, kinesthetic, interpersonal, and intrapersonal learning through the small cooperative grouping, the various activities, and the assignment. The parts of this lesson that relate to each of these learners are noted throughout the lesson in parentheses.

- *Students with Disabilities*: These students will be given all the accommodations as required from their Individual Education Plans, such as, but not limited to, preferential seating, extra time on assignments, clear agenda, checking for comprehension beyond what is normally required, etc. Plus, this lesson utilizes small group cooperative learning whereby low-level students can be assisted by high-level students.
- *English Language Learners*: Visuals will be used to aid ELL students (e.g., when telling students to get a piece of paper out, the teacher should literally pull out a piece of paper as they give the directions). Also, the teacher should try to translate the key vocabulary words into a student's native tongue, if possible. Furthermore, the teacher can have these students complete their work by writing in their native language and then attempting to translate it at a later date.

> **FYI:** Meeting the individual needs of all learners should be standard practice. Here you want to plan appropriate accommodations for your students.

Character Education Connection

- Tolerance: This lesson teaches that prejudices are wrong.
- Respect: Students are encouraged to treat everyone regardless of ethnicities or skin color with respect.
- Responsibility: Students are apologizing for the actions taken by earlier generations of Americans. This will help students learn from previous mistakes and learn to apologize for future wrongdoings that they may do.
- Caring: Students are encouraged to care for others who may not have a voice or who face prejudices.

> **FYI:** Character education is considered a foundational goal of public education and is mandated in many states. Here you want to detail how you will be addressing character-related traits/topics/themes.

▶ LOOKING BACK

The quality of planning makes a difference in the quality of teaching. Teachers fail to give adequate time to planning for a variety of reasons, but by determined systematic effort, planning can add to teaching effectiveness and satisfaction.

The term *curriculum map* is most often used to describe the long-term planning a teacher does to outline the curriculum for an entire year/semester. The term *unit* is used to describe the planning a teacher does to teach a large topic to a group of students. The teachers' editions of textbooks use the term to describe the activities provided for teaching particular content, usually chapters. Whether a textbook unit or a teacher-made unit, considerable planning is involved. Teacher-made units may be of several types, including collaborative or team units, which are usually resource units.

Short-term planning most often takes the form of daily lesson plans. The format of lesson plans varies, depending on your state/district. Russell's Basic Components of Lesson Plan format and Hunter's lesson sequence are two different formats for planning a lesson. In the standards and accountability era we live in, lesson plans typically have common attributes, including lesson topic, objectives, standards, materials, procedures, evaluation, and accommodations.

EXTENSION ACTIVITY

SCENARIO

Even on a Friday afternoon, the front office at Yourtown Elementary School (YES) was a circus of activity as you emerged from your meeting with your principal, Dr. Russell. Before you could even make it to your classroom, the word had spread among the faculty about the elementary social studies committee, and you heard quite a few teachers express interest in being on the committee. Some teachers seemed excited about helping reform social studies at YES. Others seemed interested in protecting the status quo. You were relieved to get to your classroom, grab your stuff, and head off for the weekend. After all, Monday would be more than the start of a new week; it would be a new beginning for social studies at YES.

QUESTIONS

1. Dr. Russell charged you with a task of forming a social studies committee to advise him on planning/reforming the curriculum. What are the advantages/disadvantages to having a committee like this in a school?
2. Do you think having teacher input into curriculum planning/reform would produce a better curriculum for the students? Why or why not?
3. What are the qualities a teacher should possess to be on this committee? Of these qualities, which are the most important? How should these teachers be selected?

ACTIVITY

Once the committee has been formed and organized, the teachers get to work. Imagine your group is the committee. Create a curriculum map (what will be taught and when) for your grade level's social studies curriculum. Be sure that you meet all required state standards. The scope and sequence should be detailed and be for the entire school year.

CHECKING FOR UNDERSTANDING

1. What are some reasons teachers cannot always plan as effectively as they should?
2. What is a curriculum map?
3. What is the difference between long-range planning and short-term planning?
4. What is a collaborative unit?
5. What are the necessary elements in a unit plan?
6. What are the basic components of a lesson plan?

▶ HELPFUL RESOURCES

Volusia County School District has an array of curriculum maps online:
http://myvolusiaschools.org/K12-Curriculum/Pages/ElementaryCurrMaps.aspx
Watch this video of an experienced teacher detailing how she maps the curriculum and
   aligns it with standards and the C3 Framework:
https://youtu.be/Cq0Z06xzQTQ
Watch this short video about writing objectives:
www.teachertube.com/video/writing-learning-objectives-introduction-423152
Check out this video about writing learning objectives based on Bloom's Taxonomy:
www.youtube.com/watch?v=4DgkLV9h69Q
Federal Resources for Educational Excellence (FREE) is a U.S. Department of Education
   website that houses more than 1,500 federally supported teaching and learning resources.
   The website includes a great many primary sources and photos, along with ideas and
   suggestions for instruction:
https://www2.ed.gov/free/index.html
Watch this first-year teacher explore writing effective lesson plans:
www.teachertube.com/video/new-teacher-survival-guide-planning-423156
The PBS Teachers website provides teachers with complete lesson plans and free media
   resources, spanning multiple subjects for all grades:
www.pbs.org/teachers
The Gateway to 21st Century Skills is one of the oldest publicly accessible U.S. reposito-
   ries of education resources on the web. The Gateway contains a variety of educational
   resource types from activities and lesson plans to online projects to assessment items.
   Gateway is supported by the National Education Association:
www.thegateway.org

▶ FURTHER READING

Roberts, P., & Kellough, R. (2006). *A guide for developing interdisciplinary thematic units* (4th
   ed.). New York: Prentice Hall.
This book provides a step-by-step approach to using interdisciplinary thematic units to
   help students acquire the knowledge and develop the problem-solving skills required for
   today's changing – and challenging – times.

▶ REFERENCES

Ball, D. L., & Feiman-Nemser, S. (1988). Using textbooks and teachers' guides: A dilemma
   for beginning teachers and teacher educators. *Curriculum Inquiry*, *18*(Winter), 401–423.
Educational Market Research. (2012). *The complete K-12 report: Market facts and segment
   analysis*. Rockaway Park, NY: Educational Market Research.

5

Assessment and Evaluation

▶ **LOOKING AHEAD**

Assessment is essential to effective elementary social studies teaching, not because politicians say so or because there is so much stress on grades and test scores, but because it informs teachers and learners. Effective assessment tells us what we are doing right and what we need to improve. Assessment, at its best, should reflect what teachers and schools are trying to accomplish.

This chapter focuses on the tools that elementary teachers use in assessing students. We want to stress that all assessment in elementary social studies should be firmly based on the goals and objectives of the social studies program. We also want to stress that the students need to be involved in the assessment process.

A lot has been written about authentic assessment over the past decade. Authentic assessment means that the focus is on what students do and produce rather than on test scores. The notion of authentic assessment is consistent with the problems approach. Solid authentic assessment involves students in the evaluation process, making them aware of what needs to be accomplished and learned.

CAN YOU? DO YOU?

Can you . . .

- Explain why grades and test scores are so emphasized in schools?
- Explain how teachers go about determining grades?
- Explain authentic assessment?

Do you . . .

- Know why evaluation is always comparative?
- Know how evaluation should be different in the problems approach?
- Know the strengths and weaknesses of objective and subjective tests?

FOCUS ACTIVITY

Before reading this chapter, try the following focus activity.

Think back on your educational experiences. What was your favorite social studies assignment/project when you were a student? Why? Share experiences with others. Discuss the details of the assignment/project and compare. Does your favorite social studies assignment/project share common attributes with others'? If so, which attributes?

▶ THE ROLE OF ASSESSMENT IN SOCIAL STUDIES

Teachers and students tend to equate terms such as "assessment" and "evaluation" with grades. This is like thinking that art is a paint brush or that music is a voice or a piano. Grades and standardized tests are tools by which assessments are done. They are indicators of student progress and learning, of the degree of teaching success, and of areas of strength and weakness. Teacher-made tests, teacher observations, and the various kinds of work that students produce provide teachers indicators. It is extremely important that teachers not lose sight of the purpose of evaluation in social studies, which, as in any other area of instruction, should be to improve student learning.

Assessment, especially achievement test scores, as well as summary grade evaluations on report/grade cards, takes on special importance to administrators, teachers, students, and parents. Grades and tests are important because they are the major form of feedback to students and parents. In addition, they are a concrete and permanent record based on performance data.

Feedback is only part of the reason for student assessment. Student assessment is also related to finding out how well a teacher has taught, how well a student has learned and performed, and what still needs attention. At best, evaluation guides and improves teaching and learning.

All types of student assessment involve comparison of student performance. Many people like grades and test scores because they provide the easiest comparisons and have many bases of comparison. Student performance can be compared in a quantitative way to some particular criteria of success built into school or teacher objectives, to a performance standard, to classmates, to the whole school, to a national average, or to personal past performance or perceived potential. Normative performance, for example, is the basis on which most standardized test scores are analyzed. Norms or averages can be computed and used to compare the performance of one person or group to average performance of either an age or grade group or even among all people who have taken a particular test.

Another basis of comparison is criterion-based assessment. Criterion-based assessment is the extent to which an individual can meet indicators of success that relate to particular characteristics. Levels of performance are set in advance based on some preconceived notions of what constitutes mastery.

When a teacher plans instruction, a criterion-based assessment is often useful. The pre-selected criteria of success identified for a lesson or a unit are called objectives. Objectives describe the specific knowledge or skills that are expected to result from the teaching/learning activities. Objectives identify the desired learning outcomes. Objectives can be more clearly defined and evaluated if they name a behavior that might be an indicator that the objective has been achieved, and these are known as behavioral objectives.

Assessment and teaching will be more effective if based on objectives or desired learning outcomes that we can then use as indicators of the degree of success we have had in teaching. When the learning outcomes provide direction, both teaching and evaluation are more focused, and purposeful learning is more likely to occur. One approach to teaching, often referred to as mastery learning, is based entirely on the notion that instruction about any basic learning needs to continue until that standard has been achieved.

Social studies has been struggling for a long time with some particular dilemmas that educators in other curricular areas may just now be starting to see. One of these dilemmas has to do with the overall evaluation of students, but especially with the assigning of grades. Social studies learning outcomes involve the acquisition of knowledge; the development of skills; the variables of interpersonal relationships; very complex and often subtle changes in personal values, philosophies, and beliefs; and other criteria that relate to performance and to development of products that are often intricate and elaborate. For some of these outcomes, it is very easy to design ways of assessing that can be easily measured. For what may be considered the most important learning outcomes, though, measurement and assessment are much more difficult and subjective.

▶ PRINCIPLES OF ASSESSMENT

Assessment is important to teaching and learning when it helps teachers, students, parents, and administrators improve on what is already being done. Well-constructed assessment gives students and parents, as much as teachers, ownership of the learning process. This can only be accomplished if all are involved in deciding what the assessment will be and how it will be used.

Alleman and Brophy (1999) discuss the changing nature of assessment in the social studies. They point out that assessment should be focused on curricular goals and objectives and be used as a means of improving both the curriculum and the instructional program. They go on to assert that "evaluation of student achievement should be used solely to improve teaching and learning" (p. 336).

The standards movement in social studies has had a profound influence on how social studies teachers view assessment. Historically, success in the traditional elementary classroom was based on the ability to remember specified information and the mastery of particular technical skills. The job of assessment has become much more complex. Information and skills are now viewed differently, with emphasis on students learning how to obtain information and how to learn skills. Learning to learn and becoming an independent learner are stressed. The foci of evaluation are expanded to include such factors as the ability to identify and define problems, flexibility to handle new situations, ability to apply knowledge in different settings, and openness to many ideas and solutions. The real concern is the ability of students to handle problems.

An illustration of how the tools of evaluation and grading have changed is shown in Table 5.1. The table is hypothetical but reflects observed differences in general.

Social studies educators argue that assessment can be important to teaching and learning when it helps everyone involved think about and better understand how they are doing and how they can improve in relation to the goals of social studies (Alleman & Brophy, 1998; NCSS, 1990). Authentic assessment gives students as well as teachers ownership of

Table 5.1 The Extent to Which the Tool is Used in Student Assessment

Evaluation Tools	Traditional Teaching	Standards-Based Teaching
Daily assignments	2–3	1
Short quizzes, review	2–3	1
Short quizzes, problems	1	2–3
Objective tests, recall	2–3	1
Objective tests, application	2–3	2
Essay tests, informational	2	1
Essay tests, problems	1	2–3
Individual projects	1–2	3–4
Reports, written	1–2	3–4
Reports, oral	1	3–4
Group/collaborative		
projects	1–2	2–3
Reports, written	1–2	2–3
Reports, oral	1	3–4
Teacher observation	1	2–3
Self-assessment	0–1	1–3
Journals	0–1	1–3
Stories and other writing	0–1	1–3
Games and active discussion	0–1	1–3
Problem-solving activities	0–1	1–3
Dramatic activities	0–1	1–3
Participate in community service projects	0	1–3
Personal portfolios	0	2–3

Key:

0 = Not Used at All
1 = Used Sparingly/Occasionally
2 = Used Frequently
3 = Of Critical Importance in Evaluation

the learning process (Avery, 1999). Both goal–centered assessment and authentic assessment can only be accomplished if we consider at least five major principles:

1. The aim or purpose of all assessment in education is to improve learning by:

   a. Making sure the curricular goals are understood by all.
   b. Identifying specific areas of student strengths and weaknesses.
   c. Identifying effective and ineffective teaching practices.
   d. Being sure that assessment tasks themselves involve organization of information and decision making.
   e. Identifying the need for additional and/or different instruction.
   f. Bringing about self-assessment and independent learning.

2. To be authentic, assessment must be an ongoing process, and a variety of tools must be used with understanding.

3. Everyone must realize that all assessment is imperfect and that flaws are inescapable. Types of errors include:

   a. Sampling error: What we choose for assessment does not allow us to effectively identify what the student knows and does not know, what they can do and what they cannot do. (This could be a bad test item or an unrepresentative sample of the student's work.)
   b. Assessor error: The person doing the assessment makes the wrong assumptions, and/or inappropriate interpretations, and/or incorrect judgments.
   c. Communication error: The assessment message sent to and/or received by the student is incorrect, misunderstood, or otherwise constructed so that it does not result in learning improvement.

4. Students need to develop ownership of the goals of assessment.

5. All assessment should relate to the goals of the curriculum, and classroom assessment should be directly connected to soundly conceived and well-stated objectives.

6. Classroom evaluation should be based on what you intend to teach, what you teach, and what you intend for students to learn from that teaching.

▶ GUIDELINES FOR ASSESSMENT

Assessment may require many different types of instruments and forms in social studies, including quizzes, tests, examinations, observations, oral examinations, interviews, conferences, checklists, self-evaluations, portfolios, holistic evaluation of projects and papers, and a host of others. Even if we limit our concern to just grading and the other formal ways of providing students and parents feedback, the complexity of the assessment process is sometimes overwhelming. That complexity might be illustrated by looking at a typical six-week grading period. An elementary social studies teacher, even a traditional one, might have the following variety of information on which he or she would like to base grades:

- Scores/grades on one or two unit tests plus quiz grades.
- Scores/grades on homework and/or seat work completed.
- Evaluations of student map work of different types.

- Grades from several pieces of evaluated written work (stories, poems, essays, reports, outlines, questions answered).
- A holistic evaluation of a group project involving working together to produce a group report and some display (diorama, mural, table scene).
- Grades for an individual research project given both in writing and orally with artifacts made by the student.
- Observations of participation in class activities and discussion.
- Notations on volunteer projects, including some very elaborate ones showing a great deal of energy and interest.
- Student self-evaluation and peer evaluation of projects.

The first obvious problem is that, if some numerical averaging is to be used to determine a grade, this teacher has more than one option for determining each of the various numbers to plug into the grade mix. The second problem has to do with coming up with an overall formula that accounts for or weighs differences in importance and effort for each activity. Subjective decisions are made about the relative value or percentage of a grade to be allotted for different tasks and performances. A third and even more important difficulty, though, is that only some of the activities on the list may be evaluated in such a way as to yield definitive and objective grades. Some of the most important student work simply has to be evaluated in very subjective ways. Even checklists, which can produce questionable quantitative information, just will not provide any true evaluation of this work.

The point is that assessment, even the small part of it that we call grading, is never easy and never without flaws. Teachers have to make difficult decisions. These decisions can be, and probably will be, questioned and debated. To provide at least some help in the decision making, we want to offer ten broad principles or guidelines for assessment:

1. Both the form and the substance of assessment tools can best be defended if based on teaching objectives. Think through in advance what learners are to accomplish and ways to effectively evaluate these accomplishments.
2. We need to assess what we teach, not what we should teach; both teaching and assessment should reflect what we want as learning outcomes.
3. We need to focus assessment on what is important rather than on what is easy to measure.
4. Ongoing assessment is preferable to endpoint; we need to incorporate evaluation into regular activities.
5. Assessment of teaching should be based on what students learn rather than on what they already know and can do; therefore, we need to find out what they already know before we teach.
6. If we give students a clear understanding of the purposes of any assessment and the reasons for the assessment, they will perform a lot better.
7. Students need to perceive the assessment as fair and honest, not tricky or directed at "catching" them.
8. Assessment procedures should be built around the notion of finding ways of improving instruction.
9. Effective assessment involves the student in self-evaluation, thinking about how he or she can do better, and taking responsibility for his or her own learning.
10. A teacher should always remember that assessment is, at its very best, a subjective and risky affair:

a. Anyone *can* be wrong about a grade or any kind of assessment, and everyone is sometimes wrong.
b. Anyone can make mistakes about the information upon which evaluation is based.
c. Anyone can misjudge a student or a student product.
d. Anyone can be wrong about what they should be evaluating and teaching.

Everyone will be guilty of faults *a* through *d* on this list on a regular basis. Many of the approaches, techniques, and tools of assessment are well known because we have experienced them as students ourselves. Even so, an overview of the various tools of evaluation can help teachers find a more purposeful and fair personal approach to grading and evaluation.

▶ AUTHENTIC ASSESSMENT AND PORTFOLIOS

Educators have become more concerned in the last decade about how well the various means of assessment are working. One issue is that tests alone are inadequate as measures of ability and learning. Educators can easily identify students who do poorly on tests and produce and do wonderful things in class or show great knowledge and skill in conversation. They see the same kinds of discrepancies with students who have high test scores and do poorly outside the tests. There are many questions about the validity of the tests themselves since scores seem to be influenced by reading ability and cultural background.

Then, of course, there is real concern that the quality of learning simply does not lend itself to being quantified. Going beyond issues relating to testing to the broader one of giving grades, many educators feel that students need to take an active part in the evaluation, instead of having the traditional receptive and even passive roles. In even the best situations in the past, students have taken part in only a limited number of in-class experiences in which they have graded their own work or that of other students. Students have been given few, if any, experiences in which they have had the opportunity or the need to examine their own thinking and work reflectively and diagnostically.

The term "authentic assessment" describes a broader approach to student evaluation that tries to bring teachers, parents, and students together to look at the whole body of work that reflects student ability and potential. The term "authentic" is used because the basic premise of the approach is that we need to look at all types of real work that students do in order to see their accomplishments and potential. Types of assessment that have been used in the past, especially tests, simply do not have any relation to the ways that skills and knowledge are used in the real world and in jobs later in life. Educators involved in this effort are looking more to methods of evaluation, which involve all kinds of performance and products of performance that show what students can do, particularly what they can do over more extended periods of time.

Authentic assessment is an approach that relies on authentic or alternative means of assessment, such as individual portfolios or collections of student work assembled over time. The student takes an active and important role in the development and organization of the portfolio. Students usually help decide what goes into the portfolio. Students may also be responsible for organizing and record keeping with regard to the contents of the portfolio. Emphasis may be given to student initiative in conferences with the teacher. The individual items in the portfolio become the basis for student-teacher conferences and the base of comparison for future work. Students who learn to gather and organize material for a portfolio and to select the best material for it are not only more active in evaluation but also learning skills that will be of benefit in the world of work.

One way that a teacher can control the size of a portfolio and ensure that students actually do some selective decision making is to limit each portfolio to a certain number of pieces/artifacts. Another way is to require that the portfolio include examples of particular types of work (e.g., book reports, essays, answers to comprehension questions, poems, stories, maps, pictures, problem-solving activities, and group reports). The form that portfolios take can also help the teacher manage the size in order to make them meaningful, evaluated work instead of unorganized collections. In some cases, the portfolios may be organized physical scrapbooks, but they can also be electronic portfolios.

Ideally, portfolios bring teachers and students together in ways that help students improve work. Even so, there are obvious problems when it comes to how they are used in evaluation. The success of portfolios depends upon several factors:

1. The students, teacher, and others have to see them as important and purposeful.
2. Time has to be spent between the teacher and student, both in the development of the portfolio and in its evaluation.
3. Acceptable procedures for organizing and evaluating the portfolio have to be developed.
4. There have to be clear-cut ties between the portfolio assessment and traditional grades.

Portfolios can be evaluated in several ways, including group and individual conferences, written descriptive feedback, and diagnostic and evaluative checklists. The evaluation, whatever form or forms it takes, should make the best sense to the teacher and student.

▶ ASSESSMENT THROUGH TESTS

In a world of high-stakes testing, the very first thing many people think of is standardized tests when the subject of assessment is mentioned. Tests always involve performance and are used because they are an efficient method of finding out what people know or can do. Nationally normed standardized tests, although not as well known in social studies as in reading and mathematics, are given system wide and statewide because they have been viewed as a way of comparing and evaluating students as to their mastery of information and skills. Though many educators are dissatisfied with standardized tests and the way the data are used, there currently is a movement toward national testing programs.

In social studies, the most widely used forms of tests are written ones that involve answering questions or performing specified tasks. Generally, tests that involve little or no judgment in grading are called objective measures. Included in this group are true-false tests, multiple-choice tests, labeling of diagrams and maps, matching, and some short-answer and fill-in-the-blank tests. Most of these tests can also be called "high-cue" tests because they contain a lot of clues and may even supply the correct answer (e.g., matching). The kind of thinking that is required may involve recognizing and basic rote memorizing.

The advantages of objective-type measures mostly relate to the unchanging quality of the test items. The correct answers are thought to be verifiable and absolute. Except when the teacher makes a detectable and documentable error, there is little or no danger of misinterpreting or wrongly grading an answer. In addition, such questions can cover the material to be tested by sampling what is important in a very equitable way based on pre-established criteria, and performance data can be gathered to establish the value of individual items. Once such tests are established, the teacher can correct them fairly quickly.

However, there are many criticisms of objective tests. Some point out that these tests are really not objective at all. Many deal with test-item construction. Here are some criticisms of objective tests:

- Insufficient information is given to call for one specific answer (multiple-choice stems and completion or fill-in-the-blank: e.g., All of the ___ were ___).
- Items are written deliberately to be tricky or misleading (e.g., True or False: Cortez conquered the Incas in Mexico).
- Test items tend to concentrate on the less important and even trivial aspects of a topic of study (e.g., Short Answer: How many Pilgrims survived the first winter in Plymouth?).
- Test items require the students to share an opinion (e.g., True or False: The greatest woman of the nineteenth century was Florence Nightingale.).
- Questions are often long, wordy, and confusing.
- More than one alternative is plausible as an answer.
- It is difficult to write objective items that involve creativity, evaluation, and application, and few objective tests include such items.
- Objective tests often work to the advantage of lucky guessers, and chance plays too large a role.

Elementary teachers are still going to find objective tests useful. First, there is no doubt that objective tests are efficient. They can be taken and graded quickly. Students easily learn the skills needed to answer objective test questions. Furthermore, the skills developed taking these tests are useful for future standardized tests.

Elementary teachers who use objective tests can improve the quality and usefulness of the tests over time. First, they need to make sure that every question relates to some important objective or learning outcome. They also need to realize that a high success rate on the test is their goal, because if most students do poorly, it is an indicator that they have not taught effectively. If many students miss a particular question, something is wrong. It probably means that the question was either worded in a way that was vague or difficult to understand, that the material was not taught, or that the information was either not understood or had no impact.

Tests that require value judgments in evaluation are described as subjective measures. Subjective measures include nearly all types of essay and problem-solving work, where the process is as important (if not more important) as the answer and where thought and creativity are often part of the judgment. These can be called "low-cue" test items because they depend almost wholly on the ability of students to understand and retain information relative to the question and use it. Little or no information is supplied.

Subjective tests require students to think and to structure thinking, recalling the appropriate information and applying the information. They also allow different students to use different arguments and information. There are as many common criticisms of essay tests as an objective measure. Critics claim the following:

- There is no fair and consistent way of grading an essay test.
- Students who do not write well do not do well on essays.
- Many students are able to be too creative in their answers.

- The kind of thinking required in essay tests is beyond the ability of most students, so the measures are unfair indicators of what they know.
- Essay tests can only sample a small amount of the material covered, not all the objectives.
- Essay tests take much more time to grade and must be graded by someone who knows both the material and how it was taught.

An answer to these criticisms is called holistic evaluation. In this approach, the preparation procedure includes supplying students with thorough descriptions of various performance levels for essays. These descriptions range from descriptions of characteristics of poor answers on up to the attributes of superior essays. These criterion-based descriptions become the basis for the grading, which is the process of categorizing essays into levels. They are generally referred to as rubrics.

Holistic evaluation has been a way of responding to legitimate recognition of a testing problem. It is a good way to show that simply by knowing the pitfalls of any form of test or test question, it is possible to avoid or at least reduce the dangers. The form of a test and the kind of test questions that a teacher uses should be a matter of sense and judgment. Some tests provide information specifically to help planning and teaching (formative evaluation); some are merely diagnostic; and others are intended to be final, exit evaluations (summative). Any good test for elementary social studies, whether it includes subjective or objective questions or both, and regardless of its intended use, is going to do the following:

- Measure what it is supposed to measure (prerequisite knowledge, what is important, what has been taught and learned, etc.).
- Require the thinking skills that the teacher wants students to use.
- Allow the teacher to evaluate how well the objectives have been achieved.
- Be an additional learning experience for students.
- Be constructed and evaluated with fairness.
- Be carefully and clearly worded and understandable to students.
- Not be a test students fail because of a lack of reading ability.
- Be constructed so that students can be expected to complete it in the time allowed.
- Relate to all objectives in an equitable way.
- Be of a length and type that is appropriate to students, the material covered, and the way the material was covered.

Developing a test and even deciding to use one that has been prepared to go with a textbook or other educational material should be a thoughtful and purposeful procedure. The first consideration should be the purpose that the test is going to serve. Several additional steps are needed, which might include the following:

1. Think about your specific purposes in the evaluation. What are you trying to find out about what the students have learned or what they can do with that knowledge?
2. Consider how much time you want the test to take, accounting for attention span, ability level, the breadth and depth you want in the evaluation, and the importance attached to the particular evaluation.
3. Decide what kind(s) of activities or behaviors you want the test or quiz to include.

4. Develop a plan for dividing the test into its component parts. This may take such forms as outlines, sets of objective statements, and organizational plans allocating percentages.
5. Prepare the individual items.
6. Carefully check the items for content, wording, clarity, readability, and so on.
7. Have someone else read the items to see if they understand them as you intended them and if they see any ambiguity, possibility of multiple interpretations, trickiness, and so on.
8. If possible, have someone do the test to see how that person interprets it and answers the questions and how long it takes to complete. (As a rule of thumb, multiply adult time by three to get an estimate of student completion time.)
9. Observe students as they take the test to note ease or frustration, commonly experienced difficulties and individual problems, and differences in rate of completion.
10. When grading tests, become aware of instances in which student answers consistently vary from the correct answer.

▶ ASSESSING PROJECTS AND REPORTS

Projects are extremely difficult to assess. They often involve art ability or other abilities outside those that are directly related to elementary social studies learning and thinking; sometimes reflect parent help and/or differences in financial and other resources; and, even for a similar assignment, vary immensely in type, complexity, and learning value. When projects are done by cooperative learning groups, various members may make vastly different contributions. All this is an almost essential part of the nature of this type of activity. Project work, at its best, involves a tremendous amount of thought and effort in conceptualization, which may not be reflected to the evaluator in the finished product. One of the problems of project work is that students may turn it into copy work, reflecting almost no thought or originality. The teacher may or may not detect this when it happens, depending on how carefully the material is read, how familiar the teacher is with the resources and/or the style of the language used in them, and what the teacher expects from a style. Flashy and impressive projects may, finally, reflect little learning or teaching; unimpressive projects, on the other hand, may be the result of much more time and thought.

Even so, it is within the very qualities that make projects difficult to evaluate that the true value of project work is found. Projects involve students; they make them think and apply what they learn; they require conceptualizing, problem solving, and solution finding; they provoke research and questioning; they necessitate planning and organization; and, in the case of cooperative learning projects, they involve group interaction skills and teach some valuable lessons about how other students operate and think.

Reports, whether oral or written, present all the same evaluation difficulties. They involve language abilities of different types, and the student's self-confidence and ability to communicate to and/or in front of others may influence how good the report seems as much or more than the actual thought and work involved. Availability of resources may also be a factor, as may the nature and form of the assignment. A well-structured report assignment, for example, should produce better results.

Projects and reports may be evaluated in several ways. The most common of these are any number of types of subjective evaluation with or without comment, checklist evaluation, analytical evaluation, rubrics, peer evaluation, and self-evaluation.

▶ SUBJECTIVE ASSESSMENT

The teacher's overall subjective judgment has always played a role in assessment. It is authoritarian in style and relies almost entirely on the teacher's professional judgment. The reasoning is that the teacher observes a project or report through its development, has an intimate knowledge of individual students, and has had a great number of past experiences with student projects and reports. Subjective assessment assumes the authority of the teacher and his or her right to be the judge. Students are discouraged from questioning any grade or judgment from the very beginning. At least an unconscious reason for this discouragement is that the criteria for judgments are not easily verbalized and are not very consistent. In fact, a teacher or student could bring almost any factor into a justification argument. It is very difficult to give instructive and useful diagnostic feedback in this approach. When instructional suggestions and comments are made, they tend to be interpreted by the student as the teacher's rationale for the grade given. This may not actually be true.

Flaws in writing mechanics (or the absence of such flaws) and the appearance of projects sometimes influence teachers' judgment of substance and ideas. Often ideal models/examples are used to show students in advance what a good report or project looks like. This may or may not have positive effects. Seeing the models/examples may reduce creativity in some cases or even cause student frustration at not feeling able to complete equivalent work. It may also cause students to simply repeat or copy the model/example, making minor changes. On the other hand, models may provide students with clarification about expectations.

▶ PEER ASSESSMENT AND SELF-ASSESSMENT

Peer assessment and self-assessment by students represent the aim of all evaluation. Elementary teachers need to be constantly working toward the point at which they can develop constructive ideas about what constitutes good work and make adjustments to achieve it. The basic process, whether involving peer assessment or self-assessment, begins with educating students to think of first efforts as preliminary stages. The process also means that students develop high standards, a desire to produce quality work, and an acceptance that such work can be achieved through revision. Students become involved in actively seeking to understand what it takes to produce good work. This is always a goal, and the process of moving students in the direction of the goal is at the center of standards-based teaching as well as the problems approach. Students perceive success in terms of work that they can take pride in; intrinsic goals replace extrinsic ones.

The process is one in which students learn to judge their own reports and projects as well as their peers', to know what they need to contain, and to have a refined concept of the features that distinguish outstanding efforts. Obviously, this is an ideal and, as such, is something that teachers need to work toward, not expect at the outset. Teachers need to carefully structure instruction so that students learn how to make judgments. Follow through is needed, and a developmental approach is an absolute requisite to achieve more than superficial assessment.

▶ CHECKLIST AND RUBRIC ASSESSMENT

Using checklists or rubrics to assess produces an assessment that is criterion based. A checklist or rubric may identify the features that the project or report is to include and the characteristics that the teacher expects in a report or project. When checklists and rubrics are given to students in advance, they help students clarify the teacher's expectations and provide a sense of security about how they can be successful in meeting expectations and getting a good grade. Such thinking may produce regimented work and cause students to work too much on meeting the criteria and too little on creative problem solving.

An example of a checklist that might be used with a third-grade reporting activity is detailed in Table 5.2. The items on the checklist might be treated with a simple check mark indicating acceptability or might be rated in some way showing how well each criterion has been met.

Items on a rubric will be marked indicating the level of acceptability or might be rated in some way showing how well each criterion has been met. Table 5.3 depicts an example of a rubric that was used to assess a project on monuments around the world. The rubric is suitable for fifth or sixth grades.

▶ ANALYTICAL ASSESSMENT

Analytical assessment is based on careful examination of student behaviors or products in the light of clearly identified criteria. This approach may take several forms. When projects or reports are evaluated analytically, the teacher usually examines them very carefully and gives a detailed reaction. Sometimes this is a preliminary evaluation after which the students can revise, change, and improve. This view treats the work that has been done as a phase in the process of learning how to do this type of project. It is a draft. Whether the analysis is merely a step in the process or comes as a final feedback session, it can take one of two basic forms. One approach is for the teacher to begin with no criteria, basically letting the work itself dictate how it is analyzed. The idea is to give feedback on the strengths and weaknesses that will allow students to improve. Another analytical approach involves the examination of a report or project to see how well it meets a few standards. Comments would then be made relative to each of these standards. For example, the following categories might be the basis for evaluation of a project:

- Topic (What thought is evidenced in the selection of the basic idea?)
- Approach (How unique and interesting is the approach?)

Table 5.2 Example of Third-Grade Checklist

The report . . .
- _Has a clear, creative, descriptive title.
- _Attempts to solve a problem or answer a question.
- _Deals with an important topic.
- _Is well organized with at least three subtopics.
- _Has a list of references (in correct form).
- _Shows that the references have been used.
- _Covers the topic completely.
- _Is presented in an interesting way.
- _Shows that the writer or presenter is knowledgeable about the topic.
- _Uses visual material (pictures, charts, maps, etc.).
- _Shows concern for mechanics (grammar, punctuation, and spelling).
- _Has a good summary and conclusion.

Table 5.3 Example of a Rubric

	Unsatisfactory 0–1	Satisfactory 2–3	Excellent 4–5	Points Earned
Location	-The monument was not located within the assigned country. City and significance of location was not provided	-The monument was located within the assigned country. City and significance of location was briefly discussed.	-The monument location, city, and significance of location were all addressed clearly and accurately.	
Demographic Information	-The project did not include demographic information.	- The project included some of the demographic information but with a few errors.	-The demographic information was accurate and useful.	
Historical Monument	-No background information or analysis of the monument was provided.	-The monument was located within the assigned country and some background information was provided, but with little analysis.	-The monument location, background information, and analysis were all clear and informative.	
Rationale for Visiting Monument	-Did not provide a rationale.	-The rationale was somewhat detailed.	-A detailed rationale was provided.	
World Monument and Cultural Guide	-The guide was not completed and/or contained multiple instances of incorrect information.	-The guide was completed, but some of the information was inaccurate or irrelevant to the project.	-The guide was fully completed with accurate and useful information.	
Presentation	-The information was not shared with the class	-The presentation was too brief and difficult to follow.	-The presentation was clear and informative.	
Technical Aspects and Grammar	-There were multiple misspellings or grammatical errors.	-There are a few misspellings and/or grammatical errors.	- There are a no misspellings and/or grammatical errors.	
Comments:			Total /35 pts.	

- Effort. (Does the project show industry and care?)
- Purpose. (Is the project purposeful and instructive?)
- Visual quality. (Does the project attract attention and interest?)
- Mechanics and content. (How well does the project reflect research and knowledge, and is it done with a care for correctness?)

▶ TEACHER OBSERVATIONS AND ANECDOTAL RECORDS

Descriptions of your observations of students do not easily translate into a form that can be considered in grading. Teacher observations are considered informal assessments, compared to formal assessments like tests, projects, etc. Nonetheless, teacher observations are an invaluable tool in evaluation. One of the reasons is that the development of the student is full of subtleties and nuance. Teachers need to be reminded that the essence of an individual is not really something that can be quantified.

The best elementary teachers are those who are reflective educators. The records of day-to-day actions of students often give teachers the best substance on which to reflect. In addition to the paper trail of students, these records are of two broad types: criterion-based quantitative observations, which usually take forms such as checklists, and qualitative observations that take the form of narrative descriptions. If either type is used, it needs to be done in a systematic, regular way, and it needs to be kept up over a longer period. This record keeping cannot be done when teachers are presenting to the class; the logical times for such record keeping are when students are engaged in activities that allow the teacher to quickly reflect and make notes and at times when students are not present, like during lunch, planning, recess, and the end of the school day.

What becomes obvious with only a little knowledge of the techniques of teacher observation is that they incorporate checklist techniques in a particular way. In observation, checklists are shortcuts to developing systematic records of how students are behaving and progressing. They give the teacher a record that helps him or her make sense of the class, and they do so with very little time spent outside class, beyond determining and setting up what qualities the teacher is seeking. Checklist assessment also relates well to determining the actual accomplishment of at least certain kinds of objectives.

Observational checklists may take many forms. One of the most common is a list of very specific competencies or knowledge (e.g., knows the cardinal directions). When a student masters an item on the list, his or her name is checked. A checklist might be set up to keep systematic track of group activity as well. The teacher might carry the checklist outlined in Table 5.4 about the room during an independent cooperative learning activity.

While checklists save time, anecdotal teacher observation records demand a lot of time. Anecdotal material may reflect specific observations during the day. It is narrative in form and describes actual behavior. Such comments may not need to be lengthy or provide a lot of detail, but they do need to be complete. The teacher may or may not want to create categories for such notes prior to observation. Some may be behavioral; for example, "When John lost his place in line at lunch, he shoved several students and made threatening remarks." Others may reflect participation; for example, "Caroline raised her hand for several questions in discussion. On two occasions that I called on her, she answered correctly and completely."

The time required by anecdotal observation approaches to evaluation demands that such observations be focused on particular problems or particular students. The data can be very helpful in instances when faculty are going to meet and discuss a student or when reference material is being gathered to recommend special attention for a student. This type of information may also help a teacher deal with a classroom management issue.

Table 5.4 Example of an Observational Checklist

Name	Works without conflict	Gets on task	Problem solves	Shows leadership	Behavior is appropriate
Group 1					
William	❑	❑	❑	❑	❑
Benedict	❑	❑	❑	❑	❑
Juliet	❑	❑	❑	❑	❑
Lynn	❑	❑	❑	❑	❑
Group 2					
Olivia	❑	❑	❑	❑	❑
June	❑	❑	❑	❑	❑
Penelope	❑	❑	❑	❑	❑
Rae	❑	❑	❑	❑	❑

▶ LOOKING BACK

Assessment is an important and complex part of elementary social studies. Assessment tools allow teachers to examine their own effectiveness as well as the learning of their students. Sound evaluation begins by comparing what has been learned to what the teacher intended to teach. In other words, achievement is measured against objectives.

Teachers assess this learning through student behaviors and student products. They need to be constantly aware of the need to focus on what is important, not just on what is easy to measure. Authentic assessment advocates argue that tests and other traditional measures do not measure in a "real" way what a child is capable of doing. One approach to authentic assessment is through student portfolios. The most traditional assessment tools are tests, quizzes, and papers, but evaluation based on these tools alone does not give a true or authentic picture of student capability. Other student activities are as important, or more important, than tests and written papers. Teachers may attempt more complete assessment by using observational tools, including checklists and criterion-based rubrics, for projects and other assignments.

EXTENSION ACTIVITY

SCENARIO

Currently, you are teaching at Yourtown Elementary School (YES), and everything is going wonderfully. However, on Monday morning, you arrive at YES, and you are inundated with students giving you flak about their grades on a social studies project. You explain to the students why they received the grades, and the day goes on as is normal. It is almost 5:00, and you are preparing to leave school for the day, but just as you are about to leave, the principal of YES, Dr. Russell, comes in and wants to meet. He has received numerous complaints regarding your grading procedures from parents and students. Unaware of your grading procedures, he asks to see your assessment plan for the assignment receiving the complaints; however, you do not have one. He explains that all effective teachers have an assessment plan, and he expects you to create assessment plans in the future. Embarrassed, you apologize and agree to create an assessment plan from now on. Furthermore, you promise to complete an assessment for the next social studies lesson you will be teaching and email it to him by tomorrow morning.

TASK

For this activity, an assessment plan is simply a plan for assessing students' learning and is a basic component of any effective social studies lesson plan. Your assessment plan should have measurable learning objectives and multiple forms of assessment. The learning objectives and forms of assessment must align.

Select a social studies lesson topic and create an assessment plan. The assessment plan should include learning objectives and forms of assessments to measure those objectives. Create assessments that align with the learning objectives.

CHECKING FOR UNDERSTANDING

1. What does the term *basis of comparison* mean in assessment?
2. Explain why both the method and the content of assessment should be based on the teaching objectives.
3. What is meant by the term *authentic assessment*?
4. Identify the criticisms of both objective and subjective tests.
5. Can you describe an example of an informal assessment?

▶ HELPFUL RESOURCES

Watch this video created by Teachings in Education about authentic assessment:
https://youtu.be/rQPCk27tM4U
Watch this video from NCSS about authentic assessment and the C3 Framework:
https://youtu.be/Ci0KF35ENII
Former classroom teachers created the Internet 4 Classrooms website as a forum for educators to gain up-to-date and relevant information about assessment and evaluation issues and ideas in public schools. Teachers will find useful updates about social studies testing, curriculum developments, and evaluation processes for states all over the U.S. at:
www.internet4classrooms.com/index.htm
Watch this video that briefly highlights the pros and cons of standardized testing:
https://youtu.be/tUyjJEY3o6A
Watch this video that highlights various teachers and their utilization of formative assessments in the classroom:
https://youtu.be/mMDVzRy8bJU
Watch this video that clearly outlines summative and formative assessments and how they can be utilized:
https://youtu.be/rJxFXjfB_B4
Watch this video, which highlights a history fair and how the social studies projects impacted students:

https://youtu.be/cpkQZYF7jY4

Watch this video explaining the foundation of project-based learning:

www.youtube.com/watch?v=LMCZvGesRz8&list=PLvzOwE5lWqhSgJVgg7VfRkBis
   bmm-BFUL&index=9

This valuable and free website allows teachers to construct rubrics for classroom assignments
   in a clear fashion. The site is very user friendly and walks teachers through the step-by-
   step process of creating rubrics to enhance classroom instruction and assessment. See
   Rubistar for Teachers at:

http://rubistar.4teachers.org/

Watch this video by Teachings in Education that outlines and explains rubrics and a rationale
   for utilizing rubrics in the classroom:

https://youtu.be/b4shMaSel00

▶ FURTHER READING

NCSS. (1991, September). Position statement: Testing and evaluation of social studies students. *Social Education, 55*, 284–285.

This position statement issued by the National Council for the Social Studies analyzes how
   testing and evaluation of social studies students can contribute to the development of
   more engaged citizens. The organization addresses how testing and other kinds of evaluation can help teachers weigh the appropriateness and effectiveness of social studies
   instruction while also providing recommendations for evaluation instruments and student
   achievement evaluations.

Vinson, K. D., Ross, E. W., & Wilson, M. (2011). Standards-based educational reform and
   social studies education: A critical introduction. In W. Russell (Ed.), *Contemporary social
   studies: An essential reader* (pp. 153–172). Charlotte, NC: Information Age Publishing.

This book chapter examines contemporary social studies curriculum and assessment within
   the contexts of standards-based educational reform. The authors discuss the impact of
   curriculum standards on social studies assessment, evaluation, and instruction.

▶ REFERENCES

Alleman, J., & Brophy, J. (1998). Assessment in a social constructivist classroom. *Social Education, 62*(January), 32–34.

Alleman, J., & Brophy, J. (1999). The changing nature and purpose of assessment in the
   social studies classroom. *Social Education, 63*(October), 334–337.

Avery, P. G. (1999). Authentic assessment and instruction. *Social Education, 63*(October),
   368–373.

Dewey, J. (1944). *Democracy and education*. New York: MacMillan Company.

NCSS. (1990). *Social studies curriculum planning resources*. Dubuque, IA: Kendall/Hunt.

Chapter 6

Reading and Writing in Social Studies

▶ LOOKING AHEAD

If we were to imagine social studies as a huge monument, the very base on which the weight rested would be an area called information and communication skills. Social studies cannot stand without these skills. We simply should be able to find, process, and use information in order to problem solve and/or make decisions. When we have questions to answer, our success depends on either knowing or being able to find the specific information that those questions require. In addition to all these information skills, social studies requires us to interpret information and create from it. What this all means is that students' ability to deal with information is critical.

This chapter deals with the development of those information skills essential in the social studies. It focuses on some of the types of materials and assignments that teachers traditionally have found to be useful as well as on types of materials that have become available in this age of technology. The chapter also speaks to the pitfalls and problems that teachers and students encounter in using these tools.

CAN YOU? DO YOU?

Can you . . .

- Name the four basic purposes for reading and writing assignments in social studies?
- Identify the specific reading abilities students need in social studies?
- Explain how to use textbooks with students who cannot read?
- Think of ways to use fiction books in social studies?
- Help students use the internet for research?

Do you . . .

- Know what students dislike most about using references?
- Know how to break students out of the "copy from the internet" loop?
- Know how to make social studies book reports interesting?

- Know how to help students learn to organize their writing?
- Know several ways to teach new concepts and new vocabulary?
- Know some ways to actually shorten what students have to read?
- Know why it is important for students to understand the organization of reading material?

FOCUS ACTIVITY

Before reading this chapter, try the following focus activity.

Think back on your educational experiences. What was your favorite book as child? Why? Do you remember reading it or having it read to you by a parent or teacher? Share experiences with others. Discuss the details of the book and how you might use it in your classroom.

▶ READING AND WRITING ASSIGNMENTS IN SOCIAL STUDIES

Reading and writing have long been important and necessary skills for social studies. Obviously, students need to read to obtain information. On the other side of the coin, many kinds of social studies activities require writing. Students must often write to demonstrate that learning has occurred.

> **FYI:** "If we encounter a man of rare intelligence, we should ask him what books he reads" (Ralph Waldo Emerson).

Both teachers and students first need to understand the purpose that a particular reading and/or writing assignment serves in order for it to be completed in an effective, meaningful way. An effective assignment will exhibit several traits. An effective assignment will be:

- *Interesting* and will provoke the curiosity of students.
- *Teacher facilitated*. Though students need to overcome difficulties and solve their own problems, the difficulties and problems cannot be so great as to cause students not to do the assignment. Make work challenging without making it impossible.
- *Devised to be accomplished in an amount of time that is appropriate to the age and the ability of students*. Students need to believe that they can accomplish the tasks. Sometimes we have to break large assignments into segments in order to accomplish this.
- *Clearly organized and understandable*. A lack of clarity is the most common problem with assignments. Students need to have a clear and complete understanding of what and how to accomplish the assignment.

▶ READING SKILLS NEEDED IN SOCIAL STUDIES

Many identifiable reading activities and skills are important if students are going to get meaning from textbooks and other reading materials. The following is a list of those activities and the skills involved:

1. Recognize the organization of reading materials:

    a. Show students how to use boldfaced headings as cues to content organization and that they can use these to make the content more meaningful.

    b. Help students learn to recognize topic sentences and show them how to use these in skimming and scanning.

    c. Teach them to identify main idea(s).

    d. Model and give them experiences in finding supporting ideas and facts that relate to main ideas.

2. Bring meaning to reading:

    a. Help students learn vocabulary and concept meaning by recognizing and using context definitions and identifications.

    b. Show them how to use glossaries and outside resources to find the meaning of vocabulary.

    c. Give them experiences that help them learn to use structural analysis and context clues to obtain vocabulary meaning.

    d. Help them to relate what they read to personal experiences, observations, and past learning.

    e. Relate new material to previous studies.

    f. Teach them to recognize and follow relationships in text (e.g., sequence, chronology).

    g. Help students relate what they read to particular problems and purposes brought to the reading act.

3. Read for a purpose:

    a. Before they read, help students understand questions and problems so that they will recognize appropriate solutions when they encounter them.

    b. Teach them how to skim for overall meaning.

    c. Teach them to scan for specific information, answers to questions, and useful related ideas.

    d. Help them develop the habit of using the table of contents and index to find specific information.

    e. Show them how to obtain information from maps in the text and how this can contribute to overall understanding of the reading material.

    f. Teach them how to use and interpret charts and graphs in the text.

4. Read critically:

    a. Help students learn to recognize author bias.

    b. Teach them to recognize discrepancies, contradictions, and missing information.

    c. Teach them to identify relationships among elements (e.g., cause and effect).

    d. Help them learn to distinguish opinion from fact, description from interpretation, and so on.

▶ HELPING STUDENTS READ SOCIAL STUDIES MATERIALS

There are a variety of strategies and techniques for helping students read social studies–related material. Some are simple and direct while others are complex. What you want as a teacher is for students to be able to get maximum use of social studies material of all types. We would like to suggest a four-step strategy:

1. Pre-teach difficult vocabulary prior to reading.
2. Reduce the length of independent reading tasks.
3. Provide specific clear purposes for reading.

4. Help students get a sense of the "story" that the reading material is telling, developing their predictive skills so that students use features of the text (such as pictures and boldfaced headings) and features of tasks (such as key-in question words) to anticipate more accurately.

By specifying a series of steps, we are not suggesting that this is a locked-in, lockstep sequence. The precise order of the steps as well as the decision to include any one of these specific steps may change greatly according to individual teaching style, the topic of study, and other individual and classroom factors. More importantly, we do not want to give the impression that these steps can only be carried out in one way. We want to suggest general approaches, not specific techniques. Some notion of the range of possibilities is indicated in the examples that are given in the following sections describing each step, but the possibilities are far greater.

Strategies for Developing Vocabulary

The single most important factor in reading comprehension is vocabulary meaning (Shanahan, 2001; Gersten & Baker, 1999). Every student develops and extends four basic vocabularies throughout his or her education: reading, listening, speaking, and writing. For most students, substantial listening and speaking vocabularies exist when they enter school. They attach a set of meanings to many words they hear and use a large number of words in speaking. Most of the materials designed specifically for early reading instruction are limited to include only those words that the student is likely to know. Since listening vocabulary far exceeds all other vocabularies throughout the elementary years, this is not a particularly limiting factor. Most of the words they encounter in reading are words they have heard and for which they have conceptualized meanings.

However, social studies deals with world cultures, historical times, social and governmental processes, and an endless variety of often unique names of people and places. This makes the field vocabulary rich. Many words are introduced for which students have few, if any, related experiences or concepts. Proper nouns, particularly names of people, places, and events, are abundant. Many complex and abstract concepts are also given word labels in social studies. The new words that students encounter in social studies reading materials are terms that are entirely new to them, terms that are not in their speaking or listening vocabularies. Teachers are responsible for providing enabling experiences and building necessary concepts and vocabulary. New vocabulary to be understood by the student must be fitted into perceptions and experiences that form the child's existing view of the world (Smith, 1975). New concepts then become part of the student's worldview only when they can be related to that view as it already exists.

If students are to be successful in understanding and making sense of social studies reading tasks, they must learn to think about new words before they read. Pre-teaching of essential new words and the concepts they represent prior to any reading task will save both teacher and student frustration. Many types of activities and techniques can be used for developing vocabulary meaning prior to reading. A few ideas are suggested and described.

Teacher Explanation of Meaning

Often the most efficient way of introducing vocabulary words is for the teacher simply to explain the meanings of crucial terms prior to reading. If several terms are involved, writing the words and definitions on the board or providing a duplicated list may help. A list may even be provided in the text, but unless the teacher pays attention, students will most likely ignore it. For individual assignments, the teacher should provide a vocabulary list before material is read. However, once the new vocabulary is introduced, teachers need to help students see each word in context, relating the importance of the terms for the particular reading assignment. The words need to be seen and heard by students.

At its simplest, the teacher explanation involves pointing out to the students where the text uses and defines terms. Teacher definitions might point out pictures, maps, and charts in the text that illustrate the concepts involved in particular terms. For some words, actual objects can be used from which students might get term-related multi-sensory experiences.

Though it is the most efficient way to introduce vocabulary, direct teaching may also sometimes be an ineffective method. Students will not always feel a need to listen or look, particularly if the routine of the explanations becomes too tedious and regular. When the teacher uses this approach, presentations of words and definitions need to be varied, exciting, and with reinforced student involvement. This way of teaching vocabulary should be interspersed with other approaches to vocabulary development.

The Frayer Model

The Frayer model is a graphic organizer used for concept development and vocabulary building. The model requires students to think about and describe a concept. The model is designed to have students analyze a concept, synthesize the concept, and apply the information. The Frayer model was designed by Dorothy Frayer (1969) and her colleagues at the University of Wisconsin. The Frayer model is an extremely valuable tool for helping students grasp a meaning and truly understand a new concept. Concept development is key for understanding social studies content. For example, if a student does not understand the concepts of abolitionists, slavery, freedom, and/or equality, then they may have a difficult time understanding and meeting the learning goals surrounding a unit on the Civil War. There are two versions of the Frayer model that elementary teachers will find valuable. Table 6.1 depicts version A, and Table 6.2 depicts version B.

As a class or individually, students complete the Frayer model to obtain a deeper understanding of a concept. Common steps for implementing the Frayer model follow.

1. Describe and explain the Frayer model to the class.
2. Give an example of how to use the model. Use a simple and common concept to demonstrate the sections of the model.
3. Assign a new concept(s).
4. In collaborative groups, pairs, or individually, have students complete the model with the assigned concept(s).
5. Have students share their conclusions.

Table 6.3 depicts a completed example of version A of the Frayer model, which can be used to help students gain a better understanding of the concept of culture. Table 6.4 depicts a completed example of version B of the Frayer model, which can be used to help students gain a better understanding of the concept of dictatorship.

Table 6.1 Frayer Model Version A

Definition (In Own Words)	Characteristics
Concept	
Examples (Personal)	Non-Examples

Classifying Experiences

Using classifying charts helps students see how terms fit into various systems of concepts. Charting is an effective way to help students categorize and see relationships among words and terms. Though such charts are more often used in reviewing after reading, they can also help students build a conceptual framework for new words. For example, the terms *bayou* and *canal* might be understood better if depicted using the charts in Table 6.5 or Table 6.6.

Other classifying experiences may simply involve students in sorting and prioritizing terms and words or a series of questions that bring out previous associations that will enable them to classify the terms.

Extended Teacher Definitions

If one or two terms are central to understanding total reading selections, then the teacher may need to give a more extended definition that includes illustrations. For example, the terms *pioneer* and *frontier* are both abstractions. Both would be crucial to understanding entire units and entire chapters of text in the study of American history. Since the terms have several meanings and describe very complex and involved ideas, the teacher may want to go to elaborate lengths to develop the depth of understanding needed. The teacher may want to read aloud descriptions of features of pioneer life, show audiovisual materials and websites, plus provide a wide range of real experiences prior to reading. An extended discussion to reach a group consensus about the definition would be still another way to introduce terms.

This in-depth approach might need to be used with many critical abstractions. The following questions might serve as a guide for developing a consensus definition of the abstract term *democracy*:

- What are your first thoughts about the meaning of democracy? (This might start a round of association play.)

- What are the features or characteristics of a democracy? (Prepare a list on the board.)
- Do all leaders in this country have the same concept of democracy? (Depending on student knowledge, you might ask about particular contemporary or historical individuals and their differences.)
- Does democracy mean equal opportunity? Participation in government? Equal wealth? Freedom (what kind of freedom)? Equality?
- If a country has democratic ideals, does this mean it will have democratic practices?

Teacher-Provided Experiences

Some terms may be better understood if the teacher can provide real or vicarious experiences to illustrate the concepts involved. Names of articles of clothing or utensils from

Table 6.2 Frayer Model Version B

Essential Characteristics	Non-Essential Characteristics
CONCEPT	
Examples	Non-Examples

Table 6.3 Frayer Model – Example of Version A

Definition (In Own Words)	Characteristics
The ideas, values, beliefs, and ways of doing things that I share with the people who live in my area.	• Shared ideas • Shared beliefs • Shared practices
CULTURE	
Examples (Personal)	Non-Examples
• What I wear • What I eat • How I speak	• What I wear • My hair • The weather • My eye color

Table 6.4 Frayer Model – Example of Version B

Essential Characteristics	Non-Essential Characteristics
• State exerts control • Central planning • Autocratic ruler (one person in control) • Power to govern without consent of those being governed	• Violent transition • Genocide • Inequitable distribution of goods and services
DICTATORSHIP	
Examples	Non-Examples
• Cuba • North Korea • Germany (Hitler) • Russia (Stalin)	• USA • UK • Mexico • Canada

Table 6.5 Classifying Chart – Example 1 for *Bayou* and *Canal*

Term	Features	Natural or Constructed	Examples	Related Geographic Features
Bayou	Shallow; sometimes navigable	Natural	Bayous in Louisiana delta	Low-lying marshlands; may drain into ocean/river
Canal	Shallow; navigable; may have locks to change elevations; often connects two bodies of water	Constructed	Erie Canal Suez Canal Panama Canal	Major transportation route links

Table 6.6 Classifying Chart – Example 2 for *Bayou* and *Canal*

Waterways	Landform	Types of Vegetation
Bayou	Isthmus	Deciduous trees
Canal	Delta	Savannah
Lake	Cape	Taiga
River	Island	Desert

a culture, for example, may be better understood if students see the objects and try to use or wear them. Foods that can be tasted may leave an impression.

Where real experiences are impossible, vicarious experiences may also be useful in developing concepts. These experiences may include hearing or reading fictional stories, seeing and hearing audiovisual presentations, and other activities in which students can identify with the people involved.

Student-Centered Experiences

Finding meanings for new words can be an exciting new adventure for students if well planned. On the other hand, it can also be routine, unpopular "busywork." The number of words must be limited with special thought to age and ability. Student involvement and participation in the discovery of new definitions will slow the instructional process but will help ensure a greater understanding. The techniques are numerous, and only a few can be described here.

- *The word experts:* Each student is responsible for just one word (or, at most, two) that appears in a unit to be studied. The job of the expert is to become so knowledgeable about that word that if any question about its meaning is raised, he or she will feel comfortable in attempting to answer.
- *Picture definitions:* The students are responsible for the meaning of a term or word in visual form. Posters, collages, and rebuses are among the many possible forms these defining visuals may take. Collages may be especially useful in depicting abstract concepts such as democracy, as well as in developing a concept of a particular person, their character traits, and their accomplishments.
- *Sound pictures:* A few particular social studies terms lend themselves to sound pictures as a way of vocabulary introduction. In some cases, a student may have to take a tape recorder to the best place to collect the sound picture. For example, the call of a muezzin or the singing of a cantor might be ways of gaining concepts of what these individuals do in a study of religion. A foreign language or dialect, a musical instrument, a type of song or dance melody, and other similar concept words can be defined through experiencing the sound.
- *Word look-outs:* Each student is responsible for one or two words and their meanings. Over a period of several days' class activities, every word will come into discussion. When an individual's word comes up, that person is responsible for noticing, defining, and writing the word on the chalkboard or on a classification chart.
- *Contextual locating:* Many terms are defined either directly or indirectly by the reading context. As a skimming exercise, have students look for and read definitions of words and terms as the text defines them.
- *Creating context:* Often the best way to learn what a word means is to use it. In this technique, students are demonstrating that they know the meaning of a word by inventing a context in which the word can be used properly. The particular context required of the student may vary greatly from a story, a descriptive paragraph, a single sentence, a poem, a poster or cartoon caption, a bumper sticker, a picture title, and/or a type of poem. These and many others can be creative applications of words through written contexts. An example of a "diamonte" (a diamond-shaped poem) that defines the word *scimitar* can be found in Figure 6.1. A descriptive paragraph for the word *senators* might look like this one:

Senators

No matter how big your state is or how many people it has, there are always two *senators. Senators* are elected every six years. There are fewer *senators* than there are representatives.

```
┌─────────────────────────────────┐
│                                 │
│            Scimitar             │
│                                 │
│             Keen                │
│          Curved blade           │
│         Defense of Islam        │
│            Saracen              │
│             Sword               │
│                                 │
└─────────────────────────────────┘
```

Figure 6.1 Example of a Diamonte

▶ LESS CAN BE MORE: QUALITY READING IN SOCIAL STUDIES

Reading is the means, not the end, of dealing with social studies materials. Understanding the content is the goal. Therefore, more comprehension can be achieved by cutting the number of actual pages of reading. For some students, a reading assignment of two pages versus one of ten or twenty pages of reading may mean the difference between doing or not doing the reading.

One of the most creative ways a teacher can help a student read is to control the amount of material that the student should read. The trick is to find ways of focusing the student's reading effort on the particular information that he or she absolutely needs to know. Since social studies materials are most often written at or above elementary grade–level reading ability, reducing reading may be helpful for many students. The following are several ways of reducing the reading load:

- Use student-written summaries instead of the text.
- Use teacher-written summaries instead of the text.
- Use textbook cut-ups.
- Try textbook highlighting.
- Experiment with question write-ins.
- Cooperate with class divide-ups.

Using Student-Written Summaries

One way to reduce reading is to collect, over a period of several years, student-written summaries of chapters or sections of printed material. These can be put in binders, folders with illustrations, and/or electronic files on a computer and then used as reading material for students. The time needed to collect good summaries puts the beginning teacher at a disadvantage. A teacher may need several classes before enough good summaries can be assembled. Cooperation from a teacher and class in a high grade may be one way of overcoming this difficulty temporarily. Good student-written summaries have several advantages:

- They are usually closer to the language that students speak and hear daily, both in sentence structure and vocabulary, than are materials.
- They reflect digested rather than raw content. That is, they include the message that one student has received from the readings.

- They are usually brief and to the point, leaving out many things a teacher would include.

Before student summaries are used as a substitute for textual materials, the teacher must do some careful editing. This can be very time consuming. Summaries may be duplicated and used with an entire class, with groups of students, or with individual students with special reading problems. A sixth-grade student did the following example. The teacher read and corrected the paper, and, after a conference, the student rewrote it. This summary is a student's view of an entire chapter of a textbook (Figure 6.2).

Using Teacher-Written Summaries

Well-prepared teacher summaries of materials also take a great deal of time to produce. Such summaries are especially useful because they may be written to include all specific facts and ideas that the teacher especially wants students to understand. Vocabulary can be specifically controlled and limited. The teacher should have a clearer and more complete understanding of the conceptual content of the material than students and be able to give the purposes and themes more emphasis. Clear references to pictures, diagrams, and other features of the text can be inserted.

Because of the time that summaries require, the teacher usually should not try to write summaries for all readings. Summaries may be duplicated and used with an entire class, with groups of students, or with individual students with special reading problems.

Figure 6.3 is a teacher's summary of the same selection covered by the student write-up. Similarities and differences in style and completeness can be noted, but the one

The first industry to grow in the United States was the textile industry. This happened after Samuel Slater brought the idea of cotton spinning machines to the United States and Francis Lowell built machines for making cotton cloth. Eli Whitney came up with the idea of mass production and interchangeable parts.

After the Civil War, more money went into industries and many industries grew. Andrew Carnegie built the steel industry into an empire. When he was 66, he sold all his companies and retired. Other industries that grew were the banking industry and the oil industry. Industries got so big that they became monopolies.

There were also new farm machines and scientific developments during the industrial revolution. One famous scientist was George Washington Carver. People moved off the farms and into the cities. Many people also emigrated from other countries to the United States. In the cities, people began having problems because of houses with poor safety and sanitation.

FIGURE 6.2 Example of a Student Summary

crucial quality of shortening the material read is the same. Thus, both make good substitute reading materials.

Textbook Cut-Ups

Textbook cut-ups require that the teacher have a free rein with the materials. It also demands extra copies of materials and a ruthlessness in destroying books and similar materials that repels many teachers automatically. It may be an especially good way of salvaging texts no longer in use.

Two copies of each page to be used may be needed for every cut-up version unless the material is printed on only one side or careful editing is done. The teacher cuts out only the most important sentences, pictures, and other things appearing on the pages and glues or pastes them in order on a clean sheet. A textbook chapter can usually be reduced to a few pages. Textbook cut-ups eliminate the overpowering and discouraging number of pages that may keep many students from ever attempting to really do an assignment.

Textbook Highlighting and Write-Ins

Go through the chapter before the student does and highlight the parts that he or she really needs to pay attention to, or have students highlight as they read. Warn students about what is important and what is not. Make sure the student knows what has been done and why before he or she reads the material.

Writing in the text is something that teachers have usually discouraged. This technique causes a breaking of the taboo. It is a technique that is easier if only a few problem readers are involved, and the teacher aids them by marking up their texts.

The teacher draws attention to major points and to questions answered by writing notes in the text. If textbook questions are used, they may even be cut out and taped directly next to the answer. Arrows can be drawn to maps, pictures, and charts from the descriptive references to put these in context.

Class Divide-Ups

Instead of having every student read every part of the text, assign only portions of the text to each student for reading. All can still have the benefit of the information in the entire reading. Each student might be assigned half the chapter and have a partner assigned the other half. The partners then prepare one another with the important and useful information in the other half. Another way to work this is to have various groups each assigned sections. After reading the section, the group meets to decide what they need to teach the class from their section and how this can be done most effectively. Until students become good at this, it will be necessary and helpful for the teacher to sit in on the meeting of every group to provide guidance.

▶ READING TEXTBOOKS

Reading is an interactive process. Real reading is not taking place unless the reader is finding meaning. For that to occur, the reader should be making a conscious, purposeful effort to be mentally engaged and involved and be showing at least a small amount

The Industrial Revolution brought changes to life in the United States. This "revolution" began in the first half of the 18th century with the textile industry in New England. Two men made this happen—Samuel Slater and Francis Lowell. Slater was an Englishman who built the first cotton spinning machines. Lowell built factories with weaving machines that made cotton cloth. The Industrial Revolution was also aided by Eli Whitney, the inventor of the cotton gin, who introduced the ideas of mass production and machines with interchangeable parts.

After the Civil War, the development of a national market due to transportation developments made more money available for industry. Among the great industrialists was Andrew Carnegie who built the large steel making industry and J.P. Morgan, who built a large banking industry and later bought Carnegie's steel empire. Another leader was John D. Rockefeller who founded Standard Oil. This was one of the businesses that grew so large that it could put competition out of business. The government became so concerned about such businesses that it tried to regulate them through a law called the Sherman Antitrust Act (1890).

New farm machines and scientific developments revolutionized farming and caused many people to move to the cities where jobs were available in factories. Large numbers of immigrants also came from Europe and Asia to the cities. Cities grew so quickly that they developed problems due to crowded areas and poorly built buildings. Sanitation and safety in tenement (apartment) buildings was very bad.

Attempts to deal with the problems were called reforms. Limits were set on immigration. Laws were passed to improve housing and sanitation. Settlement houses were founded to provide services. One of the reformers was Jane Addams who founded a settlement called Hull House in Chicago.

FIGURE 6.3 Example of a Teacher Summary
A four-paragraph example of a teacher summary. This summary describes the industrial revolution and its impact on America.

of interest. Effective reading involves coupling decoding and comprehension skills with background knowledge and an awareness of the interrelationships of elements in the text (Vacca & Vacca, 1993). The questions that a teacher needs to ask before using textbooks with students in social studies include the following: How can we make textbook assignments have the most meaning and usefulness to the greatest number of students? How can we aid students in relating background and in seeing the interrelationships of parts of the text? How can we maximize interest in the reading? The fundamental issue is making anything that students do with the textbook meaningful, important, and purposeful.

If textbook units are to be used effectively, students are going to have to view work as something more than a series of things to be completed, and teachers need to see curriculum as more than many pages to cover (McCutcheon, 1981). This is going to be true of any social studies approach in which students are using any kind of print or non-print materials to get information or ideas. Let us look at what teachers need to do to use textbooks and similar reading materials effectively:

- Give specific, purposeful assignments. Not only does the teacher need to have clear and important purposes for having students read material, but the students also need to understand what these purposes are. Talking with students about what they are reading for should be as important as telling them what to read. It also means that the teacher will need to have a fair degree of certainty that the students can accomplish those purposes.

- Stimulate interest in doing the reading. Fortunately, teachers have several ways available to arouse interest, and most of them involve creating curiosity. The teacher can, for instance, ask questions that can be answered by the reading material, point out curious and interesting illustrations that are explained or further described in the text, start and leave incomplete stories that are finished in the assigned reading, or give thumbnail sketches of people, places, or events in the text.

- Make sure that students have the skills needed to do the assignment. Many reading skills are needed in the social studies. A partial list of these appears earlier in the chapter. If the teacher does not know the mastery level of a needed skill, it is a good idea to provide at least a review demonstration and monitored practice before the students do the assignment.

- Provide supervision, monitoring, and help where needed. Monitoring is important for many reasons. First, it is an effective form of teaching and, at least in some instances, allows the teacher to keep students from deep learning of incorrect ways of doing assignments. Second, it helps teachers spot cases of "frustration" easily so that directions can be clarified or help given to students who do not understand assignments. Such help, particularly the right kind of help, is not always available to a child outside the classroom. Third, monitoring gives the teacher feedback about the effectiveness of the pre-teaching, the clarity of the assignment, and the ability of the students.

- Follow up on reading assignments. If students are required to read and do tasks associated with reading, it should be because this will help them learn important things. What they learn needs to be applied and used in ways that make learning from print important.

Helping Students Develop a Sense of the "Story" by Aiding Predictions

Every reading, textual or otherwise, has a message or story. Knowing the story – a sense of its purpose, organization, and direction before we read – helps us better understand. Effective previewing or surveying of reading material helps in the following ways:

- It provides purposes for reading in the form of expectations.
- It heightens anticipation and interest.

- It helps determine in what way materials relate to particular interests, questions, hypotheses, and so on.
- It provides advance organizers for thinking about what is read.
- It aids in predicting.

According to Smith (1975), greater accuracy in prediction is highly important to reading comprehension. That is, if the individual has a better idea about the nature of the reading content before reading, he or she will understand it better. The SQR3 technique (Herber, 1978) is a five-step procedure consisting of steps labeled Survey, Question, Read, Recite, and Review. Of these steps, surveying or previewing the material seems to be most important because effective surveying helps all other phases. If the student can predict, he or she can follow the direction of the writer and anticipate his or her thoughts. A number of teaching techniques, including the following, can help students predict more accurately the content of reading materials:

- Point out the headings and boldface type so students recognize them as organizers.
- Have students discuss speculations from titles and headings about what content is logical.
- Point out pictures before reading and discuss them. From the pictures and the captions, intelligent guesses are possible about the accompanying written material.
- Point out specific references in the text to maps and illustrations so students will know to look for these during reading. For example, the text might refer to stone ruins, which an illustration will show.
- Provide an outline or introduction overview and discuss it. A simple outline for the selection involved in the student and teacher summaries used previously might be:

    I. The textile industry grows in the United States.
   II. Transportation aids the growth of industry after the Civil War.
  III. Machinery revolutionizes farming.

Purposeful Reading

If asked, "Why are you reading this?" most students respond with a shrug of the shoulders or, at best, answer, "Because the teacher told me to." The most effective readers are very aware of their purposes for reading and areas where they can find very specific types of information. This alertness to the purposes of reading allows students to read material more rapidly, use context and format clues in locating information, access and use such features as an index or table of contents, and even determine appropriateness or inappropriateness of the material. Reading to achieve specific purposes aids in developing the predictive skills described earlier.

To help readers use their social studies textbooks and other reading materials with a better sense of purpose, elementary teachers need to set purposes for students that are specific and clear, guide them so that they read to understand those purposes, and follow through to emphasize the importance of the purposes.

The major learning students need for some purposeful reading is that the objective of reading in social studies is not simply to read the material. In fact, reading is incidental and only a tool by which the student gains the necessary information. Some very common procedures of social studies textbooks focus on providing purpose for reading, regardless of whether the teacher is aware of this purpose. These procedures include:

- Providing guiding questions before reading that identify specific types of information and understandings the student is to gain.
- Providing study questions that ask the student to identify the ways an author thinks and to go beyond the author's thoughts. For example, after reading material on historical periods, questions might be asked to get the student to explain how people in those eras might think about the way we live in the present.
- Alerting students prior to reading to follow-up tasks that will employ particular knowledge and concepts. For example, in the chapter on the industrial change in America, students might be asked to build a model of a farm before the change and another to show how farming was revolutionized.

When tasks related to reading are given to students, the purposes need to be made clear. It should not be assumed that students understand why they are reading or know what to look for.

Practice exercises such as skimming and summarizing for facts, details, or headings can help students become more aware of the importance of purposes in guiding how and what they read.

▶ READING QUESTIONS AND TASK STATEMENTS

Many students have difficulty in reading social studies materials simply because they do not make effective use of question clues that could help them be more purposeful in their reading and more accurate and correct in the way they respond. Elementary teachers can incorporate direct teaching about question clues into social studies or reading study skills instruction. One of the most fundamental skills in dealing with questions should be getting an immediate idea of what a question is asking and being able to relate that to the reading material. One of the ways that effective readers do this is by being sensitive to the nature of question words and to the nature of the answers these words demand.

Question words such as *who*, *what*, *where*, and *when* call for particular kinds of answers. One does not have to have any knowledge at all of the reading material itself to know that the answer to "Who was the English king and leader in the Third Crusade?" will not be "the Longbow," "the Battle of Agincourt," or "the Holy Roman Empire." *Who* dictates a particular kind of answer, including the name or description of a person or group of persons. Therefore, we know the answer could be Richard the Lionheart. Any question, in fact, offers clues to the length and nature of acceptable answers by the question words that appear in it. Many students intuitively learn this as they develop their skills in reading and the social studies. For some, though, it is crucial that teachers develop their sensitivity to the influence of key words on question meaning.

Even alerting students to organizational features of textbooks related to questions may be useful to them. For example, students should realize that answers to lists of questions in the text are usually found in the same sequence that they are asked. As simple and logical as this may seem, there are many students who may need to be reminded often.

Another feature that students should recognize is to question reversal and parallel structure. These both refer to questions that are written in the same language as the text but with a change in sentence order. A question such as "What was the ruler of Ancient Egypt called?" will probably be answered in the text with a statement such as "The ruler of Ancient Egypt was called the Pharaoh."

Elementary teachers constantly grapple with problems students have in grasping and retaining social studies content through reading. Teachers need to remember that the objective of social studies is not to have students read so much as it is to have them learn to use reading as one way to master concepts, learn new content, and obtain information relative to problem solutions.

▶ READING SOCIAL STUDIES-THEMED TRADE BOOKS

Students need to learn how to identify, use, and appreciate trade books. Trade books are common in the elementary classroom and are written at various levels. Trade books include a variety of reading topics and formats, including biographies, fiction, and poetry. An excellent resource for teachers regarding social studies–related trade books is the National Council for the Social Studies' annotated bibliography, *Notable Trade Books for Young Readers*. The books that appear on the annotated book list are evaluated and selected by a book review committee appointed by the National Council for the Social Studies (NCSS) and assembled in cooperation with the Children's Book Council (CBC). The annotated bibliography is published annually and includes

> books that emphasize human relations, represent a diversity of groups and are sensitive to a broad range of cultural experiences, present an original theme or a fresh slant on a traditional topic, are easily readable and of high literary quality, and have a pleasing format and, when appropriate, illustrations that enrich the text.
> (National Council for the Social Studies, n.d.)

Visit www.NCSS.org for the *Notable Trade Books for Young Readers* annual list for the past few years.

Reading Biographies and Other Nonfiction

Increasing numbers of nonfiction books that are boldly exciting and informative are being written for students. Biographies are written at many levels. Some nonfiction books have real depth and feeling as well as interest-arousing information. Such books can be used in a lot of ways in addition to standard classroom browsing "interest" tables and reporting activities.

Through elementary school, well-written, carefully researched, colorfully illustrated nonfiction picture books of high quality are abundant. These can be used for highly effective read-aloud experiences in social studies through the elementary grades. Some of these describe other cultures or life in other places. Others richly describe events and the details of life in different times. The accurate illustrations add to the delight that students experience and to the learning value.

Elementary biographies are full of anecdotes and stories. Some of the best ones have eye-catching illustrations, and many have humor that this age group can understand. Table 6.7 lists some recently published biographies that elementary teachers may find useful when teaching social studies. The list includes title, author, publisher, grade level, and connections to various NCSS themes.

Table 6.7 Examples of Trade Books: Biography

Title (Year)	Author	Publisher	Grade Level	NCSS Themes
A Taste of Freedom: Gandhi and the Great Salt March (2014)	Elizabeth Cody Kimmel	Walker Children's Books	K–5	1, 3, & 10
Friends for Freedom: The Story of Susan B. Anthony and Frederick Douglass (2014)	Suzanne Slade	Charlesbridge	3–6	5 & 10
The Right Word: Roget and His Thesaurus (2014)	Jen Bryant	Eerdmans Books for Young Readers	3–6	2
The Amazing Age of John Roy Lynch (2015)	Chris Barton	Eerdmans Books for Young Readers	3–6	3, 5, & 10
Gordon Parks: How the Photographer Captured Black and White America (2015)	Carole Boston Weatherford	Albert Whitman & Company	K–5	2, 5, & 10
Marvelous Cornelius: Hurricane Katrina and the Spirit of New Orleans (2015)	Phil Bildner	Chronicle Books	K–5	1 & 3

Reading Fiction and Poetry

Another way that social studies learning can occur is through fiction that students encounter in the reading and language arts curriculum and as recreation. Fiction is about people, events, and places, often about real ones. Even animal characters in stories often personify human qualities. Fiction deals with solving problems and often centers on values and emotions. Fiction is often culturally routed, and story forms such as myths, tall tales, and folk tales tell much about the culture of their origin.

Poetry also offers social studies learning opportunities. We can learn and remember a lot about the beginning of the American Revolution, for example, by doing a readers' theater based on Longfellow's "Paul Revere's Ride." Poetry is the most economically worded, intense, and focused form of verbal communication. The basic job of poetry is to express personal feelings and thoughts either in song or story form. What this means, in effect, is that the content of all fiction and poetry can be called social studies.

One reason for using fictional material in social studies is that fiction is most often more appealing to students than nonfiction. Good stories just read better than textbooks, where the task of covering specific content controls the writing. Fictional characters and plots are imaginative, exciting, and appealing to the emotions, while bare fact material of any sort is not always so interesting. Many students who give only minimum effort to textbooks and other nonfiction materials are avid fiction readers. They can often be led to discover history, geography, and other social studies content through fiction. In fact, many grow to love the social studies after first having their interest stimulated by fiction.

What kind of fiction do you want to guide students to? We often think a book is going to be good social studies material if it meets some, but not necessarily all, of the following conditions:

- It tells a good story well.
- It develops strong, real characters who are confronted with important and believable problems.

- It contributes something to the reader's knowledge and understanding of the world (other people, other places, other times, the self).
- It provokes the reader to think and feel about some human problem or situation.
- It helps the reader deal with his/her own problems.

There are many types of fictional and poetry books that relate to social studies. Though far from complete, Table 6.8 provides a fair sampling of the varieties of story types that can be used as part of social studies.

Some excellent teachers make it a daily practice to find time to read aloud to classes, exposing students to at least a portion of some powerful and interesting books with solid social content. One reason for doing this is that students really enjoy it. In addition to the motivational value, reading aloud to students is good modeling; students see the teacher, whom they admire and look up to, reading. Students can often listen with understanding, memory, and appreciation to books and stories that are too difficult for them to read themselves.

Fictional books and stories as well as poems are usually rich in drama and can be turned into skits, role plays, pantomimes, and other acting-out experiences. Some poetry lends itself to choral reading and independent read–aloud activity. Fictional books are an alternative to topical assignments for students to practice reporting skills.

Trade books designed for younger readers are full of invigorating stories and eye-catching illustrations. Table 6.9 lists some recently published fictional trade books that

Table 6.8 Types of Fictional and Poetry Books Related to Social Studies

Fiction

Folk tales and myths
Legends and hero stories (Robin Hood, King Arthur, William Tell)
Tall tales
Historical novels that focus on particular events or times
Biographical novels with real and important individuals as their subjects
Biographical novels written about real but relatively unknown historical figures
Novels in different geographic settings
Books dealing with personal survival
Books dealing with the problems of family living
Books that deal with contemporary social problems
Books that present characters who have admirable and desirable qualities

Poetry

Poems that tell the story of real or legendary events
Poems that deal with historically significant individuals
Poetry that is a folk art form of a particular culture
Problem poetry
Lullabies
Work songs
Holiday and calendar-related poetry
Geography and weather poems

Table 6.9 Examples of Trade Books: Fiction

Title (Year)	Author	Publisher	Grade Level	NCSS Themes
Abe Lincoln: His Wit and Wisdom from A-Z (2016)	Alan Schroeder	Holiday House	3–5	3, 6, & 10
Dear Mr. Washington. (2015)	Lynn Cullen	Dial Books	K–2	2, 3, & 4
Frederick's Journey: The Life of Frederick Douglass (2015)	Doreen Rappaport	Disney – Jump at the Sun	K–6	2, 4, & 8
Heroes of History (2016)	Anita Ganeri	Little Bee Books	K–6	5, 6, & 10
Can We Help? Kids Volunteering to Help Their Communities (2015)	George Ancona	Candlewick Press	K–5	5 & 10
Sitting Bull: Lakota Warrior and Defender of his People (2015)	S. D. Nelson	Abrams Books for Young Readers	3–8	2, 3, & 5

elementary teachers may find useful when teaching social studies. The list includes title, author, publisher, grade level, and connections to various NCSS themes.

▶ CONNECTING READING AND WRITING IN SOCIAL STUDIES

Fiction and nonfiction reading can add meaning to social studies learning. Sharing the reading is important, yet connecting what was read to written form can be difficult and meaningless if not completed effectively. This is often completed as a book report. Here are ten alternative and unique book reporting activities that can be more effective and have much more impact on the reporter and on the audience.

1. *Economic reports:* For a story or book, draw two circle graphs. On one, show the expenditures of the main character. On the other, show that character's income. The circles should be segmented, estimating the percentage of the total budget the character would have had to pay in today's market for the goods and services received in the story and the sources of income.
2. *Archaeology reports:* Create a shoebox dig for a book or story. Having read the story, try to imagine that archaeologists are digging into the site of the main story events hundreds of years after the story happened. In the shoebox, create in miniature the artifacts they might find at the site.
3. *Story museum reports:* Create a miniature museum exhibit commemorating the events depicted in the story. This can be done as a diorama or through a series of drawings.
4. *Comic book reports:* Create a comic book for the book or story using cartoon drawings to show the story events.
5. *Shoebox story parade:* Read a fictional book about a historic event or a biography of a historical character. Create a float out of a shoebox showing the most significant or memorable scene from a book or story. When everyone in the class

has done a different float, they can be formed into a parade with each person serving as commentator as his or her float passes by.

6. *Book trials:* After a significant number have read the same book or story, stage a mock trial of one of the story characters or a trial of the author(s) for "corrupting the youth." Assign the roles of attorneys, defendants, witnesses, and jurors.

7. *Historical creation reports:* Create documentary evidence that traces the history of a book.

8. *Story geography:* Map a book or story showing the location of the episodes and events described. Then give a map talk taking the major character(s) through these events step by step.

9. *Sociometries of books:* Develop diagrams showing the relationships of people in a book. Small circles represent individuals; dotted lines show kinship ties, and solid lines with arrows stand for positive feelings of like or love. The oral report consists of explaining the diagram.

10. *Publicity and review reports:* Do a promotion for a book as it might be sold in a television commercial, or develop a review that might be given on a television review program if the book were a movie.

▶ ORGANIZING TO WRITE

Reading and writing activities or assignments in social studies may take several forms. The follow-up to a class or group reading assignment might include having students do any of the following activities:

- Answer questions.
- Write a summary.
- Write a solution to a problem using information from the reading material.
- Make up a story involving the time or place described.
- Write a description.
- Write book reports on single books read independently (e.g., biographies, books about events, "You are there" type books, viewpoint books, etc.).
- Write summaries of articles in magazines and newspapers.
- Make written plans for a project or activity.
- Write letters requesting information or materials.
- Write letters of appreciation.
- Imitate literature types from other cultures or times (e.g., Japanese haiku poetry, tall tales, ballad-type songs, etc.).
- Do in-role writing activities in which the student pretends to be in another culture, place, time, or position.
- Write dramas and skits related to unit topics being studied.
- Write narrative reports of library research on a topic using one or multiple resources – an experiment conducted, a series of observations, an interview or conversation.
- Make up rules, generalizations, hypotheses, cause-and-effect statements, etc.

Students experience two major kinds of difficulties with writing assignments in social studies. The first of these has to do with the clarity of the assignment. The teacher simply needs to be sure to explain an assignment clearly and completely. The teacher needs to cross-check, asking students to repeat and even paraphrase and explain in their own words the expectations. The second difficulty has to do with how well prepared students are for an assignment. Avoiding this difficulty involves being assured that students have the ability or readiness to do the assignment. It also means that they have been taught how to do the assignment.

The base or prerequisite skills needed for many if not all writing jobs include note taking, writing answers to questions, and outlining. All these skills involve having the ability to see what is most important and the ability to discern what is relevant for particular purposes. For students to develop these abilities, they should, first, be able to see the essential purpose of the writing job itself. Second, as they read, listen, or observe, they must be able to pick out central messages. Third, they need to be able to scan for messages related to particular criteria.

Do not assume that students have already developed the necessary skills. Once you have determined the skills they do and do not have, you can set about to gradually develop the needed abilities. Note taking, question asking and answering, and outlining can be boring, especially if students do not understand the assignment or if the content is dry. Utilize interesting and relevant topics to help students learn the skill(s). Outline the sports section of the newspaper or the lyrics of a pop song, for example, or take notes on a comic book or a travel brochure. Be sure that students understand what it is they are supposed to do. One procedure to try is the following:

1. Define the skill that you want students to have and analyze the steps they will have to go through in performing that skill.
2. Find out what students can do by giving them a very simple and short supervised task involving the skill.
3. Model the skill, using a question-and-answer format to get students to look at what you are doing analytically.
4. Repeat the model, going step by step with new content, allowing students to do the work as a class. Monitor to make sure that they are all with you.
5. Supply exercises in which part, but not all, of the structure is in place.
6. Gradually withdraw the structure until students can perform without it.

Such a systematic procedure sounds simple and logical, but many teachers seldom follow this kind of procedure. Research indicates that teachers rarely make certain that students understand the questions in textbook assignments (Anderson, 1984) and that there are often major comprehension problems inherent in the questions themselves (Cooper, 1986). The questions may be unclear in their wording. Students may lack the background knowledge needed to understand them or may be unable to see just what it is that the questions are seeking.

Despite these problems, research supports post-reading questions as contributing to learning (Walberg, 1986). This would seem to indicate that if teachers were more careful about assignments and about preparing students for them, such assignments could be beneficial.

Plan to keep an assignment within reach of a group of students. By "within reach," we mean that the assignment is one that students can do in a reasonable amount of time. Reducing assignment length (the number of questions to be answered) while providing more guidance and feedback is beneficial (Barron et al., 1998; Slavin, 1987). Mechanisms for doing this include dividing work among students, segmenting assignments, and identifying assignment mentors (Turner, 1989).

The following are guidelines that may make textbook question assignments more meaningful:

- Assign questions only after reading them carefully.
- Give clear, complete directions both in writing and orally, taking time to explain and answer questions.
- Call attention to special problems and trouble spots students are likely to encounter.
- Point out where questions call for the student to evaluate, be creative, or give interpretation.
- Teach the students about question words and that questions in texts are answered in the order that they are asked.
- Follow up completed assignments by going over them in a meaningful way.
- Wherever possible, use visual graphic organizers.

▶ DEVELOPING RESEARCH AND REPORTING SKILLS

The Common Core Standards (2012) and the C3 Framework (NCSS, 2013) emphasize research skills throughout the standards. Students are often asked to research, write, and present reports in social studies. Such activities can serve several purposes including, but not limited to, the following:

- Writing both necessitates and helps thinking. By asking students to do reports, we are giving them valuable practice in thinking skills.
- Writing develops with practice. By involving students in writing activities, we help them develop their writing skills.
- Reporting activities allow students to pursue individual interests and work at their own levels.
- Giving a report gives a student a sense of authority. He or she becomes an expert and gains ownership of a unique and special knowledge.
- Reporting can help a student develop and improve self-expression.
- Presenting a report can be an application of the entire spectrum of language skills.
- Reports can give oral and visual display of writing and/or speaking.
- Reporting can be structured to foster social interaction.
- Reports provide checkpoints where student learning is observable and in a form where such learning can be evaluated.

Reports can be written, oral, or both. The first reporting activities for kindergarten and first-grade students are often informal, such as show and tell. Writing an experience story as a class in early school experiences is also a preparation for reporting, especially if one student reads the entire story back after the class has composed it. Reading, writing, and oral language skills are combined in reporting. Among the most common problems associated with reporting assignments are wholesale copying from books and the internet, students' lack of comprehension of their own work, stumbling and stiff presentation of oral reports, lack of meaningfulness or purpose, and inattention of students to one another's reports. It is easy to see that these problems are somewhat related. Fortunately, they are also avoidable.

None of the problems associated with student reports is attributable to the nature of reporting itself. They seem to be more related to the lack of thought by teachers relating to the clarity of reporting assignments and the readiness of students for particular types of reporting assignments. Problems also arise due to the failure of teachers to teach students how to prepare and write a report and presentation.

Let us first look at the assignment stage. Reporting assignments may be set in several contexts:

1. As an assignment all students complete (everyone reports on the same thing).
2. As parts of sets of assignments from which all students choose (students may choose among two or more projects).
3. As a form of recognition or distinction to better students (reporting activity is done only by students the teacher sees as capable and likely to put forth the effort).
4. As volunteer activities that are encouraged and rewarded (History Fair, extra credit, praise).

None of these forms is inherently better or worse than any of the others. What is important is that students know and understand which set of rules is operating. A logical rule of thumb is to keep the system simple, especially with younger students.

There are several types of reporting assignments. The earliest reporting activity in elementary school begins with sharing or show-and-tell activities and with language-experience approaches. Sharing activities are important because they develop students' ability to talk in front of an audience and can help them learn to distinguish important and appropriate things from those that have less significance and relevance. Language experience approaches, which are a form of teacher-led corporate reporting, have similar value and teach students sequencing and ordering skills as well.

One type of individual reporting that can begin very early is experiential reporting. "What I Did/Learned/etc. on My Summer Vacation," the tritest example of this kind of report, gives this type of assignment a bad name. At its best, an experience report is a positive learning experience. It involves having students give true accounts of events that have reality to them. There is a natural narrative and sequence and an opportunity to learn the importance of supporting detail, noting cause-and-effect relationships, and drawing conclusions.

The same can be said for observational reports, which are accounts of events witnessed and sometimes staged and orchestrated by the student. Observational reports can be made about movies, television programs, dramas, field trips, and other events witnessed by students both as individuals and as groups. They may even be done collaboratively.

Face-to-face, phone, and/or Skype interviews can be the basis of interesting reports. Students need to be given a structure of questions to ask in the interview. This can be provided by the teacher or developed in a guided class discussion. Audio or video recordings of the interview can be useful both in report write-ups and in segments as part of oral reports.

Reports may also take the form of demonstrations. Students can show either directly or by simulation how something was or is done in a culture. They may also use drama as the vehicle for the report.

A real danger in reporting is that of mindless, copied reports. This danger can be averted by clear directions that specify how the report is to be organized. Whatever form of reporting or writing students may be asked to do, success rather than failure can be expected if the teacher follows certain principles:

1. Assignments should be stimulating, interesting, and challenging to students.
2. Writing assignments need to be clear. Teachers need to provide both a written description and an oral explanation of the assignment and seek feedback about how well students understand the expectations.

3. Assignment length and complexity need to be within the capabilities of students. This can be achieved by
   a. limiting the length of the assignment, or
   b. segmenting the assignment into logical steps or components.
4. Provide a structure for the report. Among the many structuring devices that might be used are outlines, sets of questions, dramatic devices (e.g., job applications for biographical reports on historic characters), a list of key points, or chronologies.
5. Successful writing assignments result from embedding the teaching of necessary directions and skills development into the writing assignment process:
   a. The assignments should specify and direct length by specifically defining length (number of words or sentences or pages) or space provided.
   b. The assignments should embed the teaching of such skills as summarizing, paraphrasing, skimming, and scanning in the development of the assignment.
   c. The assignments should provide a structure of steps to follow in doing the assignment.
   d. The assignments should specify and provide the resources to be used and direct students on how to use them.

▶ WRITING CREATIVELY

Writing can make social studies more engaging. The variety of creative-writing tasks that can relate to any social studies topic is really limited only by the teacher's imagination. Any idea used needs to be tested with three questions before it is tried:

1. Is doing this task really going to serve a purpose related to understanding what is being studied?
2. Can students do this task and in a reasonable amount of time?
3. How is this task going to affect or relate to the other activities that we are doing?

Many beneficial writing activities can be described as in-role writing. In-role writing means that the writer is pretending to be someone else as he or she writes. One kind of in-role writing involves trying to go through some authentic writing exercise from a particular time period, such as writing letters, wills, and epitaphs for famous and non-famous historical characters. Another type of in-role activity involves imagining how a historical character might deal with some of the paperwork we deal with today. For example, how would that character fill out a job application or some questionnaire? Students can also write in-role autobiographies and poems.

Another type of creative writing strategy involves imitating a writing form of a particular culture. Students studying Japan can, of course, write haiku poems. The study of Germany and France invites fairy tales, the American West suggests tall tales, ancient Greece and Rome might produce myths and fables, and the New England colonies bring sampler messages and hornbook-type sayings and stories. Reading stories or poems that come from any culture can provide models for meaningful creative writing.

A third type of writing that holds exciting promise is problem-solving stories. Usually, the teacher provides a story starter that is a problem scenario. Students then write a story in which the central characters try to solve the problem. For example, a fifth-grade class was given a scenario about two students from the North who found themselves deep in the heart of the Confederacy at the outbreak of the Civil War. They had to write a story in which the students figured out how to find their way back.

One activity utilizes simple stories that students make up about fictional students they imagine in the cultural setting they are studying. With older students, try to get them involved to the extent that they feel that they are doing research in order to write the story. It gives them what amounts to a real scholar's purpose for studying. This might be in the form of a diary that they make entries in daily. These could involve such events as traveling with Columbus, Marco Polo, or any explorer; going on a cattle drive with cowboys; taking a wagon train or a railroad train West; going on a modern trip to a pre-selected set of sights; or any one of a host of other journeys.

Collaborative writing is another effective strategy, in which students write a story as a group. Their story is structured by the skeleton story in a series of topic sentences. Each student or pair of students independently writes a paragraph beginning with one topic sentence. When finished, the group works together to smooth out the inconsistencies and write in transitions. Here is an example of a set of topic sentences that might be used for students to collaboratively write a "Robin Hood" story.

▶ COLLABORATIVE WRITING SAMPLE TOPIC SENTENCE SET

Many a good and honest man had turned outlaw because of the greed and the cruelty of the Norman nobles. These outlaws roamed the king's forests, foraging what they could. The most famous of all the outlaws was Robin of Locksley, better known as Robin Hood. Robin was himself of noble blood but had been dispossessed of his land and titles by trickery. Along the roads that led through Sherwood Forest, no rich Norman traveler was safe from Robin's merry band of outlaws. According to legend, Robin Hood robbed from the rich and gave to the poor. You can help build yet another story to add to the Robin Hood legend.

1. The Sheriff of Nottinghamshire, unable to catch the outlaw known as Robin Hood, at last hit upon what he thought would be a foolproof plan.
2. Disguised as peasants, the Sheriff and three of his archers slipped into Sherwood Forest quietly.
3. As they passed through a glade in the forest, an arrow whistled through the air, missing the Sheriff's ear by little more than an inch.
4. The Sheriff did not realize that Robin Hood had seen through his disguise immediately and told a story of how he and the others had been forced off their land in the north.
5. Blindfolded, the four strangers were led through a twisting, turning way to a secret glen.
6. Secretly, the Sheriff left a trail of white pebbles for his soldiers to follow.
7. When the blindfolds were removed, the Sheriff's men were amazed at the great group of busy and happy people they saw.
8. The outlaws treated their visitors royally, feasting and toasting them through the late afternoon.
9. With a mischievous grin, a small man came strolling through the boisterous, crowded tables to pour out a bag of white pebbles in front of the Sheriff.
10. As Robin and a half dozen or so men surrounded them, the Sheriff and the archers looked at each other fearfully.
11. The Sheriff and his men, relieved of the weight of their purses, their weapons, and their shoes, wandered in the forest for days before they were found, and the Sheriff was not a happy man.

▶ **LOOKING BACK**

Social studies is knowledge based, and that knowledge has been most readily communicated through print and the internet. Students need reading and writing skills to succeed in social studies. Teachers give reading and writing assignments for reviewing information, preparing for new studies, extending what goes on in the classroom, and developing creativity.

There is a growing unity of purpose between social studies and the language arts as the literature connection becomes more apparent in social studies with the Common Core Standards. Writing skills are emphasized in all content areas and are a requirement of most state assessment tests. Educators know that reading and writing abilities grow through practice and that reading and writing are linked to thinking.

When students have problems reading content material, there are several strategies that teachers can use. Among the most important of these is pre-teaching vocabulary, reducing the actual length of reading assignments, providing sufficient and clear purposes for reading, and developing predictive skills.

EXTENSION ACTIVITY

SCENARIO

Wednesday, the middle of the week and an early release day, arrives more quickly than normal at Yourtown Elementary School (YES). As students are leaving school for the day, you have a brief conversation with your devilishly handsome principal, Dr. Russell. As you are talking, Dr. Russell asks if you are ready for trade book adoptions. Knowing that you have not started working on the adoption list, you explain that you are planning to start this week. Dr. Russell reminds you that trade book adoptions are due next Wednesday.

Feeling a little stressed about the trade book adoption timeline, you consider alternatives. In the end, you decide you only have two options. Option One: Develop your own list of 20 books you could use in your classroom to help teach social studies. Option Two: Partner with your other grade-level teachers and develop one list of 20 books that all the teachers in your grade will utilize to help teach social studies.

QUESTIONS

1. What are the advantages and disadvantages of having your other grade-level teachers' input and adopting one set of trade books?
2. What are the advantages and disadvantages of selecting your own list of books for adoption?
3. What qualities, topics, etc. would you seek in the new books?

TASK

Select either Option One or Two, and once an option has been selected, get to work developing a trade book adoption list. The list should include at least 20 recently published trade books. The list should also include all bibliographic information, summaries of the books, discussions of how you could use each book in social studies, and possible state and national standards addressed.

CHECKING FOR UNDERSTANDING

1. What are the four basic purposes for which reading and writing assignments are used?
2. What are the qualities that you need to look for in a nonfiction book?
3. What are some different kinds of fictional material that can be used in social studies?
4. What are the purposes of learning research and reporting skills?
5. How are guidelines useful in making textbook questions more meaningful?
6. Why do teachers have students write reports and present them orally?
7. Describe several ways of teaching concepts and vocabulary to students.
8. What is meant by the term *purposeful reading*, and why is the concept important?

▶ HELPFUL RESOURCES

Watch this video, which explores a sixth-grade teacher and how she teaches scaffolding for reading comprehension:

https://youtu.be/gleNo8dqHb8

Watch this video that details the importance of literacy in the history/social studies curriculum and how it can be effectively incorporated:

https://youtu.be/sF0BpowS4Gg

Watch this video about building literacy in elementary social studies from the National Council for the Social Studies:

https://youtu.be/1Nf3qZ2kDd0

Watch this video about how to use the Frayer model:

https://youtu.be/AdjN09VouaU

Watch this video, created by the National Council for the Social Studies. The video explores informational text and how to make text more readable and enjoyable:

https://youtu.be/8UE3b2N16zk

TumbleBooks is a great website for both students and teachers in the elementary social studies classroom. The website takes children's literature books and adds animation, sound, narration, music, and images to produce a very user-friendly experience for children who may struggle with reading. They also offer books in multiple languages to address students who may be learning English as a second language:

www.tumblebooks.com/

The Great Books Foundation is a useful website for teachers looking to incorporate reading into their classroom instruction. Books are recommended for a variety of topics, including social studies, with additional ideas on how to create meaningful activities and assessments from the suggested books:

www.greatbooks.org

This website was created by the Screen Actors Guild and contains videos of several popular celebrities reading children's books aloud. Students will be excited to see famous actors from their favorite television shows or movies reading stories to them in these videos. Also, and perhaps this is the best part, the website is free! Teachers and parents can easily bookmark this site on computers so students can access these stories any time they want!

www.storylineonline.net

Watch this video about mastering essay writing:

https://youtu.be/oegC9JWi2xw?list=PL96_6089u0OWHB5KhnHRp7MTU2fNa-dP8

Watch this video created by the National Council for the Social Studies. It highlights how teachers can teach argument writing in the social studies:

https://youtu.be/7GRnQviAshM

▶ FURTHER READING

Libresco, A., Blantic, J., & Kipling, J. (2011). *Every book is a social studies book: How to meet standards with picture books, K–6*. Santa Barbara, CA: ABC-CLIO, LLC.

This book is a wonderful resource for elementary school teachers interested in teaching social studies with picture books. The authors present a variety of social studies topics common in elementary social studies, then provide examples of picture books and supporting activities for the readings that could be used in the classroom.

▶ REFERENCES

Anderson, L. W. (1984). What teachers don't do and why. *Education Report, 27*, 3.

Barron, B., Schwartz, D., Vye, N., Moore, A., Petrosino, A., Zech, L., Bransford, J., & The Cognition and Technology Group at Vanderbilt. (1998). Doing with understanding: Lessons from research on problem and project-based learning. *The Journal of the Learning Sciences, 7*, 271–311.

Common Core Initiative. (2012). *Common core standards*. Available at: www.corestandards.org

Frayer, D., Frederick, W. C., & Klausmeier, H. J. (1969). *A schema for testing the level of cognitive mastery*. Madison: Wisconsin Center for Education Research.

Gersten, R., & Baker, S. (1999). *Reading comprehension instruction for students with learning disabilities: A research synthesis: Executive summary*. New York: National Center for Learning Disabilities.

Herber, H. L. (1978). *Teaching reading in content areas* (2nd ed.). Englewood Cliffs, NJ: Prentice Hall.

McCutcheon, G. (1981). Elementary social studies teachers' planning for social studies and other subjects. *Theory and Research in Social Education, 9*(Winter), 45–66.

National Council for the Social Studies. (2013). *The College, Career, and Civic Life (C3) Framework for social studies state standards: Guidance for enhancing the rigor of K–12 civics, economics, geography, and history*. Silver Spring, MD: NCSS. (www.ncss.org/c3)

National Council for the Social Studies. (n.d.). *Notable trade books for young readers*. Available at: https://www.socialstudies.org/notable-social-studies-trade-books.

Shanahan, T. (2001). *The National Reading Panel: Teaching children to read*. Newark, DE: International Reading Association.

Slavin, R. E. (1987). *Cooperative learning: Student teams*. Washington, DC: National Education Association.

Smith, F. A. (1975). *Comprehension and learning: A conceptual framework for teachers*. New York: Holt, Rinehart, and Winston.

Turner, T. N. (1989). Using textbook questions intelligently. *Social Education, 53*(1), 58–60.

Vacca, R. T., & Vacca, J. L. (1993). *Content area reading* (4th ed.). New York: HarperCollins.

Walberg, H. (1986). Synthesis of research in teaching. In M. Wittrock (Ed.), *Handbook of educational research: A project of the American Educational Research Association* (3rd ed.). New York: Macmillan.

Chapter 7

Social Studies and Diverse Learners

▶ LOOKING AHEAD

Social studies as a subject is diverse, as are the students in your class. Teaching diverse learners can be a challenge if you are not properly equipped. Teaching an array of students who are from different countries, speak different languages, have different cultural beliefs and values, and learn and retain information differently are some of the many requirements of an elementary teacher.

This chapter begins by discussing the various learning styles you will see in your classroom. The chapter then moves into a discussion regarding multicultural education and what it means to be a culturally responsive teacher. From there, the chapter focuses on teaching English language learners (ELLs) social studies and various teaching techniques that can be utilized to accommodate the needs of English learners. The chapter concludes with a discussion of teaching exceptional education students and details various strategies elementary teachers can utilize to accommodate social studies instruction. It should be noted that the techniques and strategies detailed in the chapter can be utilized and have been found to be effective with many, if not all, student populations.

CAN YOU? DO YOU?

Can you . . .

- Identify Howard Gardner's multiple intelligences?
- Describe the common characteristics of a culturally responsive teacher?
- Identify the ideals of multicultural education?

Do you . . .

- Understand what it means to be a culturally responsive teacher?
- Know how to adapt instruction to meet the needs of English language learners?
- Know two strategies to accommodate instruction for exceptional education students?

FOCUS ACTIVITY

Before reading this chapter, try the following focus activity.

Think about your various learning experiences. Think about how you learn. Do you know how you learn best? If so, move to Option One; if not, move to Option Two.

1. Option One: How do you learn best? When did you become aware of how you learn best? Share your answer with others.
2. Option Two: Since you are unaware of how you learn, try to discover how you learn best. Think of things you have learned and how you have gone about learning the information. For example, maybe you remember making flash cards for a test that you aced. Maybe you remember building a birdhouse that helped you understand measurement. Spend time reflecting about how you learn. Once you realize how you learn, it will make learning more meaningful, enjoyable, and efficient. Share your experience with others.

▶ MULTIPLE INTELLIGENCES

Since the beginning of the twentieth century, the concept of intelligence has been carefully studied. Intelligence tests, conceived early in the century, have continued to be developed and refined. Early psychologists generally believed that intelligence could be defined as overall intellectual capacity and potential. Toward the end of the century, the most widely used intelligence tests were challenged as being culturally biased. However, the concept of a single quality of intelligence remained largely intact. The psychologist who has offered the greatest challenge to this idea, when it comes to learning, is Howard Gardner (1983). Gardner has discounted the idea of considering intelligence in the limited dimensions assessed by the kinds of tests that have been used in education. In fact, he has argued that schools often fail because they have concentrated exclusively on verbal and mathematical ability; Gardner has contended that individuals have different kinds of intelligence and that schools should provide learning activities that allow students to learn as they learn best. Originally seven in number, Gardner's intelligences offer possibilities for expansion.

Currently, eight intelligences are being considered in many teacher education programs. Table 7.1 shows Gardner's eight intelligences (1999) and presents an abbreviated explanation of each.

In sum, Gardner's work relating to multiple intelligences demonstrates the need to diversify instruction to meet the students' individual learning needs. It is essential, because students learn in different ways, that teachers utilize a variety of teaching techniques, strategies, and methods of instruction.

▶ MULTICULTURAL DIRECTIONS IN SOCIAL STUDIES

Multicultural education has been a transforming force in social studies since the 1960s, yet even its strongest advocates differ widely about what exactly multicultural education should be. Beginning in the 1980s, scholarship emerged related to multicultural

Table 7.1 Gardner's Multiple Intelligences

Intelligence	Explanation
Linguistic-Verbal	The ability to read, write, and communicate with words
Logical-Mathematical	The ability to reason and calculate in a logical, systematic way
Visual-Spatial	The ability to think "in pictures"
Musical	The ability to make or compose music
Interpersonal	The ability to work effectively with others
Intrapersonal	The ability for self-analysis or reflection
Bodily-Kinesthetic	The ability to use the body to solve problems or to create products
Naturalist	The ability to recognize flora and fauna, to make other distinctions in the natural world

education. Agreement has emerged about the ideals of multicultural education. Gorski (2000) asserts that the ideals of multicultural education include:

- All students should have equal chances of achieving their full potential.
- Students must be prepared to live and work in an increasingly intercultural society.
- Teachers should be enabled to effectively facilitate learning for every individual student, no matter how culturally similar or different.
- Schools have to be active in ending oppression and prejudice, first within their own walls, then by developing all students to be socially and critically active and aware.
- The role of schools is essential to laying the foundation to change society and eliminate oppression and injustice.
- The goal of multicultural education is to effect social change.

Multicultural education goes beyond teaching tolerance and

> advocates the belief that students and their life histories and experiences should be placed at the center of the teaching and learning process and that pedagogy should occur in a context that is familiar to students and that addresses multiple ways of thinking.
>
> (NAME, 2003, p. 1)

Multicultural education means reaching comfort levels with curricular issues that give us discomfort, raising and addressing issues that are difficult, and asking questions that challenge thinking and beliefs. To bring about the changes advocated for multicultural education, these ideals must be embodied in all social studies curricula. Teachers themselves need to become more sensitive and aware of both obvious and subtle incidents of prejudice, bias, and/or intolerance. Educators need to become culturally responsive teachers. Culturally responsive teaching requires all educators to develop an understanding of students' learning contexts (Gay, 2000). Culturally responsive teaching is a pedagogy that recognizes the importance of including students' cultural references in all aspects of learning (Ladson-Billings, 1994). Common characteristics of culturally responsive teaching are (Gay, 2010):

1. Positive perspectives on parents and families.
2. Communication of high expectations.
3. Learning within the context of culture.
4. Student-centered instruction.
5. Culturally mediated instruction.
6. Reshaping the curriculum.
7. Teacher as facilitator.

Culturally responsive teaching is much more than teaching the notable and iconic figures of color. It requires teaching alternative perspectives inclusive of gender and race (Ladson-Billings, 1995).

▶ SOCIAL STUDIES AND ENGLISH LANGUAGE LEARNERS (ELLS)

Non-English-speaking students are a reality in the contemporary classroom. The most popular and accepted term for non-English-speaking students is English learners (ELs) or English language learners (ELLs). However, depending on your state and district, ELLs are also referred to as English as a second language (ESL) students, limited English proficient (LEP) students, or English speakers of other languages (ESOLs).

According to the National Clearinghouse for English Language Acquisition, the percentage of ELLs across the U.S. increased by 51 percent to over 5.3 million students between 1998 and 2009 (2011). Furthermore, ELLs are considered to be the fastest-growing segment of the student population when compared to other subgroups in U.S. schools (Cruz & Thornton, 2009).

California, Florida, and Texas are a few of the states in the nation that face an enormously large ELL population. Nonetheless, teaching ELLs is not limited to those states. No Child Left Behind (see Short & Fitzsimmons, 2007) requires adequate yearly progress across all student populations. This means that attention must be given to the needs of ELLs. It can be extremely challenging for ELLs to demonstrate progress in an English-only curriculum. According to the NCLB guidelines, ELLs are required to be tested in English within two years of entering a U.S. school. In 2005, only 4 percent of all eighth-grade ELLs achieved proficiency on the National Assessment of Educational Progress (Short & Fitzsimmons, 2007).

Communicating With ELLs

When communicating with ELLs in an elementary classroom, speak clearly. However, you do not need to speak louder; they are not deaf. When communicating with ELLs, use props, pictures, drawings, gestures, signals, objects, graphic organizers, etc., to help explain the directions and/or the social studies content information. If you are communicating in written form, be sure to print legibly or type information. Sloppy handwriting and/or cursive adds an additional challenge for ELLs. In all forms of communication, be sure to avoid slang terms (e.g., "cool"), colloquialisms (e.g., "y'all"), and idioms (e.g., "kick the bucket") (Szpara & Ahmad, 2007).

Managing the Classroom

As in any efficiently and effectively run classroom, students need to be aware of requirements and expectations. Develop classroom rules, procedures, and routines for everything – from using the restroom to turning in assignments to getting make-up work, and so on. Just as you would teach the American Revolution or any other topic, be sure to teach the class rules, procedures, and routines. Post your rules in English and in your respective ELLs' language(s). For translating, try the school/district foreign language department. Classroom structure will help ELLs function in the classroom environment. Furthermore, involve ELLs in day-to-day activities. Do not isolate them. However, be sure to foster an environment that allows all students to feel safe, secure, and comfortable.

Promoting Social Interaction

One of the core components of social studies is social interaction. Some elementary social studies teachers do not promote social interaction because they prefer the "stand and deliver" method or the "read and answer the questions" method. ELLs need social interaction, and fostering an environment that encourages social interaction will allow ELLs to be more comfortable, thus increasing their chances of success. Social interaction promotes discussions among students. Discussion can increase students' interest in content and improve basic interpersonal communication skills (BICS) (Cruz et al., 2003). Oftentimes, English-dominant classrooms can subject ELL students to subtle segregation unless teachers are prepared to address their needs. Provide ELLs with opportunities to work with partners and/or in cooperative learning groups. Social interaction with peers can help ELLs with basic vocabulary, building BICS, and increasing self-esteem and, most of all, can prevent segregation.

Embracing the Culture

Another core component of social studies is culture. However, some elementary teachers shy away from discussing the cultures of students. Embrace your ELLs' culture(s) by incorporating them into the curriculum. Display photos, books, and images around the classroom. Have all students share artifacts, experiences, and/or stories about their cultures. Utilize oral histories to have all students explore and learn more about their classmates' cultures. This will provide all students with an opportunity to highlight themselves and their cultures without segregating the ELLs.

Delivering Content

Use a variety of instructional methods and present information in a variety of ways when teaching ELLs. Utilizing a variety of instructional methods can increase student achievement and understanding. ELLs will benefit from kinesthetic-related activities. Being hands on allows ELLs an opportunity to complete a task and feel validated. Place new content terminology on the board and provide as many visual aids and demonstrations as possible. Using visual aids increases student understanding and comprehension of the material being presented. When delivering new content, give simple directions. Relate new information to students' everyday lives and help make connections to students' prior knowledge. Repeat and rephrase information frequently. List the lesson objectives and activities on the board and provide ELLs with step-by-step instructions. Allow students to interact. Be sure and check for comprehension. Have them demonstrate their learning to check for comprehension. Do not ask, "Do you understand?" Usually ELLs will reply "Yes," even if they do not understand.

Visual Aids for ELLs

Teachers should utilize various visual aids to accommodate instruction. The utilization of visual aids is an essential feature of effective instruction because it provides the support needed to contextualize learning. Visual aids include real objects from the field, photos, images, drawings, charts, graphs, maps, music, video, and graphic organizers. Specifically, graphic organizers support ELLs' understanding of complex and difficult concepts and text (Weisman & Hansen, 2007).

▶ SOCIAL STUDIES AND EXCEPTIONAL EDUCATION STUDENTS

Approximately 4 to 6 percent of students are considered exceptional education students because of a learning disability. Additionally, 1 percent of students have a diagnosed behavior disorder (Steele, 2008). Newman (2006) reported that approximately 70 percent of students with learning disabilities and/or behavioral disorders receive inclusive education. Inclusive education requires that exceptional students spend all or part of their time with non-exceptional/non-special education students (Minarik & Lintner, 2016). Elementary teachers often have students with exceptional needs in their classrooms; however, many teachers are uncertain what the label might imply regarding instruction. Most exceptional educators agree that students with learning disabilities have "normal" intelligence but do not process information in the same manner as students without learning disabilities. Students labeled exceptional can have difficulty with academic and daily living skills. A student with a behavior disorder may lack positive peer relationships, demonstrate non-age-appropriate behavior, lack academic abilities or achievement, and appear unhappy or depressed. No single method can reach all learners. Thus, a teacher must approach the curriculum with a diverse set of instructional strategies.

Reading Adaptations

Selecting various reading materials, including textbooks from lower grades, can help accommodate students' individual learning needs. Provide students with instruction on the components of the textbook. Many students with disabilities require instruction regarding how to use the glossary, appendix, and table of contents, as well as headings, boldface terms, and illustrations.

Study guides can promote comprehension of the text and encourage active learning. We recommend supplemental readings for students with disabilities. The supplemental readings component includes newspaper articles, historical fiction, and internet historical sites (e.g., the Library of Congress), as well as magazines, such as *Newsweek*. Supplemental materials associated with curricula are significant because the materials more often relate to the lives of those who lived in the time period. Historical fiction can be compared with factual text, engaging critical thinking and analysis of materials.

Reading the newspaper builds community awareness and critical thinking skills and can be used to initiate cross-curricular relationships. Supplemental readings add depth to the content in the textbook and assist students with disabilities in clarifying themes, events, abstract ideas, and topics.

Writing Adaptations

Many students find writing difficult. Students with disabilities often need assistance, guidance, and modifications to writing requirements. Elementary teachers need to combine a variety of writing strategies like summarization, collaborative writing, specific product goals, word processing, sentence combining, pre-writing, inquiry activities, process writing approach, study of models, and writing for content learning. Elementary teachers should use mnemonic writing strategies to assist exceptional education students. Scholars (Graham & Perin, 2007; Mason & Graham, 2008) have developed various examples of mnemonic strategies. which are listed below:

> *PLAN* (*P*ay attention to the prompt, *L*ist the main idea, *A*dd supporting ideas, *N*umber your ideas).
> *WRITE* (*W*ork from your plan to develop your thesis statement, *R*emember your goals, *I*nclude transition words for each paragraph, *T*ry to use different kinds of sentences, and *E*xciting, interesting, $10,000 words).

For paragraph-specific writing strategies, students can follow the SLOW CaPS mnemonic writing strategy:

> S = Show the type of paragraph in the first sentence.
> L = List the type of details you plan to write about.
> O = Order the details.
> W = Write the details in complete sentences and cap off the paragraph with a
> C = Concluding,
> P = Passing or
> S = Summary sentence.

For sentence-specific writing strategies, students can follow the PENS mnemonic writing strategy:

> P = Pick a formula.
> E = Explore words.
> N = Note the words.
> S = Search and check.

Teachers can use the COPS mnemonic strategy to help students proofread written work:

> C = Capitalization – Have I capitalized the first word in the sentences and proper nouns?
> O = Organization – Have I made any errors related to overall appearance such as handwriting, margin, messy, or spelling errors?
> P = Punctuation – Have I used end punctuation, commas, and semicolons correctly?
> S = Spelling – Do the words look like they are spelled right? Can I sound them out, or should I use the dictionary?

Teachers can use the ANSWER mnemonic strategy to assist students in formulating answers to essay questions:

A = Analyze the action words in the question.
N = Notice the requirements of the question.
S = Set up an outline.
W = Work in the detail.
E = Engineer your answer.
R = Review your answer.

Graphic Organizers

Graphic organizers facilitate comprehension and prepare visual representations of materials for all students. Graphic organizers are also known as knowledge maps, concept maps, story maps, cognitive organizers, advance organizers, and/or concept diagrams. Graphic organizers can be used to organize large amounts of material, creating timelines, cause-and-effect comparisons, and event relationships. Elementary teachers can use graphic organizers before, during, and/or after classroom activities, such as assigned readings, direct instruction, discussions, and presentations. Graphic organizers help students create meaning of text, sort information, and promote easy and efficient information recall. Graphic organizers enable students to acquire information through their preferred learning style. For visual learners, it creates a visual representation of content. For auditory learners, graphic organizers can become the focus of discussion of materials with peers as the student explains the organizers. For tactile or kinesthetic learners, the activity requires creative thought processes and writing and could involve bodily movements. When utilizing graphic organizers, teachers should use the following evaluation criteria for selecting suitable and appropriate graphic organizers (Merkley & Jefferies, 2001, p. 351):

1. Analyze the learning task for words and concepts important for the student to understand.
2. Arrange them to illustrate the interrelationships and pattern(s) of organization.
3. Evaluate the clarity of relationships as well as the simplicity of effectiveness of the visual.
4. Substitute empty slots for certain words in order to promote students' active reading.

In addition to analyzing the usefulness of a graphic organizer, teachers should model the use of a graphic organizer and scaffold instruction from classroom to small group to independent utilization and writing. Teachers should have explicit instructions and model how to use the graphic organizer to ensure students' effective application of graphic organizers.

▶ LOOKING BACK

The ability to teach and accommodate the individual needs of all learners is a skill all teachers must acquire. As stated earlier, the techniques and strategies detailed in this chapter can be utilized and have been found to be effective with many, if not all, student populations. Social studies is as diverse a subject as the learning styles, cultural make-ups, spoken languages, and/or exceptionalities in your classroom. Teachers need to equip themselves with the tools, skills, and knowledge necessary to effectively teach and accommodate instruction to meet the diverse learning needs of all students.

No matter what the students' learning style, first language, exceptionality, and/or cultural background, elementary teachers will surely need to modify content and instruction. This chapter detailed Gardner's multiple intelligences, ideals of multicultural education, and what it means to be a culturally responsive teacher. In addition, this chapter shared numerous techniques and strategies for helping English language learners and exceptional education students learn social studies. One of the most significant changes to the world of education over the past 20 years is the increasing emphasis on diverse learners and meeting the needs of all students.

EXTENSION ACTIVITY

It is the Monday right after winter break at Yourtown Elementary School (YES). Your students arrive to school on time, well rested and eager to learn. As you greet students at the door, students shower you with sweet and heartfelt comments about how they missed you and they hope you had a wonderful winter break. As you are about to greet the last student, you realize that you do not recognize her. You say "Hi," and ask her "Where are you supposed to be?" She does not answer. Just then, the guidance counselor, Mrs. Benedict, comes from around the corner and explains: "You have a new student, and her name is Carlota." You walk Carlota into the classroom and place her at an empty desk. Mrs. Benedict follows and explains: "Carlota just moved here from Brazil. Her first language is Portuguese, and she has a very limited understanding of English." Mrs. Benedict recognizes the look of concern on your face and asks, "Are you capable of effectively teaching English language learners?" You nod and say, "Yes." Pleased, she smiles and explains: "Be sure you accommodate your content and instruction to meet her learning needs."

TASK

Imagine Carlota is in your class. How will you accommodate your social studies content and instruction to meet her learning needs? For this activity, select a social studies topic and grade level. Then develop an engaging lesson plan that includes accommodations to meet the needs of all students, including Carlota. Share your lesson plan and accommodations with classmates.

CHECKING FOR UNDERSTANDING

1. List and explain Howard Gardner's eight multiple intelligences.
2. Describe the common characteristics of a culturally responsive teacher.
3. Identify and explain the ideals of multicultural education.
4. Describe two strategies you could use to accommodate instruction for exceptional education students.
5. How can you adapt instruction to meet the needs of English language learners?
6. What does it mean to be a culturally responsive teacher?

▶ HELPFUL RESOURCES

Teaching Tolerance is a respected website and journal published by the Southern Poverty Law Center; they offer a free journal for educators interested in teaching tolerance. The journal highlights various teaching activities and practices for multicultural teaching: www.teachingtolerance.org

Teachers of English to Speakers of Other Languages is a respected professional organization devoted to advancing professional expertise in English language teaching and learning for speakers of other languages worldwide. The association offers numerous publications, which include research and practice applicable to teachers: www.tesol.org

Watch this video, which discusses the unique characteristics of ELLs and their learning needs. The National Council for the Social Studies created it: https://youtu.be/L9_cok-NYOE

Watch the following video of a first-grade teacher exploring different families and cultures within her classroom: www.teachingchannel.org/videos/first-grade-social-studies

Watch this video, which shares how an experienced teacher teaches U.S. geography to ELL students: https://youtu.be/-BEnlxdtzRM

Watch this video of an ELL student sharing his story and describing what he sees in a visual aid: https://youtu.be/L44XW88fe5Y

The Council for Exceptional Children is a respected professional organization devoted to the teaching of students with exceptionalities. The website includes instructional strategies and lesson ideas for teachers. The association offers numerous publications, which include research and practice applicable to teachers: www.cec.sped.org

▶ FURTHER READING

Baum, S., Viens, J., & Slatin, B. (2005). *Multiple intelligences in the elementary classroom*. New York: Teachers College Press.

This book is a great resource for elementary educators interested in designing curriculum for students with diverse learning abilities.

National Council for the Social Studies. (1992). Guidelines on multicultural education. *Social Education, 56*(4), 274–293.

This article is a position statement of the National Council for the Social Studies detailing how multicultural education should be incorporated into social studies.

Chandler, P., & Hawley, T. (Eds.). (2017). *Using inquiry to teach about race in social studies*. Charlotte, NC: Information Age Publishing.

This book addresses teaching race in the classroom. It provides concrete lesson ideas for engaging learners in the social studies.

Hickey, G., & Clabough, J. (2017). *Digging deeper: Activities for enriching and expanding social studies instruction*. Charlotte, NC: Information Age Publishing.

This book showcases best practices and includes research-based lessons and activities that enrich and expand social studies instruction.

Minarik, D., & Lintner, T. (2016). *Social studies and exceptional learners*. Washington, DC: NCSS.

The authors provide background information on categories of disability and laws driving disability services in schools and recommend best practices for educating these exceptional students in an inclusive classroom setting. The book also offers carefully designed lesson plans for teaching economics, geography, history, and civics to exceptional learners.

Lintner, T., & Schweder, W. (Eds.). (2011). *Practical strategies for teaching K–12 social studies in inclusive classrooms*. Charlotte, NC: Informational Age Publishing.
This book blends best practices in social studies and special education instruction and details how to make social studies meaningful, relevant, and engaging for all students.

▶ REFERENCES

Cruz, B., Nutta, J., O'Brien, J., Feyton, C., & Govoni, J. (2003). *Passport to learning: Teaching social studies to ESL students*. Washington, DC: National Council for the Social Studies.

Cruz, B., & Thornton, S. (2009). Social studies for English language learners: Teaching social studies that matters. *Social Education, 73*(6), 270–273.

Gardner, H. (1983). *Frames of mind: The theory of multiple of intelligences*. New York: Basic Books.

Gardner, H. (1999). *The disciplined mind: What all students should understand*. New York: Simon and Schuster.

Gay, G. (2000). *Culturally responsive teaching: Theory, research, and practice*. New York: Teachers College Press.

Gay, G. (2010). *Culturally responsive teaching: Theory, research, and practice*. New York: Teachers College Press.

Gorski, P. (2000). *Multicultural education*. McGraw Hill Supersite. Available at: http://www.edchange.org/multicultural/papers/edchange_history.html.

Graham, S., & Perin, D. (2007). *Writing next: Effective strategies to improve writing of adolescents in middle and high schools: A report to Carnegie Corporation of New York*. Washington, DC: Alliance for Excellent Education.

Ladson-Billings, G. (1994). *The dreamkeepers*. San Francisco: Jossey-Bass.

Ladson-Billings, G. (1995). Toward a theory of culturally relevant pedagogy. *American Educational Research Journal, 32*(3), 465–449.

Mason, L. H., & Graham, S. (2008). Writing instruction for adolescents with learning disabilities: Programs of intervention research. *Learning Disabilities Research and Practice, 23*(2), 103–112.

Merkley, D. M., & Jefferies, D. (2001). Guidelines for implementing a graphic organizer. *The Reading Teacher, 54*(4), 350–357.

Minarik, D., & Lintner, T. (2016). *Social studies and exceptional learners*. Washington, DC: NCSS.

NAME (National Association of Multicultural Education). (2003). *Definitions of multicultural education position statement*. Available at: www.nameorg.org/definitions_of_multicultural_e.php.

Newman, L. (2006). *Facts form NLTS2: General education participation and academic performance of students with learning disabilities*. U.S. Department of Education Institute of Education Sciences National Center for Special Education Research. Available at: www.nlts2.org.

Short, D. J., & Fitzsimmons, S. (2007). *Double the work: Challenges and solutions to acquiring language and academic literacy for adolescent English language learners*. Report to Carnegie Corporation of New York. New York: Alliance for Excellent Education.

Steele, M. M. (2008). Teaching social studies to middle school students with learning problems. *Clearing House: A Journal of Educational Strategies, Issues and Ideas, 81*(5), 197–200.

Szpara, M., & Ahmad, I. (2007). Supporting English-language learners in social studies class: Results from a study of high school teachers. *Social Studies, 98*(5), 189–196.

Weisman, E., & Hansen, L. (2007, January 1). Strategies for teaching social studies to English-language learners at the elementary level. *Social Studies, 98*(5), 180–184.

Social Studies and the Acquisition of Skills

Chapter

8

▶ **LOOKING AHEAD**

Information is important only if it can be put to use. Students often feel that they are asked to learn information for which they have no use at all. As a result of this and other factors, students do not always learn in school the skills they need to use information.

If the teacher's goal is for students to become independent learners, and if the ability to solve problems is a major factor in that independence, then finding and analyzing information have to be viewed as critical tool skills. The focus of this chapter is on those skills that are needed to make the best use possible of information in every problems context. The chapter begins with general information skills, decision making, and historical thinking before moving into two specific areas that have special importance to elementary social studies: map skills and time skills.

CAN YOU? DO YOU?

Can you . . .

- Identify several ways that you can stimulate curiosity in students?
- Explain why map and globe skills are challenging for students?
- Explain the three types of memory?
- Utilize a DBQ?

Do you . . .

- Ever get the "Columbus urge" or have "Aha!" moments?
- Know and understand the term *mnemonic device*?
- Know how students develop time and space concepts?

FOCUS ACTIVITY

Before reading this chapter, try the following focus activity.

Think about how you learned to read a map and follow directions on a map. Do you consider yourself to be good with directions? Do you know people who are directionally challenged? Why do you think some people lack this skill? Share your experiences and opinions with others. Do your experiences and opinions share common attributes with others'? If so, what attributes?

▶ BUILDING THE DESIRE TO MASTER STUDY SKILLS

Students must master some very complex and difficult information-processing skills. What makes learning more difficult is that students must master these skills during a period when they are going through physical and emotional changes and facing stressful social changes. Many students in the world today are in stressful home situations, and that complicates the mix. A growing number are latchkey kids on their own for hours after school. Many are from single-parent homes. Many face physically or mentally abusive situations. Unemployment of parents, insufficient family income, or other major economic problems add to the insecurity.

There is an expression: "the urge gives you an edge." What it means is that the strong desire or wanting to do something well gives an individual a distinct advantage; it helps them do well. Students often wonder how they will ever use the learning that educators and parents are forcing upon them. The best opportunities that teachers have to help students acquire the strong urge to learn occur when they give students opportunities to put information to use. Learning to use knowledge is the heart of a problems approach. Once students learn that knowing information and how to get it is useful in solving real problems, it gives knowledge purpose.

Teachers should convince students that knowledge really does empower because it can enable them to solve existing problems and anticipate and head off potential problems. If they believe this, students will learn because they need to know and want to learn, not because the teacher tells them it is important.

Students deal with information that comes from an array of sources, an almost endless variety of print, electronic, and mobile-accessible materials. Not the most exciting of these materials or the easiest to handle is the textbook. More exciting, but sometimes requiring more interpretation, is other information that comes from technology or print in audio or visual forms, from artifacts and other objects, and directly from other people. Reading, observation, and listening skills as well as technological competencies are needed as the basis for study.

First, students need to be able to know where and how to find the information needed. As an accompanying processing skill, they should be able to decide if information is true and accurate, relevant, important, and useful. Finally, they should be able to remember, use, and present the information.

▶ FINDING INFORMATION

Locating information requires a particular kind of mindset, and teachers can help students acquire it. Mastery of accessing skills is needed, as are using various types of indexes and tables of contents, computer applications, and search engines. Students need to be taught skimming and scanning skills. However, these can be learned over time with effort if students develop the right mindset. We like to call that mindset the "Columbus urge." It is that irresistible desire to explore, to find out. Corny as the expression may sound, the "Columbus urge" causes students to seek the thrill of discovering and the sheer satisfaction of knowing that they know transforms them into self-motivated students. If students can acquire this one quality, they will be driven to learn all the necessary skills that it takes to gather information.

The "Columbus urge" can only be encouraged, never created, by the teacher. Key teaching elements that contribute to its growth include the teacher modeling an excitement about learning and developing a classroom that is a busy, exciting, stimulating place where provocative questions are constantly being asked and where tidbits of curious information of interest are constantly being unearthed and celebrated. Here are a few ideas to help students develop the "Columbus urge":

- Regularly give students things to find out that really catch their interest and stir their curiosity. Find out about their cultures and what interests them. You are likely to find that things like "first," "longest," "shortest," and "most" work consistently.
- Leave questions dangling and unanswered and challenge them to find out.
- Model the excitement of researching and finding out.
- Celebrate when students discover solutions, making a big thing out of it.
- Challenge students to come up with questions and curiosities for you and for their classmates.
- Obtain and have students see and use as many interesting resources as possible.
- Give students opportunities to find information and then use it.
- Remember that "knowers" love to show off, so do not just let them; encourage them and even plan opportunities for them to do it.
- As a time filler, play the "I know something" game. In it, the students try to discover what it is that the teacher, or someone else, knows. Students have to be trained to know that their first job is always to find out where the information can be found (e.g., dictionary, atlas, etc.).
- Have constantly changing displays and bulletin boards where students encounter people, actions, and things that are different and that create curiosity.

Last, yet far from least, among the classroom elements that the teacher can and must provide for students to develop their own "Columbus urge" is a structure that ensures students' ownership in repeated successes. The greatest payoff that self-motivated problem solvers can experience is an "Aha!" moment. "Aha!" moments are those times when students feel the thrill of a breakthrough; a problem that they have worked on that has eluded them suddenly has a solution; the pieces of the puzzle fit together; the unexplainable makes sense. When a teacher can make these times of elation for students, then both have satisfaction.

Decision Making

Give students lots of practice in decision making. You can start with questions about how they distinguish things in popular culture. Here, they are the experts. What makes a video game or toy different from another? How do you tell the differences among cartoon characters? Play along as if you do not know the answers. Ask them about attributes of the video games, toys, or characters that are not relevant but are, nonetheless, observable traits. All Dalmatian puppies are white and black and little. All cars have four wheels. These are characteristics, all right, but they do not help us tell things apart. With younger students, who are very ego centered, go to the students themselves as examples. "Why do I like Penelope? Is it because she is wearing a pink shirt?" You can easily see where this questioning would go. The important thing is that through it, students are learning that what may be important and relevant to one question has no merit or use with another.

You can also do a listing of traits. This can be transferred to unit study. For example, if you are teaching a country, a city, a state, or a geographic area, make a list of the characteristics of the area with students. Do this as part of a "Would you like to live there?" activity. That way, you can have two columns: one of traits that make a difference and one of traits that do not. You can do a similar listing with historical people or current candidates for political office. You are just deciding different things: whether they did their jobs well, whether they are suited for the office, and so on.

Once they have the idea, move to some type of game activity. A favorite across grade levels is one called "mysteries." These are multi-clue riddle activities, and they can even be done in groups cooperatively. The number of clues and the difficulty need to meet the individual needs of your class. The idea is to reveal a series of clues one at a time, beginning with the hard clues that could apply to any number of possible answers and going to easier, more obvious ones. In some of these games, some clues may be irrelevant or unimportant.

Sorting activities also help students learn to distinguish relevance. A sorting activity that works very well is called a card sort. The activity begins with a deck of cards with facts or single words written on them. Have labeled category boxes ready and sort the cards into these. After you have done this sorting a few times as a group discussion activity, it may be assigned with multiple decks as a cooperative group activity as well. After the groups finish, they can explain their logic. It is good to include cards that do not fit any category in the deck. Using concrete materials is good for explaining similar sorts that can be done with large amounts of information with the proper computer software.

▶ HISTORICAL THINKING

For many years, the objective of history courses in schools was the mastery of specific content. Teachers would share stories, names, dates, and facts about past people and civilizations while students were largely expected to remember and recall this information on assessments to prove mastery or understanding. Historical thinking is an approach to teaching history that challenges the aforementioned model of instruction and encourages teachers to allow students to actually be engaged in the process of "doing history." With historical thinking, teachers should include a variety of primary and secondary sources from multiple perspectives that push students to think critically and deeply about how historical narratives are constructed over time. While the content itself remains important, historical thinking puts more of the focus on students developing critical skills necessary to understand the past, such as inquiry, analysis of sources, citing evidence to support conclusions, and constructing narratives. One common activity used by social studies teachers to engage students in historical thinking is using document-based questions.

Document-based questions, or DBQs for short, are a teaching strategy or assessment that asks students to utilize their own background knowledge and analysis of provided sources (documents) to construct a narrative demonstrating understanding using textual evidence. Most often, students are asked to construct a written response or short essay explaining their understanding of the historical issue, person, or trend using the provided documents to support their arguments. While most frequently utilized in secondary classrooms, document-based questions can be introduced in upper elementary grades as a way to promote critical and historical thinking. Naturally, the advanced reading levels of many primary and secondary sources coupled with varying reading and writing abilities of elementary students mean that teachers will need to take great care in planning and scaffolding DBQ instruction.

Retaining Information

In social studies, students are required to retain information for three reasons: (1) they have to understand and retain information just long enough to work through a single lesson or class; (2) they have to understand and retain information for a while longer, perhaps a few days, in order to do more extended, long-term assignments; and (3) finally, there is information that teachers want students to retain over a long period of time. Driscoll (2009) refers to these as sensory memory, working memory, and long-term memory. It is important to realize that all three components of memory are important. An elementary teacher's job is to help students learn how to decide what is important and how to retain the information.

Part of the secret of getting students to retain information and ideas is to present that information to them in memorable ways. That means it should be interesting, even exciting if possible. If you do not think this is important, think about the fact that students can tell all about a movie they saw but remember nothing they read in a dull textbook. There are several ways that teachers can help their students learn and retain information:

- Work on a can-do attitude. This requires both encouragement and task control to keep the amount of information at a level that students can handle. Students need to feel confident that they can remember. (If they feel they cannot memorize something, their own prediction of failure will be one more hurdle to overcome.)
- Understanding precedes remembering. Yes, nonsense words can be memorized, but generally, anyone is more likely to remember what they understand than what they do not understand.
- Talk with students about what they already know. If students can relate or associate information to their own experiences, it will make it easier for them to remember.
- Organize the information for them in a way that makes sense. Isolated pieces of information are often more difficult to remember than information that has patterns and structures that relate individual facts.
- Provide mnemonic devices for sets of information. Memory-jogging associations that are catchy and full of images really do work (e.g., Never Eat Soggy Waffles for remembering North, East, South, and West on a compass).
- Make memorizing work as much fun as possible. Play memory games and quick fun practices.

When it comes to reviewing for the purpose of remembering information of all types, the approach most often used is drill. Drill can be meaningless, boring, and totally useless as a learning activity. If students are tuning out mentally, they are not learning. This means that you must make it engaging and relevant. This can happen even if drill is the method. Even the rote learning drill can be so structured that it makes the fact that students are learning mean something. A good drill is going to help the learner put the information into logical and meaningful structures. It will put the stuff together in a way that makes sense and seems useful. Equally important, the drill has to be one that the student will participate in completely. If students find the drill uncomfortable or boring, they will start tuning out or daydreaming.

A drill is effective and more engaging when everybody is getting the answers quickly and correctly. Students are also more likely to learn if they experience information with as many senses as possible repeatedly. Picture flash cards, actual associated objects, actions or movements, even odors can be part of a drill.

One of the best ways to make drill effective is to turn it into a game. A drill game should be one that students will enjoy and one that covers the necessary information repeatedly. The best drill games are those that keep many students mentally engaged. Games that give the information in written and oral form require more from students and increase participation.

Many commercial board games and card games, as well as television game shows and sports activities, are adaptable to fact-learning activities. Games do not have to ask questions about the facts. They simply should get the students to see, say, and hear the information repeatedly. Monopoly or Candyland types of games can be adapted so that the various board spaces and playing pieces are labeled to represent historic or geographic facts related to a topic being studied. This will enable students to encounter these words and images over and over. Similarly, many common games played with cards can be fact-learning games with specially made cards.

▶ MAPS AND GLOBES

Today, with GPS and other mapping applications, students often complain that map reading is not an important skill to learn. However, despite the ease that technology provides, it is still important. Consider learning math. If schools and teachers had eliminated mathematics from the curriculum once the calculator was invented, students and society would be in trouble. Why should map reading and other social studies skills be different?

The skills needed to use maps and globes depend on an extensive knowledge base regarding the types of maps and their purposes. Furthermore, they require the knowledge and understanding of map conventions, symbols, and the nature of different land forms. To use these tools effectively, one must know something of the structure, functions, and terminology of different types of maps and globes. Maps and globes are sources of information about the geographic world. From them we can learn about the location, size, and names of places; the economy; weather and climate; and natural features. Maps and globes provide important information that can help students understand their world and are tools for problem solving.

Choosing Maps and Globes to Use

We want to make students feel comfortable with maps and globes and to fascinate them with the kinds of information that they can find with them. We also want students to gain an understanding that different kinds of maps and globes can be used for different purposes. By the time they have reached the fourth or fifth grade, if not before, students should be able to use maps and globes to answer questions and solve problems.

We can define a globe as a three-dimensional representation of the Earth's surface or the surface of another astronomical body. A map, on the other hand, is a two-dimensional representation of an area. Since maps are flat, maps depicting a very large area, such as the Earth's surface, are going to be distorted from reality in some way.

It is important to choose maps and globes for classroom use wisely and carefully. Maps can be found in an atlas or on the internet; additionally, interactive maps like Google Earth are excellent resources for exploring and examining the Earth. To begin with, teachers need to keep in mind that the best globe or map (print or electronic) for a lesson will depend on several factors, including:

- The conditions under which it is going to be used.
- The number of students who will be looking at it (e.g., whole class, small group, individuals).
- The ability, background, and skill levels of students.
- The purpose(s) for which it is going to be used (i.e., the type of information that the map will need to show).
- The types of tasks that students are going to have to complete.
- The available technology.

In purchasing and collecting classroom maps and globes (electronic or print) over time, teachers need to think about several things, especially the following:

- Relative cost.
- Accuracy.
- Readability.
- Durability.
- Write-ability. (Maps on which you can write, draw, and erase are very useful in the classroom.)
- Store-ability. (Teachers have limited space.)
- Usability (Maps must be useful for a variety of teaching purposes.)
- Technology requirements.

Maps and Globes in Grades K–3

Among the key geographic concepts that K–3 students need to learn is what a map is. They begin learning the concept by working with very simple maps showing areas they can see. The classroom, the scene shown in a sand table, and the location of items in a desk drawer are examples of places to map.

Students need to learn that objects on a map have a directional relation to one another and that you must turn a map a certain way if you are to follow it. They also need to learn that maps use symbols and that maps simplify and summarize a lot of information. They can learn all this and more by making and then following maps of their home, school, and/or playground or of places they visit on field trips. These experiences early on will also help them learn that maps show very real places and will teach them the importance of accurate depiction of relative size on a map.

The following are a few ideas for consideration that might help students learn more effectively from and about maps:

- Try to orient maps in a horizontal rather than a vertical position with young elementary students because that is the way they see the world. This also prevents a confusing misconception that "North is up, and south is down."
- Give students a lot of experiences with maps of places they can see, places they have been, and places they will and can visit.
- Give students plenty of multisensory, manipulative experiences with maps (working with jigsaw puzzle maps, map outline and route tracing, feeling high and low places in relief maps, etc.) and, when a manipulative is used, orally affirm things like place names and names of geographic features.
- Whenever place names are mentioned in reading stories, in class discussions, and so on, it only takes a minute to show them on maps and globes.
- Acquaint students with a variety of types of simple colorful maps, including pictographic maps, to make them aware of the map legends and symbols and to teach them that different maps show different types of information.
- Teach about scale, map distances, and direction experientially and at a developmental simple-to-complex pace.
- On a regular basis, have specific attainable but challenging objectives that relate to what students should learn about place location and geographic and map concept terminology.

Maps and Globes in Grades 4–6

Students should be able to work with maps and globes containing differing amounts of information with increasing independence. As they spend more time learning about different cultures and regions, increasingly, information is presented to students in map form. By the time they have completed the elementary grades, students should be able to read, use, and make maps and globes in a way that shows mastery of the four basic map skills: (1) reading direction, (2) reading distance, (3) understanding map legends, and (4) orienting the map to the real world. They should be able to recognize and understand the purposes of the basic types of world-map projections and different thematic maps (rainfall, vegetation, product, etc.). Students at this level need to understand several terms related to maps and landforms.

Teachers need to assign map activities carefully and often to develop map skills. Many of the guidelines that were suggested for K–3 students apply as well to older elementary students.

- Never assume previous knowledge and/or skills in using maps without verifying whether students really do possess that knowledge or skill.
- Ask questions in discussion and writing that require students to get information from maps and globes.
- Have several easy-to-play map location and jigsaw-map assembly games and activities available in the classroom and encourage their use during free time of any sort.
- Have plenty of activities, such as treasure hunts, scavenger hunts, and mapping of field trips, that involve using or following maps as a means of reaching objectives.

▶ USING MAPS

One of the reasons students have trouble learning map skills is most map work in school is too often just a series of questions and tasks for which students see no purpose. They really need to be exposed to maps in ways that seem meaningful and purposeful.

It seems amazing that we teach map skills without having students really use maps in the ways that adults do. Although GPS and other navigation systems are available, reading and understanding a map are a much-needed skills for a variety of reasons: to find out where they are going or how to get there (GPS is not always accurate); to find alternate routes when there is some problem with the original; to help them decide about a new job; to locate a friend or relative; to find their way around some place they are visiting; to make business decisions that require a knowledge of distance and routes; to consider distance to supplies, equipment, or marketing; to determine the weather's effect on their travel; to determine meeting places; etc. In short, maps can be used to plan, understand, solve problems, and dream about the world. Unfortunately, the teaching of map skills to students contains too little of this. Map skills are taught in a way that says to students that maps are to look at; to answer questions from worksheets; and sometimes to color, draw on, or mark. Students fail to discover that maps are useful items and that they can help in real-life activities.

This appears to cause any number of problems relating to sequential development of skills and concepts. One of these problems is that students tend to see map work as lacking in purpose. A second is that they never really learn to use maps to find specific information or to follow routes.

The following are map-using activities in which students can participate and from which they can learn how maps can be used. "Map-using activities" is a descriptive title for this type of exercise. It includes any method by which students experience relating maps to physical space or to problems involving that space. To be effective, such activities should be perceived by students as having sensible purposes and should involve short-term, specific tasks that are tightly structured.

Map-Reading Scavenger Hunt

A scavenger hunt taxes students' abilities to follow directions given on a map or in a set of written directions accompanying a map. It is an adaptation of the gaming sport of orienteering. Groups of students are asked to find a treasure by following a precise route in the shortest possible time.

Each group is equipped with a compass, a yardstick, and a set of directions or a map showing the route to and location of one portion of the team's treasure map. Each group's route is different from the others'. The teacher will need to prepare in advance a treasure map or set of directions for each team. The treasure maps or directions are each cut or torn into sections and each section put into a separate capped plastic bottle or a can with a tight-sealing lid. This enables the teacher to place the containers in advance without worry about weather damage. Of course, they cannot be set out too far ahead of time. Chance discovery and removal can happen too easily. The cans or bottles of all teams should be indistinguishable from one another. However, the maps inside might be color coded by team so as to be recognizable when discovered. The containers are then hidden in a pattern shown on the map or described in the directions. The sets of directions are written so that the discovery of one container gives a new set of directions leading to another. A team may, by following its own map, discover all of its own map pieces or directions. The activity should be monitored, and any group that opens another team's container simply because it is discovered and not by following the map should be penalized by adding time (say, one minute). Teams are staggered in starting, but turns are recorded. The team completing the map in the shortest time wins.

Site Stakeout

For site stakeouts, students are divided into groups of six to ten. If possible, work with one group at a time and keep accurate record of the time it takes a group to complete the task and any errors corrected or help needed. Each group is assigned a different site. Sites may be such things as castles, forts, museums, public buildings (e.g., city hall, the school, jail or prison), typical small frontier towns, factories, or colonial farms. Groups are given sketch map drawings showing their own site in detail. Other information about activities on the site is also provided. The group's job is to "stake" its own site by outlining the perimeter and interior features as accurately as possible. Each group uses string and small wooden or plastic stakes. (Clothespins work well, too.) Stakes are driven into the ground and string stretched between the stakes. All groups show such things as dimensions, relative size, and so on. All parts of the site are labeled corresponding to diagram labels. Upon completion, the staked-out sites are evaluated on the basis of their accuracy, the time elapsed in completing the stakeout, and the amount of adult assistance required.

Orienteering Scavenger Hunt

For the orienteering scavenger hunt, some advance work will need to be done. Cooperation is needed among several people in the school and community. It is also recommended that an adult volunteer be recruited to accompany each team of students. The initial task is to identify places in the community, students' homes, places of business, offices, and so on, simply based on the willingness of people in these places to participate in helping the students learn. A map of the community is drawn, indicating by a number each of the places where a cooperating person is to be found. No names of people or place titles are listed on the map.

Each team is given a copy of the map and the order in which they are to visit each place. The order is indicated only by the number (the order of the places is different for all teams). Teams are sent out at five-minute intervals. Their job is to use the map to find, in proper order, the places listed in their directions. At each stop, the team records the name of the person or the location and the time of arrival. The teams must get a verifying signature from the cooperating person at the site. (They may wear badges or caps if there are several people about.) The objective for each group is to finish all scheduled stops in the correct order on a timed schedule or in the shortest possible time.

Fantasy School Map

The fantasy school map activity is designed to help students understand the concepts of miniaturization and symbolism as they apply to maps. It is a map-making activity in which students try to translate a part of the world onto a map. Imagination and policing are needed, but it can be well worth the effort in terms of practical learning. The amount of space used may vary. A large area, such as a cafeteria, gymnasium, or playground, is best. Students imagine that the area used for the map is a part of some larger, distant geographic area. For example, it might be an area of the gold fields of California, a township in the Northwest Territory, an area of land being opened for homesteading, a feudal manor, a Roman military encampment, or a contemporary community in any country.

The size of the actual area being imagined would be much larger than the actual space used. The first job of the group of students is to arrange and label the features of the area. Existing furnishings should be incorporated. A chair may be used to symbolize a building; a bookcase may be a mesa, and so on. But added features may be created simply by labeling sheets of paper. The students then map the area they have laid out.

Best Route

Best route involves students in using maps to determine the best way to get from one place to another. For this activity, students are put into small groups. Each group has a map of the local community around the school and a list of jobs to do. The tasks may simply be finding specific purchasable items (students need not buy, only locate where items may be purchased) or finding the best prices or set of items to deliver. But jobs could also include involvement in volunteer citizenship activities at several locations, community improvement, or helping elderly or disabled individuals.

Each group is to determine the most efficient route for performing the tasks and the time it will take to complete those tasks. Groups go together and will need to use the map. They must anticipate delaying factors (such as hills or unmarked construction sites, heavily trafficked roads where crossing may be difficult or even incur backtracking) and keep in mind such effort and time influencing such factors as distances to carry heavy loads. A route plan and estimated time for each stop should be submitted before the trip is taken. Afterwards, students can discuss alternative, better routes and factors influencing how well their plans worked.

Map Labeling

Provide students with an unlabeled map of a familiar area and have them fill in the labels. The location may be one seen and traveled regularly, such as some part of a local neighborhood or one visited one or more times. If the latter is used, informing students before the actual trip can improve observation.

Where Does It Come From?

Divide students into groups. Each group is given a world map and a list of ten products, ten animals, or ten plants. Using reference books and the internet, the group must determine locations where the items on their list may be found. They then must chart the shortest possible route for obtaining them.

Shortest Route to the Habitat

Give students a list of ten animals and ask them to pretend that they have been commissioned to return each animal to its natural environment. Have students discover the shortest distance that these animals may be taken by plane to a safe habitat that is like the one in which they are naturally found. The catch is that they cannot carry animals beyond a specified total weight or animals that are natural enemies on the same trip. The list of animals should include some relatively heavy ones, some that are prey, and some that are predators.

Mapping a School Activity

Have students make and use a school and school grounds map to set up plans for a school activity. These might be a school carnival (with specific locations for all attractions), a walking field trip (with specific places of interest noted), a class party, parents' night, or open house.

Story Maps

Have students do story maps as book reports. A story map charts the geographic areas used as settings for the book. Inferences and direct statements of the author about relative distances, landmarks, and features are used by students; movements of protagonists and other characteristics can also be charted. Interior as well as exterior maps may be made. Fantasy and realistic stories set in fictitious places may be mapped almost as easily as those whose settings are real places.

A caution and guideline: depending on school policy, these activities may be designed in such a way that they take students around the neighborhood for variety and interest. Local school policies, community cooperation, and the neighborhood will be determining factors in deciding if and how to use orientating approaches. Parent or other adult volunteers are essential precautions for many. However, simple adaptations may be all that is needed to use some such activities within school grounds.

▶ CHARTS, GRAPHS, AND MAPS

In today's classrooms, teachers are encouraged and/or required to incorporate "tested subjects" (e.g., English, reading, math) into "non-tested subject areas" (e.g., social studies). However, it should be noted that many elementary teachers already utilize many math-related concepts and skills within social studies curriculum. Mathematics-related skills are essential for learning about the world. It is important to help students learn to apply mathematical skills.

Begin with items that are relevant to students' everyday lives. The experience can begin as a class activity and then slowly move to group and individual practice. Charts and graphs can be used to show such information as:

- Students' attendance.
- Teacher conferences.
- Students' independent reading.
- Class opinions.
- How related ideas are alike and different.
- Days remaining until some special event.
- Competition among groups.
- Numbers of different kinds of objects.
- Work completed.

The use of measurement as well as charts and graphs can provide important, conceptually related experiences as students study other cultures and other times. They can measure areas equivalent to the sizes of the ships of explorers and colonists or of the log cabins of famous historical characters such as Abraham Lincoln. They can look to the contents and weight of pack-loads of soldiers of various eras. In fact, measuring is one of the most important ways of making verbal descriptions visual and tactile. Mathematics enables students to look comparatively at such things as personal income, shipping, manufacturing, mining, and farming in very concrete ways.

Mathematics is also an important tool for making and reading maps. Practice in measuring distances on maps is a critical part of learning about scale and about place relationship. You can have students create their own ruler from a piece of string and then make a game out of measuring distances. Making grids to draw smaller and larger maps can also help students with measurement skills. Younger elementary students can begin with a map divided into four numbered quadrants, where they locate places by quadrant.

▶ TIME CONCEPTS

Students are very aware of time. Developing time concepts and skills not only helps them understand history but also enables them to better understand the events in their own lives. Their awareness of time and time words should become increasingly specific as they progress through the elementary grades.

Time understanding for students begins with a mixture of vague and precise time references in their lives and in the language around them that is most likely to be confusing. For example, when someone says, "in a second" or "in a minute," they do not mean precisely 1 or 60 seconds. In fact, the reference, in a student's experience, might have meant several hours and is no more precise than the very uncertain "in a little while." Other seemingly precise time references also have had a wide range of meaning to students. "Tomorrow" may have meant just that, or it may be a word used for when something was not going to happen for days, if at all. Part of the job of the school is to help students clarify and distinguish both the vague references and the more precise ones.

Table 8.1 describes each stage of a student's understanding of time based on Thornton and Vukulich (1988).

As students grow in their understanding of and ability to deal with time, they begin to have increasingly more precise reference points on the clock, on the calendar, in their

Table 8.1 A Student's Understanding of Time

Age (in years)	Stage Description
3–5	Capable of sequencing daily events; can rank order family members by age
6–8	Develop the ability to use "historical numbers" to represent the past; can sometimes match dates with major events (e.g., Christmas is December 25)
9–11	Become capable of matching persons and events with textbook descriptions (e.g., colonial period)
12–14	Able to use time classifications with increasing ease (e.g., decade)

own history, and in the histories of different elements in their world. They begin to understand that one of the ways to understand time is to visualize time passage as space distance. Visualizations through a variety of types of timelines help students better see events in relation to one another. In the process, students begin to learn:

- The meanings of time and calendar words.
- The precise meaning of time words used in the measurement of time (second, minute, hour, day, week, month, year, decade, century, millennium) and that some of these words are used with indefinite meanings as well.
- How time is sometimes represented by distance (timelines including calendars and some clocks).
- How to use clocks.
- Ways of using calendars.
- How to use different types of timelines.
- That events occur in sequence and knowing this sequence can be useful.
- That the relation of events to one another is sometimes a function of the times when each occurs.
- What the relationships between events are.

Students learn about time by developing meaningful reference points. The schedule for the school day is one of the major devices used to learn about clocks and acquire shorter time references. Scheduled events at school and outside school, as well as the so-called Holiday Curriculum, are the major means through which students learn about the calendar. Multisensory experiences that add meaning to events and associate their occurrence with dates help students remember the time and place of the events.

A calendar is one of the earliest timelines that young elementary students are exposed to both in and out of school. Early elementary teachers, for example, often use the space above eye level on all four walls of the classroom to make an "in-the-round" pictorial calendar. On it they show the seasons, the months, the weeks, and the days. Events are given particular attention. School starting might rate a picture of the school, birthdays a student's name and picture or a crown, holidays some other picture or symbol. Such a timeline not only teaches time concepts, including the cyclical nature of the year, but also develops self-concepts.

Learning about the relationship between events and people through timelines continues with many different possible activities. Examples include:

- Have students make a personal timeline of their own lives. This can be illustrated with drawings, photos, and/or cut-out magazine pictures showing themselves, their families, their interests, and the events of their lives. This may require taking time with each child to help them recognize, remember, and reconstruct what has been important to them.
- Have students line up according to birthday.
- Let each child do a stair-step family timeline, tracing one strand of his or her forebears:
  - _____ Great–Great–Grandmother
  - _____ Great–Grandmother
  - _____ Grandmother
  - _____ Mother
  - _____ Me

- Help students do human timelines in which everyone represents events and historical people. Chalk marks or masking tape on the floor can show precisely measured distances to represent decades, centuries, etc. Costume creation and reporting-type activities can be added to make it even more fun.
- Human timelines can be used to represent events relating to one another during a relatively brief period of time (e.g., events surrounding the break-up of the Soviet Union), the time relations of different people or events (e.g., inventions that changed our lives), or the relationship of several important events over a broad span of history.
- Make clothesline timelines. Have students add events as they are talked about, clipping the new events to the timeline using a squeeze clothespin.
- Give students in groups of three or four a deck of cards, each labeled as a different holiday. Have students experiment sorting and ordering the holidays in different ways, including chronological order.

▶ ECONOMIC SKILLS

Economic skills that students begin to learn in elementary school should have to do mostly with their roles as consumers. However, they also need to learn something about how producers and others operate. Among the economics concepts and skills that students need to learn to use are the following:

- Different types and values of money.
- How to manage their own money and time.
- How businesses and governments use money and time.
- What are needs and wants, and how do we tell the difference?
- What is meant by such concept terms as *value*, *cost*, and *price*.
- The relative costs/values of different goods and services.
- How to do comparative shopping.
- How and why exchange occurs.
- The skills needed for using bank accounts.
- What credit is and how it works (including what interest is).

Situational scenarios and hypothetical problems related to economics can be created and used at almost any level. Even in kindergarten, economic thinking can be part of many types of learning centers set up in the classroom: kitchen centers, post office centers, building construction centers, and so on. Students of all ages learn from trading and swapping activities, which can provide an experiential basis for discussion of relative merit and relative value. Many commercial games, perhaps the best-known being Monopoly and Pit, involve swapping activity and can be the basis for classroom activity.

- Teachers can make up card decks related to units. On each card, an item of property related to the unit can be listed. When cards are distributed, students can have a trading period. The follow-up should relate to issues such as scarcity and abundance, the costs of production and transportation at the place and time of the unit, and other factors relating to the trades.
- At a small cost to the teacher or perhaps with items from a school sponsor, the teacher may set up a "store." Students, over a period, can "work" for "store money," which they can exchange for items on a given day.

- Student groups can be set up as countries with sets of resources and needs. The game involves exchanging their resources for what they need.
- Card decks can be created with suits of cards based on items of value. Card games can involve exchange with the purpose of getting a monopoly by collecting a complete suite of one item.

Lots of commercial games deal with banking, budgeting, and using and conserving resources. The teacher needs to find out which of these the students are familiar with, extend their experiences with these games, and help them understand what these games teach. Beyond the commercial games, numerous valuable classroom activities are possible. Class banks can be set up with accounts involving checks, balances, and other factors. Income and expenses can be assigned. The whole experience then can be used as the basis for discussion. Students can deal with pretend shopping lists for events like Thanksgiving or other holiday meals and make a visit to a grocery store to cost out their lists. Field trips to banks and businesses may be valuable. They can be urged to ask questions of directors of zoos, hospitals, and other enterprises about their own expenses and budgets. Students can deal with hypothetical budgets for families in any period of history or in any culture being studied.

Activities that can build economic skills should be carefully planned to suit the level of ability and the interests of students. The following is a list of a few possible activity types:

- Planning dream vacations.
- Practicing exchanging play money representing different values or currencies of different countries.
- Price-following activities and games (e.g., stock market, home prices, automobile prices, etc.) over time.

▶ LOOKING BACK

Well-developed study skills give students a winning advantage, an edge, when it comes to learning tasks or success in life. The most important study skills include knowing how to find necessary information, being able to make decisions about information, and being able to organize and retain information. Some study skills are specifically associated with the social studies because they relate to one or more of the social sciences. One of these is reading and using maps and globes. Students are more likely to develop map competency if they are exposed to many experiences interacting with maps, map problems, and problems that involve using maps. The maps used in these experiences need to be simple and purposeful. The experiences themselves should teach about distance, direction, scale, and map symbols at a developmentally appropriate level. Maps should be used purposefully in the classroom with a variety of applied map-reading and map-making activities. It should be stressed that maps can be engaging, and there should be an abundance of map games and other activities that students enjoy doing. Time skills also require concrete hands-on activities with concrete materials that expand the student's awareness of the time relationships among events. Lots of experiences with clocks, calendars, and other forms of timelines can help students understand the abstractions of these time relationships.

Ours is a society in which the development of economic skills is essential to survival. Students need experiences in dealing with money and exchange, as well as a growing understanding of credit, banking, budgeting, and economic planning, at a personal level as well as for communities up to the size of nations.

EXTENSION ACTIVITY

SCENARIO

Your Monday at Yourtown Elementary School (YES) begins the same as any normal Monday until you are approached by YES's assistant principal, Dr. Waters, requesting a meeting. Dr. Waters asks, "Can you meet with Dr. Russell and me after school today?" You say, "I sure can." Each of you smiles and goes your separate way. Throughout the day, you can't stop thinking about your meeting this afternoon and what it's about. However, the day goes by, and you find yourself sitting in the principal's office, waiting for the meeting.

The meeting starts with Dr. Russell explaining, "Dr. Waters and I are pleased with your performance and would like you to create a sample skill development activity that we can share with all YES teachers. Your ability to help students build skills is remarkable, and we think that you should share that information with other teachers here at YES." You feel silly for having worried about the meeting the entire day, but you relax, smile, and say, "Thank you for the kind words. I would be happy to create a sample skill development activity." Your response is met with delight.

TASK

Select a skill and K–6 grade level of your choice. Develop a new and unique activity that can help students master the selected skill while learning social studies content. The activity should be in written form and utilize the lesson/activity format required by your school/district/university. Share your response with peers and/or instructor.

CHECKING FOR UNDERSTANDING

1. What are some ways to create the "Columbus urge" in students?
2. What is a mnemonic device?
3. Describe the three types of memory.
4. What are some guidelines for using maps and globes?
5. Why is it important to teach maps in a way that involves maps as tools of problem solving?
6. What are some of the time concepts?
7. How can I promote historical thinking in my classroom?

▶ HELPFUL RESOURCES

Watch this short video providing an overview of what historical thinking is and why it matters in the classroom:
www.youtube.com/watch?v=mSJLmWnxrPg
Watch this video about the DBQ project, an initiative focused on promoting the use of DBQs at all levels of education:

www.youtube.com/watch?v=y8MlNzi1s_k

Visit this website for a list of several social studies games that could be utilized in the elementary social studies classroom:

http://pbskids.org/games/social-studies/

Visit this website (Video #4: China Through Mapping) to see an example of a second-grade teacher using a variety of map resources and activities to explore China:

https://www.learner.org/series/social-studies-in-action-a-teaching-practices-library-k-12/china-through-mapping/

Watch this short video about the importance of map skills:

www.flocabulary.com/unit/map-skills/

Watch this video of an example lesson showing a middle school teacher using maps to explore emigration and migration:

www.teachingchannel.org/videos/teaching-human-migration

Share this video with elementary students as an introduction to understanding longitude and latitude:

www.flocabulary.com/unit/longitude-and-latitude/

▶ FURTHER READING

Wineburg, S. (2001). *Historical thinking and other unnatural acts: Charting the future of teaching the past*. Philadelphia, PA: Temple University Press.

For much more detailed information on historical thinking, consider this seminal book by Dr. Wineburg.

Sumrall, J., Russell, W., & Carter, L. (2007). Yard sale! Challenges for young geographers. *Social Studies and the Young Learner*, 20(2), P1–P4.

This article discusses an engaging geography lesson. The lesson activity requires students to be actively engaged in map reading, measuring distances, and determining varying costs by using yard sale addresses found in a local newspaper. Through location and plotting, they determine the shortest or, in some cases, the best path for going from sale to sale. Map reading and elements of problem solving are emphasized throughout the lesson. Determining the cheapest route based on fuel used, making multiple conversions, and finally deciding on a "best route" are some of the open-ended/real-world connections made in these activities.

McIntyre, B. (2011). History scene investigations: From clues to conclusions. *The Social Studies*, 23(3), 17–21.

In this article, the author introduces a social studies lesson that allows students to learn history and practice reading skills, critical thinking, and writing. The activity is called History Scene Investigation or HSI, which derives its name from the popular television series based on crime scene investigations (*CSI*). HSI uses discovery learning and inductive reasoning. It requires students to use artifacts in a mock scene from history as clues for drawing conclusions about the scene. By selecting the appropriate types of artifacts to present to the students, the teacher can adjust the level of difficulty of an HSI lesson, making it appropriate for middle- or upper-elementary grade students.

Council for Economic Education. (2003). *The great economic mysteries book: A guide to teaching economic reasoning grades 4–8*. New York: Council for Economic Education.

This book introduces students in grades 4–8 to an economics way of thinking by exploring the mysteries of everyday life. Students solve each mystery by responding to hints provided by simple true/false questions and by reference to a logical system of thinking.

Johnson, T. (2012). Exploring the options: Teaching economic decision-making with poetry. *The Social Studies*, 103(2), 61–66.

In this article, integrating instruction in poetry and economic decision making is presented as one way to maximize the use of scarce instructional time. Following a brief introduction to the role of economics in children's lives and a rationale for using poetry to teach significant economic concepts, summaries of four appropriate poetry collections and a description of a recent experience teaching economics with poetry in a fifth-grade classroom are presented.

▶ REFERENCES

Driscoll, M. P. (2009). *Psychology of learning for instruction* (4th ed.). Needham Heights, MA: Allyn and Bacon.

Thornton, S. J., & Vukulich, R. (1988). Effects of students' understanding of time concepts on historical understanding. *Theory and Research in Social Education, 16*(Winter), 69–82.

Critical Thinking and Problem Solving

Chapter

9

► LOOKING AHEAD

In a democratic society, developing students' abilities to think critically and solve problems is a pivotal goal. The aim is to develop students into independent and self-motivated learners. Embodied in this goal is the notion that effective teachers allow, encourage, and challenge students to understand how to find, evaluate, and use information. If the development of independent learners is truly the goal of education, then it is important to teach students how to think, not what to think.

Thinking and problem-solving skills are the core purpose of social studies. The National Council for the Social Studies Task Force on Early Childhood/Elementary Social Studies (2009) explains that "The purpose of elementary school social studies is to enable students to understand, participate in, and make informed decisions about their world." The NCSS Task Force goes on to explain that social studies content provides the "skills for productive problem solving and decision making as well as for assessing issues and making thoughtful value judgments."

Presentation-style social studies, where the teacher does most of the talking, is not likely to develop students' thinking skills. To ensure students become problem solvers, students must be involved and participate in the learning process. This means that discussion, teacher questioning, and carefully constructed assignments are critical.

CAN YOU? DO YOU?

Can you . . .

- Explain three ways to teach students to think logically?
- Identify the functions of the mind that relate to critical thinking?
- Identify problem-solving tasks?

Do you . . .

- Know how to help students to understand and retain information?
- Understand the term *story map*?
- Know the functions of the mind?

FOCUS ACTIVITY

Before reading this chapter, try the following focus activity.

Think back on your education and life experiences. Can you recall an important decision you had to make in your life? How did you go about finding the ultimate solution? Share your decision-making experiences with others. Discuss the details of the decision-making experiences and compare. Does your decision-making process share common attributes with others'? If so, what attributes?

▶ **THINKING SKILLS**

Learning can be viewed in two different ways. The first we usually call rote learning. Rote learning means that information is memorized with little or no understanding of its meaning. For example, you may have learned a poem, speech, or song or learned to spell and pronounce words but had no idea of their meaning. Rote learning does not provide us with useful information because if we have no idea of the meaning of what we have learned, we cannot conceive how to put it to use.

The second way of learning begins with our understanding of what we learn. The more sense we can make of something, the more it fits into patterns and stories in our minds, the more likely we are to retain it. Constructivism is the learning theory that explains how people come to understand new ideas and information by relating it to previous experiences. From a constructivist point of view, the way that new information is presented may be as important as or even more important than the information itself, because it will determine how we make sense of the information or how we give it meaning. The quest to develop students as problem solvers in elementary social studies can be traced at least to the beginning of the twentieth century, when a few innovative schools began to look at a life-centered problems approach as central to the curriculum. Beginning in the 1960s and 1970s, the notion of learning to learn became crucial to every social studies program as an approach called the inquiry method was widely advocated. The inquiry classroom differed from a traditional classroom. The students were to learn to ask questions, not just answer them. The teacher's role became less that of information provider and more that of coach, facilitator, and guide.

The term *thinking skills* refers to all the mental processes that individuals use to obtain, make sense of, and retain information, as well as how they process and use that information as a basis for solving problems. The process of taking in the information likewise involves thinking skills, especially those related to observing, listening, and reading. Obtaining information and ideas is a sensory process, and all the senses are used in information gathering. For many students, learning is easier through one sense than the others; thus, teachers need to utilize multisensory learning materials wherever possible. Even so, learning to listen and observe are trainable skills acquired through directed and disciplined practice. Therefore, teachers need to help students acquire these important skills in a systematic and developmental way.

Schema is a term used to describe relating new ideas to experiences (Driscoll, 2009). *Schemata* (the plural) are the various ways that we group ideas and knowledge in our minds. Our best chance at understanding new concepts is to tie features of those concepts to one or more of these schemata. To do this, we look for similarities, make assumptions, create analogies, and generally relate information to ourselves.

Another factor in comprehension is metacognition: a student's awareness of his or her own thinking processes and of the thinking processes of the people with whom he or she is communicating. The term has come to be used to describe a student's awareness and understanding of the organizational patterns of reading material and of speakers. Individuals who can form clear and accurate story maps of reading material or spoken material have a clearer overall understanding of that material. This, in turn, helps them understand the meaning of specific parts of the communication as it relates to the organization and purposes.

To maximize student understanding, teachers should provide story maps for students before they listen to, read, or view material. In effect, this means that teachers need to provide both sensitive and clear overviews of oral presentations, audiovisual programs, and reading material before students are exposed to it. A reflective review of material will also help students develop their metacognitive skills. Such reviews increase learning and retention in a clearly measurable way. These reviews generally involve teacher questioning so that students become intellectually involved and, therefore, active in forming clearer cognitive maps of material covered.

Generally, teachers can help students understand and retain information by following a few principles:

- Associate new information with experiences that students have had in the past.
- Connect each piece of new information to other pieces of information using a pattern that students can follow. (Sensory or visualizable patterns are best.)
- Repeat information and patterns often.
- Provide a shared purpose or use for the learning.
- Give opportunities for practice with feedback.

▶ LOGICAL THINKING AND ANALYZING SKILLS

In social studies, elementary teachers help students gain logical thinking and analyzing skills in at least three ways: by modeling, through discussion, and through guided practice with feedback. Table 9.1 details thinking skills and possible activities.

Critical and Creative Thinking

The chief dilemma of teaching is to show students where to look without telling them what to see. Helping elementary students learn to think logically should lead them to critical and creative thought processes, not telling them what to think. The elementary teacher wants the student to be able to make informed decisions based on the information available and to have the ability and the mindset needed to come up with multiple and original ideas as solutions to problems.

Critical thinking can be defined as making evaluations or judgments of experience. When evaluation is based on analysis, then critical thinking involves often complex logical reasoning. Critical thinking requires comparing a personal set of experiences and values to current experiences, newly encountered data, and decision- and judgment-demanding situations. We think critically whenever we try to reason out decisions or judgments. Critical thinking relates to some very important functions of the mind. Those functions of the mind can be seen in Table 9.2.

Creative thinking also requires evaluative thinking as well as other abilities. Creative thinkers come up with new ideas, new ways of looking at things, and different ways of

Table 9.1 Thinking Skills and Activities

Thinking Skill	Type of Activity
Interpreting or explaining	Paraphrasing, rephrasing
Relating information	Advanced organizers for reading assignments
Applying previous knowledge	Charting, drawing parallels
Identifying implicit assumptions	Discussion of motives
Identifying key features and characteristics	Defining, describing, giving background
Summarizing and synthesizing	Writing summaries, reviewing, giving closure to lessons
Comparing and contrasting	Identifying attributes, pattern finding
Organizing information	Outlining, sequencing
Classifying and categorizing	Charting, sorting
Inferencing and concluding	Cause-and-effect exercises, following clues, guessing games, problem solving
Determining truth, accuracy, completeness, reliability	Cross-checking, maps of errors, peer evaluation

Table 9.2 Functions of the Mind

Process	Definition
The symbolic process	We allow words, numbers, and other symbols to stand for ideas
Visualization	We make mental pictures that represent our perceptions
Characterization	We notice the qualities of things and that which we notice, in turn, builds our perceptions of likes and differences
Classification	We sort things into classes, types, families, and so on
Structure analysis	We notice how things are made and divide classes into component parts
Operations analysis	We notice how things happen, successive stages, and so on
Paralleling	We see how situations are alike

synthesizing or combining existing ideas. They see several logical possibilities in solving problems and also are open to illogical methods. They are not so much looking for the solution to a problem or answer to a question as they are trying to see various possibilities. Part of the creative mindset is a fluency and flexibility of thought. Creativity implies originality: the ability to come up with unique and unconventional approaches. However, creative thinkers follow through with the same openness, having the ability to develop and elaborate ideas in solving problems. Creative thinking is what we need when we try to find new and different ways of solving both new problems that we have never encountered before and older ones that have remained without satisfactory solution.

It would be an oversimplification to say that creative thinking is the ability to solve problems; however, that ability is at least a focus of creative thinking. Creative thinking differs from most thought required in school chiefly because of its emphasis on alternative approaches and on multiple solutions.

Problem Solving and Inquiry

Problem solving most often begins with a situation that demands a solution or a response. A creative problem-solving experience is one in which the individual must figure out both what to do and how to do it. Creative problem solving, as it relates to elementary social studies, can involve any one of the following thinking difficulties:

- Dealing with a negative or difficult situation.
- Overcoming an obstacle.
- Bringing about some desired outcome.
- Bringing about change.

To understand and use information, we must be able to put that information into a variety of logical structures. As this skill develops, it involves curious playfulness and a willingness to experiment with different ways of ordering and looking at information. As we learn to do this, we learn to identify relationships and patterns, to put information from different sources together, to make inferences and judgments, to recognize qualities such as relative importance, relevance, and usefulness, and to differentiate among degrees of partial, convincing, decisive, and conclusive evidence.

A critical issue in problem solving is the ability to recognize and identify the real problems. Once the critical problems are clearly and specifically identified, ways to find solutions are more easily determined.

Inquiry teaching models use variations of the "scientific method." Most of us learned some version of this method in middle and/or high school science class. The scientific method is simply a sequence of the steps involved in any research. The following steps describe the basics of the scientific method:

1. Sense the problem (beginning with a doubt or uncertainty).
2. Define the problem.
3. Come up with some hypotheses (possible solutions to the problem).
4. Gather evidence.
5. Draw conclusions.

Inquiry has changed the way we look at teaching elementary social studies and has provided problem-solving tools that continue to be useful in teaching students to become independent thinkers and problem solvers. One contribution of the inquiry approach has been the development of a variety of creative problem-solving strategies. These strategies were conceived with a problem that defies solution in mind, and they can be learned easily through experiences in which the teacher models them in discussion formats with specific problems. Successful strategies for approaching difficult problems are detailed in Table 9.3.

The best way to get students to become active problem solvers is to give them lots of problems to solve. Real-life problems are most effective. The teacher needs to treat situations in the classroom as problem-solving activities. Give students a set of guidelines like those found in Table 9.4. When students encounter problems, lead them through the list and ask them their thoughts about the problem in relation to each of the guidelines. Point out that every guideline does not have to apply to every problem.

Table 9.3 Successful Strategies for Approaching Difficult Problems

Restate the problem	Simply putting a problem into different words may make it more understandable and, therefore, more solvable. It gives the problem solver a fresh perspective.
Segment the problem	Dividing the problem in some way, whether into identifiable components or simply into smaller pieces, is a useful strategy. Divided, the problem can be attacked as a cooperative learning task by a group or can be dealt with one piece at a time.
Tangential problems	Try solving tangential problems. Look at the impact of the problem and identify side effects. Work on solving these relatively minor problems, and they may provide a key to the central problem.
Analogies to the problem	Look for analogies to the problem and try solving these analogous problems. For example, if we said that our polluted rivers are like clogged arteries and then looked at the solutions doctors suggest for clogged arteries, it may help us identify remedies for the rivers.
Reduce the problem	If we try to say the problem in the minimum number of words and as simply as possible, then we may understand its essence more fully and be better able to solve it.

Table 9.4 Sample Guidelines for Problem-Solving Activities

1. The best way to get super ideas is to get lots of ideas and then discard ideas that are not so great.
2. Write down your ideas before you forget them (within 5 minutes).
3. Begin with the obvious and then look for more than one right answer.
4. Ask questions, even ones you may consider stupid.
5. Remember that nearly all words have several meanings.
6. Visualize the problem. See it backwards, forwards, inside out, and all mixed up.
7. Ask how nature would solve the problem.

Attempt to tolerate and encourage offbeat and unique, but appropriate, responses and comments. Also, keep the classroom atmosphere relaxed and welcoming. Help students realize that the true secret of problem solving is perseverance and that the process is often as valuable as the outcome.

▶ TYPES OF PROBLEM-SOLVING TASKS

Once students learn to recognize and verbally describe problems, they need to learn to identify critical elements within these problems. Recognizing the presence of patterns and features in a problem may signal a possible way of solving it. A problem of one type can be approached in much the same way as other problems of that type. Knowing the elements of a problem will be of enormous help in identifying and using the most promising approach. Once the approach is identified, following a series of steps used in similar problems will often lead to a solution. The following are approaches that can be used as models for students. Each relates to problems of a certain type. Sample activities are given with each approach.

Identifying All Factors of a Problem

Identifying all factors of a problem requires looking at all related factors and issues involved. In these problem-solving strategies, the emphasis is on the nature of problems that have multiple possible answers. The approach is one that is effective for complex problems for which there is no perfect set of right answers. The actual number of possible answers will vary with such problems. However, the problem solvers' task includes defining criteria for examining the appropriateness of answers. Examples of this approach follow.

Example 1: Identifying All Factors of a Problem

Pilgrims' Progress: If you were embarking with the early Puritans or Pilgrims who came to settle in New England, what sort of supplies would you take with you? Make a list that includes necessities as well as other things you might like to have. Remember that this is the 1600s. What kinds of supplies are going to be available, and what things simply will not be? Think about the kind of place that you are going to and the kind of place you are coming from.

Example 2: Identifying All Factors of a Problem

Invention Brainstorm: Suppose we put the word *invention* in the middle of the board. Now let us think of other words that represent related ideas; we will place these words all around the board and connect the ones that are related to one another with lines.

Prioritizing a Problem

Prioritizing a problem requires setting priorities within the problem. Prioritizing is a lifelong problem. There are always too few resources or goods and too little time or money for the demands. Individuals, communities, and nations continually have to decide which needs and wants to meet first. Prioritizing problems in social studies usually involves looking at lists of equipment or provisions as they relate to a problem or being faced with a series of problems in a given situation and having to decide in what order these problems need to be solved, based on immediacy, importance, or a combination of the two. The following is an example of a problem-solving task.

Example: Prioritizing a Problem

Shipwreck Rescue: You are the commander of a sailing ship bringing new colonists and supplies to the New World in the seventeenth century. Your ship has been caught in a terrible storm as you approach the coast. You have been unable to keep the ship from going aground on the rocky shore. The storm still is raging all about and may at any moment either wash you out to sea or break the ship into pieces. The water rushing all around is only about six feet deep, and you can see a solid beach perhaps a hundred yards away. Here are all the problems that you must handle. Number them according to the order in which you think they need to be handled. Suggest a solution for each.

- Sharp rocks can be seen dead ahead.
- There is a gaping hole in the hull. and some water is rushing in.
- You fear that hostile natives may inhabit this area of the coast.
- The food supplies are in the hold, which is fast filling with water.
- The crew members are unhappy and are arguing among themselves.
- One of the ship's cannons has broken loose and is careening across the deck.
- A woman on board is about to give birth.
- A small fire has broken out in the ship's kitchen.
- One of the ship's masts has been broken by the storm and has fallen, pinning a crew member, perhaps breaking both of his legs.
- Some of the colonists are trying to break into the powder magazine containing all the ship's weapons and gunpowder.
- A passenger is demanding that he and his scientific records be put ashore in the ship's boat.

Multiple Perspectives of a Problem

Multiple perspectives of a problem require examining differing, conflicting, and opposing points of view. Understanding, accommodating, and relating to ideas and opinions of others are problems of cooperation. They are also the foundation of understanding conflict of all kinds. Problem-solving exercises require students to identify the likely opinions of others. Examples of this type of exercise include the following.

Example 1: Multiple Perspectives of a Problem

The Telephone: Think about how people in the nineteenth century felt about the invention of the telephone. Think about the impact that the first telephones might have had on different people's lives. Just after the turn of the century, there were only a few hundred telephones in use. Even then, people were beginning to see the change that a telephone network was going to bring. Write down a few sentences about the views of the people that follow. Then, we will assign roles in groups and discuss what our feelings would have been if we had lived at the turn of the century, exploring:

- The opinion of the owner of the telegraph company.
- The opinion of a messenger boy whose job might be threatened.
- The opinion of a New York businessman.
- The opinion of a New York housewife.
- The opinion of a conservative country minister.

Example 2: Multiple Perspectives of a Problem

Programming: Pretend that you are the programming director for a major television network. You are considering the eight o'clock Monday night slot, where this program will be up against established shows that have had good ratings. You are considering a long-running comedy program that has been revamped after being canceled by another network (as the ratings reached an all-time low); a new comedy with a star who once had a hit drama series but may not have comedic ability; a show aimed at pre-teen, teen, and young-adult viewers and starring several young, unknown actors; a news program presenting controversial issues and public opinion; and a hard-hitting action show with an up-and-coming African American star and lots of violence. What would be the views of the following people:

- The conservative network president.
- The president of a fast-food chain that is a big sponsor.
- The head of an organization of concerned parents.
- An 11-year-old boy.
- A 9-year-old girl.

Problems With Alternative Solutions

Problems with alternative solutions begin with a problem that has several plausible solutions, none of which can ever be absolutely identified as the single correct solution. The basic question the problem solver must ask is, "What is the impact of each solution identified?" For example, the teacher might begin with a series of contemporary problems like drugs, gangs, pollution, prejudice, or terrorism and suggest, or have students suggest, several of the partial solutions that have been articulated by social scientists and politicians. Students would then try to think hypothetically about what positive and negative impact each of these solutions would have if implemented.

Identifying Purpose Problems

Identifying purpose problems involves identifying the aims, goals, and objectives of a problem. The focus in this type of problem is on identifying the purposes that people might conceivably have. It sometimes involves looking at our own aims as well. The basic strategy uses analogies, stories, and situational scenarios. The problem solver has to examine the wants, needs, and hopes of people involved in the particular setting. In each case, the key problem is to identify the major aims, goals, and purposes that the individual or group is pursuing in the situation. This kind of problem focus should help students become more purpose oriented and help them understand the reasons for the problem.

Examples: Identifying Purpose Problems

- Identify the central aims, goals, and objectives of the main characters in a children's book or story (e.g., *Harry Potter, Treasure Island, The Seven Dancing Princesses*).
- What are the main goals and objectives of police officers?
- What are the main goals of the school rules?
- What were the aims, goals, and purposes of African Americans during the civil rights movement?

Problems With Proposed Solutions

Problems with proposed solutions emphasize identifying advantages, disadvantages, and unique and interesting features. In this type of problem solving, the problem is an assertion or an idea to be examined. The purpose in the problem-solving process is for students to be able to see possible advantages and problems or disadvantages that the implementation of that assertion would bring. A secondary purpose is to have them analyze the unique and interesting features of this assertion. The teacher might want to begin by having students show agreement by hand signals or standing up.

Examples: Problems With Proposed Solutions

Students should volunteer when they know the answer.

- There should be a law that all containers and print materials be recyclable and that users recycle such containers.
- Abraham Lincoln should have issued the Emancipation Proclamation immediately when the Southern states seceded.
- People need to be able to do whatever they want with property that they own.

▶ PROMOTING CRITICAL THINKING WITH MODULES

Modules provide for a series of lessons, sometimes consisting of several activities centered on one or a series of closely related ideas, usually concept statements or generalizations. Modules may be used in isolation, as part of or in conjunction with a unit, or in clusters. Built into modular teaching is the notion of mastery. Mastery, in this case, means that the module teaches the idea to a point at which some specified or at least defined level of understanding is reached. Evaluation and re-teaching, then, are necessary for module construction.

As the following examples of topics for modules might indicate, modules may aim at developing definitional understanding of concepts, at helping students reach evaluation judgments, or at providing experiences that cause students to arrive at a commonly shared generalization as a way of thinking. The following are examples of definitional topics:

- A map is a model representing some part of the surface of the Earth or some other area, and it is subject to various inaccuracies.
- A president is the head of a nation, organization, or business, having specific executive functions and powers for a defined length of time and under restricted conditions.
- Laws are rules recognized by a governing body as binding upon the members of the group.

The following are examples of evaluation judgments:

- A good country.
- Responsibility.
- Playing fair is more important than winning.

The following are examples of generalizations:

- Urban communities tend to change more rapidly than rural communities.
- Though all members of a community are consumers, only some are producers.
- A single event may have several causes and produce more than one outcome.

Once the topic is identified, the module consists of an array of activities, including examples and identified non-examples, along with identifying experiences. The activities have the express purpose of bringing an understanding or mastery of the topic, requiring students to analyze and think critically about the topic.

▶ PROMOTING INQUIRY WITH CASE STUDIES

The case study approach has become increasingly more viable with the development of computers and databases. The term "case study" implies a kind of intense examination of an event, person, or thing or a grouping of these. The one case is looked at as an example or model that can be studied over time. In medicine, a doctor might study the medical history of a few patients. From these selected cases, it is hoped that insights about others who have a similar medical history may be derived. In law, a case study may be chosen because it represents a landmark decision or provides a precedent in court procedure. Sociologists, historians, and psychologists may construct fictional cases to demonstrate typical behavior. In fact, the case study approach is used by almost all professions looking at human behavior simply because of the complexity of human thought and action.

A case study is an intensive use of examples. The example provides a database for inquiry and concrete illustration of principles, concepts, and ideas. Case studies used in social studies can help students see the personal and human aspects of a culture or of a time. Students look at one person, one family, or one village rather than reading generalizations about a country, culture, or period. Human qualities seem less abstract. The following are some basic procedures for preparing a case study.

Procedure in Preparing a Case Study

1. Identify the problem to be studied and the purpose to be accomplished.
2. Tentatively identify a research procedure for students to follow.
3. Select the appropriate example (or case).
4. Develop detailed procedural plans.
5. Collect resources related to the case. Examples of resources include:
   a. Maps of varying sorts.
   b. Background information sheets.
   c. Interviews on related topics.
   d. Letters.
   e. Descriptions of objects.
   f. Diaries and journals.
   g. Records and public documents.
   h. Newspaper clippings.
6. Organize the materials and data related to the case. For example, one usable pattern of organization consists of:
   a. A single narrative or a series of narratives describing the facts of the case. These may include first-hand accounts, scholarly summations, and even slanted or biased descriptions.
   b. First person (witness) interviews with principals in or witnesses to the case (transcripts or tapes of these).
   c. Pictures (photographs, drawings, etc.), films, and other media visualizations (including actual film coverage of an event) of the setting, the people, and the chain of events in the case across the time period involved.

    d. Exhibits (artifacts, realia).

    e. Maps, graphs, charts.

    f. Background information (including anecdotes).

7. Plan activities and materials structured to help or guide students as they examine the case or inquire into the evidence.

A Few Types of Activities to Use With Case Study Material

- Research-based discussions and individual reports of controversies.
- Problem-solving situations calling upon data in the case.
- Role plays involving the principals of the case.
- Developing reports or answering questions drawing from data.
- Debates involving controversies or points of view regarding the same or related cases.
- Creative writing to or about the principal characters in the case (e.g., letters, hypothetical diaries, fictional stories, etc.).
- Question-generating sessions.
- Data-generating sessions to build additional cases or to extend the data bank.
- Reenactments of events.
- Artistic endeavors (e.g., murals, models).
- Projective analysis. (What are outcomes to be anticipated beyond the data?)
- Analysis sheets and questions to be answered by studying the data.

▶ INCORPORATING THINKING AND LEARNING SKILLS IN SOCIAL STUDIES

Problem-solving and decision-making skills are the core of effective teaching. Only if elementary students are mentally engaged in social studies are they going to learn. The major thrust of social studies is to develop the ability of students to think and learn for themselves. If they can do that, then they are ready for any social studies topic. If they cannot think, then each topic and each encounter with content requires the teacher to present and guide them through, and the student is always a dependent learner. Students who need such guidance will not fully develop into the ideal citizens that a democracy requires to survive.

▶ LOOKING BACK

There is increasing concern over the development of thinking in social studies. If the major goal of teaching is to help students become independent learners, then there must be a real emphasis on the development of the ability to think and solve problems.

    Obtaining, understanding, and retaining information are among the thinking skills that are important to social studies learning at the elementary level. Generally, students can learn to relate new information to previous knowledge, to identify the patterns and relationships of information and ideas, and to identify purposes for learning. They can be aided in learning to remember through planned repetition of information accompanied by appropriate feedback. Thinking skills can be taught through modeling by the teacher, through carefully planned discussions, and through guided practice. Problem solving is the most essential thinking ability and is an important part of the inquiry process. The use of alternative problem-solving strategies can be taught directly through structured activities. Among these strategies, the following are useful as models:

- Identifying all the factors of a problem.
- Prioritizing a problem.
- Multiple perspectives of a problem.
- Problems with alternative solutions.
- Identifying purpose problems.
- Problems with proposed solutions.

EXTENSION ACTIVITY

You are at the end of the third nine weeks at Yourtown Elementary School (YES). It is almost spring break, and you are finishing semester report cards. The devilishly handsome YES principal, Dr. Russell, stops by your classroom to see if you are ready for spring break. During the conversation, Dr. Russell says, "I enjoy your problem solving–based classroom activities, and after spring break, I would like you to share a new classroom activity with the superintendent, Dr. Turner; YES assistant principal, Dr. Waters; and a local reporter. I would like to see the new dynamic activity on the Monday after spring break." You agree to the challenge and say, "I am excited for the opportunity. Thank you."

TASK

For this activity, develop a new and innovative problem solving–based classroom activity for the elementary grade level and topic of your choice. The activity should be in written form and utilize the lesson/activity format required by your school/district/university. Share your response with peers and/or your instructor.

CHECKING FOR UNDERSTANDING

1. What are thinking skills?
2. What does the term *schema* mean, and how does it relate to thinking?
3. What does the term *critical thinking* mean?
4. What is meant by the term *story map*?
5. Can you list five thinking skills and describe a class activity for meeting each thinking skill?
6. Can you identify and describe types of problem-solving tasks?

▶ HELPFUL RESOURCES

Watch this video created by C3 teachers detailing the importance of students asking questions:
https://youtu.be/GAzvec-cQpk
Visit this website (Video #7: Caring for the Community) to see an example of a K–3 classroom engaged in creative thinking and problem-solving activities:

https://www.learner.org/series/social-studies-in-action-a-teaching-practices-library-k-12/caring-for-the-community/

Watch the video of a master teacher teaching a model lesson from the C3 Framework: https://youtu.be/tbWapv3m6y8

Watch this video of an elementary teacher reflecting inquiry learning in the social studies classroom:

https://youtu.be/1JVOFrCORQ4

This website has an array of useful information, including sample critical-thinking social studies lesson plans:

www.criticalthinking.org

Visit this website (Video #12: Using Primary Sources) to see an example of a fifth-grade teacher implementing a case study lesson using primary resources:

https://www.learner.org/series/social-studies-in-action-a-teaching-practices-library-k-12/using-primary-sources/

Watch this video of the creators of the Inquiry Design Model of the C3 Framework. They explore the model and how it can be utilized in the classroom:

https://youtu.be/FdypkpuKUy4

▶ FURTHER READING

Boostrom, R. (2005). *Thinking: The foundation of critical and creative learning in the classroom.* New York: Teachers College Press.

This engaging book encourages educators to think about the ways in which the practice of teaching unintentionally promotes non-thinking. The author makes suggestions and recommendations to promote a thinking environment.

Russell, W. (2007). A picture is worth 20 questions. *Middle Level Learning, 30*(3), 16.

This article highlights how students can utilize asking questions to better understand the content.

Erickson, L. (2007). *Concept-based curriculum and instruction for the thinking classroom.* Thousand Oaks, CA: Corwin Press.

This book details proven curriculum design with teaching methods that encourage students to learn concepts as well as content and skills for deep understanding across all subject areas.

Sewell, A. M., Fuller, S., Murphy, R. C., & Funnell, B. H. (2002). Creative problem solving: A means to authentic and purposeful social studies. *The Social Studies, 93*(4), 176–179.

This article argues that CPS has the potential to support the development of many citizenship skills, especially problem-solving, communicating, critical-thinking, and information skills. The authors describe how CPS was used to solve problems by students in grades 2 and 6 of a primary school in a small New Zealand farming community. The case studies show how ordinary classrooms can be transformed so that learning is embedded in purposeful and authentic participation, which fosters a community of learners responsible for the direction of their learning.

Hickman, M., & Wiggington, E. (2009). *Cooperative problem-solving activities for social studies.* Thousand Oaks, CA: Corwin.

This book details various activities to engage students in problem solving. The book is written for middle and high school, but many of the ideas can easily be adapted for upper elementary.

Bennett, L., & Hinde, E. (2015). *Becoming integrated thinkers: Case studies in elementary social studies.* Washington, DC: NCSS.

The book discusses the importance of case studies in elementary social studies and includes model lessons that are aligned with the objectives of the C3 Framework and Common Core Standards.

Kracl, C. (2012). Review or true? Using high-level thinking questions in social studies instruction. *The Social Studies, 103*(2), 57–60.

This article provides a foundation for K–12 teachers to begin the implementation of asking higher-level questions in their classrooms and engaging students in critical thinking activities. Using the work of Benjamin Bloom (1956) and Kagan Publications (1999), actual questions and ideas that can be used before, during, and after readings in the classroom will strengthen the ability of all students to think.

▶ REFERENCES

Bloom, B. (Ed.). (1956). *Taxonomy of educational objectives: The classification of educational goals.* New York: Longmans.

Driscoll, M. P. (2009). *Psychology of learning for instruction* (4th ed.). Needham Heights, MA: Allyn and Bacon.

Kagan Publications. (1999). *Higher-level thinking questions.* San Clemente, CA: Kagan.

NCSS Task Force on Early Childhood/Elementary Social Studies. (2009). *Powerful and purposeful teaching and learning in elementary school social studies.* Available at: www.ncss.org/positions/powerfulandpurposeful.

10

Experiencing Social Studies

▶ LOOKING AHEAD

Teaching aims at "impact." We want to make the learning environment so powerful that students remember what goes on there as well as the information and skills. If students can *experience* social studies, it is more likely to be impactful. Several factors contribute to the impact of teaching, including: (1) the ability and interest of the learner; (2) previous background knowledge and experience; (3) how well particular teaching/learning experiences are understood; (4) the amount of practice or repetition; (5) student perceptions of the importance of learning; (6) the degree to which students feel or do not feel safe, secure, and accepted; and (7) the senses and intelligences involved in the learning experience.

Elementary teachers who think about meaningful learning experiences, the impact of the activities, and the pacing of the school day will more likely do high-impact teaching. If the way that we teach creates excitement, what we teach will be retained. School experiences that are truly educational will intellectually and emotionally involve students, commanding both interest and response. If a lesson does not, it will have little or no positive impact on how students learn, think, and feel about people, places, and events. Utilizing teaching methods such as drama, role play, simulations, field trips, and service learning in the classroom will help teachers foster meaningful learning experiences.

The focus of this chapter is to discuss impactful learning experiences that elementary teachers can utilize. This chapter examines the utilization of drama, role playing, simulations, field trips, and service learning in the elementary classroom. This chapter details how problem solving is a natural and intrinsic element of drama and how dramatic techniques can be a vitalizing and energizing force for elementary social studies. This chapter offers explanations and examples of a wide variety of dramatic techniques. Furthermore, this chapter explores the utilization of field trips and service learning, along with mock trials and simulations.

CAN YOU? DO YOU?

Can you . . .

- Explain how drama is a problem-solving activity?
- Identify reasons for using dramatic activities?
- Describe different forms of mock trials?
- Organize a service learning project?
- Plan an effective and meaningful field trip?

Do you . . .

- Understand the term *dramatic tension*?
- Understand how to use a variety of dramatic techniques in social studies?
- Know the forms of mock trials?
- Know what steps to take to plan a field trip?

FOCUS ACTIVITY

Before reading this chapter, try the following focus activity.

In small groups, generate a list of powerful quotes from the speeches and writings of historic figures. Here are a few examples:

"I have a dream." Martin Luther King, Jr.
"A date which will live in infamy." Franklin Delano Roosevelt
"Ask not what your country can do for you." John F. Kennedy
"Ain't I a woman?" Sojourner Truth
"We hold these truths to be self-evident." Thomas Jefferson
"Four score and seven years ago, our fathers brought forth on this continent a new
    nation, conceived in liberty and dedicated to the proposition that all men are created
    equal." Abraham Lincoln
"Give me your tired, your poor, your huddled masses yearning to breathe free." Emma
    Lazarus

Repeat each quote several times, going around the group with each person trying to express the quote as dramatically and differently as possible. Discuss the meaning of each quote, and the nuances that the different ways of stating the quote add. What does this say about how we learn from dramatic and eloquent figures in history and what we can learn from using drama in teaching? Share responses with others.

▶ THE IMPORTANCE OF DRAMA IN SOCIAL STUDIES

Every lesson in every classroom on every school day should be a dramatic experience. If the teacher does well, the classroom experience is going to be interesting, exciting, and eventful. If the teacher has no flare for the dramatic, then the classroom is likely to be a somewhat lifeless and unexciting place where only routine learning occurs.

Drama is more than putting on a play, more than a category of techniques that teachers can use in elementary social studies. Drama is a way of looking at the entire learning thrust of the classroom. That thrust is the product of the emotional atmosphere, the teaching style and range of the instructor, and the kinds of activities in which students are engaged. When dramatic tension is the focus of the classroom, then there is a positively charged atmosphere that can be felt. This kind of tension is the distinguishing feature in the very best classrooms regardless of the teacher's style. It is an almost visible glow of anticipation on students' faces. It is evidenced in the way students come into the room, in what happens when class is begun, in how small groups and large groups are handled, in the things that contribute to order and management, in the kinds of assignments that are made and how and when they are made, and in when and how oral reading is done.

Positive dramatic tension in the classroom can be created by challenging students with little mysteries and surprises. To create the best kind of suspense, teachers need to see themselves as constant stage setters. The teacher promises a surprise. A mysterious visitor is coming. A kindergarten class, for example, can build excitement for several March days over the strange visits of an invisible leprechaun who leaves activity materials and green tracks (made of construction paper) whenever the class leaves the room. Teachers need to challenge students with provocative questions, problems to solve, and interesting anecdotal stories. What happened to the Roanoke colonists? Was Booth aided in his assassination of Lincoln by Washington insiders? What happened to Amelia Earhart or to Meriwether Lewis? What can be done to preserve the ozone and the rainforests or to reverse global warming? What is being built in the construction site down the street, and how will it change the neighborhood?

Teachers are always performers in the drama of the classroom, but their roles and the ways they play them vary. Some are wonderfully dramatic solo performers, good storytellers, and powerful mood setters. There are others who develop their own dramatic flair best while interacting with their students. Still others star at evoking passion and excitement and curiosity in a class while remaining quietly in the background. Many are talented organizers and catalysts to unleash the impassioned thoughts and feelings of the student. You can be a good teacher without being a ham, but not without enthusiasm and a flair for lighting the flame in others.

Teachers need to be stage managers, providing students with a dramatic vision of history, of culture, and of human relationships. This allows students to experience and to become involved in the conflicts and controversies, the personalities and plottings – in effect, the drama – implicit in the very name *social studies*. They make students aware of the dramatic moments of the past and of the present, the elements of conflict, climax, comedy, and tragedy; plot or story; suspense and resolution; setting, character, and dialogue. As stage managers, teachers can also utilize several dramatic techniques that get students involved, provoke curiosity and give reason for research, develop a sense of event sequence, develop skills of oral and written expression, and develop sensitivity to the feelings and ideas of others. The use of drama as a teaching approach makes social studies come alive. Most importantly, drama can stimulate interest and often give purpose and meaning to the content.

Only when the perspective of drama is understood is a teacher really going to be able to use the spectrum of dramatic techniques purposefully and effectively. Dramatic techniques are almost always involving. In almost every type, a variety of problem-solving opportunities occur. Fortunately for teachers, there are variations of drama that can be done with almost any ability level and require amounts of time varying from a few minutes to weeks. The amount of teacher centeredness and control also varies, and students can be moved slowly from dependence toward independence in planning and carrying out dramatic activities.

▶ DRAMA THROUGH READING

The dramatic power and eloquence of the printed word can be used to create images and suspense when read aloud. The following techniques have been found effective.

Guided Fantasies

Guided fantasies, also called visualizations, are dramas in which even the shy students can participate because no acting is required: only good listening, concentration, and sensory imagination. Students are asked to sit with their eyes closed and to envision as vividly as they can a scene as a reader describes it. If students are expressive readers, they can be involved in this capacity as well as being listeners. This is especially true in the upper elementary grades.

A special kind of listening needs to occur when reading fantasy. The teacher wants students to get the feel of what it is like to be in another time and/or another place. The teacher wants students to be able to envision the scenes, smells, and sounds. What is wanted, in short, is a very imaginative sensory kind of listening, the kind that involves students and makes them want to interact with and know more about what is being described.

The readings need to be fairly short, certainly within the concentration span of students. They need to be very descriptive, sensory, and specifically detailed to the point of being graphic. The scenes that they describe should, of course, be relevant to the curriculum. They should help students envision the settings, the culture, and the sequence of events. You want them to smell the smoke of the battlefield, the stench of the prisons, the perfume of the flowers, and the aromas of the feast spread before the king. You want them to almost hear the royal court, the noises of battle and of the marketplace, and the voices and clatter that fill the city and the streets. In their mind's eye, you want students to see as clearly as they can the panorama and the detail of everything.

The scenes described can be historical or contemporary. The amount of imagery created in the story is an important process in getting students involved. Step out of the story to tell them to breathe in the smells and ask them what they smell. See if they can add detail to the vision. Reread short segments of the description that are particularly strong in the images they create. Pictures and objects and things to touch, hear, and even smell can be examined to add to the intensity of the sensory experience and to increase input into the discussion from students.

Guided fantasies can describe a range of times from the distant past to the events in the news today. Newspaper and internet accounts can be used. Since guided fantasies may be just too stressful and powerful, teachers should be careful what they choose to use with elementary students. For example, you would not want to use the radio account of the destruction of the Hindenburg or the contemporary accounts of the killings at Columbine or the World Trade Center attack. But you could use descriptions of opening events at the Olympics, a World Fair, or description of life in a historic mansion.

As a follow-up activity, the guided fantasy can be reenacted as a pantomime. Through pantomiming the event while the fantasy is read aloud, students can intensify the visualization and express the images they have seen in their minds.

▶ **DRAMATIC EXAMPLE #1**

THE TORNADO

Set-up

Students are seated in a circle or perhaps on the floor so that there is a sense of closeness in the group. At its best, the technique allows the listener to be totally immersed in the images being created and suspend disbelief in their reality.

Teacher

"Close your eyes and let your mind go blank for a minute. Form a picture in your mind. Try to make this picture as clear and as filled with vivid detail as you possibly can. This story is based on accounts of the destructive tornado that swept the Midwest on April 13, 1974."

Story

It has been an uneventful April day in the town of Xenia in central Ohio. It is a quiet kind of old-fashioned town most days. This part of Ohio is fairly flat, and you can see from one end of town to the other. The carhops at the local drive-in root beer stand are taking orders. Along with other girls and boys, you are waiting for a ride in front of the school. The air seems strange, kind of heavy and oppressive, and there is quietness in the air that does not seem normal even by the standards of a Midwestern American town. Though it is not raining, dark clouds are hanging low, and daylight seems to be going early.

Something catches your eye. Off to the southwest, a huge darker cloud has formed and seems to be revolving. In minutes, it is funnel shaped. You have been listening to radio weather, and you know that conditions are dangerous right here in the "tornado alley," so you have no doubt. That cloud is now a tornado! And this one looks like a bad one, headed right into town.

You run back into the school screaming, "Tornado! Twister coming and coming fast!" Looking out the window of the school, you and the other students and teachers can now see with horror a terrible fearsome twisting cloud only a few hundred yards away. Everyone hits the floor in terror as the tornado slams into the building with screaming force. Crashing, banging, and grating sounds fill the air along with the screams of terrified people. It is raining rocks, slabs of concrete, tree limbs, bricks, and great chunks of earth that have been ripped from the ground. Daggers of broken glass twirl through the air everywhere. The huge beams of the school are falling everywhere.

The tornado funnel moves across the town at 40 miles per hour, leaving a trail of destruction and rubble. Wood-frame houses are crushed or swept from their foundations. Huge old trees are torn from the earth and hurled into the air. The air is filled with objects, from furniture to cars and trucks, all now being hurled with monstrous force.

The black twisting tornado hits the rear of a train moving through town. Several train cars are thrown from the tracks across the main street where they crash into the red brick post office, a museum, and a restaurant.

Finally, the destructive tornado passes. Thirty-three people have been left dead and hundreds injured. Over 1,300 buildings have been destroyed. Of course, you do not find this out until later. For now, you can only see the awful damage everywhere. You and the rest are left dazed and unbelieving, but you feel lucky to have survived.

Class Action Dramas

A class action story is one that is read aloud. Students listen for particular words or phrases. When they hear them, they must quickly respond in a prescribed way. You may have done these little stories and called them by a different name or had no name for them at all. What they involve, more than anything else, is listening skills. Students should listen carefully to the story as it is read. The required words and actions usually involve only rudimentary drama, and generally even the shyest student will participate in most roles.

The stories themselves may include stereotypes and may even contain misinformation. The stories may also contain blatant exaggerations. Often the responses are made to look ridiculous. The stories can provoke solid discussion of issues and values.

For some words and phrases, a response may come from a single individual. For others, a group within the class may be asked to respond. In many cases, though, the entire class may be required to react when a key word is read. Scripts can be adapted from historical events or from books and can even be written as class projects. The first job after writing the story and determining the key words and the responses is to assign the roles within the group. It is usually good to rehearse responses before doing the entire story. The story should be read with as much excitement and expression as possible, but the rate must be regulated to allow everyone to see, hear, and participate in the responses. Here is an example based on a familiar version of a series of historical incidents involving the famous Revolutionary War figure Paul Revere.

▶ DRAMATIC EXAMPLE #2

PAUL REVERE'S MANY RIDES: A CLASS ACTION STORY

This example involves whole-class participation. Use the bold prompts to indicate when the class has to perform the relevant action.

When the Reader Says . . .	You Do and Say . . .
English	Shout, "The Regulars are coming!"
Paul Revere or Paul	Pretend to jump on a horse and ride.
Tea	Raise a pretend cup and pretend to drink while saying, "Mm, good!"
Taxes	Shout, "No taxation without representation!"
American(s)	Whistle the first line of "Yankee Doodle."
Horse	Shout, "Get your dogs, cats, and chickens off the road!"
Boston	Shout, "Is that where they invented baked beans?"
Philadelphia	Shout, "Is that where they invented cream cheese?"
Ride, Rode, Riding, or Ridden	Make the sound of a horse: "Neigh, Neigh."
Lexington/Concord	Shout, "BANG! BANG!"

The **English** wanted to tax everything in their **American** colonies, and **Paul Revere** and his friends in **Boston** didn't like it one bit. First, the **English** put a **tax** on everything the **Americans** printed. Then the **English** wanted to **tax tea**, glass, and paper. The **Americans** protested so strongly that the **English** took back all the **taxes**: all, that is, but the **tax** on **tea**. The **Americans** liked their **tea**, but they refused to pay the **English tax**. One night, **Paul Revere** and some other **Americans** dressed up as Indians and boarded three **English tea** ships in **Boston** Harbor. They threw all the **tea** into **Boston** Harbor. Afterwards, **Paul** jumped on his horse and rode to tell other **Americans** in Massachusetts, Connecticut, and **Philadelphia**, Pennsylvania. For the next year, **Paul Revere** kept an eye on the **English** soldiers who were now all over **Boston**. He **rode** his horse from **Boston** to **Philadelphia**, all the time carrying messages about what the **English** were doing. One night, a friend of **Paul Revere's** found out that the **English** soldiers were going to march to the towns of **Lexington and Concord** to capture guns and ammunition that the **Americans** had stored. The **English** also wanted to take two **American** leaders, Samuel Adams and John Hancock. **Paul Revere** and others were sent to warn the **Americans** in **Lexington and Concord**. So, off rode Paul on his **horse**. Before he even got to **Lexington**, he was almost stopped by two **English** officers, but **Paul** got away and woke up Hancock and Adams. **Paul** and two others started out on their **horses**, **riding** toward **Concord**, warning farmers along the way. But the **Americans** were stopped by **English** soldiers, who took their **horses**. **Paul** had to walk back to **Lexington**, where he met the **American** leaders, Adams and Hancock, just getting in their carriage to leave. **Paul rode** out with them but had to walk back to save a trunk full of secret papers that they had left behind. **Paul** walked back to **Lexington** to find it full of **American** farmers armed with muskets. In fact, **Paul** was just carrying the trunk out when the **English** troops arrived, and he heard the sound of gunfire. So **Paul Revere** actually heard what was later called "the shot heard round the world."

Readers' Theater

Readers' theater involves turning a story that is written in narrative form into a play. A group of students read the story and then plan together how to alter it so that it can be read as a play. Young, Chase, and Rasinski (2009) found that the readers' theater enhanced reading fluency and comprehension. A critical benefit and dimension of readers' theater is that it focuses on the drama planning process. Students have to figure out how they can change the way that the story is told. They have to develop a thorough understanding of the characters; a feel for the setting; and a mental map of the purpose, themes, and the plot line or sequence. They literally rewrite the story, putting in dialogue to cover narrative passages. They are made to think about what character would be most likely to relate the information and how it can be fit in as conversation or as monologue. Of course, one of the natural tendencies is to fall back on the device of a narrator, but ideally, the use of this voice should be minimized, if not prohibited.

The focus of dialogue is human interaction. A monologue reveals inner thoughts, dreams, and concerns. Stories that place a lot of emphasis on character, are written in the first person, and/or are already rich in dialogue usually take less adaptation. For social studies content purposes, folk tales, biographical episodes (such as those in the books of Jean Fritz), historical fiction (such as *Nettie Goes South*), and stories that emphasize culture and human relationships (such as *Ming Lo Moves the Mountain* or *Frog and Toad Are Friends*) are most useful.

After the story is planned and usually rewritten, students can try reading through it different ways, running through it several times. This can allow different students to express themselves in the roles and allow rewriting and rethinking different parts of the story.

▶ DRAMATIC READING

There is a wealth of short dramatic material that students can read expressively. This can be funny and/or serious, depending on the material. The trick is finding and/or adapting it. For adaptable material, popular descriptive histories and historical fiction are good sources. Good material can also be found in popular history and geography magazines such as *National Geographic*, *Smithsonian*, *Cobblestone*, and others. It is also productive for students to prepare their own readings as creative writing assignments and creative reporting exercises.

The teacher needs to set it up so that more than one student reads the material aloud. That way, they can begin to envision the range of expressive possibilities. Seven types of readings – brags, cliff-hangers, character monologues, in-role reports, first-person poems, expressive poems about human feelings, and historical poems – are detailed next.

Brags are comic devices. They are humorous partially because boasting is considered inappropriate behavior in mainstream society and partially because of the use of exaggeration that is implicit in all bragging. Most students' social interactions are filled with boasting claims, from the stereotyped "My father is stronger than your father!" to the "dares" that are so common to youth society and on to the name-dropping of adults. Brags involve strength, ability, status, possessions, and relationships. Bragging has become and continues to be an art form in some societies (including that of frontier America).

Written brags make excellent oral reading devices. They invite competition and imitation. They make excellent models for creative writing, and they can incorporate a great deal of knowledge of a culture. Here are two brags, one from a fictitious inventor, the other from a real one. They might be used in a unit on invention and discovery or one dealing with a period of history when invention was a major theme. Have the students read these to see who can read most expressively. Then have them write their own brags.

▶ DRAMATIC EXAMPLE #3

PROFESSOR IMA CHEENIUS

Of course, *I* am the greatest inventor of all time! *My* inventions will one day be household words. Why, *I* have inventions in process right now that will make life easier for everyone, save energy, repair the ozone, cure cancer, get us to other planets, make clothes and shoes and cars that will never wear out, and solve the energy shortage. And here is my little secret – I am inventing an engine that will run entirely on polluted air. Too much for you? Well, try this! I am going to invent instant water to save the world from a water shortage. All you need to do is add water. Can you believe how clever I am? I just don't know what I'll come up with next: maybe chew-less gum or a math pill that helps children get their math homework done twice as quickly! Why, next to me, Edison was a bulb head, Newton was a fig cookie, and Bell was a ding-a-ling. And, just between you and me, I think Franklin flew a few too many kites in the lightning. I am just *so* clever!

▶ DRAMATIC EXAMPLE #4

GEORGE WASHINGTON CARVER BRAG

I am George Washington Carver. I am a modest man, so it is hard for me to brag. I worked my way through high school and was the first Black student ever to attend Simpson College in Iowa. I worked as a janitor there until I got my degree in agricultural science, then went back and got a master's degree. You think it is tough to do now; it was a thousand times tougher for a Black man in the 1800s. But I was a worker and a man who looked – looked closely at things. I once said, "When I talk to the little flower or the little peanut, they will give up their secrets." And they did just that to me, too.

Another thing I said was, "Ninety-nine percent of the failures come from people who are in the habit of making up excuses." And that I never did. In 1897, Booker T. Washington asked me to come to Tuskegee. I was there for 50 years. I invented 325 products from peanuts alone and 228 from sweet potatoes. My inventions would fill a large hall. I created synthetic rubber, synthetic marble, vanishing cream, wood filler, mucilage, rubbing oils, instant coffee, insulating board, linoleum, creosote, bleach – why it would be hard to name something that I could not create a version of. I even taught the Black farmers to rotate their crops and restore the worn-out land.

Now this part you really are not going to believe. Most of my inventions I just gave away. I wanted people to benefit, not to make a lot of money for myself. I told people, "God gave my ideas to me; how can I sell them to somebody else?" In fact, in 1940, I gave my life savings for the establishment of a research foundation at Tuskegee.

But I did get my honors. Simpson College gave me an honorary doctorate in 1928. I became an honorary member of the Royal Society of Arts in London and received the Spingarn Medal from the NAACP. In 1939, President Roosevelt even gave me a medal for saving Southern agriculture.

Cliffhangers are readings in which the central characters are depicted in impossible situations, dire straits from which it may seem impossible that they can ever extract themselves. It is best to design these as problem-solving readings. After they have been read aloud a few times to try alternate expressions, have students try to suggest ways out of these truly solution–defying situations. Generally, the decisions do not involve moral dilemmas so much as insurmountable difficulties. They can really test students' problem-solving abilities. When faced with many impossible problems, one has to look at them individually *and* together, often beginning with the initial task of identifying the least impossible one to solve.

▶ DRAMATIC EXAMPLE #5

THE SEA CAPTAIN EXPLORER

There I am. My ship has run aground in uncharted waters. There is a gaping hole in the hull, and even if it were fixed, there seems to be no way to get this heavy ship back out into the water. Speaking of water, there isn't any, and thirst is a terrible killer at sea. The stores are in short supply, and we've been eating wormy ship's biscuits for a week. The crew, which is made up of the worst cutthroats who ever signed sailing papers, has been grumbling and refusing to take orders. The sailors are beginning to plan a mutiny, and some pretty nasty-looking types are starting to edge toward me with cutlasses and belaying pins in their hands. Out of the jungle-like growth just a few hundred yards away, a large group of hostile natives, wicked-looking spears at the ready, are moving toward the beached ship and me. Out to sea and moving toward us, I can see a fierce seasonal storm, the kind that can pick my poor ship up and break it entirely on the rocks. It is coming fast. The only path of retreat is the sea, which will soon be stormy. But that may not be the worst part. Out on the bay, I can see a half dozen black fins slicing through the water. What am I going to do?

▶ **DRAMATIC EXAMPLE #6**

THE NEW COUNTRY EXPLORER

I am climbing the mountain trail where no Englishman has gone before. The mountains tower all around me, and the only trails are those made by animals. A single misstep along a narrow ledge and I go crashing down through underbrush and scrub trees, hitting every rock as I go. Desperately grabbing at trees and rocks, I try to break my fall, finally sliding to a stop only inches from a 200-foot drop-off. Badly bruised and shaken, I try to struggle to my feet, only to find one leg twisted grotesquely underneath my body. For a moment, there is no feeling at all in the leg. Then the pain hits me with a jolt and, in a cold sweat, I nearly pass out. Just then, I hear a snarling, growling noise. The hair on my neck stands on end as a giant brown and gray grizzly bear rises on its hind legs not more than a hundred feet away. Pitifully, I struggle to drag myself away. Suddenly, there is a whizzing sound, and an arrow thuds, quivering in a tree trunk a few feet away. I look up to see a party of dreaded Blackfeet warriors with bows drawn on the ledge above me. It is at that exact moment that I hear the warning rattle of the rattlesnake at my feet. What am I going to do?

Character monologues are readings that reveal the history, philosophy, or plans of an individual. Shakespeare's plays are filled with them: Caesar, Hamlet, and so on. Browning's poetry as well as the writings of people like Dickens, Poe, and Twain give other examples. Children's books, from Diane Stanley's book on Mozart (2009) to Margie Palatini's version of Aesop's "Fox and the Grapes" (2009) or Fritz's treatment of the Jamestown colony (2010), are excellent sources. In addition, there are many usable primary resource materials, particularly letters, diaries, and newspaper accounts. Generally, first-person writing is best, but individual examples should be judged on their own merits. Whatever the example, it should help students get a feel for the person and his or her cultural context and value system.

In-role reports represent one device that can be used to get students to write their own dramatic reading. In-role reports bring a refreshing change from standard student reports. It has been common practice for decades for students to copy reports directly out of an encyclopedia or some other reference and then read with little comprehension what they have copied. With in-role reports, students take a character role and give the report from the perspective of that character. Characters may be real or created. Students have to pick a point in time for the character and report as if they knew nothing from that point on. For example, someone taking the role of Lincoln on the first of April 1865 would know nothing about the assassination and might even end the report by describing plans to see *Our American Cousin* when it plays at Ford's Theater. The point of these reports is to get into the feelings or perceptions of the characters involved.

First-person poems are one of the most personal forms of writing. Poems express feelings in their most essential form. Poetry is also designed for oral display by its very nature. A number of kinds of poems are excellent material for dramatic and expressive reading. First–person poems are especially useful, especially when their subjects are historical and geographic characters. The poetry of Robert Service (2006) or Walt Whitman, as well as more modern poem renditions, help students get the "feel" of a place and time.

▶ ROLE PLAYS AND OTHER STRUCTURED DRAMA TECHNIQUES

Structured Role Play

Structured role plays are dramatic activities in which character information and a scenario are provided to students. Some device is used so that the teacher controls the sequence of the drama.

▶ DRAMATIC EXAMPLE #7

STRUCTURED ROLE PLAY

Set-Up

Create two groups of six to eight students each, the Roller-Coasters and the Merry-Go-Rounds. Other students can be observers, or activity participation can be doubled if space and control variables are favorable.

Scenario

The Roller-Coasters and the Merry-Go-Rounds live in neighboring villages, but their cultures are very different, and neither group knows much about the other. The Roller-Coasters have decided to invite the Merry-Go-Rounds to a big getting-to-know-you party. The fact that no one in either village speaks the other's language causes some problems, but the invitation is finally sent and understood. There are some differences in culture, however, that may cause the people of the two villages to believe certain things about what one can and cannot do.

Only the Roller-Coasters know the following:

- You honor your people by always letting your guests eat first.
- The most honored people (your guests) are always served apples.
- Your teachers have taught you always to wear something blue.
- You must give a gift to a guest.
- During a meal, it is impolite to talk or stand, but just before and after the meal, everyone shouts, "Yeow!" very loudly several times.

Only the Merry-Go-Rounds know the following:

- It is impolite to start eating before your hosts take a bite.

- Apples are a forbidden and profane food. Any of your people who eat apples are thrown out of the tribe.
- Blue is a sacred color of the sky and sea, to be worn only by the most holy person in the village. When anyone else wears blue, it is a terrible, wicked thing.
- It is rude to take gifts from a host.
- When one is a guest, a good Merry-Go-Round does everything he or she can to please the hosts.
- One is silent before and after meals, but, while eating, a polite guest shouts, "Gooba!" and jumps up and turns around after every bite.

The role-play event involves the party. It can be played two ways: either with the two cultures able to speak to one another or with both ignorant of the other's language. The role play can be suspended at any moment with a "freeze" signal for discussion of questions about the nature or culture or about the culture clash that is occurring. This role play has children discuss the differences in how cultures resolve problems.

Sociodramas

Sociodramas involve acting out the solutions to problems. The major difference between role play and sociodrama is that in sociodrama, you are playing yourself. The essential problem situation begins, "If you were in this situation, what would you do, and what would you say?" Quite often, the problems are essentially of the sort that students encounter, such as someone wanting to copy their homework, seeing someone cheating or stealing, meeting someone new, relating to someone who is very old, getting directions when lost, giving "how to" directions, making a complaint in a store, or going to the principal about an unfair rule. However, students may be projected into a situation in which they are asked how they would act in parent or career situations if they were involved.

Children's Theater

Shotick and Walsko (1997) have described a structured approach they call children's theater, which they use to teach economic concepts. The term may be somewhat confusing since "children's theater" has long been the term to describe scripted dramas of any type done for a juvenile audience, but the idea itself is a useful one. A story is presented to the audience in play form with the audience being asked to interact with the actors, usually answering specific questions as the play develops. It is in some ways like the notion of interactional drama described later in this chapter. Morris (2009, 2001) and Morris and Hickey (2003) described a similar approach involving historical incidents and leading to writing activities for the students themselves.

▶ ART- AND STORY-RELATED DRAMATIC TECHNIQUES

There are any number of techniques that specifically utilize art and literature. They not only develop cultural appreciation and expose students to exceptional examples but also show the relationship of the arts to culture and to history. The following two techniques have been found to be effective.

Picture Pantomimes

Picture pantomimes require prints of paintings showing historical or legendary events or people in action in cultural settings. Students look at the painting and isolate and focus on two or three motions they see that they can do in sequence. They then do these motions and each person's response is discussed, at the same time drawing out the meaning and explanations of the paintings.

Story Play

Story play is a technique in which stories are acted out without pre-written scripts. The story line, at least to begin with, is a familiar one. Students have a solid understanding of "how the story goes." This is either because the story is an extremely familiar one or because the teacher has taken them through the reading or the telling of the story enough times to give them a good sense of who and where in the story the characters are and where the plot line goes. Students then plan how to play the story and then act it out based on their plan. The actual dialogue is improvised as they go. Students can do the story as it is written, experiment with different endings or different twists on the plot, or try putting the story in different contexts (doing parodies such as a modern version of "Cinderella" called "Successerella," based on economic problems, for example).

Usually these story plays are done not for an audience but for the experience of doing them. Students delight in having these videotaped or in doing a radio drama on audiotape. They also can profit from the opportunity these dramas afford for experimenting, redoing the same stories, using different students in the same roles, treating closed-ended stories as though they were open ended, and so on.

One device that can be incorporated into these story plays is story cards. The teacher or students in the planning process create a storyboard of the story. Each story card on the storyboard represents an advancement of the plot, a different scene, or an event in the sequence of the story. For example, the first card from "The Brave Little Tailor" might read, "While working in his shop, the Little Tailor swats at some irritating flies, killing seven of them, and is so proud of his feat that he goes out to seek his fortune." All the story cards are then put in a stack on the chalk ledge and revealed one at a time as the story play is enacted. This gives students a better metacognitive map of the sequence of the story. It keeps the drama moving, and when students are in on the planning of these stories, they learn about sequencing and writing a story. This enables them to develop a sense of the importance of sequence in any chain of events.

Story cards allow students to plan and create new endings as well. Most importantly, they give students an experience in drama that can be the basis of discussion. After students become familiar with using the story cards as a way of developing and pacing the drama, they can use them to develop entirely new story dramatizations. A sixth-grade class created and dramatized the following story using their own story cards, creating various endings each time they played it out.

1. Story Card 1. The expedition was alert for any sign of danger as the horses moved at a slow trot along the dusty trail.
2. Story Card 2. The explorers were looking for a route that would lead them to the Pacific Ocean.
3. Story Card 3. From the dense undergrowth, the captain of the expedition felt hostile eyes watching his small party.

4. Story Card 4. In a small glen, a spring bubbled up out of the rocks, and there the party stopped for a refreshing drink.
5. Story Card 5. The captain felt rather than heard the footsteps on the path behind them and turned to see a large party of armed natives moving toward him.
6. Story Card 6. The small party of explorers was helpless to do anything but follow the natives back through the undergrowth.
7. Story Card 7. The walls of the strange city loomed high in front of the party, catching the explorers by surprise.
8. Story Card 8. Where the explorers had been expecting primitive natives, they found a people who were far advanced in every way.
9. Story Card 9. The explorers were led into the magnificent halls of the king's palace.

▶ REENACTMENT

Reenactment groups across the country work at staging authentic Civil War and Revolutionary War battles. At various historic sites, local preservationists and employees go through the motions of living and working as early settlers as a part of the attempt to show visitors what life was like. Various plays and other performance pieces are staged at various times by theater groups. When teachers have students participate in any form of reenactment, they find that students can become very motivated to do the needed research. That purposeful research aimed at doing an authentic and accurate job in a reenactment role can be an invaluable experience.

The general guidelines for any reenactment begin with the selection of some event that will put students in touch with the historical and cultural world heritage. The event should be one that students can reproduce with some faithfulness to history, but it should also be one with an internal sequence that is simple enough for students to follow. Another consideration also might be that the event should be one that they can reenact without doing any violence to one another. (Battle scenes, so popular with reenactment hobbyists, are almost always excluded by this consideration.) The event should be one in which the sequence of actions by participants can be researched and reproduced.

Among the events that reenact well with young students are ceremonies and cultural rituals (greetings of two people, home entry rituals, tea ceremonies, a military group from a period setting up a camp, etc.), historic document development, exchanges and land sales (the Louisiana Purchase, the Purchase of Manhattan, etc.), and parades and celebrations (women march for the vote, labor movement picket lines, etc.). Once the event is selected, students need to do basic research, identify the sequence of events, and then plan how they are going to replay the event. If possible, go through the reenactment in the early stages of the research and then again after the research is complete. It gives the teacher and the students a better sense of what they know to begin with and what they have learned. It also gives some ideas about the kinds of questions that need to be answered in the research. During the planning period, the teacher needs to help discuss the meaning of what they are doing as well as the things that they cannot accurately or fully portray.

▶ INTERACTIONAL DRAMA

Interactional drama involves an outsider or outsiders playing out a scenario from a historical context in front of students. The actors, usually in costume, play in such a

Table 10.1 Types of Interactional Drama

Type	Description
Interview	The visitor introduces him- or herself and then answers questions. The actor really should have a good background on the character to do this, and students will do better if prepared so that they can ask better questions.
Storytelling	The visitor, in character, tells stories about his or her life.
Eavesdropping	The visitors have a conversation staged so that students seem to be overhearing something they were not meant to hear. There may be a "freeze" signal that causes the actors to seem to become statues while the teacher and the students talk about what has been said.
Recruitment	Different actors, taking different sides, try to get students to side with them.
Confrontation	The actors are set up to have a conflict. One of the characters wins the sympathy of students and gets them to help defend him or her against the adversary.

way that they draw students into the dialogue, either by asking direct questions or asking students about what they think (in such a way that they solicit both opinions and viewpoints). The dramas are not scripted and are usually open ended, leaving students to solve the problems and conflicts the actor(s) brought.

Though interactional drama usually involves no role taking by students, the success of the technique depends on suspended disbelief: the ability of students to think and act as though what is happening is real, instead of just pretend. Suspended disbelief is what enables anyone to enjoy a play, a movie, or a television program, thinking of the characters as real people instead of as actors playing people. To make this happen in interactional drama, older classes especially may need to be coached beforehand. Convincing actors who stay in character and know their material are essential. It may be helpful but not essential to use actors who are not recognized by the class.

It may be best if the historical persons who visit the classroom for these dramas are not famous figures. In general, famous characters are more difficult for students to believe, especially if they already have an image of how the person looks. Ordinary people or less well-known historical personages are easier to impersonate. See Table 10.1 for several types of interactional drama that visitors can utilize.

The following sample scenarios indicate various types of interactional dramas.

SCENARIO ONE

It is September 1776. Two revolutionary figures enter, arguing. One says that Washington's situation is so hopeless that he ought to retreat from Long Island, burning New York City behind him so the British cannot quarter there for the winter. The other argues that this is too drastic because it would destroy a lot of American property and leave many people homeless. The other replies that two-thirds of the property in New York belongs to Tories anyhow. Both try to recruit students to their side.

SCENARIO TWO

Two people dressed in turn-of-the-century garb enter, arguing. One thinks that women should be given the right to vote. The other is convinced that this is the wrong thing to do. The two (ideally both are women) try to recruit students to their view, limiting themselves to arguments of the period.

SCENARIO THREE

A young man (or woman) dressed in ancient garb sneaks into the room looking frightened and wary. He claims that he is a Roman slave and that his master was killed in his home during the night. Because the murderer cannot be identified, Roman law says that all the slaves of the household can be jailed. He asks students to hide him. After he hides, a burly Roman enters looking for the runaway slave. He tries to get students to reveal the hiding place. When the young man is found, the teacher convinces the Roman officer that they should debate the law right there in the classroom before he is allowed to take the young man away. It is admitted in the debate that the circumstances of the death indicate that a much stronger man than this youth and probably an assassin from outside the house committed the crime.

▶ DRAMA UNITS

Entire units can have a dramatic focus. One approach is what Fulwer and McGuire (1997) call "Storypath." It utilizes a story line as the effective organizer for a study. A story scenario is the point of departure, with students creating roles for themselves consistent with that scenario. Discussion and artwork allow students to elaborate on the scenario. As events unfold in the scenario, students construct meaning for themselves. As stakeholders in the story line, they have both character sympathy and a real need to solve the problems in the evolving plot line. Social interactions and involvement are natural. The technique is highly adaptable and may be used to create "neighborhoods" for stories set in any culture or period. One of the advantages of Storypath is that it can be used with primary age students, and McGuire has published multiple units (Cole & McGuire, 2011; McGuire, 2005) that elementary teachers will find useful.

▶ STORYTELLING IN SOCIAL STUDIES

Storytelling is experiencing a worldwide revival. Throughout human history, storytellers have passed on the culture, created and preserved heroes, and passed on the history. Storytellers were often both the best historians and the foremost entertainers of bygone times.

Storytelling is included as a dramatic technique not because professional storytellers are consummate actors, but because every good teacher is something of a storyteller. Story makes the past come alive and humanizes other people, no matter how different their culture or the geography of where they live.

Both elementary teachers and students learn and benefit from becoming better storytellers. Telling a story to an appreciative audience is extremely satisfying. More importantly, a story provides a context in which information is given meaning and may be remembered. There are only three steps in becoming a storyteller: learning to choose a story that is worth telling and fits your purposes, learning how to learn a story, and learning how to tell a story (Turner, 1994). Choosing a story may be as easy as contacting the school librarian. Simply find a story that you like; that teaches something important; that is simple, suspenseful, exciting, and/or funny. Learning a story comes more easily once you learn how to "map" it out into a sequence of incidents and master a style of practice that fits you. Four suggestions for effective storytelling are listed here:

1. Know your story so well that you do not have to concentrate your attention on what comes next: in fact, so well that you can change it and add material to it. If you do forget something, do not "double back." Either add what you lost later, make up stuff to cover, or forget it all.
2. Work on expression, putting a lot of emotion and change in your voice.
3. Involve your audience by asking questions in the story, getting them to do stuff, pretending that each one is a character, etc.
4. Keep the story simple and direct and human.

▶ PROCESS DRAMA IN SOCIAL STUDIES

Process drama is an approach to drama that involves students deeply in the content that they are studying (Rosler, 2008; Baldwin & Waters, 2010). According to Baldwin (Baldwin & Waters, 2010), this approach has several key tools, including improvisation; teachers taking roles; meetings in which students talk about and plan the course of the dramatic action; thought tracking, in which individuals in character are asked to talk about their private thoughts about events; collective role play, in which multiple students play the same role simultaneously; and hot seating, in which students question the teacher, in character, about his or her role. The teacher's role is to guide the drama, stepping in and out of character as necessary, providing encouragement and motivation to students, who are treated as experts. Narration and storytelling are used with the speaker directly addressing the audience (Hillyard, 2011). Process drama is rich in empathy and purposeful problem solving (Rijinbout, 2003). The following scenarios are examples that can be used with the conventions of process drama:

• The class is told about the terrible conditions under which colonial prisoners of war are held by the British during the American Revolution. They are on a rotting decommissioned ship in leg irons and on short rations of mealy, spoiled gruel. They are treated with cruelty and threatened with hanging.
• The town is meeting to set up a volunteer fire department. The effort needs funding for equipment, vehicles, and training. Where do they get the money, and how will they stop the growing number of fires in the meantime?
• The settlers in the new settlement are having trouble. Some of the people are lazy and do not want to work. Others are doing jobs that do not need to be done.
• One of the students in the class has lost his puppy. Everyone wants to help him find the young dog.

▶ EFFECTIVE USE OF DRAMA IN SOCIAL STUDIES

Drama in elementary social studies can produce the kind of memorable Camelot moments that students will carry with them throughout their lives. It can help develop the research drive in lifetime students and make research purposeful and important to even marginal ones. It can make the classroom an exciting place to be and can help students remember historical and cultural concepts and facts that they would otherwise forget. It can teach about social interactions and develop self-concepts in a way that traditional "lecture, read, and recite" social studies can never do. However, dramatic activities used without instructional purposefulness can be a waste of time. In fact, drama can even become disturbing. The difference lies in the way the teacher handles drama.

If drama is to be effective in elementary social studies, the teacher has to first feel comfortable with it. He or she must be attracted to dramatic techniques and feel very positive about the potential to make the entire classroom a more exciting and interesting place. Teachers should avoid using techniques that make them feel uncomfortable or as if they are losing control of the classroom. Dramatic techniques require high student involvement and sometimes include student planning and student leading in different directions. Teachers also need to feel that what they are doing with drama is solid and purposeful (McCaslin, 2006). Drama cannot be used as a mere time filler or entertainment. It must have curricular importance and value, and the teacher has to effectively communicate that to students, parents, and administrators.

Drama requires preparation. If there is a first rule of effective use of drama in the classroom, it is, "Be prepared!" The teacher has to know what he or she is about, find the right material, plan and structure the dramatic activity, and lead the students through planning and rehearsal and up to the dramatic enactment moment. The plan and the material cannot be developed along the way. The teacher who shoots from the hip with drama is likely to fall flat or, worse, waste a lot of valuable learning time.

Drama only works in a positive, accepting atmosphere. That atmosphere is one that is open and experimental and charged with exciting stimuli. It also offers emotional security so that students feel safe psychologically. To take the kind of personal risks that drama demands, students should be sure that peers will not be ridiculing or demeaning them for their efforts. No student wants to appear to be foolish or ridiculous. Paradoxically, some students will act silly on purpose to avoid looking silly while trying to be serious. The safe, conducive atmosphere for drama comes only with a series of positive experiences in which the teacher slowly edges the class toward dramatic expression that involves more risk taking.

▶ SIMULATION GAMES

Perhaps the most familiar of social studies dramatic techniques is simulation gaming. Simulation games have become part of the culture. Fantasy simulations are played out recreationally by young people worldwide, and there are many well-known computer games (e.g., SimCity) that are simulations. Many popular board games, including the perennial favorite Monopoly, have elements of simulation gaming in them.

Essentially, simulation games are structured decision-making activities in which students assume roles and then solve problems. Participants are given problem scenarios and additional information related to the problem and their roles. Their job is to come to the decision points in the simulation game and then make the best choice among the options available. Decisions and actions of students participating are limited by sets of restrictive rules. These rules make simulations more patterned than other role-play activities. The decisions often result in consequences and, often, at least some chance is involved in those consequences. The problem scenario itself, which serves as the beginning point, may be based on some very current or historical situation or on a hypothetical one.

Like any school activity, simulation games should be more than just for fun. Both the choice of simulation games and the way that the activities are conducted are critical. There are several important considerations in choosing and playing such simulation games at any level. Perhaps the most critical of these is that the simulation should serve an important curricular purpose. Simply put, when students participate in simulations, they should be learning social studies content and skills. The simulation should help them understand the concept and/or topic better. Once that is the prime consideration, other concerns follow logically. Students need to be aware of and understand what they are doing. The game should be one that students truly enjoy, and they will immerse themselves in the issues and the content. The best simulations provoke questions, reading, and research. These considerations should make elementary teachers aware that how the teacher sets up the simulation and follows through after the dramatic playing is complete are critical to using simulation activities effectively. These are often referred to as briefing and debriefing, and few simulations have much meaning or learning value without them.

At the elementary level, simulation games need to be relatively simple. The amount of reading required to play the game is a factor that needs to be controlled to fit the abilities of the group of students. It is usually advantageous to use simulations that can be played in one day (from about ten minutes in the early grades to just under an hour in upper elementary and middle school), depending on the attention span and involvement level of the students. This reduces the possibility of students continuing the game in unsupervised settings. Another factor that the teacher may want to consider is the ability of students to work independently. Several different simulations are presented next. Each is a model that can be duplicated with similar information for many different units.

▶ SIMULATION EXAMPLE #1

THE PRESIDENT'S CABINET

Type of Simulation: A Real Information Simulation

Mr. President, Whom Will You Choose?

The president's Cabinet helps in the decision making and directs the day-to-day operations of the executive branch of the government. While the first president had only five members in his Cabinet, more recent presidents have had far larger Cabinets. The following is a list of some of the various Cabinet offices held over the years. Which five of these do you think Washington would have had in his first Cabinet?

State	Commerce	Housing and Urban Development
Labor	Defense	Transportation
Energy	Justice	Attorney General
Education	War	Health and Human Services
Interior	Treasury	Health, Education, and Welfare
Navy	Agriculture	Postmaster General

President George Washington had the same problem as every other president when it came to selecting the people to help him take on the job of chief executive: Whom should he ask to serve on his cabinet, and in what jobs should he place them? Because his Cabinet had only five members, the choices, even among the people Washington had known and worked with, were many. Washington's Cabinet offices and brief descriptions of people who might have been considered are detailed in the potential Cabinet members section.

Mr. President, Choose Who Will Serve!

Pretend that you are George Washington and make your choices and placements for your Cabinet. Before you begin, you will need to answer one question: In choosing a Cabinet, Mr. President, which factors do you think are more important? To help you answer this question, nine of the factors Washington might have considered are identified on the following list. Rank order the factors (plus one factor of your own) to get your mind set for making your final selections among the ten finalists for your Cabinet:

- Represent all regions of the country on the Cabinet.
- Choose the people who are best qualified for the jobs.
- Represent the small states as well as the large states.
- Select friends who are loyal and true to you.
- Favor people who have great political influence.
- Have people with the most experience in government.
- Reward those who gave outstanding military service.
- Have people who have opinions and views like your own.
- Include people who have outstanding accomplishments.
- Other _____.

Actual Offices of Washington's Cabinet

State

Treasury

Attorney General

War

Postmaster General

Potential Cabinet Members

The teacher may want to assign each of the people under consideration as roles to students and let them try to make a case for themselves for a Cabinet post.

1. Boston bookseller; forced to flee Boston in disguise in 1774; Revolutionary War general; served as an artillery officer with Washington's army; developed a reputation for being able to move equipment and supplies quickly; known as sound, solid, and dependable.
2. Revolutionary War general; served with distinction and bravery; considered a strong, brilliant leader in battle whom men would die for; fought guerilla-type warfare from the swamps of his native state for a considerable period of time while the British were in control of the area.
3. Strong-minded, clear-speaking champion of individual rights; opposed to a central government that is too strong; extensive experience in dealing with other nations; took a leadership role in Congress during the Revolution.
4. Supporter of a strong national government and a strong executive branch (may even want a king rather than a president); Revolutionary War officer of Washington's personal staff and strong supporter of Washington; good organizer and thorough planner; wants to establish a national bank and be sure that the new nation has a strong economic base.
5. Supporter of strong central government; Southerner from a powerful state; lawyer by occupation; took a leadership role in the approval of the U.S. Constitution; keen observer and careful record keeper.

6. Elder statesman with ambassadorial experience; had a strong role in both the Declaration of Independence and the U.S. Constitution; extremely well liked; inventive and scientifically curious; writes extremely well and has many publications.
7. Outspoken critic of the U.S. Constitution and defender of states' rights; spirited public speaker whose words caused many to support the Revolution; experienced as a state governor and a long-time member of a state legislature; has a real vision for the future.
8. Lawyer from a powerful Northern state; took a key role in the effort to gain separation from Britain and helped in the writing of the Declaration of Independence; considered uncompromising, unyielding, but a man of principle; advocate of a strong central government.
9. Boston merchant; Harvard graduate; served in the Revolution, first as a captain and later as a colonel; strong supporter of the U.S. Constitution; first Commissioner of the U.S. Treasury, 1785–1789.
10. Virginia lawyer; aide-de-camp to Washington; governor of Virginia; member of Congress; attended Constitutional Convention but refused to sign; urged the ratification of the Constitution on the grounds that the union was necessary.

Students may want to compare their choices to Washington's and know the names of the people who were candidates. This is one case in which it is not as important that their choices line up with the first president's. (The numbers identify which of the descriptions correlate to the historical names.)

Actual Selections (First Term)

State	Thomas Jefferson (3)
Treasury	Alexander Hamilton (4)
War	Henry Knox (1)
Attorney General	Edmund Randolph (10)
Postmaster General	Samuel Osgood (9)

Not Chosen by Washington

Francis Marion (2)
James Madison (5)
Benjamin Franklin (6)
Patrick Henry (7)
John Adams (8)

▶ **SIMULATION EXAMPLE #2**

WHO WILL GO WITH THE KING'S ENVOY?

Type of Simulation: A Real and Hypothetical Information Simulation With One Decision

The people do not have to be real for simulations, and the situations can be more general.

It is the fourteenth century. The English king is sending you as his envoy to the court of the king of France. You are to pick a party of five to go with you on the journey and to work with you at that court. Although there is currently peace between your country and France, it is an uneasy peace. There has been a series of wars spanning over half a century. Even recently, the two nations have been tottering on the brink of war. Your job is to make sure the peace continues so the king can fight wars in Scotland and Wales. You obviously want to pick the five people who can best help you. As ambassador, your task will be to keep things smoothed over, avoiding war if that is possible. You also are to find out as much about what France is planning as you can.

Sir William of Dobret speaks French fluently and has spent some time at the French court. He is a capable knight of 35 who rides well, has a reputation as a swordsman, and has battle experience. He is from a noble family of French descent and knows the people and the geography of the area well. He has never been disloyal to the king, but his loyalty has not really been put to the test, and there is a widely held belief that he is more French than English.

Rowan of Logansby is a trusted friend and a seasoned fighter of unquestioned loyalty. He is a free man and a commoner, but his family has served your own for four generations. At 29, he is the best man with a longbow you have ever seen. He speaks a little French and has a good ear. Unusual for one of his class, he reads and writes. He is a blunt-speaking, hot-tempered Englishman through and through.

Bertrand Dorsett is a clerk in the king's court. He is a source of knowledge about everyone and everything. He makes it his business to know. A young man in his early 20s, he is very ambitious, but he is loyal to none but himself. As a clerk, he has mastered both Latin and French, and he speaks, reads, and writes fluently. He is an intriguer who will learn all the ins and outs of the French court. He is very anxious for advancement.

The Count of Edwingham is an experienced diplomat of 50 who is somewhat resentful of you because he feels that he should have been selected as the ambassador. He is an old campaigner, still fit for battle. He has served in the French court in the past and knows many influential members of the French nobility. He speaks the language well and is totally loyal to your king.

Sir Geoffrey of Couran is not the type to love battle, loving the life at court and especially gifted as a minstrel. In his early 30s, he has managed to avoid serving in most of the constant wars. He has the ability to charm men and women alike, and he is especially adept at smoothing ruffled feathers and calming those who are angry. The king is particularly fond of him because of his wit, his charm, and his ability to sing and play the lute. Since he sings and speaks French as well as English, his skill as a minstrel will make him popular at the French court.

John Fitzhugh has been very helpful to the English king in identifying plots against the crown and helping identify agents of other kings. He is second to none in his skill at espionage, having a devious mind himself. He is a secretive, careful, and very thorough kind of man who likes to work behind the scenes. He can speak French with a variety of dialects and pass as a native. He is also a master of disguise. It is said that his father was a French knight and his mother the young widow of an English merchant.

Henry of Selfield is one of the most successful merchants in England. His ships have been trading at important ports in Europe for 20 years. He is neither a soldier nor a courtier and is not a member of the nobility, but he speaks several languages, including French, and knows the importance of commerce to the future of England. He has been of great help to the king in financing some of his military campaigns.

Lady Jane Selridge is a cousin of the queen and highly thought of in the English court. She is witty, charming, an excellent hostess, and speaks flawless French. She knows all the intrigues of most of the royal courts of Europe and would offer the added advantage of having access to the talk of the ladies of the court.

▶ **SIMULATION EXAMPLE #3**

WHAT DO WE NEED IN OUR NEIGHBORHOOD?

Type of Simulation: A Speculative Information Simulation With Many Decisions

Pretend that you are planning a new neighborhood with a shopping center. There is room for only ten businesses in the shopping center, but there are spots for four other businesses at other locations in the neighborhood. It is important to know that you and your family, as well as other people in the neighborhood, may have to travel a long way to get those services and goods not offered in your community. So be very careful as you choose the 14 different types of goods and services you want. You also want to take care as to where the businesses are located within the community. Be very thoughtful as you place them on the map so that each business is at exactly the right spot. Here is a list of potential businesses:

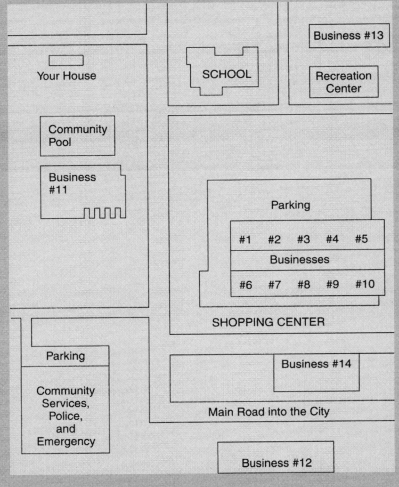

Figure 10.1 What Do We Need in the Neighborhood?

Auto Supply Store	Bakery	Bank
Barber Shop	Beauty Salon	Bicycle Shop
Bookstore	Bowling Alley	Candy Store
China Shop	Clothing Store	Convenience Store
Craft Store	Delicatessen	Department Store
Dentist	Doctor's Office	Drug Store
Dry Cleaner	Eye Doctor	Fabric and Sewing Store
Fast-Food Restaurant	Flower Shop	Furniture Store
Garden Supply Store	Grocery Store	Hardware Store and Plant Nursery
Hospital	Ice Cream Store	Jewelry Store
Laundry	Library	Miniature Golf
Music Store	Pet Store	Post Office
Produce Market	Restaurant	Service Station
Shoe Store	Skating Rink	Souvenir Shop
Toy Store	Variety Store	Veterinarian
Video Store	Video Game Arcade	Zoo

▶ **SIMULATION EXAMPLE #4**

ESTABLISHING A COLONY

Type of Simulation: An In-Basket Simulation

In-basket simulation games are prioritizing activities. They are based on the notion that, quite often, life choices require us to decide what we must do first and what can be put off or done later. In-basket games begin with a list of activities or jobs that a single individual must do. The central question is, "In what order should these jobs be done?"

You are the leader of a group of colonists who have come to the New World during the seventeenth century. You have sighted the coast and sailed along it for several days, finally dropping anchor in a quiet cove. There is a likely area for a colony just ashore, and a small river flows into the sea here. The area does not appear to have any permanent settlements, but you have seen natives peering at your ship from shore. You have no idea whether they are friendly or hostile.

You do not own your ship but have hired it, along with the services of its crusty old sea captain, who wants to hurry you off his ship so that he can return home to take on other cargos. A number of tasks face you. The following is a list of some of them:

- Send scouting parties to explore the surrounding area to be sure that the best possible site for a colony was chosen.
- Find fresh water to replenish the ship's stores.
- Send a group to try to meet with the natives who have been seen looking out from the shore.
- Hold a meeting of all the colonists to decide on the rules of government for the new colony.
- Land all passengers from the ship.
- Pay the captain what is still owed him for the voyage.

- Draft a letter to the patrons of the colony telling of your safe arrival and suggesting what you will do now.
- Determine your exact location and how far your colony is from other New World colonies.
- Build a stockade for defense.
- Start building shelters for the colonists.
- Plant crops.
- Send out a hunting party to find fresh meat.
- Unload all supplies.
- Plant the flag of your country on the shore, claiming the land for your sovereign.
- Hold a Thanksgiving celebration.

▶ **SIMULATION EXAMPLE #5**

NUCLEAR WASTE DISPOSAL

Type of Simulation: A Single-Choice Decision Simulation Based on Vested Interest

Set-Up

For this game, you will need a large map of the United States and one of the world. The scenario is that there is a need to dispose of certain waste products from nuclear reactors and other sources. These waste products are radioactive. Students are divided into five groups, one representing the Congressional committee that will be making the recommendation and the others representing various potential sites. The Congressional committee and the four area groups meet as groups first to plan strategy. Then the Congressional committee listens and asks questions while each group makes its case indicating why its area should not be chosen. Then the groups all meet separately again, the Congressional committee to make its final decision and the area groups to come up with a contingency plan in case their area is the one chosen. This plan may include a set of safety recommendations, recommendations regarding specific site priorities, and some recommendations about how the amount of nuclear waste might be controlled (recycled, etc.).

Group 1: Congressional Committee

The committee is made up of seven members of Congress, one from each of the regions being considered and three from unspecified other areas of the country. A chairperson and a secretary are appointed. The chairperson should be an uncommitted individual. It is the job of the chairperson to keep the hearings flowing smoothly and to present the final recommendations of the Congressional committee. The four options that the committee is considering are the following:

1. Burial of the waste in sealed containers in a Southwestern state that has a small population.
2. Burial of the waste in sealed containers in a Southeastern state relatively close to the majority of the facilities producing the waste. There is, of course, danger of spills and contamination whenever radioactive materials are moved.

3. Disposal of the nuclear waste by putting it in sealed waterproof containers that are then taken out to sea and placed on the ocean floor in a specified site, away from major shipping lanes or ocean currents.
4. Disposal in airtight sealed containers at a specific site in a mountainous area in a Northwestern state with a low population.

Group 2: Representatives of a Southwestern State

They feel that their state does not get much, if any, benefit from the plants producing the nuclear waste. Neither does it profit from the products, which are largely military in nature. This state is one of the few areas of the country where pollution has not yet become a problem, and they wish it to remain that way. They also point out that their state has many Native Americans in it and that putting the waste disposal site there would be yet another blow of oppression and discrimination against that population.

Group 3: Representatives of a Southeastern State

Their state has a potential high population growth as part of the Sunbelt. They feel that, as a producer of nuclear products for the nation, their population is already exposed to enough danger. They also know that their population density already far exceeds that of the two Western states.

Group 4: Representatives of a Coastal State

There is great fear in this state that no containers can be designed that can withstand the sea over time. If the waste is disposed of in this manner, it is believed that eventually leakages and seepage will bring about further damage to coastal plant and animal life and pollute the coasts themselves. This area already has one of the biggest pollution problems in the nation.

Group 5: Representatives of a Low-Population Northwestern State

The severe weather of the mountainous region and the difficulty of burying anything in the rocky area make the container problem a serious one. Falling rocks or cold weather could damage a container very quickly. and a nuclear leak problem would then exist. This is a nearly pollution-free area, and the population is very independent and wishes to stay that way. They also feel that the creation of this waste is not their problem and that the people who benefit from the nuclear energy produced should be the people who have the waste product disposal site.

▶ ## MOCK TRIALS

The activity of the courtroom offers many possibilities for drama. Because the justice system is so integrally important to understanding democracy and the democratic process, various kinds of dramatic activities can be built around the legal process. This can be useful in helping students understand the constitution and the legal system as well as the various conflicts and controversies that have been and continue to be important issues. Understanding the legal system seems nearly as important as understanding the democratic process itself and developing the knowledge and attitudes needed to participate. Most people will be involved in the legal system several times in their lives, and the more students learn about the law and the courts and how they operate, the better prepared they will be to deal with these legal encounters throughout life.

By far the most used dramatic activity related to the legal process is the mock trial. Mock trials enable students to reexamine history and to look at questions of right and wrong as they relate to the law and the legal system. Mock trials can take numerous forms and be developed with varying degrees of thoroughness and detail, depending on such factors as the teaching purpose, the ability level of students, and the time available. Nine forms of mock trials are detailed next.

1. *Re-creation of real trials from the past*: An attempt to reenact the trial as it took place. The more thorough the research and the more preparation done, the more completely this can be accomplished. Because of the court record-keeping system, almost exact reenactments are even possible if desired. With elementary students, giving the broad picture of what happened is likely to be more comprehensible.

2. *Staging trials from the past with open verdicts*: This type of mock trial is like the first in all but one respect: the verdict can be changed. In fact, we want to see if a jury of students is going to come to the same decision that was reached at the original trial. When comparisons are made, the question is always going to be why the verdict was the same or different.

3. *Hypothetical trials of historical and contemporary figures who have never stood trial*: With this type of trial, the students' sense of justice and fairness and even their natural curiosity are served, as well as their biases. Trials of historical characters like Oswald, Hitler, and Custer have been the subject of speculative movies and novels. The question is, what kind of evidence and testimony might have been given if the figure had gone to trial? Figures from centuries ago, such as Attila the Hun, Brutus, King John of England, Jack the Ripper, or Ivan the Terrible might be tried. More recent figures, such as Richard Nixon or Harry Truman (the atom bomb) also give insight.

4. *Creating cases to retest a landmark decision of the Supreme Court*: The emphasis is on discussing the issues and the circumstances of the original case and then attempting through discussion to come up with a parallel case that might cause the Supreme Court to offer a modern opinion.

5. *Trials related to current controversies and issues*: The cases come right out of the newspapers and news broadcasts, and relatives and friends have information and opinions. The issues of current events become relevant and important to young learners as they try to make their own case.

6. *Reenactment of trials suggested in fictional books*: Trials are a popular subject in fiction. Having students develop the detail to enact one of these trials can help comprehension and test their creativity.

7. *Fantasy trials of story and book characters*: Moral themes are almost universal in children's fiction. Putting a fairy tale character like Jack or the wolf on trial can be a delightful learning experience. The advantage is that students are very familiar with the story line and the characters. The trial gives them a new perspective on the events of the story.

8. *Creation of a new crime scenario and then staging the trial*: This is a creative experience in which students create a crime, a victim, witnesses, clues, and an accused

perpetrator of the crime. The teacher can exercise some control with a discussion in which specifications regarding the nature of the crime are carefully drawn.

9. *Development of a classroom court to try discipline offenders*: Several systems, ranging from very simple to very elaborate, may be used to put members of the class on trial for breaking the classroom rules. The major benefit of the exercise is that students develop clearer, more meaningful ideas about such issues as reasonable doubt, the relationship of punishment to crime, and punishment as a deterrent to crime. The technique has been used successfully by teachers as part of their classroom management plan.

Trial-Related Activities

There are various activities that can help students learn about the legal system. Role playing a crime with various witnesses giving independent accounts of what they saw can teach students that people see and remember events differently. Visits to law school mock trials or to one of the mock trial competitive programs put on at the high school or visiting a courtroom can be a real learning experience if carefully planned. Classroom visits by attorneys, judges, and police officers are also profitable if such guests can relate to students. Students can examine laws and go through the process of debate and enactment of a law. They can also go through structured writing exercises to write trial briefs.

▶ FIELD TRIPS

Many of us have participated in a variety of field trips throughout our educational experiences. The experiences and information learned during these adventures often have a meaningful and lasting impact on us (Kenna & Russell, 2015a). A field trip is an experiential activity that "consists of grasping an experience and then transforming it into an application or result" (Behrendt & Franklin, 2014, p. 236).

Whether you went to a local history museum for the day or on an overnight field trip to Washington, DC, the experience was unique and often impactful. (See Table 10.2 for a list of field trip ideas.) Despite these memorable adventures, many educators tend to focus on field trips as rare learning experiences that are expensive and difficult to plan. These issues are compounded in many contemporary schools, where increased pressures to improve standardized test scores and teacher accountability measures have made both teachers and administrators more cautious about spending instructional time outside the classroom (Kenna & Russell, 2015b). Now more than ever, teachers must

Table 10.2 Possible Field Trip Ideas

Airport	Courthouse	Library
Aquarium	Farm	Memorial
Archeological dig	Fire Station	Monument
Art Gallery	Harbor or Port	Museum
Battlefield	Health Clinic	Police Station
College or University	Historical Site	Post Office
Congressional Session	Hospital	State or National Park

purposefully and thoughtfully plan field trips that are engaging and fun but still align with instructional objectives and state standards. Despite these challenges, we maintain that field trips can be powerful and wonderful learning experiences for students, and elementary teachers should spend the time necessary to plan learning experiences outside the classroom setting. While types and scale of field trips certainly vary in terms of cost and planning (visiting a local history museum is quite different than an overnight trip to Washington, DC), the important thing for teachers to remember is that the purpose of the field trip is student learning, and they should align it to local, state, or national standards.

As with any effective lesson, a successful field trips starts with a detailed plan. Teachers should adhere to Russell's guide when conducting an effective field trip.

RUSSELL'S GUIDE TO PLANNING AND IMPLEMENTING A FIELD TRIP

Step 1: Instructional Planning

You need to have a clear plan. Establish the purpose and goals of the field trip. The following questions will help you get started.

a. Where are you going?
b. What is the purpose of the trip?
c. What are your instructional goals?
d. What subjects are you teaching?
e. What standards are you meeting?
f. Is this the best way to allow students to meet the standards?
g. Are other teachers participating in the field trip?

Step 2: Organizing the Trip

Once you have the instructional component down, you will need to organize the field trip. You will need to do the following:

a. Schedule with site, museum, or location and obtain costs.
b. Plan transportation to and from the location and obtain costs.
c. How many chaperones will you need? What is the cost for chaperones?
d. Plan for all meals, beverages, restroom breaks, and first aid emergencies.

> **FYI:** Will students buy lunch or bring lunch? What about students on free/reduced cost lunch? You will need to talk with the lunchroom staff. Will meals other than lunch be needed? What about snacks? What about drinks? You have a lot to organize and plan.

a. Develop a backup plan. If you plan to eat lunch outside but it rains, you need to have a plan.
b. Outline a detailed itinerary, accounting for all educational time.
c. Outline a detailed budget of the field trip costs, along with how the trip will be funded (e.g., each student pays six dollars).

Step 3: Obtain Administration Permission

Once you have planned and organized the trip, you will need to submit a proposal to your administration for written permission. A typical proposal should include a detailed rationale for the field trip. It should include curriculum standards and academic goals. It should also include a detailed itinerary outlining a minute-by-minute schedule. Plus, you need to have a detailed budget of the field trip and how it will be funded if approved.

> **FYI:** Every school/district has its own procedures and policies regarding field trips. We recommend talking with your administration about their specific protocol.

Step 4: Obtain Parent/Guardian Permission

Once you have approval from your administration, you are ready to obtain parent/guardian permission. Do not wait until the day/week before the field trip. Start early! Typically, parent/guardian permission will come in the form of a permission slip. Send home a letter to parents explaining the field trip and its value. Include your instructional goals, the purpose of the trip, and the standards you will be meeting. Also include the cost, what students need to provide (e.g., bag lunch or sunscreen), and any special instructions. Also, this is the point in the process at which you want to solicit parents to be chaperones. Be sure parents complete all required documentation to be considered as chaperones. Be sure you have a signed permission slip before you allow a student to go on field trip.

Step 5: Conducting the Field Trip

This step is where you will go on the field trip. Make sure to account for all students before, during (multiple times), and after the field trip. Develop an accountability system – whether every student has two friends or every student is assigned to a chaperone who constantly monitors their small group. You cannot be too cautious.

> **FYI:** Possible tasks/duties can include having a parent be responsible for bringing the coolers with all the kids' lunches to the picnic area or having a guardian responsible for collecting all the headphones from the audio tour.

While on the field trip, make sure everyone has an itinerary and try your best to stay on schedule. Be sure to assign certain tasks/duties to chaperones.

You also want to clearly explain students' responsibilities and what they should be doing. Sometimes, students will have a study guide or activity to complete during the field trip.

Assessing Field Trip Experience

During the field trip, you can continually utilize informal assessment questions to obtain an understanding of the students' experience. If students complete a study guide or activity during the field trip, this can be one way to assess student learning. Additionally, at the end of the field trip or when you return to campus, you can often utilize more formal assessments to measure student learning. Ultimately, as the teacher, you will need to determine the best means to assess student learning. You know your students best; you decide what assessment strategies are needed to meet their individual learning needs.

▶ SERVICE LEARNING EXPERIENCES

Service learning allows students to truly demonstrate character civic mindedness. A service learning experience is simply having a student provide some type of service to an individual, group, or community. It is volunteering with the purpose of learning and obtaining something meaningful from the experience. You do not participate in a service learning project to have good karma. Instead, the purpose is to demonstrate and better understand your role as a citizen and your responsibility to your community and the world (Montgomery et al., 2017). For example, if your school has a problem with litter, maybe you can have your class organize a campus clean-up. This event can be spontaneous or a one-time event. These types of events are referred to as short-term service learning projects. However, you can also plan and organize service learning projects for longer terms. For example, you could work with your administration and plan an ongoing campus-wide beautification project. In such a project, each class adopts a section of the school and is responsible for keeping it clean and improving the space throughout the school year. These types of events are referred to as long-term service learning projects. Long-term projects can also be more robust service learning projects and can include multi-year agreements or arrangements with an outside agency or partner. For example, you could forge a partnership with a local retirement home that allows your students opportunities to visit and spend time with the elderly multiple times throughout the year. Students can be assigned a resident, and the students can build relationships with individuals and assist the residents with games, storytelling, memory keeping, and more.

All service learning projects require that students selflessly serve others in some capacity. The action students take to complete a service learning experience is often either social or political. Social action service learning experiences are projects to help the community or society without changing policy or laws. For example, if the beach or a local body of water is polluted with debris and trash, you may have your students

Table 10.3 Possible Service Learning Ideas

- *Food drive* – This can be a short- or long-term service learning experience. It most likely will be a social action project but could easily be adapted to political action if students seek to change policies. For example, students could seek to change the way government disburses food rations to those in need.
- *Volunteer at a retirement home* – This can be short- or long-term service learning. Most likely this will fall into the category of social action. Students will have the opportunity to learn from the retirees but also teach them as well (Fair & Delaplane, 2015).
- *Assist at an animal shelter* – Assisting at a local animal shelter would be a social action and could be short- or a long-term service learning project. However, you could adapt this project to political action if you had students seeking to increase the funding for the shelter by contacting local representatives.
- *Plan an international relief effort* – Most likely a short-term project, but there are existing programs available to teachers that would be considered long-term projects like American Red Cross (www.redcross.org), Boys and Girls Club of America (www. bgca.org), UNICEF (www.unicef.org). If a hurricane devastates the coast and your class packs shoeboxes full of toiletries and food, this would be considered a social action service learning project. However, as a political action service learning project, you may have students write letters to the president of the United States pleading that the area be acknowledged as a disaster zone and federal aid be provided.

help clean the polluted waters. If this were a political action service learning experience, you might have students write letters to city/state officials seeking better enforcement of environmental laws or letters to the local business responsible for polluting the waters. Both types of service learning experiences can be social and political, and they all hope to make a difference. For a list of service learning ideas, see Table 10.3.

▶ LOOKING BACK

Elementary teachers who have a stronger sense of allowing students to experience social studies in the classroom are going to add suspense and excitement to their teaching. They create a dramatic atmosphere; prompt meaningful experiences; and give students visions of history, geography, culture, government, and society that are vivid, interesting, and memorable.

Among the many meaningful ways that drama can be used in elementary social studies instruction are dramatic reading, class action dramas, mock trials, story play, sociodrama, simulations, and role play. Drama can even be the focus of entire units. Even if other forms of drama are not used, certainly all teachers and many students can become storytellers and, by doing so, make social studies more memorable and more involving. Drama activities of all types become memorable experiences themselves, and those experiences can provide the basis for learning new concepts and information.

Meaningful learning experiences, such as field trips, provide elementary students with unique experiences and memories. They often can provide elementary students with an up-close and hands-on perspective of places, people, and events. Like field trips, service learning is meant to provide students with memorable learning experiences. Service learning can provide students with an appreciation for volunteering and a better understanding of their role in the community and the world.

EXTENSION ACTIVITY

The fourth nine weeks at Yourtown Elementary School (YES) are off to a fabulous start. Dr. Russell, the YES principal, stops by your classroom to inform you that he would like you to join his in-service training team. He explains your role would be to develop and implement in-service training sessions for current teachers at YES and other schools in the district. Realizing this is truly an honor, you accept. Appreciatively and enthusiastically, Dr. Russell explains that your first task is to share three different sample activities that have students experiencing social studies into the curriculum.

TASK

For this activity, you will need to develop three separate original activities.

Activity 1: Develop a lesson that incorporates drama into the social studies classroom.
Activity 2: Plan and organize a field trip. Draft a field trip proposal for your principal. Be sure you plan for all aspects of the trip.
Activity 3: Plan and organize a service learning project.

All activities should be developed for elementary social studies (K–6 level and topic of your choice). The activities should be engaging and informative. Share your products and all the required resources necessary to teach the activities with peers and/or your instructor.

CHECKING FOR UNDERSTANDING

1. What is a simulation game?
2. What are some basic components of a field trip?
3. Describe three types of mock trials.
4. What is readers' theater?
5. What is service learning?
6. How can service learning be used in the elementary classroom?
7. What is role play?
8. What are some ways in which a teacher or student can become a better storyteller?

▶ HELPFUL RESOURCES

Watch this experienced teacher discuss how she utilizes drama in the elementary classroom:
www.youtube.com/watch?v=_c40Zpz0Ltk
Visit this website for a useful collection of readers' theater scripts:
www.Teachervision.com
Watch a group of elementary students work through a role playing activity:
https://youtu.be/yeW_PnOeMyU
Watch an example of a mock trial titled *State vs. Golden Locks*:
https://youtu.be/qw7Z4dLkPko
Watch an example of a mock trial of an elementary principal on trial for being mean to students:
https://youtu.be/6sZ4-q6JE7g
Watch an example of a mock trial titled "Fairy Tale Trial":
https://youtu.be/gFeYUgGccvw
Watch this video about how one elementary school is utilizing service learning to promote
    meaningful learning experiences:
https://youtu.be/KjjMD3nxewM

▶ FURTHER READING

Farmer, D. (2011). *Learning through drama in the primary years*. Raleigh, NC: Lulu.
This book details drama strategies and lesson plans for use with primary school children
    across the curriculum. The book provides guidance to teachers who have never taught
    drama before but are considering using it in a subject area such as science or history and
    offers new approaches to those familiar with common drama techniques.
Pogrow, S. (2008). *Teaching content outrageously: How to captivate all students and stimulate learn-
    ing*. New York: Jossey-Bass.
This book explains how dramatic practices can serve as powerful tools for enlivening lessons
    and captivating students, even the most resistant learners.
Whaley, C. (2002, March). Meeting the diverse needs of children through story telling.
    Young Children, 57(2), 31–34.
The article discusses how story enactments can be used in preschool and kindergarten class-
    rooms to allow children to take on the role of story maker and to provide experiences for
    children to draw upon as they learn to read.
Kenna, J., & Russell, W. (2015). Tripping on the Core: Utilizing field trips to enhance the
    Common Core. *Social Studies Research and Practice, 10*(2), 96–110. Available at: www.
    socstrpr.org.

This article discusses the utilization of field trips in the era of accountability and provides procedures for conducting field trips and details of sample field trip ideas.

Morris, R. (2010). *The field trip book: Study travel experiences in social studies.* Charlotte, NC: Information Age Publishing.

This book provides educators with ideas for using field trips in the social studies classroom.

Wade, R. (2000). Beyond charity: Service learning for social justice. *Social Studies and the Young Learner, 12*(4), 6–9.

This article describes how elementary school teachers can develop service learning projects that educate for social justice in order to promote change as opposed to charity. Provides examples of how charitable projects can be changed into social justice projects. Discusses how service learning projects can be done without leaving the school grounds.

▶ REFERENCES

Baldwin, P., & Waters, M. (2010). *School improvement through drama: A creative, whole class, whole school approach.* Bel Air, CA: Network Continuum Education.

Behrendt, M., & Franklin, T. (2014). A review of research on school field trips and their value in education. *International Journal of Environmental and Science Education, 9*(3), 235–245.

Cole, B., & McGuire, M. (2011). The challenge of a community park: Engaging young children in powerful lessons in democracy. *Social Studies and the Young Learner, 24*(September), 24–28.

Fair, C., & Delaplane, E. (2015). It is good spend time with older adults: You can teach them, they can teach you: Second grade students reflect on intergenerational service. *Early Childhood Education Journal, 43*(1), 19–26.

Fritz, J. (2010). *Who's saying what in Jamestown, Thomas Savage?* New York: Puffin.

Fulwer, B. E., & McGuire, M. E. (1997). Storypath: Powerful social studies instruction in the primary grades. *Social Studies and the Young Learner, 9*(January/February), 4–7.

Hillyard, S. (2011). *Introduction to process drama conventions.* Available at: https://tesoldrama. files.wordpress.com/2011/01/process-drama-conventions.pdf.

Kenna, J., & Russell, W. (2015a). Tripping on the Core: Utilizing field trips to enhance the Common Core. *Social Studies Research and Practice, 10*(2), 96–110.

Kenna, J., & Russell, W. (2015b). Elementary teacher's utilization of field trips in an era of accountability: A research study. *Curriculum and Teaching, 30*(1), 51–66.

McCaslin, N. (2006). *Creative drama in the classroom and beyond* (8th ed.). Boston: Allyn and Bacon.

McGuire, M. (2005). Using Storypath to give young learners a start. *Social Studies and the Young Learner, 18*(2), 20–23.

Montgomery, S., Miller, W., Foss, P., Tallakson, D., & Howard, M. (2017). Banners for books: "Mighty-hearted" kindergartners take action through arts-based service learning. *Early Childhood Education Journal, 45*(1), 1–14.

Morris, R. V. (2001). Drama and authentic assessment in a social studies classroom. *The Social Studies, 92*(1) (January/February), 41–44.

Morris, R. V. (2009). *Bringing history to life.* Lanham, MD: Rowman and Littlefield Education.

Morris, R. V., & Hickey, M. G. (2003). Writing plays for the middle school social studies classroom: A seventh grade case study. *International Journal of Social Education, 18*(1), 52–58.

Palatini, M. (2009). *Lousy, rotten, stinkin' grapes.* New York: Simon & Schuster.

Rijinbout, F. (2003). The unbearable lightness of process drama. *Stage Art, 15*(3), 6–11.

Rosler, B. (2008). Process drama in one fifth grade social studies class. *The Social Studies, 99*(6), 265–272.

Service, R. (2006). *The cremation of Sam McGee*. Tonawanda, NY: Kids Can Press.

Shotick, J. A., & Walsko, G. (1997). Using children's theater to teach economics. *Social Studies and the Young Learner, 9*(January/February), 11–13.

Stanley, D. (2009). *Mozart: The wonder child: A play in three acts*. New York: Collins.

Turner, T. N. (1994). Storytelling: It's never going to be easy. *Tennessee Education, 24*(Spring), 5–10.

Young, C., Chase, J., & Rasinski, T. (2009). Implementing readers' theatre as an approach to classroom fluency instruction. *The Reading Teacher, 63*(1), 4–13.

Technology and Media in Social Studies

▶ **LOOKING AHEAD**

What is technology? This seemingly simple question will undoubtedly produce a wide variety of responses from teachers and members of the general public for that matter. For many people, technology today is simply a synonym for computers. To be sure, technology covers a wide range of devices, such as televisions, DVD players, LCD projectors, CD players, overhead projectors, Smart Boards, document cameras, and a variety of other things that can and should be used to enhance classroom instruction.

Technology advancements of the late twentieth and early twenty-first centuries have greatly altered the world, changing how people interact and access information. As society becomes more accustomed to and dependent on new technologies, the need for the presence of technology in schools increases greatly. Many jobs of the twenty-first century now require an understanding of technological hardware and software in order to function. Skills such as word processing, web browsing, and sending electronic mail are now considered very basic abilities required in a variety of workplaces.

This chapter focuses on various types of technologies and the ways that teachers can effectively utilize these valuable resources to enhance social studies instruction in the elementary school. Since students in elementary schools will likely bring with them a variety of different prerequisite skills and knowledge regarding technology, this chapter will detail everything from basic software and hardware uses in the early primary grades to more advanced uses of contemporary technology resources for more proficient students. It is important to remember that technology serves as a tool for instruction and should only be utilized to supplement or enrich the curriculum.

CAN YOU? DO YOU?

Can you . . .

- Explain how technology benefits students learning and enhances your instruction?
- Describe your own skills and abilities in utilizing technology?
- Identify or describe specific technology skills that are important for your students to master?

- Think of activities in which children could have experiences in utilizing classroom technology?

Do you . . .

- Know where to find valuable resources using the internet?
- Know what technologies are typically found in schools and how they should be used?
- Know the definition of *media* and *visual literacy*?
- Understand different ways of using technology to enhance classroom instruction?

FOCUS ACTIVITY

Before reading this chapter, try the following focus activity.

Think back on your experiences in the classroom as a student. What types of technology did your teachers use in the classroom? Consider how technology from your experiences as a student has evolved over the years. What technology do you expect to see in contemporary classrooms? What resources and technologies do you feel comfortable working with, and which technologies might you need more support utilizing? Share your experiences with others.

Rank the following technologies based on how important you think they are for classroom instruction (1 being most important, 10 being least important). Use this list as a basis for discussion. Why are some resources more valuable to you than others? How do you envision technology being used in your classroom? You might also like to generate additional resources not listed in this overview. Share your conclusions with others.

____ Television
____ Internet Access
____ Document Camera
____ Video Recorder
____ DVD/VCR
____ Mobile Device (e.g., iPad) (for student use)
____ Computer (teacher use only)
____ Interactive White Board (Smart Board, Promethean, etc.)
____ Liquid Crystal Display (LCD) Projector
____ Computers (student use)

▶ GETTING STARTED: TECHNOLOGY AS A PRODUCTIVE TOOL

Before any advanced discussion can take place about the use of technology as an educational tool, we must first consider the basic skills expected of twenty-first-century teachers. The rapid development of new and emergent technologies has drastically changed the way people live, and in turn, these developments have also changed the perception of what it means to be a technologically proficient teacher. Teachers are now expected to bring with them certain prerequisite skills regarding the use of technology. For example, when was the last time you heard of a school offering professional development for teachers about composing typewritten documents or sending electronic mail (email)?

As schools continue to place increased emphasis (and funds) on classroom technology, it is important to consider the expectations placed on teachers. Many contemporary classrooms now come equipped with a great deal of technology. Resources like classroom computers, televisions, LCD projectors, document cameras, internet access, and even interactive white boards are becoming increasingly present in contemporary classrooms. However, the mere presence of technology does not ensure a better education for the students. Teachers must continually work to gain proficiency and knowledge about technological innovations, specifically focusing on how these devices can enhance instruction and/or student learning. Learning about the best applications of classroom technology is a process critical to the success of beginning and experienced teachers alike. Rapid innovations and developments in the technology realm mean that nearly every teacher will need some support or training in emerging uses of new devices.

Luckily, teachers often have several options for acquiring skills to use new technologies. The most common and accessible form of training typically comes from professional development offered by schools or districts. Nearly every public school in the country has "teacher training" days that provide some form of professional development to classroom teachers. While many schools frequently use this time to help train teachers, it is safe to say that this may not always be the case. Classroom teachers interested in more training should always discuss the issue with school administrators. Whether the training is offered during in-service days or sometime outside school operation hours (before class, after class, weekends), teachers need to actively seek support in the use of instructional technology. Other options outside school-offered professional development could include taking courses at a college or university focusing on instructional technology or attending professional conferences designed to improve the teaching profession.

▶ TECHNOLOGY AND STANDARDS

Like all areas of education in the era of accountability, advocates for the inclusion and increased presence of technology in the classroom have created specific standards and benchmarks to guide instruction. These standards are significant for teachers to be aware of because they are the indicators of what is deemed "important" in curriculum and pedagogy on national and state levels.

The International Society for Technology in Education (ISTE) has created a set of National Educational Technology Standards (NETS) for students, teachers, and administrators. ISTE lists the following five main standards for teachers and contends that effective teachers should model and apply the NETS as they "design, implement, and assess learning experiences to engage students and improve learning; enrich professional practice; and provide positive models for students, colleagues, and the community" (ISTE, 2008, p. 1):

1. Facilitate and Inspire Student Learning and Creativity.
2. Design and Develop Digital-Age Learning Experiences and Assessments.
3. Model Digital-Age Work and Learning.
4. Promote and Model Digital Citizenship and Responsibility.
5. Engage in Professional Growth and Leadership.

The National Council for the Social Studies (NCSS), the largest organization dedicated to social studies in the U.S., also has issued standards, bulletins, and position statements that specifically highlight the importance of integrating technology into the social studies curriculum. One aspect that makes NCSS positions different from those of other organizations is that they go beyond advocating for inclusion of instructional technology by also promoting the exploration of the effects of technological developments on society to provide context for students about the social, economic, and political impact technology has on the world. The eighth strand of the National Council for the Social Studies themes is titled "Science, Technology, and Society." NCSS states under this theme that "social studies programs should include experiences that provide for the study of relationships among science, technology, and society" (National Council for the Social Studies, 2012, www.socialstudies.org/standards/strands). The following are a few examples of key questions that the National Council for the Social Studies believes social studies educators should address under the technology theme:

1. What can we learn from the past about how new technologies result in broader social change?
2. Is new technology always a good thing for society?
3. How should society cope with rapid changes and potential inequities caused by technological innovations?
4. How can we manage technology so that the greatest numbers of people benefit? How can we preserve fundamental values and beliefs in a world that is rapidly becoming one technology-linked village?
5. How do science and technology affect our sense of self and morality?
6. How can technology advances help alleviate global issues such as poverty, human rights violations, etc.?

In addition to the overview of national standards provided here, teachers should also be aware of state standards. Many states have recognized the importance of technology in the classroom and have incorporated this significance into state standards at all grade levels. State standards should always be closely monitored when planning lessons not just for content but also for skills that are deemed a valuable part of students' education.

▶ ONLINE AND VIRTUAL TEACHING

2020 was a year that brought forth many changes around the world due to the rise of the COVID-19 pandemic. The impact of this virus spread across all aspects of society, and schools were no different. As schools began to close, many also explored the prospect of pivoting to online/virtual learning environments. To be sure, online and virtual teaching have been around for many years. However, schools and teachers have never seen anything quite like the shift that took place in 2020. Seemingly overnight, teachers were required to create online learning materials, Google classrooms, and digital resource libraries and become Zoom teachers all at the same time. These issues were even more prominent in elementary schools, as teachers, students, and parents struggled with the shifting role of learning in a virtual setting. Aside from the normal technical issues associated with virtual learning (lacking technology, internet, at-home supports, etc.), elementary teachers also found themselves teaching in new and unfamiliar ways, designing lessons dependent on technology, rather than using technology as a supplement to normal classroom instruction.

As most teachers are not trained specifically for teaching in virtual environments, it is safe to say that this year has been a learning experience for everyone. Fortunately, teachers and students have been using much of the technology and resources used in virtual learning for many years. For example, teachers routinely utilize the internet for supplemental readings, videos, and materials to enrich student learning. Students increasingly are using mobile and technology devices at home for personal and educational purposes. While an extensive discussion around teaching elementary social studies in the virtual setting would be outside the scope of this book, we do believe the resources and approaches covered throughout this chapter (and all the chapters, really) can be scaffolded to support the teaching and learning of elementary social studies in online and virtual environments. Additionally, for teachers interested in more general supports about designing online instruction, we highly recommend the Teaching Channel's website on distance learning (www.teachingchannel.com/).

▶ ENHANCING INSTRUCTION WITH THE INTERNET

The internet might arguably be one of the most revolutionary innovations in the history of education. Access to the World Wide Web allows people all over the world to share information, experiences, knowledge, and ideas faster than ever before. In addition, the internet also contains a vast amount of resources that enable teachers to do their jobs in a more effective, efficient, and engaging way. In fact, the popularity of web resources has increased so much that teachers and students probably need more practice narrowing down search results and determining what is actually a reliable resource than they do in the process of finding websites. For elementary students in particular, understanding what makes a website valuable and relevant is an essential process in education during the digital age. Before ever bringing any websites into the classroom, it is the teacher's responsibility to thoroughly examine the website to determine how appropriate the resource is and look for any potential problems with using the site to enhance instruction. The following section will discuss how teachers could go about evaluating websites for their classroom instruction or with students to help them understand how to critically analyze web resources.

Evaluating Websites

The evaluation of websites for classroom use is a task that should first be completed by the teacher. Before utilizing any website in the classroom, make sure you thoroughly examine the site for things like accuracy of content, author of the site, date the site was last updated, and security of the site (e.g., can the website be accessed at the school, which might have internet restrictions?). After analyzing the site and determining its appropriateness, consider going through a similar process with the students. Of course, this process will need to be modified based on the skills and developmental levels of the student population. For younger grades, it is helpful for teachers to bookmark selected websites to be used during online research projects. This will allow students to access the information more easily while also lowering the risk of students engaging with inappropriate or less useful websites. The following list provides some quality example questions that teachers should consider with students when evaluating the usefulness and relevance of a website.

- What is the title of the website being evaluated?
- What is the URL of the website being evaluated?
- What is your research topic?

- Who is the author of the website?
- Is there contact information for the author? If so, what is it?
- What is the purpose of this website?
- Is the website published by a webmaster? Or by the author?
- Is the person qualified? How do you know? Does the person list their qualifications?
- How detailed is the information?
- Does the information express any bias? If so, what is it?
- When was the website created?
- When was the website last updated?
- Did an organization, institution, government agency, or foundation publish the website? If so, what is the name of the agency?
- Is the information on the website outdated?
- Overall, what are the strengths and weaknesses of the web page?

While the aforementioned list of questions is certainly not exhaustive, it will provide teachers and students with a strong enough foundation to proceed with the utilization of websites in the classroom. Teachers should always remember that student safety is the most important component of online exploration. Helping students better understand the complexities of the internet, with all its glories and pitfalls, is an essential part of education during the digital age.

Mobile Technologies and Apps

The use of mobile technologies could be the most popular movement in contemporary classroom instruction. All across the U.S., and the entire world, schools and educators are investing a great deal of time and money into the use of mobile devices in the classroom. Laptops, tablets (iPads, Chromebooks, etc.), and even cell phones are beginning to become the norm in K–12 schools. Unfortunately, schools often do not provide the level of professional development and in-service training necessary to maximize learning opportunities with these devices. This can be extremely frustrating to classroom teachers, as school administrators not only push for teachers to use the technology, which costs so much for the school, but also expect teachers to demonstrate a connection between mobile devices and student learning gains. To be sure, the use of mobile devices certainly has the potential to improve teaching and learning. In many ways, these devices have already transformed how classrooms operate and how teachers and students access information. However, it is important to remember that these devices are simply tools and teachers need to constantly seek out training and professional development opportunities to find the best ways to utilize mobile devices to support classroom learning. As technology and its various resources are constantly evolving and updating, it would be well beyond the scope of this chapter to attempt to cover all the tools available to teachers and students. However, we would like to provide a few selected apps that we have found to be particularly useful in teaching and learning elementary social studies. For more detailed information on teaching and learning with mobile devices, see *Learning with Mobile and Handheld Technologies* (Galloway, John, & McTaggart, 2015).

Selected Apps to Consider

BookFlix – This app is a tool helpful to elementary students and teachers as a resource that pairs a piece of fiction with a nonfiction article. For example, students may read a story about cars, then follow that up with an explanatory article about the impact of automobiles on the environment.

Padlet – Teachers often utilize this free app as a digital bulletin board to help organize content. Additionally, users can work on projects simultaneously, which makes it a favorite for activities like building interactive maps or timelines.

Socrative – This assessment tool allows teachers to quickly and efficiently assess student understanding through quizzes and "exit ticket" types of features. Students can respond to these teacher-designed assessments with their mobile devices, and a report is sent to the teacher's device instantly.

Kahoot – Similar to Socrative, this assessment app allows teachers to generate interactive quizzes with time limits for each question, offering a playful "game show"–like feel for students. Students respond to the questions on their phones or mobile devices; answers are instantly sent to the teacher. If not every student in the class has a smartphone or mobile device, consider having the students work in small groups or with a partner.

Educreations – Teachers can use this app as a presentation tool or method for allowing students to explain their thinking. The app allows you to record your voice and draw/import pictures. Teachers could have students upload a primary source document, then have students circle "key words" and record their analysis of the document.

Nearpod – Mostly for use in one-to-one classrooms, this app allows teachers to control how and when screens advance for students. This is an especially effective resource for teachers when working with younger kids, who often want to click or swipe on the screens during activities.

Aurasma – This augmented reality app allows users to bring content to life. Devices can be held over selected images or objects (known as triggers), which will then bring forth some form of 3D video or animation. Teachers can create their own triggers as well, making it especially useful for field trips to local historical sites and/or museums.

Explain Everything – Teachers can use this app to transform their phone or tablet into an interactive white board. Images and files can be uploaded, manipulated, and shared with students. Additionally, teachers could use this as an assessment tool, uploading student work to the app, recording audio and written feedback directly on the assignment, then sending the video recording of the feedback directly to students and/or their parents.

Interactive White Boards

Interactive white boards are among the most popular technology features found in contemporary classrooms. While there are many different brands and variations (Smart Boards, Promethean boards, etc.), the basic function of these devices is to increase student learning and engagement by combining the features of a traditional dry erase board with an LCD projector. Teachers can use these boards for a plethora of activities, such as showing video clips, completing graphic organizers, playing games, and completing interactive maps or timelines, along with thousands of other things. Students also enjoy coming up to interactive white boards and engaging directly with the technology and content, bringing a certain level of excitement to the learning experience, which continues to be an important feature when teaching social studies in the elementary classroom. Like all other technology resources, interactive white boards require a great deal of training in order for classroom teachers to truly maximize all the potential offered through both the hardware and software available with these devices.

Media Literacy

Media literacy is particularly important for younger students because it revolves around trying to understand the intentions and motives implanted within the media. Media literacy can be defined as having the necessary skills to access, analyze, evaluate, and create media in a variety of forms (Center for Media Literacy, 2012). Students in the digital era face an onslaught of media in a variety of forms. Television programs, commercials, films, billboards, and countless other forms of advertising all attempt to deliver an assortment of messages to students about an even wider range of topics. Today's society is one infatuated with the media culture, which is the primary reason billions of dollars are spent every year by the advertising industry. Every day, students see commercials, billboards, and advertisements encouraging them to buy products and/or look a specific way. The proliferation of images facing students in the media becomes even more problematic when considering the widespread use of software programs (like Photoshop) to manipulate and alter digital images, blurring the lines of reality and making critical analysis of media messages more important than ever.

Some people may consider as media literacy the ability to effectively navigate and utilize the internet. True media literacy skills involve much more than operational web browsing. Teaching students to be media literate is about teaching them to think critically and to ask the right questions about what they are reading, watching, or hearing in the media. While finding reliable and quality resources on the internet is certainly a starting point for instruction, students still face the challenge of media influence in other forms such as television advertisements, commercials, popular films, billboards, and various other outlets. Since all these sources attempt to exercise influence over students, and social studies is concerned with developing good decision makers and citizens, it becomes necessary for teachers to help students become critical viewers of media and not passive consumers. For example, elementary teachers could show students commercials or advertisements related to popular clothing lines, shoes, restaurants, or other products. Then have students analyze and discuss what the advertisement is trying to accomplish and who the intended audiences are. Teachers could then allow students to compare popular products with substantial advertisements (such as Nike, for example) to similar or comparable products. What are the major differences between these products? Do these differences justify the disparity in costs? This is just one brief example of how media literacy skills can be explored through economic concepts and principles using technology. As contemporary media continues to use advertisements in an effort to influence society, educators should strongly consider making time to explain and instruct in this unique discourse to help the students of today become responsible consumers of tomorrow.

Visual Literacy

Visual literacy is a field similar to media literacy, but it does contain some prominent differences worth addressing as a separate topic. The purpose of visual literacy is to understand, evaluate, and create meaning from images. Braden and Hortin defined visual literacy as "the ability to understand and use images, including the ability to think, learn and express oneself in terms of images" (1982, p. 38). This definition works well when considering the implications of visual literacy for elementary students because it goes beyond simple recognition of shapes, images, and symbols by also focusing on the creation of visuals to communicate.

Traditionally, education in the U.S. has placed very little emphasis or value on visual communication (Felten, 2008). While the primary grades tend to be more liberal in the use of visuals to learn and communicate, this emphasis tends to fade as students begin to develop traditional literacy skills in the reading and writing domain. As Kress duly noted, "The visual representations, which children produce as a matter of course in the early years of schooling, are not developed and built on as a means for future communication use" (1997, p. 153). The lack of focus given to visual literacy in schools becomes more problematic when considering the technological advancements associated with the digital era. More and more in professional and commercial occupations people are asked to communicate and present information utilizing the visual arts. Consider the regularity with which Microsoft PowerPoint appears in conference boardrooms and presentations all across the country. The problem for society, and especially for educators, continues to be the false assumption that students in today's classrooms already have an understanding of visual communication because of the predominantly visual culture of contemporary society. As Felten accurately noted, "Living in an image-rich world, however, does not mean students (or faculty and administrators) naturally possess sophisticated visual literacy skills, just as continually listening to an iPod does not teach a person to critically analyze or create music" (2008, p. 60).

The good news for elementary teachers is that many visual literacy strategies are already quite popular tools for social studies instruction. Resources such as graphic organizers, historic photographs, charts, maps, monuments, and films are among the more prominent resources that can be easily woven into the elementary classroom. Social studies textbooks have also begun including more images and supplemental materials over the past 20 years. (Many now include interactive electronic materials, vocabulary guides, and student workbooks.) The purposeful inclusion of images in the classroom and supporting resources directly reflects a shift in how educators are beginning to view the importance of visuals in knowledge comprehension and retention.

The multimodal principle of learning, as discussed in James Paul Gee's *What Video Games Have to Teach Us About Learning and Literacy* (2003), addresses how "meaning and knowledge are built up through various modalities (images, texts, symbols, interactions, abstract design, sound, etc.), not just words" (p. 210). With the knowledge that students learn much more when information is presented in a variety of ways, elementary teachers should more actively pursue instructional methods that place an emphasis on multimodal learning in the social studies. Elementary students can often understand much more than they are able to express in written form. For example, many students who struggle with traditional text-based assignments can routinely recite quotes from movies or the lyrics to their favorite songs. Also, allowing students to demonstrate their learning in visual forms, such as drawing a picture or creating a photo collage, increases engagement and critical thinking when dealing with abstract concepts. Consider the prospect of trying to examine a topic such as global warming with elementary students. If students were asked to demonstrate their knowledge of this concept in the traditional form of writing a research paper, then students would spend time collecting information and preparing a paper with citations. However, say students were given the same topic of global warming but with an alternative assignment like creating a public service announcement video. Students working on a public service announcement video would go through the same research process but would be required to truly think critically about the topic because they would not be able to restate (or worse, plagiarize) information they read. This brief example is one way that elementary teachers can implement multimodal learning. By having students examine information in one form (text) and then create and convey meaning from that information in a different form (visual/video), teachers provide students with an authentic assessment that allows for the simultaneous expansion of content knowledge and visual literacy skills.

Digital History

The term *digital history* is one that has gained a tremendous amount of attention in the fields of history and social studies since the World Wide Web became available for widespread public use during the late 1990s. John Lee defines digital history as "the study of the past using a variety of electronically reproduced primary source texts, images, and artifacts as well as the constructed historical narratives, accounts, or presentations that result from digital historical inquiry" (Lee, 2002, p. 507). As the internet became faster, cheaper, and more easily accessible during the first part of the twenty-first century, historians, librarians, and teachers began to realize the potential of information sharing via the World Wide Web. As a result, countless websites all over the world began uploading millions of primary and secondary resource materials in order to place these valuable sources of information at the fingertips of anyone with an internet connection. Teachers and students in contemporary classrooms now have access to more primary and secondary resources than any group in the history of public school education. These resources, when utilized correctly, have the opportunity to turn social studies instruction into a dynamic experience. Instead of simply reading about social studies content in the typical classroom textbook, teachers can engage students with thousands of photos, video clips, interviews, and historical documents in an effort to bring content to life.

The following list provides a few examples of popular digital history websites that elementary school teachers might find useful. While some of the sites may be too complicated for students to navigate on their own, teachers should find the vast collection of resources available on these digital sites to be quite useful. A brief description of each website is provided along with the web address. Teachers should spend time carefully examining all that these sites have to offer and consider activities or teaching opportunities that could be implemented while browsing through the collections.

- *Library of Congress*: The Library of Congress website is one of the largest and most useful digital collections of historical resources available to classroom teachers. This free website will allow teachers to explore documents, photos, video clips, and a variety of other materials covering historical content. Web address: www. loc.gov.
- *University of Houston*: This website was designed and developed to support the teaching of American history in K–12 schools and colleges and is supported by the Department of History and the College of Education at the University of Houston. Web address: www.digitalhistory.uh.edu/.
- *Virginia Center for Digital History*: The Virginia Center for Digital History (VCDH) at the University of Virginia promotes the teaching and learning of history using digital technologies. Research projects from this website are useful to a wide range of educators (teachers, librarians, professors, historians, etc.) at all levels of instruction. Web address: www.vcdh.virginia.edu/index.php?page=VCDH.

Virtual Field Trips

Virtual field trips are becoming one of the more popular and practical uses of the internet in social studies instruction. A virtual field trip can be defined as an activity that allows students to visit historic sites, monuments, museums, or other locations via the internet. These trips allow teachers to guide students on a journey to faraway places in order to examine both content and context of materials being studied. Consider the Egyptian pyramids or the Taj Mahal. These are historic structures that students may never get to actually visit in person but now have the ability to explore online. Many websites now offer virtual tours that are easy to navigate even for younger students. However, as is the case with any instructional activity, teachers do need to carefully consider a few things before engaging in a virtual field trip:

1. Always visit and carefully examine the site first before introducing it to the class.
2. Make sure you have developed a clear educational purpose for the virtual field trip, as well as a way to assess student learning from the activity.
3. For younger students, bookmarking the site to be explored on classroom computers will make it much easier to find and minimize confusion.
4. If students are going to explore the site on their own, make sure to thoroughly explain and model instructions for navigating the site, highlighting key aspects of the trip that students should inspect.
5. Once the trip is complete, a discussion or debriefing activity is necessary to help clarify any questions the students may have and also to initially check for students' understanding of the virtual field trip objectives.

It should also be noted that virtual field trips are not designed to replace real-life field trips as an instructional tool. Taking students on trips to local historic sites is something that always should be included in the curriculum because it allows students to connect content with real-world experiences in a personal way. Virtual field trips should be considered a valuable option for teachers with a desire to expose children to distant locations and cultures that normally would be out of reach, helping expand the traditional classroom by making the world more accessible to students.

WebQuests

A WebQuest can be defined as any inquiry-based activity that requires students to navigate through the internet for part or all of the assignment. WebQuest activities began during the mid-1990s and have steadily evolved over the years as technology advances have increased accessibility to the internet while simultaneously making websites more inclusive and user friendly. The premise behind WebQuest activities is allowing students to explore various social studies topics by conducting online research, interacting with a variety of primary and secondary sources such as photos, news stories, film clips, etc. While these activities can be time consuming for teachers to create, as much effort is spent finding appropriate websites for the activity, there are some websites that contain large collections of WebQuest activities for interested teachers. QuestGarden (http://questgarden.com/) contains a large collection of WebQuest activities for a variety of subject areas and for teachers at all grade levels. Elementary teachers should carefully consider the pros and cons of utilizing WebQuest activities in the classroom and always preview any websites being used to make sure the site is up to date and there are no inappropriate materials for students.

▶ TEACHING WITH FILM

The use of film as an instructional tool is not a new concept in the field of education. Every day, teachers in elementary classrooms all over the country utilize this powerful tool to motivate, engage, and inform students about a variety of topics and concepts. Teaching with film is considered a best practice in classrooms during the digital age and an effective way to teach elementary social studies content (Holmes, Russell, & Movitz, 2007; Russell, 2012a; Russell & Waters, 2010a). Since numerous popular films are based on historical events, many social studies teachers view films as a reliable resource to engage students. However, as most social studies teachers know, not all films are historically accurate. While some may argue that films should not be included for this very reason, teachers could utilize the historical discrepancies depicted in Hollywood films to encourage students to view films critically. In addition to popular Hollywood films, there are countless documentaries, television series, political advertisements, commercials, and digital videos that can be utilized to actively engage elementary students in social studies content.

One major concern for advocates of using film in the classroom is the lack of formal training that teachers receive in how to effectively use film. Teachers often show films as a "time filler" or simply show historical films as a way to supplement text, without any serious critical thinking or analysis of what they are viewing. Historical films, much like texts, are examples of how history is constructed and should always be open to interpretation. As Rosenstone (2006) writes, "The past told in moving images, doesn't do away with the old forms of history – it adds to the language which the past can speak." Teachers should spend time explaining the nature of the film industry and how the primary goal of most films is to make money, not the accurate portrayal of people, places, or events. Since films about historical events can often be misleading or worse, blatantly incorrect, students need practice in analyzing not only the characters and plots of films but also how information presented relates to content from different sources, such as the textbook, newspapers, and various other primary/secondary resources.

Film is an effective and powerful tool for teaching social studies. For film to be effective, it must be used appropriately. To ensure appropriate film use, teachers should adhere to the Russell Model (2004, 2007) outlined here:

1. *Step 1: Preparation*: The preparation step includes creating lesson plans that incorporate film while still meeting instructional goals/objectives, state standards, and national standards, and adhering to all legal requirements.
2. *Step 2: Pre-viewing*: The pre-viewing step is done prior to students viewing the film. The pre-viewing step should include an introduction to the film and the purpose for viewing the film.
3. *Step 3: Watching the film*: During this step, the teacher will show students the film (in its entirety or in clips). Teachers need to ensure that students are aware of what they should be doing (taking notes, jotting down questions, etc.) and looking for while watching the film.
4. *Step 4: Assessment*: The assessment step is done after students have watched the film. The assessment step includes assessing student learning in some fashion.

There are a number of ways film can be used in the classroom. The methodologies described next are effective pedagogical practices for using film in the elementary classroom (Russell, 2004, 2012b).

1. *Film as a visual textbook*: Using film as a visual textbook is the most common method used by teachers. Teachers often will use a film as visual record to convey "what happened."
2. *Film as a depicter of atmosphere*: Using film to depict a time period or setting. This allows teachers to display architecture, living conditions, clothes, weapons, etc. Thus, conveying the atmosphere to the students only requires short film clips, which saves instructional time.
3. *Film as an analogy*: Using film as an analogy includes using films that are similar to events, people, places, etc. but otherwise different. There are many films that can be utilized as analogies for various issues, events, and/or people.
4. *Film as a historiography*: Artifacts (like films) created during a time period can be a valuable resource. Many older films, as well as contemporary films, portray the relevant issues of society. The film is used to demonstrate important societal issues and topics relevant to the time period.
5. *Film as a springboard*: This often is done with short film clips to provoke interest and discussion, but entire movies can be used. The film is used as a motivator to jump start or springboard into the material.

Beyond dealing with historical-based or themed films, elementary teachers can find several other types of films useful in the classroom for helping teach social studies–related topics. A major focus of elementary social studies content in the early primary grades K–3 typically deals with topics such as the child, family, neighborhoods, and communities. Much of this content is designed to help younger children better understand themselves and the world around them on a level that they can handle developmentally and emotionally. Films can be a great way to help students relate to abstract concepts, such as communities, on a level that can help facilitate a better understanding. For example, teachers wanting to discuss the theme of communities could show students a child-friendly film like *Charlotte's Web* (2006). In this film, a young pig named Wilbur befriends other animals in the barn (community), and these animals all work together to help Wilbur during his time of troubles. This classic story can offer interesting talking points regarding the composition of communities (all the animals are different and look different, like people in local communities) and the responsibilities of community members to help others (much like Charlotte and the other barn residents help Wilbur). In addition to abstract social concepts, films can also help students better understand character concepts. As character education is a mandated aspect of the elementary school curriculum in over 30 states, teachers might consider using film as a tool to help bring many character education themes to life. Themes such as honesty, responsibility, respect, trustworthiness, and caring are routinely present in many popular films targeted at elementary students. For a more detailed look at using film to teach character education, see *Reel Character Education: A Cinematic Approach to Character Development* (Russell & Waters, 2010b). The following list details alternative strategies for using film in the classroom.

1. *Films to entertain*: Have a discussion with students about the nature of the film-making industry. Explain the different types of films and how most films are

made with the explicit purpose of entertaining to make money. Have students examine popular Hollywood films that are based on historical events, such as *Pocahontas* (1995), to determine the historical inaccuracies or exaggerations in the film. Teachers could also have students reenact or rewrite specific scenes in the film that were particularly misleading about the true nature of the event being covered.

2. *Exploring social issues with film*: Many controversial and important contemporary issues are depicted in the film industry. Issues such as teenage pregnancy, violence, drug use, bullying, discrimination, and poverty all routinely appear in many Hollywood films. Allowing students to examine social issues with film will provide them with insight into the complex dynamics of these topics while also building an emotional connection through relationship building with characters. This type of activity can be done at all grade levels with all types of students, but teachers must be sure the topic and film being explored are age appropriate. For a more complete look at teaching social issues with film, see *Teaching Social Issues with Film* (Russell, 2009).

3. *Using film to examine civic and character concepts*: Similar to social issues, the film industry also has a certain level of influence on public perception regarding civic and moral behaviors. Students should be given the opportunity to analyze films to see what messages they are attempting to convey or promote through characters in the story. Teachers could show students films created during different time periods to critique, analyze, and compare cultural norms and how the film industry perpetuated these beliefs. For example, show students selected scenes from films created during the 1950s and 1960s. What character traits are valued in these films? Are there any negative character beliefs that are commonly found (discrimination, stereotypes, racism, etc.)? Then show students selected scenes from films created during the 1990s and 2000s, repeating the aforementioned tasks. Once completed, students can compare how films from different decades depicted controversial topics relevant to the development of good character and examine how the film industry influenced or perpetuated popular character traits at different times in our country's history. For a more complete look at teaching character education with film, see *Reel Character Education: A Cinematic Approach to Character Development* (Russell & Waters, 2010b).

4. *Creating films*: Having students create films is an exciting and engaging way to assess student learning and comprehension. This type of activity will allow students to not only demonstrate what they know but also build a skill set in media production that is becoming more and more important in the twenty-first century. Students can use popular programs like Microsoft Movie Maker or iMovie to create short films about nearly any topic. For example, teachers could have students make a documentary video about a historical figure, create a public service announcement drawing attention to important issues, or develop an informational film about social studies concepts. These types of assignments will give students another way to exhibit learning while simultaneously giving them valuable experience in the increasingly popular and diverse realm of media production.

5. *Oral history videos*: The creation of oral history videos will allow students to become historians by capturing the unique perspectives of individuals who have experienced certain events. Combining this classical form of historical research with contemporary technology will give students the chance to integrate history skills with popular digital media skills. Oral history projects can consist of

a variety of topics, ranging from the Vietnam War to the more recent War on Terror in Iraq. By giving students the opportunity to interview and carry on a discussion with individuals in the community about relevant social studies topics, learning is given a new sense of significance as students see how many events resonate in the lives of citizens and how new technology can be utilized to share these stories with others.

▶ SOCIAL MEDIA

Of all the technological developments of the twenty-first century, there are few that have experienced the growth and influence of social media websites. Social media sites such as Facebook and Twitter are now dominant fixtures in mainstream culture that have drastically altered the way information is shared and people connect. Consider Facebook, a social networking service started in 2004 by a group of college students, led by Mark Zuckerberg. Fast forward to 2021, and Facebook now has nearly 2.6 billion active users worldwide and Mark Zuckerberg is a multi-billionaire. The quick rise of social media websites like Facebook presents several unique opportunities and challenges for educators. Teachers need to carefully consider all the positive and negative outcomes that can come from social media sites – not only for their students but also for themselves.

There is much debate about the educational value and appropriateness of social media sites in the field of education. First and foremost, elementary teachers need to be extremely careful about the use and implementation of these sites in the classroom. Some sites, like Facebook, for instance, have a minimum age restriction for users to join. Since Facebook's age requirement is 13 years old, most elementary students would not legally be allowed to utilize this site. However, many tech-savvy students can find ways around this restriction, and some parents may even willingly sign their children up for the site. Other popular sites, like Twitter for example, do not have any age restrictions, so anyone could create an account and engage in the social media experience. The popularity of such social media sites makes them ubiquitous and, in turn, very intriguing to young students. Consider how many celebrities, professional athletes, famous political figures, and even businesses or corporations say things such as, "Follow us on Twitter or 'like' us on Facebook." Students are bound to be influenced by these requests, so teachers should discuss the purpose of these sites and how to use them responsibly, if at all.

A final element of consideration regarding social media sites is the impact information shared on these sites by teachers, or future teachers, might have on their careers. There has been a great deal of controversy about how information shared on sites such as Facebook can adversely affect people in the field of education. Teachers who share or "post" information about students, administrators, or other school personnel have been increasingly scrutinized over the past several years, with some cases ending in the termination of the teacher. In addition, many schools looking into hiring new teachers are beginning to pay more attention to what potential applicants are sharing on social media sites as a means to gather more information about candidates. Everyone in the field of education must approach social media interactions with extreme caution.

▶ CHALLENGES TO TECHNOLOGY INTEGRATION

As is the case with any instructional strategy or resource, there are always challenges to classroom implementation that need to be carefully considered. Teachers must always keep in mind the inherent responsibility to try to maximize the learning opportunities presented to every student in the class. Since the student population can vary tremendously based on learning styles, capabilities, etc., teachers should always ask themselves the following questions before planning any activity using technology:

1. Does the use of technology contribute to student learning?
2. Does the technology improve the learning opportunities of students?
3. If the activity involves student interaction with technology, do all students have the necessary skills to complete the activity? What modifications/accommodations might need to be made for students needing additional support?
4. Is the activity or lesson dependent on the technology, and how would you respond if the technology failed (power outage, internet down, etc.)?

Access at Home: Addressing the Digital Divide

Although technology continues to spread and widely influence the way people work and live in society, it is naïve to think that all regions have equal access to technology. Students from impoverished communities often have far less home access to resources such as the internet or computers. Teachers need to gain an understanding of the student population and the community in order to address any potential issues that might occur from the incorporation of technology. Much like any other skill set, it is likely that students will bring with them into the elementary classroom a great deal of variability regarding technological proficiency. For that reason, teachers will need to scaffold the use of technology resources and instruction based on the individual needs of the students. Teachers should also never assume that any technology resource will be available to students at home and make sure to plan assignments and homework accordingly.

Cyberbullying

As mentioned earlier, social media sites and internet communications are changing the way that people interact. This is especially true for children growing up in the age of instant messaging, text messaging, and virtual social networks. One potentially negative outcome of all these methods of communication is the possibility of abuse by the students. Cyberbullying refers to the attempt to harass or bully someone using the internet or any other types of electronic devices. Bullying in general is a major concern for elementary school teachers and is considered part of most character education programs. Teachers should help students realize the consequences of their actions online, as many students may simply think it is a joke and not understand how hurtful these activities may be to others. Since social studies is concerned with the citizenship development of students, addressing cyber etiquette and behaviors in the classroom will certainly continue to develop as a critical need in the elementary social studies curriculum.

Copyright

A great deal of attention has been given to copyright issues during the digital age. The internet has made more information available and accessible than ever, leading to a blurred interpretation of what constitutes copyrighted materials on the World Wide Web. Teachers should help students understand that not everything on the internet is reliable, free, or acceptable for educational purposes. In addition, teachers need to address the importance of citing works from the internet or giving credit to the creator of products online. This foundational information is crucial to address in elementary school as projects and activities utilizing online instruction continue to grow in early grades, potentially avoiding problems of plagiarism in the future.

Internet Safety

One of the primary goals of elementary school teachers utilizing the internet should be to ensure children's safety. Helping young, impressionable students understand the joys and dangers of the internet is becoming an increasingly necessary part of the teaching profession. While some students may have parents or guardians at home to assist in explaining the vast possibilities associated with web browsing, other students might not be as fortunate. Elementary teachers can help lay the foundation for safe internet use in the lives of students by directly discussing and implementing activities that encourage responsible web browsing. Showing students how to effectively evaluate websites is a great starting point for elementary school teachers because these activities will teach students to ask the right questions about internet resources.

▶ LOOKING BACK

Technologies' innovations continually change the way people communicate, socialize, interact, and learn. This means that teachers will also need to constantly evaluate and develop new teaching strategies to incorporate instructional technology into the curriculum. Teaching social studies is about much more than the transmission of content knowledge. Social studies is about preparing students to be good decision makers and citizens in an increasingly global society. As technology becomes more and more connected to daily life and the business world, skills in understanding these devices and their implications become a critical aspect of being an effective citizen in the digital era. Some of the skills necessary for students include the ability to understand the nature of media and visuals in our society and how to safely utilize the World Wide Web.

Social media sites and online etiquette are areas that need more direct attention in the educational environment. If teachers consistently ignore these issues simply because they are controversial or difficult to discuss, then students will be far more likely to fall victim to the dangers of the digital age, such as cyberbullying or cyberpredators. This chapter has examined several of the challenges and opportunities that are presented by incorporating instructional technology into the elementary classroom. To be sure, the vast field of technology in education surely indicates that not all aspects of this crucial area have been covered in this chapter. However, we have provided a solid foundation of essential information needed to effectively utilize technology to enhance social studies instruction in the elementary classroom. As technology will continue to develop and change over time, it is crucial for teachers to continually grow as lifelong learners and explore all the exciting educational opportunities that come with new technological innovations.

EXTENSION ACTIVITY

SCENARIO

You are at the mid-point of the fourth nine weeks at Yourtown Elementary School (YES). The end of your first year of teaching is quickly approaching, and your excitement can hardly be contained. At a faculty meeting, the assistant principal of YES, Dr. Waters, explains that the district has allotted YES some additional funding for technology for the enhancement of social studies instruction. Excited, the entire faculty starts clamoring about what they will buy. Before the meeting can get off task, Dr. Waters explains that he has selected a committee to determine what technologies are important for enhancing the teaching and learning of social studies. As Dr. Waters is finishing, he concludes by telling the faculty the selected committee members. You hear your name called. Shocked, a little embarrassed, and secretly proud, you willingly accept the appointment.

QUESTIONS

1. Dr. Waters charged you with chairing a technology committee to determine what technologies are needed to enhance the teaching and learning of social studies. What are the advantages to having a committee like this in a school? Are there any disadvantages?
2. Do you think having teacher input on technology purchases will produce better social studies instruction for students? Why or why not?
3. What are the qualities a teacher should possess to be on this committee? Of these qualities, which are the most important? How should these teachers be selected?

TASK

Once the committee has been formed and organized, the teachers get to work. Imagine your group is the committee. Dr. Waters wants you to create a list of technologies to enhance the teaching and learning of social studies. Dr. Waters did not share the technology budget, but instead requested a wish list. Your committee needs to organize how the money will be spent (e.g., grade level). As well, your committee needs to determine what technologies are important, who will use them, how they will be utilized, and how often. The committee's list should be detailed and shared with peers/instructor.

CHECKING FOR UNDERSTANDING

1. What is meant by the term *media literacy*?
2. Why is there a need to help students understand how to use technology?
3. Why is the Internet considered both a positive and a negative resource?
4. What are some ways to enhance instruction utilizing technology?
5. What areas of instructional technology are you comfortable using, and in what areas might you need more development?
6. When is it appropriate to use technology?
7. Which mobile technologies and apps do you want to use in your classroom?

▶ HELPFUL RESOURCES

Watch this video discussing tips for new teachers to consider when planning technology-enhanced lessons:

www.teachingchannel.org/videos/technology-in-the-classroom

Watch this short video about the evolving world of technology and its impact on twenty-first-century teachers:

www.youtube.com/watch?v=Ax5cNlutAys&list=PLvzOwE5lWqhSgJVgg7VfRkBisbmm-BFUL&index=2

Visit the ISTE website for a variety of helpful tools and resources:

www.iste.org

View the following video for an overview of ActivBoard possibilities in your classroom instruction:

https://www.youtube.com/b46860af-991b-4d33-9f2a-4cdcb0ec4be6

For more information on Media Literacy, visit the Center for Media Literacy website:

www.medialit.org

For more information on visual literacy, visit the International Visual Literacy Association website:

http://ivla.org/new/

Watch this video of a fifth-grade class in NY creating a public service announcement on equality:

https://themediaspot.org/2018/06/21/a-message-on-equality-from-bronx-5th-graders/

Watch this video of a middle school teacher doing a lesson on immigration using a documentary film:

www.teachingchannel.org/videos/teaching-cultural-identity

Visit the Carnegie Corporation Oral History Project website for examples of oral history videos:

www.columbia.edu/cu/lweb/digital/collections/oral_hist/carnegie/video-interviews/

Visit the Common Sense Education website for a list and overview of different social media websites and apps that could be used by teachers or students:

www.commonsense.org/education/top-picks/social-networks-for-students-and-teachers

▶ FURTHER READING

Lee, J., & Friedman, A. (Eds.). (2009). *Research on technology in social studies education.* Charlotte, NC: Information Age Publishing.

This edited book focuses on empirical research on the effectiveness of technology in the teaching and learning of social studies. Included in this book are numerous works that discuss what is being done in the social studies field in relation to the use of technology and how these important studies can guide the research of future educators.

Diem, R., & Berson, M. (Eds.). (2010). *Technology in retrospect: Social studies in the information age, 1984–2009.* Charlotte, NC: Information Age Publishing.

This edited book compiles the work of social studies professionals to examine how technology has changed the nature of instruction in social studies classrooms. This book will prove to be a valuable resource for teachers or researchers interested in the nature of social studies instruction during the information age.

Galloway, J., John, M., & McTaggart, M. (2015). *Learning with mobile and handheld technologies.* New York: Routledge Publishing.

This book explores the possibilities and pitfalls of teaching and learning with mobile devices, as well as e-learning in general. Resources and teaching project ideas utilizing devices are provided.

Cohen, D., & Rosenzweig, R. (2005). *Digital history: A guide to gathering, preserving, and presenting the past on the web*. Philadelphia: University of Pennsylvania.

This introductory textbook goes step by step in explaining to teachers, historians, and other educators how to navigate the vast amount of material found on the internet and utilize these resources for classroom instruction. It also offers information on how to set up learning projects using historical documents found on the World Wide Web.

Ferdig, R. E., & Kennedy, K. (Eds.). (2018). *Handbook of research on K–12 online and blended learning*. Pittsburgh, PA: ETC Press.

Teachers will find this book to be a valuable resource to further examine many topics related to K–12 online/virtual teaching. Added bonus: this book is currently available to download for free at https://kilthub.cmu.edu/articles/journal_contribution/Handbook_of_Research_on_K-12_Online_and_Blended_Learning_Second_Edition_/6686813.

Waters, S., & Russell, W. (2020). *Movies and moral dilemma discussions: A practical guide to cinema-based character development*. Charlotte, NC: Information Age Publishing.

This book details how film can be utilized to explore cinema-based character development through moral dilemma discussions. There is a specific chapter in the book that focuses on elementary-appropriate films with detailed questions and example activities.

Prensky, M. (2010). *Teaching digital natives: Partnering for real learning*. Thousand Oaks, CA: Corwin.

This book examines the promising practices of educating students during the twenty-first century. The author discusses how technology and new teaching methods should be combined to create a unique form of learning that is extremely beneficial to students in today's society.

▶ REFERENCES

Braden, R. A., & Hortin, J. A. (1982). Identifying the theoretical foundations of visual literacy. *Journal of Visual/Verbal Languaging*, 2(2), 97–42.

Center for Media Literacy. (2012). Retrieved April 12, 2012 from www.medialit.org/.

Felten, P. (2008). Visual literacy. *Change: The Magazine of Higher Education*, November/December, 60–64.

Galloway, J., John, M., & McTaggart, M. (2015). *Learning with mobile and handheld technologies*. New York: Routledge Publishing.

Gee, J. P. (2003). *What video games have to teach us about literacy and learning*. New York: Palgrave Macmillan.

Holmes, K., Russell, W., & Movitz, A. (2007). Reading in the social studies: Using subtitled films. *Social Education*, 71(6), 326–330.

ISTE. (2008). *Nets-t: Advancing digital age teaching*. Washington, DC: International Society for Technology in Education.

Kress, G. (1997). *Before writing: Rethinking the paths to literacy*. London: Routledge.

Lee, J. K. (2002). Digital history in the history/social studies classroom. *The History Teacher*, 35(4), 503–518.

National Council for the Social Studies. (2012). *National standards*. Available at: www.Socialstudies.org/standards/strands.

Rosenstone, R. A. (2006). *History on film/film on history*. London: Pearson Education Limited.

Russell, W. (2004). Teaching with film: A guide for social studies teachers. (ERIC Document Reproduction Service No. ED 530820).

Russell, W. (2007). *Using film in the social studies*. Lanham, MD: University Press of America.

Russell, W. (2009). *Teaching social issues with film*. Charlotte, NC: Information Age Publishing.

Russell, W. (2012a). The reel history of the world: Teaching world history with major motion pictures. *Social Education, 76*(1), 22–28.

Russell, W. (2012b). The art of teaching social studies with film. *The Clearing House: A Journal of Educational Strategies, Issues, and Ideas, 85*(4), 1–8.

Russell, W., & Waters, S. (2010a). Cinematic citizenship: Developing citizens of character with film. *Action in Teacher Education, 32*(2), 12–23.

Russell, W., & Waters, S. (2010b). *Reel character education: A cinematic approach to character development.* Charlotte, NC: Information Age Publishing.

Lesson Plans for Elementary Social Studies

12

▶ LOOKING AHEAD

No matter what grade level or subject area you teach, there is a universal need for effective planning. Planning lessons in the elementary classroom is becoming increasingly important as the emphasis on improving standardized test scores continues to place unprecedented restrictions on instructional time. Many elementary schools encourage, if not require, teachers to focus a great deal of classroom instruction on subjects directly tied to standardized testing (typically reading, math, and science). As social studies content continues to routinely be left out of standardized testing, even teachers with a desire to teach social studies concepts may struggle to find the time in a curriculum dominated by other areas. For this reason, efficient and purposeful planning needs to be considered when developing the scope and sequence of the curriculum for the school year, paying specific attention to when social studies units, lessons, and activities can be incorporated effectively into the classroom.

As you may recall from Chapter 4, there are a variety of ways to develop and plan for excellent social studies instruction. Teachers in schools all over the country routinely create lesson plans based on state, district, school, or administrative requirements. Some school administrators may require teachers to submit detailed, narrative-based lesson plans weeks in advance, while others may only require a brief outline of activities. Whatever the policy may be, it is crucial that teachers understand the lesson plan requirements and expectations of their school. The great diversity of lesson plan structures and requirements in elementary public schools is demonstrated in the following sections of classroom-tested social studies activities, written by elementary school teachers, for elementary school teachers.

This chapter provides readers with classroom-tested social studies lesson plans created by elementary school teachers at all grade levels and with various levels of teaching experience. There are two lesson plans provided for each grade level, K–6, for a total of fourteen lesson plans. As we mentioned earlier, these teachers come from different schools with a variety of different lesson plan requirements and writing styles. To provide some commonalities, we suggested categories that might be included in the lesson plans but allowed teachers the freedom and creativity warranted by professional educators to complete the lesson plans however they saw fit. Readers will find that some lessons are described in detail using narrative explanations while others contain bullet points or outlines of procedures to follow. It is also important to note that the authors did not solicit any specific social studies topics from the classroom teachers who composed these lesson plans. Teachers were simply encouraged to submit lesson plans that worked well for them while teaching social studies in the elementary classroom. We offer these lessons to you as examples of engaging classroom strategies, but also as examples of the different ways that lessons can be written. It is important for the reader to determine which style of lesson plan writing best meets school requirements and your own method of effective planning.

CAN YOU? DO YOU?

Can you . . .

- Explain how effective planning benefits classroom instruction and learning?
- Describe what a "good" lesson plan looks like?
- Identify or describe supplemental resources that improve lesson plans?
- Think of social studies activities that are engaging and encourage critical thinking at various grade levels?

Do you . . .

- Know where to find lesson plan resources using the internet?
- Know what lesson plan formats are typically expected of teachers working in your local school district?
- Understand how to engage multiple learning styles in your lesson plans?
- Understand different ways to plan for the needs of diverse learners?

FOCUS ACTIVITY

Before reading this chapter, try the following focus activity.

Think back on your experiences during your pre-service education. What types of social studies lessons did you typically see in the classroom (if any) or read about in professional journals? Can you remember any really engaging activities? What made these lessons exciting? Share and discuss your experiences with others. After a brief discussion, create a list of components you consider essential in a good lesson plan.

▶ KINDERGARTEN

LESSON PLAN ONE

Teacher: Courtney King & Janie Hubbard
Grade: Kindergarten
Unit Topic: Living in the past vs. today (technology)
Lesson Topic: Computers, Telephones, Televisions, Washing Machines

OBJECTIVES (STUDENT FRIENDLY)

- I will organize picture cards with a group and explain how we organized them.
- I will work with a group to sort pictures of past and present technology.
- I will create a picture timeline that shows my knowledge, effort, and completion.

STANDARDS

National Council for the Social Studies Standards Expectations:

- NCSS Standard 2: Time, Continuity, and Change: *Learners will understand concepts such as past, present, future, similarity, difference, and change.*
- NCSS Standard 8: Science, Technology, and Society: *Learners will understand that science often leads to new technology in areas such as communication and transportation, and results change over time.*

DAILY PLANNER

- Activating Strategy/Introduction: 10 minutes
- Whole Group/I Do: 15 minutes
- Small Group/We Do: 15 minutes
- Independent Activity/You Do: 15 minutes
- Closure: 5 minutes

ACTIVATING STRATEGY

- Before class, create four sets of past to present technology picture cards. Examples should be technological items students find familiar in their world such as telephone, television, computer, and washing machine.
- Separate the class of students into four groups, preferably at tables, and say, "Today we will discuss past and present technology. Do you know what the word *technology* means? Can you name something that you think is technology? It could be some type of machine you have at home or see at school What do you think about technology from the past? The word *past* means long ago. For example, when your parents/guardians were children or when your grandparents, older neighbors, or older friends were children, maybe they did not have computers, internet, iPhones, or microwave ovens. Maybe, when you see them, you might ask questions about what types of technology they had when they were children."
- Explain that each student group will receive a set of picture cards with five cards in each set. Student groups will closely observe the pictures, talk with group members, and sort them *in order*. At this point, do not tell students to sort them from past to present. Make sure students understand that their groups should organize the cards any way they wish.
- After groups are finished, take a quick digital photograph of each set.
- Ask groups to briefly explain to the class how they decided to order the cards. "Which technology did your group have? (e.g., telephone, computer, washing machine, television). How did your group decide to sort your cards?"

INSTRUCTION

- Tell students the purpose of the lesson is to learn about how people used technology in the past and how we use it today. We also want to learn how [familiar] technologies have changed over time. Orally provide instructions and expectations for the lesson before moving to the activities. "Sometimes, I may use the word *device* when talking about a certain type of technology or machine. For example, I may call a telephone a device."

- Open and view an Interactive Timeline such as one currently on PBS Learning Media. Show and discuss each device's progression. A washing machine timeline with color photographs is available. Washing Machine Timeline. *Sutori*. It is not necessary to read all information on the timelines. The teacher may simply point out various pictures of past technologies and discuss a bit. For example: "Before we had refrigerators with electricity to make them cold inside, some people used these wooden boxes [see the photo] and placed blocks of ice in them to keep their food cold. The iceman's job was to sell or deliver big ice blocks to people from a wagon, cart, or truck."
- Continue a teacher-facilitated discussion on the progression of technology presented in both timelines. "How are telephones [or another device] changing? How are the devices similar? Have you ever seen some of the older technologies? How do you think this technology changed people's lives?
- Display a teacher-made *Photo Analysis PowerPoint* presentation. Ask students guided questions and type their responses on the slides. Another option is to use the *National Archives Document Analysis Worksheets* for young students and/or English language learners available on the *National Archives* website.

GUIDED & INDEPENDENT PRACTICE

WE DO

- Give each student one technology picture card.
- Explain to students that they are going to look at their picture and determine if the device is from the past or in the present.
- Place two butcher paper posters on walls apart from one another. One should be labeled "PAST" and the other "PRESENT."
- Each student will take their picture card to the place labeled Past or Present (students may work in pairs for this activity).
- Encourage students to explain why they think their device is from the past or present. "What details did you see to decide if the technology was from the past or present?"
- After this activity, collect the technology picture cards from students.
- Explain to students, "Now that you have identified if the devices were from the past or present, you will place them in order from oldest to newest."
- Divide the class of students into four groups based on the devices. (i.e., telephone group, computer group, washing machine group).
- Place labels with device names on the white board [tape or make magnetic cards] and leave space for picture cards. Have students in each group come to the board to order the technology picture cards of their assigned devices from oldest (1) to newest (5) with the help of their group members.
- Continue the previous step with all groups.
- Ask students guiding questions to help them chronologically order the devices.
- "What picture should go first? Why do you think that one should be first?"
- "Which do you think should go next? Explain why you chose this one."
- Closure: Once all groups have completed the group timelines, have students return to the whole group area. Encourage all students to share anything new they know about past and present technology.

YOU DO

- Before class, the teacher will make a simple *timeline graphic organizer*. The same pictures as those on the sorting cards are used for this activity.
- Have students go to their desks or table groups.
- Orally give students directions and expectations for the activity.
- Students will work individually.
- "Take out a pencil and write your name on your paper, then put the pencil away."
- Instruct students to get their scissors, cut picture cards out, and then put the scissors away.
- "Take out your glue, paste pictures in order from oldest to newest for each device, and then put the glue away." Ask for questions and/or have another student repeat the directions for all to hear.
- Submit the paper to be reviewed and assessed according to criteria on the rubric: displayed content knowledge, effort, and completion.
- Provide students an allotted amount of time to complete the activity.
- Display a timer on the board to help students track their time.

CLOSURE

- Ask students to review their understanding of past and present technology. "We only talked about computers, televisions, telephones, and washing machines today. Can you name another type of technology?" Prompt as needed (e.g., cars, lamps, dishwashers, stoves, trains). "Do you think technology is good for people or harmful for people? What makes you say that?"
- Ask more critical-thinking questions, "When can we expect telephones to change again? Why is new technology important to me and others? Where can we get more information about different technologies? If you wanted to make a better [umbrella], how would you do it? What could we add to a bike to make it better?"
- Clear up any final misconceptions and move to the next content area.

ASSESSMENT/EVALUATION

- Student participation in initial card sort to assess prior knowledge: Observation of teacher's digital photographs.
- Student participation in group card sorting [past or present] and verbal reasoning for their choices: formative assessment checklist.
- Student-created timeline: Scored according to the extent the timeline demonstrates disciplinary content, effort, and completion: summative assessment rubric.

MATERIALS/TECHNOLOGY

- Computer and screen.
- White board and markers.
- Interactive timelines located on internet websites. See suggestions in the procedures section. Paper timelines may be created if technology is unavailable.
- Picture card sets. Teachers may choose to laminate and place magnetic tape on the backs of cards for future use. Only use realistic pictures because cartoons and/or clip art can be distracting. These are suggestions:
  1. *Telephone:* (1) Gower Bell Telephone 1880–1881; (2) Model 302 Telephone; (3) Motorola DynaTAC 8000x; (4) Blackberry 8300 Curve; (5) iPhone 11 Pro Max.
  2. *Computer:* (1) 1976 Apple 1 Computer in Briefcase; (2) Compaq Portable SLT/286; (3) Apple II; (4) Micron Laptop; (5) HP Spectra X360.

3. *Television:* (1) RCA 621TS; (2) RCA CT-100; (3) Sony TV Betamax Combo; (4) Sony Grand Wega; (5) Samsung Q800T.
4. *Washing Machine:* (1) Washing Board and Tub; (2) Drum Washing Machine; (3) Wringer Washing Machine; (4) Filter-Flo Washer; (5) Samsung Front Load Washer.

- Teacher-made *Photo Analysis PowerPoint* presentation.
- Pencils/scissors/glue.
- Posters: "Past" & "Present" to place on walls.
- Labels with device names for whole class activity.
- Teacher-made graphic organizer for independent activity.

CROSS-CURRICULAR CONNECTIONS

- Technology: identifying past and present technologies
- History: past and present technology
- Visual Literacy: realistic picture card activities
- Listening and Speaking/Language Arts: discussions, group collaboration
- Critical Thinking Questions: all curricular connections

MEETING INDIVIDUAL NEEDS OF DIVERSE LEARNERS

This lesson meets the needs of diverse learners because it is taught using multiple learning styles:

- Linguistic: collaborative group and partner work, classroom discussions, talk with older people about technologies when they were children (interviewing skills).
- Visual: several activities using picture cards; interactive internet timelines; picture analysis activity.
- Kinesthetic: card-sorting activities; moving to past/present labeled on the wall; creating a timeline.
- Auditory: classroom discussions, collaborative and partner group work, clear directions.
- Logical: purpose and procedures are briefly outlined for students before starting, distinct directions, realistic visuals.
- Intrapersonal: individual timeline activity.
- Interpersonal: collaborative and partner group work, time for asking questions and clarifying students' misconceptions, classroom discussion.

This lesson also meets the needs of English language learners (ELLs). Students will engage in picture-sort activities with the same realistic pictures several times. Many technological items highlighted and pictured in this lesson may be familiar. This lesson does not require students to read. The picture analysis frame for ELL learners from the National Archives is used. Families will receive important web links, brief videos, lesson translations, and translated messages, as needed, about the lesson's concepts. There are a number of no-cost translation websites on the internet.

LESSON PLAN TWO

Teacher: Christina Burroughs
Grade: Kindergarten
Unit Topic: Rules/Government
Lesson Topic: Rules: What are they? Why do we have them?

OBJECTIVES

- The student will create and defend a rule and its purpose in order to understand that the purpose of having rules in our daily lives is to protect our environment as well as for the fair treatment of others.
- Student-friendly "I can" statement: I can explain the importance of rules.

STANDARDS

- Common Core CCSS.ELA-LITERACY.CCRA.SL.1: Prepare for and participate effectively in a range of conversations and collaborations with diverse partners, building on others' ideas and expressing their own clearly and persuasively.
- Common Core CCSS.ELA-LITERACY.CCRA.SL.2: Integrate and evaluate information presented in diverse media and formats, including visually, quantitatively, and orally.
- NCSS Standard 4: Individual Development and Identity: Social studies programs should include experiences that provide for the study of individual development and identity.
- NCSS Standard 5: Individuals, Groups, and Institutions: Social studies programs should include experiences that provide for the study of interactions among individuals, groups, and institutions.
- NCSS Standard 6: Power, Authority, and Governance: Social studies programs should include experiences that provide for the study of how people create, interact with, and change structures of power, authority, and governance.
- NCSS Standard 10: Civic Ideals and Practices: Social studies programs should include experiences that provide for the study of the ideals, principles, and practices of citizenship in a democratic republic.

DAILY PLANNER

1. "No rules" game: 7 minutes
2. Read *Officer Buckle and Gloria* by Peggy Rathmann: 7 minutes
3. Compare/contrast activity: 8 minutes
4. Direct instruction about the purpose of rules: 5 minutes
5. Rule creation activity: 15 minutes
6. Share time/teacher assessment: 8 minutes
   Total Lesson Time = 50 minutes

ACTIVATING STRATEGY

The essential question students will ask themselves at the beginning of this lesson is what would happen if we had no rules? The teacher will then divide the students into random groups of three and hand each group a deck of playing cards while explaining that the object of the game is to win. No rules will be given to the students, and they will be given five minutes to play. Grouping based on academic level will not be a concern for this activity; however, students will be grouped based on cooperative attitude and personality. While students are "playing," the teacher will be monitoring the room, listening to conversations between the group members, and gathering examples to bring up in the discussion afterwards. At the end of the playing time, the students will return their playing cards and have a seat on the blue oval where the teacher will ask some of the following questions and allow for various students to respond: What did your group do during the playing time? How did you know how to play the game in your group? Would the game have been better if there were any rules? Why or why not? What kind of rules should there be in your group's game?

INSTRUCTION

After the discussion on the blue oval, the teacher will read *Officer Buckle and Gloria* by Peggy Rathmann as an introduction to what can happen when people do not follow the rules. Throughout the reading, the teacher will stop on strategically selected pages and ask students why it would be a good idea to follow Officer Buckle's safety tip (e.g., never stand on a swivel chair, keep your shoelaces tied, always wipe up spills before someone slips and falls, etc.). After reading, the teacher and students will create a T chart (a graphic organizer in which a student lists and examines two facets of a topic, such as pros and cons, advantages and disadvantages, facts vs. opinions, etc.) that compares and contrasts what happens when we do/don't have rules. Once the T chart is made, the teacher will spend a few minutes providing some direct instruction about how rules can protect people and the environment. The teacher will also tell students that all rules have a purpose behind them. We will look at the classroom rules as a class, and students will be able to explain what they think the purpose behind each of our classroom rules is.

GUIDED & INDEPENDENT PRACTICE

Once the teacher and students have had an opportunity to discuss the purpose behind rules and their importance in our lives (home, classroom, community, and world), students will move to their seats to work on an independent project. Each student will compose a new rule for the home, school, or community and write it down. Below their rule, they will draw two pictures: one that shows what happens when people follow this rule and another to show what can happen when people do not follow the rule. After 15 minutes of work time, the class will come back together to share their new rules with each other and explain their importance.

CLOSURE

To close this lesson, the teacher will ask students to take what they have learned about rules in this lesson and decide whether or not they are important to have. They will conclude that rules can help protect the environment and that all rules have a purpose. Lastly, the students will reflect on how rules can help them treat others fairly as well as be treated fairly by others.

ASSESSMENT/EVALUATION

To assess students' awareness of classroom rules and their purpose, students will tell one rule they know and explain how it keeps them safe or helps them be fair. This will be an informal evaluation for the teacher to quickly assess how much direct instruction the students need. A formal assessment for this lesson is to have students create a new rule for their home, the school, or their daycare and explain its purpose. Student learning is assessed throughout the lesson using Bloom's Taxonomy levels of remembering, analyzing, evaluating, and creating.

MATERIALS/TECHNOLOGY

- Decks of playing cards:1 per group
- *Officer Buckle and Gloria* by Peggy Rathmann

- ActivInspire or writing tablet to create T chart
- Kindergarten writing/illustrating paper
- Pencils and crayons

CROSS-CURRICULAR CONNECTIONS

Writing on one topic is present in this lesson as students write about a new rule of their own creation and explain its importance. While reading *Officer Buckle and Gloria*, the students will notice how pictures can help tell the story, a reading comprehension standard. Character, setting, and plot can also be reviewed as a result of reading this book. Comparing and contrasting is another reading skill that is used in this lesson as students help the teacher compare and contrast the use of rules.

MEETING INDIVIDUAL NEEDS OF DIVERSE LEARNERS

Students are learning through literature, writing, social interaction, and constructivism in this lesson. Higher-order thinking questions will be asked to extend this lesson for accelerated students; however, they can be used to scaffold across the spectrum of learners in the classroom. For a student who may speak English as a second language, the pictures in the book support the text very well to help teach the importance of having rules. Additionally, the lesson provides opportunities for interpretation of the materials as the students are creating new rules for their selected environment. If the student depicts a rule and can show through illustrations what happens with and without the implementation of the rule, full credit will be given to the student, even if it is a rule that is already in place since the communication may have affected the student's performance. Any assistance from a translator provided by the school district during this lesson to help the teacher and student communicate would only serve as positive reinforcement for the learner.

CHARACTER EDUCATION CONNECTION

Based on the Character Counts model, respect and fairness are both values related to character that are addressed in this lesson. By following rules implemented in the environment, students are learning to respect others, especially those who create the rules. Additionally, students can learn about fairness by analyzing whether or not the rules that are created are fair to those who are asked to follow them. These issues surrounding character can be addressed in the lesson when reading *Officer Buckle and Gloria* and when students are sharing the rule they create during their independent work time.

▶ FIRST GRADE

LESSON PLAN ONE

Teacher: Joe Peeden
Grade: First Grade
Unit Topic: Cultures of the World
Lesson Topic: China and Australia

OBJECTIVES

- I can identify and describe the differences in culture between Australia and China.

STANDARDS

- Common Core CCSS.ELA-LITERACY.CCRA.SL.1: Prepare for and participate effectively in a range of conversations and collaborations with diverse partners, building on others' ideas and expressing their own clearly and persuasively.
- Common Core CCSS.ELA-LITERACY.CCRA.SL.2: Integrate and evaluate information presented in diverse media and formats, including visually, quantitatively, and orally.
- NCSS Standard 1: Culture: Social studies programs should include experiences that provide for the study of culture and cultural diversity.
- NCSS Standard 3: People, Places, and Environment: Social studies programs should include experiences that provide for the study of people, places, and environments.
- NCSS Standard 4: Individual Development and Identity: Social studies programs should include experiences that provide for the study of individual development and identity.
- NCSS Standard 9: Global Connections: Social studies programs should include experiences that provide for the study of global connections and interdependence.

DAILY PLANNER

- Students will go to large carpet in front of Smart Board to begin lesson. During this time, the teacher will remind the children about proper seating arrangement and behavior and state the day's objective: 0–5 minutes.
- The teacher will show the children a map-based picture of both Australia and China on the Smart Board. The students will write some of the information they know about each on the respective image: 5–13 minutes.
- The teacher will only correct information that is either culturally insensitive or answers deemed inappropriate for the class discussion.
- Teacher describes instructions and expectations of the day's assignment and then allows the children to transition to desks: 13–15 minutes.
- Students will analyze the items laid on their group's desks and decide if they are from/about Australia or China: 15–30 minutes.
- For first 5 minutes, students are to analyze and discuss each item. The item list should be composed in a graphic organizer table and consists of the following:
- Kangaroo
- Rugby ball
- China dolls
- The Great Wall
- Sydney Opera House
- Calendar
- Chopsticks
- Panda
- Koala

The students should look for properties of each item that could show its origin.

The last 10 minutes will be used filling in the graphic organizer provided and creating an illustration of their favorite item and describing its purpose.

- Transition back to Smart Board: 30–31 minutes.
- Students will decide as a whole group which items belong to which countries. Teacher will then lead a discussion about each item: 32–37 minutes.
- Students will drag an icon of the item to its correct country. Guessed item locations will be decided upon by the class in a thumbs up/down manner. The teacher will assist by detailing some key facts about each correctly identified item and its cultural significance.
- Students work independently on passport questions: 38–44 minutes.

- The teacher will circulate the room to assist with spelling or other various problems.
- Students pack up materials and transition to next lesson: 44–45 minutes.

ACTIVATING STRATEGY

The students will begin today's lesson at our Smart Board spots. It is here that I will show the children a picture representation of China and Australia. Children will attempt to fill in each country with as much information as they know. This will demonstrate a baseline knowledge of each country for the class. The students will then be asked if there is any information that they want to learn about each country that they would like to add to the map (K-W-L chart: a graphic organizer tracking what students know (K), want to know (W), and have learned (L) about a given topic).

INSTRUCTION

I will show the students the worksheet titled "China and Australia." I will tell the students that after we have written down a vast amount of information about what we know about each country, it is time for us to use the information. I am going to let you look at a group of items, and I need you to figure out which culture each item belongs to. I will then show the students the following items: a stuffed kangaroo, a rugby ball, a china doll set, a picture of the Great Wall, a picture of the Sydney Opera House, an astrological calendar, chopsticks, a stuffed panda, and a picture of a koala. I will then model for the children how I will look at each item and, based on what I already know about each item, decide if it fits with the Australian or Chinese culture with my group. Students will then be dismissed to their desks to meet with their previously assigned desk groups. These groups are heterogeneous and are based on both personality of students and a variety of student ability. Each group contains one high-achieving student and one low-achieving student.

GUIDED & INDEPENDENT PRACTICE

The students will then be dismissed to their desks to begin their group evaluation of the cultural items. Students will decide, as a group, which country each item belongs to. The students will then write their group's answer on their worksheets. If, while the teacher is monitoring group work, the students either appear overtly stumped by an item or do not appear to be working together, the teacher will intervene and discuss the items with the student groups. Following their declaration of each item's respective country, the groups will reconvene at the Smart Board carpet to discuss their decisions. Each group will have the chance to identify their object as being from either China or Australia. As each group gives their opinion on the item's country of origin, the teacher will take a class consensus for the appropriate location. At the conclusion of item classification and agreement from fellow students, the teacher will discuss the correct answers for each item with the class. The teacher will discuss the cultural significance of each item. Students will then be dismissed to their desks to complete their individual passport answers for the China and Australia pages. The students will work quietly and independently during this time. Those students who have been previously identified as needing assistance or who appear to have difficulty with the assignment will meet with the teacher at the back table to outline their responses.

CLOSURE

After the students have completed their responses in their student passports (passport categories consist of: country visited, beliefs, traditions, customs, language, and foods), the class will gather back together at the large carpet to discuss the cultures of the two countries. Students will be asked to describe either an item or an aspect of Chinese/Australian culture.

ASSESSMENT/EVALUATION

- Group Worksheet will be graded for completion, but not accuracy.
- An individual, rubric-based grade will be given on each day's passport assignment (Table 12.1).
- Individual passports will be graded on a performance-based rubric at the conclusion of the unit (Table 12.2).
- A post–formal summative exam will occur at the conclusion of the unit.
- A pre-unit informal exam will be given to the students prior to the unit.
- The teacher throughout the lesson will make informal observations of student understanding of cultural differences.

Table 12.1 Rubric for Passport Assignment

E	S	N	No grade
Student answers all questions thoroughly with minor grammar or sight-word mistakes.	Student answers all questions but makes multiple sight-word and grammar mistakes.	Student does not complete all questions for the country.	Student does not complete any questions or does not give logical/topical answers to the questions asked.

Table 12.2 Rubric for Individual Passports

E	S	N	No grade
Student completes all pages in passport with a high level of quality in writing.	Student completes more than 2 country's questions but fails to use a high level of accurate information or answers contain a significant number of sight-word or grammatical errors.	Student completes less than 2 country's worth of questions or fails to answer most questions in a logical or accurate manner.	Student does not complete any parts of the passport assignment.

MATERIALS/TECHNOLOGY

- 1 passport per student
- 1 pencil
- Photo of Australia and China from a country-size perspective
- Smart Board
- ELMO
- 1 box for each student containing either the actual item or a photo of the following:
  - a stuffed kangaroo
  - a rugby ball
  - a china doll set
  - a picture of the Great Wall
  - a picture of the Sydney Opera House
  - a Chinese New Year calendar

- a chopstick
- a stuffed panda
- a picture of a koala

Cross-Curricular Connections

Writing is prevalent throughout the course of this unit.

Meeting Individual Needs of Diverse Learners

This lesson contains material for intrapersonal, interpersonal, visual, verbal, and logical learning styles. Due to the group-based nature of a large portion of the activities, even the most struggling students will be able to accomplish aspects of this lesson. In addition, students who are struggling with their writing will be able to work with assistance from the teacher to best meet the expectations for the students.

Character Education Connection

This lesson will help increase the level of student understanding of the differences of people around the world. In this way, I hope to foster a higher level of empathy and acceptance of differences within my students.

Lesson Resources

Choose your favorite item, draw your own illustration, and decide why it is important to that country's culture.

LESSON PLAN TWO

Teacher: Irenea Walker
Grade: First Grade
Unit Topic: African American History
Lesson Topic: Civil Rights Activists

OBJECTIVES (STUDENT FRIENDLY)

- I can identify African American Civil Rights activists.
- I can describe how African American Civil Rights activists made a difference promoting equality for all.

STANDARDS

- NCSS Standard 2: Time, Continuity, and Change: Social studies programs should include experiences that provide for the study of the past and its legacy.
- NCSS Standard 4: Individual Development and Identity: Social studies programs should include experiences that provide for the study of individual development and identity.
- NCSS Standard 5: Individuals, Groups, and Institutions: Social studies programs should include experiences that provide for the study of interactions among individuals, groups, and institutions.

- NCSS Standard 6: Power, Authority, and Governance: Social studies programs should include experiences that provide for the study of how people create, interact with, and change structures of power, authority, and governance.
- NCSS Standard 10: Civic Ideals and Practices: Social studies programs should include experiences that provide for the study of ideals, principles, and practices of citizenship in a democratic republic.

DAILY PLANNER

- Activating Strategy/Introduction: 5 minutes
- Whole Group Instruction: 15 minutes
- Guided & Independent Practice: 25 minutes
- Closure: 5 minutes

ACTIVATING STRATEGY

- The teacher will begin today's lesson on the large carpet. The teacher will inform the students that today they will learn about African Americans from the past who wanted all people to be treated equally. To initiate the lesson, the teacher will display pictures of these three individuals as most of them will recognize who they are; this will serve as an attention grabber. The teacher will explain that the past is something that happened a long time ago. Next, the teacher will call on select students to define the term *equality*. After the students have defined the term and the teacher reiterates for clarity, the teacher will show the students pictures of African American civil rights activists. These will include Dr. Martin Luther King Jr., Rosa Parks, and Harriet Tubman.

INSTRUCTION

- Explain to students that other people just like Dr. King, Rosa Parks, and Harriet Tubman also took action so everyone could be treated equally.
- Define the term *activist*.
- Inform the students that today they will listen to a story about a teacher named Clara Luper.
- Read aloud *Someday Is Now: Clara Luper and the 1958 Oklahoma City Sit-Ins*.
- The teacher will prompt higher-order thinking questions.
- What did Clara Luper do that made her an activist?
- Explain why Clara Luper wanted everyone to be treated equally.
- Call on student volunteers to explain a sit-in.
- Ask students to share why it is important to treat everyone equally.
- Explain to students that they will learn about other African American activists who wanted everyone to be treated equally.

GUIDED & INDEPENDENT PRACTICE

WE DO

- Have students report back to their assigned seats.
- Inform students that they are going to learn about three civil rights activists.
- The three individuals are Fannie Lou Hamer, Mary McLeod Bethune, and John Lewis.
- Show the students a picture of Fannie Lou Hamer.
- Explain that she wanted Blacks and women to be able to vote. Explain that she gave speeches to many people so that Blacks and women could vote.

- Have students watch the short video on Voting for Kids: Why Voting is Important? www.youtube.com/watch?v=GrG7zBUDiqQ.
- Provide students with a coloring sheet of Fannie Lou Hamer. Once students have finished coloring their picture, provide each student with a blank writing strip.
- Have students write two sentences about something they would vote to change. The first sentence should describe what they want to change. The second sentence should state why they want to change it.
- Show the students a picture of Mary McLeod Bethune.
- Explain to students that she was a teacher who believed all children should be allowed to learn. Inform them that she started a school for African American girls. Inform them that African American boys attended the school later, and it became a university known as Bethune Cookman University.
- Have students listen to this children's music video. Play the video a few times and have students sing along. www.youtube.com/watch?v=ar4xRc7-Sw4.
- Provide students with a coloring sheet of Mary McLeod Bethune. Once students have finished coloring their picture, provide each student with a blank writing strip.
- Have students write two sentences about their favorite subject in school. The first sentence should include their favorite subject. The second sentence should include details of why that is their favorite subject.
- Show the students a picture of United States Representative John Lewis.
- Have students watch the short video on John Lewis: Civil Rights Leader www.youtube.com/watch?v=V92wuGnFxK0.
- Provide students with a coloring sheet of U.S. Representative John Lewis. Once students have finished coloring their picture, provide each student with a blank writing strip.
- Have students write two sentences on how they will be nice to the peers in their class. The first sentence should detail why it is important to be nice. The second sentence should give one example of how they will be nice to their peers.
- Assist students as needed with their writing.
- Call on students to share their coloring sheets and sentences.
- After students have shared their coloring sheets and sentences, reiterate the importance of treating everyone equally regardless of the color of their skin.

YOU DO

- Place several (4–5) pre-selected magazines at students' tables. It is important that the teacher review each magazine page before allowing students to view. The teacher may have to remove several pages to ensure that the images are grade appropriate. The teacher may want to select kid-friendly magazines such as *Scholastic News for Kids*.
- Inform students that they will need to search through the magazines and find pictures of people doing nice things for others. Provide examples such as opening the door for someone, sharing crayons, and helping a friend tie their shoes. The examples provided will mostly be found in a kid-friendly magazine, but appropriate magazines (even those with adults) in which people are being nice towards each other will work.
- The students will cut out seven pictures and create a collage.
- The pictures can be from the different magazines that the teacher places at the students' tables. The pictures do not have to be from the same magazine.
- When the students are finished, have them share their collage with peers at their table.

CLOSURE

- Ask students to share what they learned about being an activist and treating everyone equally.

- Ask, "Now that you have learned about Clara Luper, Fannie Lou Hamer, Mary McLeod Bethune, and John Lewis, tell me what all these people have in common."
- Ask, "Share different ways that you will treat people in our class and people outside our class equally."

ASSESSMENT/EVALUATION

- Student responses from teacher questioning.
- Students writing sentences based on prior knowledge and new information.
- Coloring sheets to reiterate visuals of each civil rights activist.
- Students creating a collage on what they learned about African American activists in this lesson and applying it to real-world experiences.
- Students identifying ways of treating everyone equally and being kind to others.
- Activating strategy: building upon students' prior knowledge.
- Informal observations by the teacher for student understanding of treating everyone equally.

MATERIALS/TECHNOLOGY

- Children's book *Someday Is Now: Clara Luper and the 1958 Oklahoma City Sit-Ins*
- Smart Board/Interactive display
- Magazines
- Scissors
- Glue
- Construction paper
- Crayons
- Pencils
- Writing strips
- Pictures of civil rights activists discussed in the lesson
- Coloring sheets of civil rights activists

CROSS-CURRICULAR CONNECTIONS

- Writing/Grammar: Students will use what they learned about each of the civil rights activists and write sentences that focuses on each leader's specific activist role. Students will verbally share their collage with someone at their table.
- Arts: Students will color images of African American civil rights activists. Students will create a collage of people doing nice things for others.

MEETING INDIVIDUAL NEEDS OF DIVERSE LEARNERS

- This lesson contains material for intrapersonal, interpersonal, visual, verbal, and hands-on learning styles.
- English language learners – Visuals will be used (coloring sheets and pictures) to aid ELL students.

CHARACTER EDUCATION CONNECTION

- This lesson promotes equality and respect for all.

▶ SECOND GRADE

LESSON PLAN ONE

Teacher: Patti Wolfinger
Grade: Second Grade
Unit Topic: Native American Regions
Lesson Topic: STEM Project – Native American Home

OBJECTIVES (STUDENT FRIENDLY)

Students will be able to recognize that Native Americans were the first inhabitants of North America.

Students will be able to compare and contrast tribes from various Native American regions of the United States.

Students will recognize cause-and-effect relationships within the information they learn about Native Americans.

STANDARDS

- CCSS.ELA-LITERACY.CCRA.SL.1: Prepare for and participate effectively in a range of conversations and collaborations with diverse partners, building on others' ideas and expressing their own clearly and persuasively.
- CCSS.ELA-LITERACY.CCRA.SL.2: Integrate and evaluate information presented in diverse media and formats, including visually, quantitatively, and orally.
- NCSS: Theme 1: Through the study of culture and cultural diversity, learners understand how human beings create, learn, share, and adapt to culture and appreciate the role of culture in shaping their lives and society, as well as the lives and societies of others. In schools, this theme typically appears in units and courses dealing with geography, history, sociology, and anthropology, as well as multicultural topics across the curriculum.
- NCSS: Theme 3: This theme helps learners develop their spatial views and perspectives of the world; understand where people, places, and resources are located and why they are there; and explore the relationship between human beings and the environment. In schools, this theme typically appears in courses dealing with geography and area studies, but it is also important for the study of the geographical dimension of other social studies subjects.

DAILY PLANNER

Each group will be given various building materials. (Each will be given the same materials, but in varying amounts. This will require them to analyze their resources when deciding which structure to build.) Students will discuss, decide which home they will build, plan, and build as a group. When finished, students will explain why they chose their region and why their home is an appropriate dwelling for that region.

ACTIVATING STRATEGY

Teacher will access prior knowledge by reviewing five regions by using previously used PowerPoint to summarize information learned about each region. Students will participate in a "Plickers" quiz, assessing knowledge of subject.

INSTRUCTION

Teacher will give more in-depth background on what students have previously learned within their unit on Native American regions by showing visuals and discussing the architecture of the wigwam, teepee, longhouse, and adobe.

GUIDED & INDEPENDENT PRACTICE

Students will be divided into heterogeneous groups. Each group will be given a bag of misc. building supplies (cloth, leaves, pipe cleaners, etc.). Groups will discuss which type of Native American home their supplies would best build. Students will have 15 minutes to plan and make sketches.

Students will present their sketches, and the teacher will ask leading questions to help students recognize strengths and weaknesses of designs. Students will be given 5 minutes to revise plans.

Teacher will now give "supplies assignments" to students. Students will only be allowed to use the materials they are assigned. (**Do not tell them this until this point in the activity**.) This will ensure that all group members participate and work together. All students may use tape and glue. All supplies must be used.

Group 1: Cloth and straws
Group 2: Sticks and mulch
Group 3: Wire, leaves, grass, moss
Group 4: Pipe cleaners and Play-Doh

Students will have 30 minutes to build their Native American home with the supplies they have been given based on their plan. Teacher will circulate giving feedback and guidance when needed to make sure all group members are participating equally.

CLOSURE

Students will take approximately 10 minutes to complete cause-and-effect sheet as a group and present their projects. Students will state what region their home is designed for (effect) and explain why they chose this region (cause) based on the supplies in their bags and the resources, land, and climate of their region. Students discuss challenges they faced, as well as what they would do differently if they were able to repeat activity. By doing this, students will acknowledge that others may have had valuable input and recognize how each member may have contributed to a better outcome.

ASSESSMENT/EVALUATION

Summative – Plickers
Formative – collaborative group work, construction of house

MATERIALS/TECHNOLOGY

- Computer
- PowerPoint
- Plickers
- Cloth and straws
- Sticks and mulch

- Wire, leaves, grass, moss
- Pipe cleaners and Play-Doh

CROSS-CURRICULAR CONNECTIONS

- Art – constructing houses out of provided materials; drawing of sketches
- Science – understanding how to construct a house

MEETING INDIVIDUAL NEEDS OF DIVERSE LEARNERS

- English Language Learners – Visuals will be used to aid ELL students (pictures of Native American housing). The teacher should try to translate the key vocabulary words into a student's native tongue if possible.
- Multiple Intelligences – This lesson fosters visual, kinesthetic, interpersonal, and intrapersonal learning through the small cooperative grouping and activities within the assignment.

CHARACTER EDUCATION CONNECTION

- Respect: Students are encouraged to respect and treat everyone as equals regardless of culture.
- Cooperation: learning to work together.

LESSON PLAN TWO

Teacher: Elyse Trout
Grade: Second Grade
Unit Topic: Our World: Maps and Globes
Lesson Topic: Maps and Globes

OBJECTIVES

- The students will be able to analyze and identify major landmasses and bodies of water on various representations (maps, globes, etc.).
- The students will be able to identify a variety of different types of maps.

Student Friendly

- "I can identify the seven continents and major bodies of water on a map and globe."
- "I can identify a variety of different types of maps."

STANDARDS

- Common Core CCSS.ELA-LITERACY.CCRA.SL.1: Prepare for and participate effectively in a range of conversations and collaborations with diverse partners, building on others' ideas and expressing their own clearly and persuasively.
- Common Core CCSS.ELA-LITERACY.CCRA.SL.2: Integrate and evaluate information presented in diverse media and formats, including visually, quantitatively, and orally.
- NCSS Standard 3: People, Places, and Environment: Social studies programs should include experiences that provide for the study of people, places, and environments.

- NCSS Standard 7: Production, Distribution, and Consumption: Social studies programs should include experiences that provide for the study of how people organize for the production, distribution, and consumption of goods and services.
- NCSS Standard 9: Global Connections: Social studies programs should include experiences that provide for the study of global connections and interdependence.

DAILY PLANNER

Social Studies (12:00–1:00)

- Activating Strategy: 5 minutes
- Administer Pre-assessment: 5 minutes
- Whole Group Activity (Read aloud & discussion): 20 minutes
- Guided & Independent Practice: 10 minutes
- Recap/Discussion (check & interactive maps): 10 minutes
- Closure: Collect materials: 5 minutes

ACTIVATING STRATEGY

Activate Prior Knowledge

"Most of you already know what a map is. Today, we are going to learn not only what it is, but also what it is used for and how it compares to a globe."

Engaging Strategy

A K-W-L chart (a graphic organizer tracking what students know (K), want to know (W), and have learned (L) about a given topic) will be used in order to discover what students already know about this topic. They will be given some time to fill out the "K" and "W" columns of the chart in order to allow the teacher to get some insight about what they already know and what they wish to learn during the unit. Later in the unit, the students will indicate what they have learned by completing the "L" section.

INSTRUCTION

The objective will be stated, and students will be asked to repeat it again along with the teacher.

The teacher will activate prior knowledge by connecting this lesson to what they already know. "Most of you already know what a map is. Today, we are going to learn not only what it is, but also what it is used for and how it compares to a globe."

Then, the teacher will pass out the K-W-L charts and direct the students/model (I Do) how to complete the first two columns. The students should be familiar with this chart since it is not the first time that it is being used. The teacher will allow them a few minutes to fill it out as she walks around to assist low-achieving and ELL students as needed. If they are having trouble verbalizing what they want to say, she will allow them to draw pictures of what they know and want to learn rather than write it out.

Next, the teacher will present the students with a blank map of the world. There are lines on the seven continents and the major bodies of water. She will ask them to put their offices up and label as many places on the map as they can. She will assure them that this is not for a grade, but rather just to see what they already know and areas she needs to focus her teaching on. The maps will be collected and reviewed later in the day.

"Well, today, we are going to read a great book that I think you will all really enjoy called *There's a Map on My Lap* by Tish Rabe." The teacher will hold up the book and generate a brief discussion about what they see on the cover and what they predict the book will be about. "Now, let's analyze the front cover; what do you see?" After they briefly discuss the front cover, the teacher will begin reading the book.

She will come to a stopping point in the book when it discusses the orange peel demonstration, and she will actually do this demonstration for the students. She will begin with an orange and talk about how it is like the world or a globe. The teacher will then begin to peel the orange and flatten it out and ask how that resembles a map. Then, she will discuss with the students that a globe is a much better depiction of the world and ask them why they think this is the case. She will use higher-order thinking questions to generate discussion. Then, she will continue reading the book. I think this is a great read-aloud to introduce maps because it is very engaging with rhymes and great illustrations. Additionally, it discusses some key points about reading maps and globes, all of which are in child-friendly language. The book describes what a cartographer is and their work. It specifically addresses the difference between maps and globes and compares the pros and cons of each. Additionally, the book addresses latitude and longitude lines, map scales, and the use of an atlas. I also like how this book focuses on different types of maps in a fun way, such as with topographical maps for hikers. The teacher will periodically stop throughout the read-aloud to talk about these key terms in more depth.

Once the book is finished, the teacher will generate a brief discussion about why this is an important skill to recognize. Differentiating between maps and globes is very important. Then, the teacher will tell the students that today they will get to color and label their own "orange peel map" of the world. They will have several minutes to complete this activity as they use the interactive website on the Smart Board.

Then, once the activity is done and they have had time to work in pairs, the teacher will engage the class in a brief discussion about different types of maps. "What are some different types of maps that you all can think of? One in the book that we just read was a climate map. Can you think of another?" The teacher will call on volunteers and non-volunteers. After they list a few on the board, she will show them the Interactive MapMaker website where they can view all these different kinds of maps. They will first look at the climate map and then go from there, depending on what sparks the students' interests.

The teacher will close the lesson and tell them that tomorrow they will have a chance to learn more about maps and their place in the world!

Higher-Order Thinking Questions

1. What can you infer about the cover?
2. Why are maps so important?
3. What makes a map different from a globe? Can you compare and contrast them?
4. Why are globes a better representation of our world?
5. What are some different types of maps that you can think of?
6. Why is analyzing and reading a map such an important skill, even in second grade?
7. Is our world made up of more water or more land? How do you know?

GUIDED & INDEPENDENT PRACTICE

"Orange Peel Map" Activity

The teacher will put students into differentiated pairs (one high- and one low-achieving student). She will distribute the sheets and have them together to discuss for just a moment where they think certain landmasses are located.

Next, the teacher will pull up the National Geographic MapMaker Interactive website on the Smart Board. The students, along with the teacher, will locate the different landmasses and bodies of water on the interactive map. The teacher will model how to do the first one, starting with their continent, North America (I Do). She will then ask for volunteers to come up to the front of the room to locate on the map something that they are already familiar with (We Do).

The students will then be asked to continue labeling the rest of the map with their partner for just a few minutes (You Do). As they are found on the map on the Smart Board, the students will color their maps at their seat according to the coloring code at the bottom. (Teacher can decide on colors.)

After they have worked for several minutes, the maps will be checked orally, and as they are checked, the students will be called upon to come out and find the location of that landmass on the class globe. The teacher will generate a discussion about the subdivisions on the globe and discuss the equator and hemispheres as they check their answers.

Intervention

Students who have not shown mastery of the day's objective will have one-on-one re-teaching at a later time.

Enrichment

For students who finish early, I will encourage them to get a *Time for Kids: Map and Graph Skills* magazine (several copies should be made available) from the back of the room and read through it with their partner while they are waiting for the rest of the class to finish up (before the maps are checked with the whole group). This will benefit both students since they will both gain the exposure to this type of text and the above-level student can support/assist the approaching-level student as needed while they read. Also, there are activities in the magazines to discuss/complete with a partner as they go along.

CLOSURE

The teacher will restate the objective. The teacher will have them engage in a brief discussion about this in order to establish relevance. "Think of a time in your life when you would need to use this skill." She will call on volunteers to share their opinions and address future learning in order to connect to tomorrow's lesson.

ASSESSMENT/EVALUATION

Informal assessment will be used periodically throughout the lesson through informal questioning and student discussion. Volunteers and non-volunteers will be called upon to participate in order to check for understanding. In addition to informal verbal checks for understanding, there will be a variety of formative assessments administered throughout the duration of this lesson, such as the K-W-L chart, the blank map, and the "orange peel map" activity coloring map. Each type of assessment will help the teacher gain some insight as to what skills the students understand and what needs more explanation. This will allow the teacher to monitor student progress throughout the unit and adjust the next lesson as needed. Moreover, students who did not show mastery of this lesson, based on the assessment, will be pulled into a small group for re-teaching later in the day and given the opportunity to reflect and correct their work. At the end of the unit, the students will be given a summative assessment that will be used to determine their overall mastery of this skill.

MATERIALS/TECHNOLOGY

- K-W-L charts
- Blank world maps
- "Orange Peel Map"
- Crayons
- *There's a Map on My Lap* by Tish Rabe
- An orange
- Several copies of *Time for Kids: Map and Graph Skills*
- Smart Board
- Interactive National Geographic MapMaker website: http://education.nationalgeographic.com/mapping/interactive-map/?ar_a=1
- Computer

CROSS-CURRICULAR CONNECTIONS

During this lesson, students will be analyzing maps and globes. Analyzing is a skill that is relevant to all subject areas. They will also be asked to write what they already know about this topic and be encouraged to read the *TIME* magazine, which incorporates the reading and writing components. Finally, the students will look at a variety of maps that are categorized based on different topics. Categorization is a math skill that we have addressed earlier in the year.

MEETING INDIVIDUAL NEEDS OF DIVERSE LEARNERS

This lesson meets the needs of every learner. There are several visual aids that will be provided for those who are visual learners. The teacher will be using a globe and an interactive website for those kinesthetic learners. Moreover, there will be a read-aloud and stimulating discussions in order to engage those who are linguistic learners. All these activities were designed in order to engage each and every learner in the class. For those students who need extra support (ELL and low-achieving students), the teacher will walk around during the entire lesson in order to make sure they are staying on track and keeping up with the pace of activities. Moreover, if they show any signs that they are struggling at any point in the lesson, especially guided and independent practice, the teacher will call them to the back table for some small group support and scaffolding.

CHARACTER EDUCATION CONNECTION

The students will be working in partners and will need to be respectful of one another's thoughts, ideas, and opinions.

▶ THIRD GRADE

LESSON PLAN ONE

Teacher: Stephanie Craig
Grade: Third Grade
Unit Topic: Government: Here, There, and Everywhere
Lesson Topic: Global Governments and National Government

OBJECTIVES

- I can discuss the purposes of government.
- I know that government agencies try to protect the environment.
- I can describe the different structures of government.
- I can examine the way different regions govern.
- I can understand why the government has to consent to the people.

STANDARDS

- Common Core CCSS.ELA-LITERACY.CCRA.SL.1: Prepare for and participate effectively in a range of conversations and collaborations with diverse partners, building on others' ideas and expressing their own clearly and persuasively.
- Common Core CCSS.ELA-LITERACY.CCRA.SL.2: Integrate and evaluate information presented in diverse media and formats, including visually, quantitatively, and orally.
- NCSS Standard 5: Individuals, Groups, and Institutions: Social studies programs should include experiences that provide for the study of interactions among individuals, groups, and institutions.
- NCSS Standard 6: Power, Authority, and Governance: Social studies programs should include experiences that provide for the study of how people create, interact with, and change structures of power, authority, and governance.
- NCSS Standard 9: Global Connections: Social studies programs should include experiences that provide for the study of global connections and interdependence.
- NCSS Standard 10: Civic Ideals and Practices: Social studies programs should include experiences that provide for the study of the ideals, principles, and practices of citizenship in a democratic republic.

DAILY PLANNER

- Introduce standards: 1–2 minutes
- "Word splash": 7–10 minutes
- Discussion: "Why do we have a government?": 3–5 minutes
- Introduce the three main forms of government: 8 minutes
- Students design skits: 15 minutes
- Students perform skits: 5 minutes
- Wrap-up/Closure/Ticket Out the Door: 5 minutes
- Total: 50 minutes

ACTIVATING STRATEGY

"Word splash"

- I will write "government" on the board.
- Students will be given 2 minutes to write down words or phrases that they think of when seeing this word.
- Once students are finished, they will talk to their group members. (Students' desks are arranged in groups. There are four groups in the class.)
- During this time, the teacher monitors the room and facilitates discussion as necessary.
- Groups will select one person to share with the whole class.
- Selected students will share with the whole class.
- Once students have shared, it is important for the teacher to give feedback about how what the students stated is relevant to the material.

INSTRUCTION

- Introduce "I can" statements.
- Lead informal discussion on "Why do we have a government?" Ask HOT questions such as: "What would happen if we didn't have a government? Do you think every country has the same type of government?"
- Introduce the three main types of government: democracy, monarchy, and dictatorship. Place the examples of each on the ActivBoard using a document camera. (If you do not have a document camera accessible, you may import the images into a PowerPoint file. Make sure images used are age appropriate and reflect principles and/or examples of each type of government).
- Pass a handout with the images to each child so that they may follow along.
- Once the three types of government have been presented, ask students which type of government that the United States uses. How do you know? What examples can you give to justify your answer?
- What do you think happens if the people in the country don't agree with how the government is being run?
- Now that students have an understanding of the various forms of government around the world, they will create skits. For the skits, you will need three groups (one for each form of government). These groups should be grouped heterogeneously by ability so that all students are in an environment to succeed. Students should be allowed to take their handouts with them to their groups. ELL accommodations: provide handout with images and text explanations in Spanish.
- Expectations should be modeled to students:
- Work together with your group members.
- 3-inch voices (classroom strategy where students communicate softly, only speaking loud enough for someone 3 inches away to hear them).
- Directions: You are creating a skit that demonstrates the form of government that your group has. What does this form of government look like in action?
- Show students the rubric so that they have a visual of expectations.
- While students are creating their skits, teacher is monitoring the room to make sure that all students are contributing to the assignment and asking questions, as needed, to prompt students' learning.
- Once skits are completed, the students will perform them for the class. Skits will be evaluated based upon a rubric. (See resources.)
- Bring students back together and review the three main forms of government.
- Distribute Ticket Out the Door.

GUIDED & INDEPENDENT PRACTICE

We Do

- Participate in discussion of why we have governments.
- Participate in discussion about the three main forms of government.

You Do

- Complete "Word splash."
- Actively participate in all discussions.
- Work collaboratively with group to create a skit demonstrating one of the three main forms of government.
- Perform skit for the class.

- Complete Ticket Out the Door.
- Follow established classroom procedures.
- The students who need extension may be given an additional task in which they have to find examples of countries where the various forms of government are used.

CLOSURE

- Remind students of the three main forms of government that were discussed.
- Restate the objectives or "I can" statements.
- Connect democracy to America.
- Distribute the Ticket Out the Door.

ASSESSMENT/EVALUATION

1. Students will be introduced to the various types of governments that exist throughout the world (democracy, dictatorship, and monarchy). Students will participate in the discussion to create a better understanding of why governments are necessary. The teacher will note students' participation informally.
2. To show the students' understanding of the types of governments, they will perform skits that show the various characteristics of each type of government. This assessment will be a formal assessment with a rubric.
3. Students will then be given a "ticket out the door" on which they will have to list the characteristics of each type of government. They will also have to identify which type of government is used in the U.S. and use evidence to support their rationale.

MATERIALS/TECHNOLOGY

Materials

- Handout
- ELL handout
- Rubric
- Ticket out the door

Technology

- ActivBoard/document camera
- Computers for enrichment research
  Sources: Images depicting each event are included on the handout that every child receives.

CROSS-CURRICULAR CONNECTIONS

There is a cross-curricular connection made with reading and character education by establishing rules for conversation (e.g., taking turns, raising hand, asking questions).

MEETING INDIVIDUAL NEEDS OF DIVERSE LEARNERS

- Visual: Students are provided with a visual of the three forms of government while the discussion is taking place.

- Auditory: There is an oral discussion occurring throughout the lesson.
- Bodily-kinesthetic: Students are able to move around during the design and performance of the skit to encourage full understanding of the concept.
- ELL students have a handout in Spanish to refer to.

CHARACTER EDUCATION CONNECTION

Respect: While working on the skit, students should be respectful of all the members of the group. This is discussed when modeling expectations for group performance.

LESSON RESOURCES

Rubric

Table 12.3 Rubric for Performing the Skit

1	2	3 Score
I did not participate in creating the skit.	I somewhat participated in creating the skit.	I actively participated in creating the skit.
I did not perform the skit to the class.	I performed parts of the skit, but not all of it.	I performed the entire skit to the class.
I was not respectful to my peers while working in a group.	I was somewhat respectful to my peers, but I could've done a better job of listening to others' ideas.	I was respectful of my peers' ideas.

Ticket Out the Door

1. List one characteristic of each type of government:
   a. Democracy
   b. Dictatorship
   c. Monarchy
2. What type of government is used the United States? How do you know?

LESSON PLAN TWO

Teacher: Jeanne Neff
Grade: Third Grade
Unit Topic: Geography
Lesson Topic: Map Essentials

OBJECTIVES (STUDENT FRIENDLY)

1. Understand vocabulary related to geography.
2. Understand how using technology helps us gather information from primary and secondary sources.

3. Understand how thematic maps, tables, charts, graphs, and photos are used to analyze geographic information.
4. Understand how people perceive places and regions differently.
5. Understand that location affects how people live.

STANDARDS

- CCSS.ELA-LITERACY.CCRA.SL.1: Prepare for and participate effectively in a range of conversations and collaborations with diverse partners, building on others' ideas and expressing their own clearly and persuasively.
- CCSS.ELA-LITERACY.CCRA.SL.2: Integrate and evaluate information presented in diverse media and formats, including visually, quantitatively, and orally.
- NCSS: Theme 3: This theme helps learners to develop their spatial views and perspectives of the world, to understand where people, places, and resources are located and why they are there, and to explore the relationship between human beings and the environment. In schools, this theme typically appears in courses dealing with geography and area studies, but it is also important for the study of the geographical dimension of other social studies subjects.

DAILY PLANNER

Teacher will go over the key elements of a map. Students will then create their own country with key aspects of a map implemented within.

ACTIVATING STRATEGY

Warm-Up: Use Google Earth to type in the address of the school and zoom in by satellite. Explain the difference between a map and a globe.

INSTRUCTION

Lesson: Student Text pp. 10–19

1. Make sure you emphasize that we need to know how to read to learn information we want to know; refer back to the learning goal/scale and check off skills as you go.
2. Read and have students highlight or underline the text that explains the purpose of each map, then write it at the bottom of the page.

GUIDED & INDEPENDENT PRACTICE

Projects: Create a Map or Model of Your Hand Island

a. Trace your hand on a piece of paper.
b. Your map/model must contain all the required elements.

CLOSURE

Students will present pictures, explaining their maps and how/why they designed them.

ASSESSMENT/EVALUATION

- Formative: Students will be evaluated based on their applied knowledge within their hand island drawings.

MATERIALS/TECHNOLOGY

- Social Studies – McGraw Hill Textbook
- Computer
- Google Earth
- Art Supplies – Construction Paper, Pens, Pencils, Crayons, Scissors

CROSS-CURRICULAR CONNECTIONS

- Art – constructing houses out of provided materials; drawing of sketches
- Math – understanding and computing longitude and latitude

MEETING INDIVIDUAL NEEDS OF DIVERSE LEARNERS

- English Language Learners – Visuals will be used to aid ELL students (Google Earth, Google Maps). Also, the teacher should try to translate the key vocabulary words into a student's native tongue, if possible.
- Multiple Intelligences – This lesson fosters visual, kinesthetic, interpersonal, and intrapersonal learning through the small cooperative grouping and activities within the assignment.

CHARACTER EDUCATION CONNECTION

Respect: While working on their individual projects, students should be respectful of all students in the classroom and share art supplies.

▶ **FOURTH GRADE**

LESSON PLAN ONE

Teacher: Sydney Wyatt & Janie Hubbard
Grade: Fourth Grade
Unit Topic: American Monuments, Memorials, and Symbols
Lesson Topic: The Lincoln Memorial

OBJECTIVES (STUDENT FRIENDLY)

- I will discuss what I know about American memorials with my classmates.
- I will closely observe pictures and read books about the Lincoln Memorial.
- I will work with a collaborative group to create and present a Lincoln Memorial billboard.
- I will create a model memorial that shows my knowledge, effort, and completion.

STANDARDS

National Council for the Social Studies Standards Expectations:

- NCSS Standard 2: Time, Continuity, and Change: *The learners will understand the history of democratic ideals and principles, and how they are represented in documents, artifacts, and symbols.*
- NCSS Standard 5: Individuals, Groups, and Institutions: *The learners will understand this theme helps us know how individuals are members of groups and institutions, and influence and shape those groups and institutions.*

DAILY PLANNER

- Activating Strategy/Introduction: 10 minutes
- Whole Group/I Do: 15 minutes
- Small Group/We Do: 15 minutes
- Independent Activity/You Do: 15 minutes
- Closure: 5 minutes

ACTIVATING STRATEGY

- Present the concept "American memorial" to students.
- Draw a web on the board and write "American memorial" in the center.
- Ask, "What do you know about American memorials?"
- Write all students' responses around the center of the web.
- Show a series of photographs of American memorials including Lincoln Memorial, Martin Luther King, Jr. National Memorial, Crazy Horse Memorial, Pearl Harbor National Memorial, National September 11 Memorial, and other diverse U.S. memorials from various states.
- "Memorial is like the word remember. Why do you think we build memorials in the United States?"
- "What do you think memorials in these photographs have in common?"
- With upper elementary students, the teacher may facilitate discussion regarding differences between the concepts, memorials, monuments, landmarks, and commemorations (i.e., statues, parks, parades, festivals, cemeteries, forts, battlefields, iconic landforms, landmarks, iconic homes, and others). More abstract concepts to discuss are intangibles such as symbolism, patriotism, collective pride, and honor.
- "Today, we are going to discuss the Lincoln Memorial, which is located in Washington, DC."

INSTRUCTION

- Review Abraham Lincoln's impact as the 16th United States president. Show a brief yet realistic video of Lincoln's life and prominence as a leader. If technology is unavailable, read and discuss quality trade books. Examples are National Council for the Social Studies (NCSS) award winners such as *Picturing Lincoln: Famous Photographs that Popularized the President* by G. Sullivan, *Abe Lincoln Remembers* by Ann Turner, and *Abe Lincoln: His Wit and Wisdom from A–Z* by Alan Schroedar.
- Ask, "Why do you think Americans might want to remember President Abraham Lincoln?" For upper-level students, the teacher might ask, "What do you think were his most significant challenges and contributions to society?" (i.e., Civil War, Emancipation Proclamation, Thirteenth Amendment to the Constitution). Continue

to facilitate this background discussion, particularly regarding the war, proclamation, and amendment.

- Redirect the discussion back to the Lincoln Memorial. If technology is available, present a virtual tour of the memorial. Otherwise, show several realistic photographs. Explain that tourists from the United States and around the world visit Washington, DC, to see the Lincoln Memorial. About 7.81 million people visited the memorial in 2019. It is designed to resemble a Greek temple, and the interior statue of Lincoln sitting in a chair is 19 feet tall. Two of Lincoln's speeches and a quote that reads *"In this temple, as in the hearts of the people for whom he saved the Union, the memory of Abraham Lincoln is enshrined forever"* are etched into the stone walls.
- Complete whole group instruction by asking students to share their newly learned knowledge. Clarify any misconceptions students may have before advancing to the guided and independent practice.

GUIDED & INDEPENDENT PRACTICE

We Do

- Introduce students to the idea of designing a billboard that features the Lincoln Memorial. Show an example and explain how billboards often serve as advertisements for tourists to locate a special landmark.
- Small student groups work to create a "billboard" on butcher paper provided to each group. The billboards should include the most important content and images that students believe would entice someone to visit the Lincoln Memorial. This activity is used to showcase students' newly learned content knowledge.
- Before students begin the design, prepare a list of approved websites. Students may use classroom computers to search for visuals and more information about the Lincoln Memorial to include on their billboards. Alternately, groups may view Lincoln Memorial pictures previously shown in class and/or picture books about the memorial such as *Lincoln Memorial* by Julie Murray. Photographs are helpful for students to closely observe and then draw more detailed depictions of the memorial.
- Walk around to monitor computer use and make sure students are only on sites related to the Lincoln Memorial. Refocus students' attention with guiding questions relating to the Lincoln Memorial and ideas of things students might search if further directions are needed.
- Talk with each group while they are working, "Tell me about your billboard. Why did you choose to put these items/words on it? What is the purpose of a billboard? What are your thought about the Lincoln Memorial?"
- Each group will share their billboards and reasons for choosing to display the information in this way.
- Revisit the web previously drawn on the board for the introductory activation strategy. Ask students to add what they know about American memorials. Write all students responses around the web.

You Do

- Read *Vinnie and Abraham* by Dawn Fitzgerald. This NCSS Notable Trade Book tells the true story of Vinnie Ream, a young girl who became friends with Lincoln. After his assassination, she overcame age and gender discrimination for the honor of sculpting the full-size statue of Lincoln that is now displayed in the Capitol rotunda.

- Ask students to think of someone they honor, see as a role model, and trust; someone who cares about others; and/or someone who should be remembered. Note: this could be a contributor to society, community, or home (e.g., community or family member, neighbor, someone in a biography or autobiography, someone near or far away).
- Option: After students read their choices of biography/autobiography genres, ask students to create an American memorial for that person.
- Provide Play-Doh or modeling clay. Ask students to individually create a memorial to that person and add a quote. Young children might write simple quotes or messages. For upper-level students, review the quote from the Lincoln Memorial and discuss its meaning: "*In this temple, as in the hearts of the people for whom he saved the Union, the memory of Abraham Lincoln is enshrined forever.*" On the board, write concepts such as memory, memorialize, commemorate, remembrance, tribute, courage, integrity, empathy, gratitude, people, public, servant, proud, love, loved, immortalize, respected, and so forth. Explain that these are only a few examples of words that are sometimes placed on memorials, though students are not required to use these words.
- Ask students to share and discuss their memorials with the class.
- Display students' memorials and quotes in a classroom museum or more public space, such as a library.

CLOSURE

- Ask students to review their understanding of American memorials. Ask, "Is the Lincoln Memorial an American memorial? What makes you say that? Please explain other American memorials you know. Why do we have American memorials?"
- Ask critical-thinking questions: "Why are American memorials important to me and others? Where can we get more information about American memorials? Why should people know about American memorials? Why is there a need for American memorials?"
- Clear any final misconceptions and move to the next content area.

ASSESSMENT/EVALUATION

- Student participation in web discussion to assess prior knowledge: formative assessment checklist.
- Student completion and presentation of the Lincoln Memorial billboard with collaborative group: formative assessment checklist.
- Student creation and presentation of a model memorial: scored according to the extent the model demonstrates disciplinary content, effort, and completion: performance assessment rubric.

MATERIALS/TECHNOLOGY

- White board and markers
- Brief videos and/or books about Abraham Lincoln
- Computers for student research (if available)
- Photographs or whole-class images of various American memorials for viewing
- Butcher paper for billboards
- Pencils/crayons/water markers
- Modeling clay or Play-Doh for model memorials
- Small paper labels for model quotes

CROSS-CURRICULAR CONNECTIONS

- Creative Arts: Model memorials and classroom museum
- Visual Literacy: Billboards
- Listening and Speaking/Language Arts: Discussions
- Internet Research Skills: All curricular connections
- Critical Thinking Questions (Closure): All curricular connections

MEETING INDIVIDUAL NEEDS OF DIVERSE LEARNERS

This lesson meets the needs of diverse learners because it is taught using multiple learning styles:

- Linguistic: collaborative group work, verbal presentation, classroom discussions.
- Visual: web, close observation of photographs, picture books, videos, billboards.
- Kinesthetic: model memorial, museum set-up, billboards, internet research.
- Auditory: presentations, classroom discussions, collaborative group work.
- Logical: purpose and procedures are briefly outlined for students before starting. Models are available (e.g., billboard), distinct directions, pre-selected website list for students, realistic visuals.
- Intrapersonal: individual model memorial activity, internet research.
- Interpersonal: collaborative group work, time for asking questions and clarifying students' misconceptions, classroom discussion.

    This lesson also meets the needs of English language learners (ELL). The lesson will be sent to ELL parents/guardians at least a week before the lesson. Families will receive important web links, brief videos, lesson translations, and translated messages, as needed, about the lesson's concepts. There are a number of no-cost translation websites on the internet.

LESSON PLAN TWO

Teacher: Matt Hensley
Grade: Fourth Grade
Unit Topic: Indigenous Peoples Through European Exploration
Lesson Topic: Just "BEAD" It!

OBJECTIVES (STUDENT FRIENDLY)

SWBAT:

1. Define material culture and understand its role in Indigenous Peoples' communities by engaging in whole-group discussion.
   - *Student-Friendly Objective: I can define material culture (e.g., clothing, jewelry, etc.) and describe its role in Indigenous Peoples' communities.*
2. Explore the functional and cultural significance of Indigenous Peoples' beadwork using object study through visual analysis (images).
   - *Student-Friendly Objective: I can describe the significance of the adaptations that Indigenous Peoples have made with their beadwork.*
3. Make connections to content by engaging in experimental archaeology and practicing various bead-working techniques.

- *Student-Friendly Objective: I can make connections by comparing and contrasting Indigenous Peoples' beadwork to my own culture.*

STANDARDS

- NCSS Standard 1: Culture: *Social studies programs should include experiences that provide for the study of culture and cultural diversity.*
- NCSS Standard 3: People, Places, and Environment: *Social studies programs should include experiences that provide for the study of people, places, and environments.*
- CCSS 3.19: Compare and contrast the geographic locations and customs (i.e., housing and clothing) of the Northeast, Southeast, and Plains North American Indians.

DAILY PLANNER

- **Activating Strategy/Introduction:** 10 minutes
  - Essential Questions
  - Whole Group Discussion on Material Culture
  - Framing Discussions Regarding Indigenous People
- **Brief Background on Beads in North America**: 10 minutes
- **Beads & Trade in North America Object Study Group Activity:** 20 minutes
- **Beaded Bird Activity**: 30 minutes
- Revisiting the Essential Questions: Think-Pair-Share: 5 minutes

ACTIVATING STRATEGY

ESSENTIAL QUESTIONS

- What is material culture, and how has it has adapted over time for Indigenous People?
- In what ways did Indigenous People use their beadwork?
- What is the cultural and functional significance of Indigenous People beadwork?

WHOLE GROUP DISCUSSION ON MATERIAL CULTURE

What is material culture?
- What is the purpose of material culture?
- What are some examples of material culture (e.g., clothing, jewelry, tools)?
- Material culture represents the beliefs, customs, arts, etc. of a particular society, group, place, or time.
- What is communication?
  - How do people communicate ideas in our culture?
  - Can art be used to communicate?
- Explain that in the past, Indigenous Peoples did not communicate through writing; instead, they mostly told stories verbally and through material culture. Example: beadwork.
- Explain that we are going to be exploring historic (take time to define *historic*) beadwork that Indigenous People created and used throughout history for functional and ceremonial purposes in North America.
  - What do you think *ceremonial* means?
  - What about *functional*?

- Today we are going to explore the beadwork of Indigenous People of North America while paying close attention to the materials used, the designs, and the purpose of various types of beadwork.
- Direct students' attention to a map of areas inhabited by Indigenous People in North America. Explain that we are going to be discussing the beadwork of the Iroquois, Ojibwa, Sioux, and Cheyenne. Map Source: https://ohiolink.oercommons.org/courseware/lesson/1981/overview.

FRAMING DISCUSSIONS REGARDING INDIGENOUS PEOPLE

- Big message: Just because Indigenous People used materials and resources that were different from what Europeans used does not mean that they were primitive (take time to define *primitive*).
- Explain that Indigenous People had their own structured societies, political systems, cultural characteristics, and technology, just as Europeans did.

INSTRUCTION

BRIEF BACKGROUND ON BEADS IN NORTH AMERICA

Begin with brief background/overview of the origin of beads in North America.

A. Before Europeans came to North America, Indigenous People used shells, porcupine quills, natural paints, and even elk teeth for beads.
B. Wampum (early form of beads) was made from shells that were shaped and polished.
   1. How do you think Indigenous People gained access to beads?
   2. Do you think it would be easy or difficult to thread these materials?
      a. Show students images of various improvised beads (porcupine quills, shells, etc.).
C. French traders brought glass beads made in Italy to trade for fur. Pony beads were soon used to make decorations formerly made with porcupine quills. After 1850, seed beads from Czechoslovakia became very popular. (Can show images or examples for context.)
   1. What are some advantages to using manufactured beads over the organic ones?
      a. Option to show images of pony beads, glass beads, etc.
      b. May need to define the terms *manufactured* and *organic*.
D. Share with students the economic chart (see link) for the trade of beads and other goods for fur. Explain that more than just beads were traded. Many other goods were traded for fur also.
   1. Option to place charts into picture format on a slide show and have ready to pull up on larger screen.
   2. Chart source: https://eh.net/encyclopedia/the-economic-history-of-the-fur-trade-1670-to-1870/.

TRANSITION

BEADS & TRADE IN NORTH AMERICA OBJECT STUDY GROUP ACTIVITY

A. Show map of locations of the Iroquois, Ojibwa (Chippewa), Lakota (Teton Sioux), and the Cheyenne. Point out map location of the Indigenous Peoples when you get to their respective artifacts.
- Students will be broken into four groups and each group provided an image of the artifacts mentioned here, along with the corresponding guided questions. Each group may record their responses to the guiding questions on a sheet of paper. Once they have responded to the questions, each group will present their object to the class and share their responses.

1. Show image of Iroquois: Northeast Woodlands Bag.
   Image Source: https://hoodmuseum.dartmouth.edu/objects/49.25.12288.
   a. What do you notice about this bag?
   b. What design or pattern do you see?
   c. What colors are being used?
   d. What material(s) do you think this bag is made of?
   e. What do you think this bag was used for?
2. Ojibwa: Northern Great Lakes (Eastern Woodlands): Bandolier Bag.
   Image Source: https://pl.khanacademy.org/humanities/ap-art-history/indigenous-americas-apah/north-america-apah/a/bandolier-bag.
   a. What do you notice about this bag?
   b. What design or pattern do you see?
   c. What colors are being used?
   d. What material(s) do you think this bag is made of?
   e) =. What do you think this bag was used for?
3. Lakota: Sioux (Great Plains): Sheath with Knife.
   Image Source: www.brooklynmuseum.org/opencollection/objects/143144.
   a. What do you notice about this sheath?
   b. What design or pattern do you see?
   c. What colors are being used?
   d. What material(s) do you think this sheath is made of?
   e. What do you think this sheath was used for?
4. Cheyenne (Great Plains): Moccasins
   Image Source: www.naaer.hoodmuseum.dartmouth.edu/plains/clothing-regalia/work-4.
   a) What do you notice about these moccasins?
   b) What design or pattern do you see?
   c) What colors are being used?
   d) What material(s) do you think these moccasins are made of?
   e) What do you think these moccasins were used for?

TRANSITION

BEADED BIRD ACTIVITY

- Explain to students that they will now have the opportunity to engage in experimental archaeology and practice beadwork using an Iroquois pattern.
- Visit link: https://hosted.learnquebec.ca/societies/wp-content/uploads/sites/10/2015/01/Iroquois-Beadwork-Teachers-Guide.pdf.
- Activity with step-by-step directions starts on page 17 and ends on page 20.

TRANSITION

REVISITING THE ESSENTIAL QUESTIONS: THINK-PAIR-SHARE

See Closure section.

GUIDED & INDEPENDENT PRACTICE

"WE DO"

WHOLE GROUP DISCUSSION ON MATERIAL CULTURE

- See Essential Question/Activating Strategy section.

BRIEF BACKGROUND ON BEADS IN NORTH AMERICA

- See Instructional Procedures.

BEADS & TRADE IN NORTH AMERICA OBJECT STUDY

- See Instructional Procedures.

"YOU DO"

BEADED BIRD ACTIVITY

- See Instructional Procedures.

REVISITING THE ESSENTIAL QUESTIONS: THINK-PAIR-SHARE

- See Closure section.

CLOSURE

REVISITING THE ESSENTIAL QUESTIONS: THINK-PAIR-SHARE

Students will independently write their responses to these EQs using their constructed knowledge from the lesson. Once students have had time to reflect and respond to the EQs, they will pair up with a classmate and share their responses with each other.

- What is material culture, and how has it has adapted over time for Indigenous People?
- In what ways did Indigenous People use their beadwork?
- What is the cultural and functional significance of Indigenous Peoples' beadwork?

ASSESSMENT/EVALUATION

BEADS & TRADE IN NORTH AMERICA OBJECT STUDY GROUP ACTIVITY

- See Instructional Procedures.
- Students will be graded for participation in group activity.

BEADED BIRD ACTIVITY

- See Instructional Procedures.
- Students will be graded for participation and completion of the activity.

REVISITING THE ESSENTIAL QUESTIONS

- See Closure section.
- Students will be graded for completion of written responses.

MATERIALS/TECHNOLOGY

IMAGES OF MATERIAL CULTURE ITEMS

- Iroquois: Northeast Woodlands Bag
- Ojibwa: Northern Great Lakes (Eastern Woodlands): Bandolier Bag

- Lakota: Sioux (Great Plains): Sheath with Knife
- Cheyenne (Great Plains): Moccasins

WHOLE GROUP DISCUSSION ON MATERIAL CULTURE

- Map of the Indigenous Peoples' Locations in North America

BRIEF BACKGROUND ON BEADS IN NORTH AMERICA

- Economic chart

BEADED BIRD ACTIVITY

- Thread
- Beading needles
- Scissors
- Beads (various sizes)
- Felt (6" x 6" or half an 11 1/2" x 8 1/2" sheet)
- Stuffing
- Pen

CROSS-CURRICULAR CONNECTIONS

- Mathematics: Students will learn to read and interpret an economic chart for the trade of beads and other goods for fur.

MEETING INDIVIDUAL NEEDS OF DIVERSE LEARNERS

This lesson seeks to engage students in a discovery and inquiry lesson that emphasizes how Indigenous People of North America worked with beads. Through exploration, discussion, object study, and experimental archaeology, students will learn how Indigenous People in North America (particularly the Iroquois, Ojibwa, Sioux, and Cheyenne) embraced beadwork as part of their material culture. Lesson highlights include bead trade, beadwork techniques, and the functional and cultural significance of Indigenous Peoples' beadwork to express cultural identity.

CHARACTER EDUCATION CONNECTION

This lesson promotes the character education value of respect when learning and discussing cultures that are different from their own.

▶ **FIFTH GRADE**

LESSON PLAN ONE

Teacher: Kelsey Evans
Grade: Fifth Grade

Unit Topic: Historical Inquiry and Analysis
Lesson Topic: Primary vs. Secondary Sources

OBJECTIVES (STUDENT FRIENDLY)

Students will be able to identify primary and secondary sources and distinguish the difference between the two types of sources.
Students will identify the Preamble to the Constitution as an important document in our history and understand its impact on our nation's history and present day.

STANDARDS

- CCSS.ELA-LITERACY.CCRA.SL.1: Prepare for and participate effectively in a range of conversations and collaborations with diverse partners, building on others' ideas and expressing their own clearly and persuasively.
- CCSS.ELA-LITERACY.CCRA.SL.2: Integrate and evaluate information presented in diverse media and formats, including visually, quantitatively, and orally.
- NCSS: TIME, CONTINUITY, AND CHANGE: Through the study of the past and its legacy, learners examine the institutions, values, and beliefs of people in the past, acquire skills in historical inquiry and interpretation, and gain an understanding of how important historical events and developments have shaped the modern world. This theme appears in courses in history, as well as in other social studies courses for which knowledge of the past is important.

DAILY PLANNER

Hook: Students will participate in a Kahoot activity to determine prior knowledge and understanding of primary and secondary resources. After, the teacher will discuss the similarities and differences of primary sources utilizing a Venn diagram. Students will play the Kahoot again to see the growth and act as a review. Afterwards, students will analyze the Preamble to the Constitution via a close reading activity.

ACTIVATING STRATEGY

- Students will participate in a Kahoot review of primary and secondary sources, analyzing and accessing prior knowledge.

INSTRUCTION

- Teacher will review content using a NearPod presentation imbedded with summative assessments. Teacher will discuss the differences and similarities between primary and secondary sources.

GUIDED & INDEPENDENT PRACTICE

- Within the NearPod, students will use individual laptops to construct a Venn diagram. The teacher will get instantaneous feedback via the NearPod app, monitoring any need for clarification or further understanding.
- Students will redo Kahoot, post-instruction.

- As a class, students will analyze the Preamble to the Constitution. Students will participate in a close reading activity of the document to determine what the document is about.

CLOSURE

- Exit ticket: Students will write one paragraph about the Preamble to the Constitution, determining if it is a primary or secondary source and why they think the document is important.

ASSESSMENT/EVALUATION

Formative – Exit ticket, Venn diagram, close reading
Summative – Kahoot

MATERIALS/TECHNOLOGY

- Laptops
- Promethean Board
- Highlighters, green pens for the close reading

CROSS-CURRICULAR CONNECTIONS

- Reading – learning new literacy strategies through close reading.

MEETING INDIVIDUAL NEEDS OF DIVERSE LEARNERS

- Accommodations and adaptations to optimize levels of support for the unique needs of SWD, gifted learners, and English language learners: visual cues, partner learning.

CHARACTER EDUCATION CONNECTION

- Citizenship education.

LESSON PLAN TWO

Teacher: Dr. Bonnie Bittman
Grade: Fifth Grade
Unit Topic: The Great Depression
Lesson Topic: Stock Market

OBJECTIVES (STUDENT FRIENDLY)

- I will learn about the stock market and explore stocks.
- I will find out what happens when stock values decrease.

STANDARDS

- NCSS Standard 2: Time, Continuity, and Change: *Social studies programs should include experiences that provide for the study of the past and its legacy.*

- NCSS Standard 4: Individual Development and Identity: *Social studies programs should include experiences that provide for the study of individual development and identity.*
- NCSS Standard 5: Individuals, Groups, and Institutions: *Social studies programs should include experiences that provide for the study of interactions among individuals, groups, and institutions.*
- NCSS Standard 7: Production, Distribution, and Consumption: *Social studies programs should include experiences that provide for the study of how people organize for the production, distribution, and consumption of goods and services.*

DAILY PLANNER

- Warm Up/Introduction – 5 minutes
- Introduce Stock Market – 10 minutes
- We Do – 10 minutes
- You Do – 10–15 minutes
- Exit Ticket/Reflection

ACTIVATING STRATEGY

- Reintroduce or introduce the following vocabulary words to the students: *stock, stock market, risk, profit, loss.*
- Have the students use each word in a sentence or fill out a Frayer diagram to explore the meaning of each word.

INSTRUCTION

- After students understand the vocabulary words, explain to the students that the stock market is a place where pieces of companies are bought and sold.
- Ask "What are some companies that you are familiar with?" Discuss the students' responses (Nike, Google, Apple).
- Using a projector connected to the internet, show the students some of the stock prices from the companies they have listed.
- Using the line graphs, explain how stocks change price through the day, week, month, even the year.
- Make sure to explain that when the price goes up, the line goes up. When the line goes down, the price of the stock goes down.
- Explain that the companies are still making goods and services but that people buy and sell stocks to make money.
- If the stock price goes up, the person makes money; this is profit.
- If the stock price goes down, the person loses money; this is a loss.
- By buying and selling stocks, people take on risk; they might make money, but they could also lose money.

GUIDED & INDEPENDENT PRACTICE

We Do

- Explain to students that they are going to be given $1,000 to buy stocks. They will be tracking it over the next week to see who has the most money.
- As a class, have students pick two or three stocks to buy.

- Look them up using an internet-connected projector.
- On the board, and in student's notebooks, subtract each CLOSE PRICE (the price the stock closed at the day before) from the $1,000.
- Explain that students will be individually or in small groups (no more than three) tracking their stocks day by day.

You Do

After the class example, students will be given their own independent work.

- Student will create a sheet (or will be given a handout) with columns for the name of the company, the symbol, the close price, and whether the stock price increased or decreased from the previous day.
- Students will, individually or in small groups, choose what stocks they want to buy with their $1,000.
- They will fill out the paper or worksheet with the correct information.
- The teacher will need to make sure that the students are not going over $1,000 and that the students are getting close to the maximum. How close is up to the students.
- Each day, as the unit continues, students will spend five to ten minutes listing their chosen stocks' closing prices.
- At the end of a week, students will add up the amount of money they made or lost during the week.
- There can be a prize for the student who made the most money (up to the teacher's discretion).
- The debrief for the activity will need to highlight what happens when stock prices increase (more people make money) and what happens when stock prices decrease (people lose money). This will connect with the stock market crash of 1928.

CLOSURE

- In their notebooks, ask the students to explain why they picked the companies they picked.
- The first day, ask why they thought the stocks would increase.
- On subsequent days, ask the students to report what happened to their stocks in words. They can also explain why they thought some stocks went up and others went down.

ASSESSMENT/EVALUATION

- Student responses from teacher questioning/class discussions: teacher checklist.
- Student-created definitions using sentences or Frayer diagrams can be checked with the other entry ticket items.
- Each day's chart of closing prices can be checked by the teacher or can be assessed at the end of the project.
- The debriefing exercise can refer solely to the stock market game or can be a longer essay connecting the modern-day stock market to the market during the Great Depression.

MATERIALS/TECHNOLOGY

- Projector with internet capability
- White board

- Paper
- Writing utensil
- Classroom computers (or other devices) with internet capabilities

CROSS-CURRICULAR CONNECTIONS

- Mathematics: Students will be examining line graphs, as well as adding and subtracting. This is a skill that is taught and practiced within this content area over multiple grade levels.
- Writing/Grammar: Students will be creating their own sentences using the new terms. Also, students will be justifying their ideas through writing.

MEETING INDIVIDUAL NEEDS OF DIVERSE LEARNERS

This lesson meets the needs of diverse learners because it is taught using multiple learning styles:

- Visual: charts, illustrations in group and independent work.
- Kinesthetic: movement around the classroom in groups, as well as the use of the internet.
- Auditory: oral instruction.

This lesson also meets the needs of English language learners. During class discussions, ELLs will be able to choose what companies they follow. If the teacher allows it, ELL students can use the stock market from their home countries.

CHARACTER EDUCATION CONNECTION

This lesson promotes values by providing students a safe way to understand risk.

▶ SIXTH GRADE

LESSON PLAN ONE

Teacher: Cyndi Mottola Poole
Grade: Sixth Grade
Unit Topic: Immigration
Lesson Topic: Immigration Interview

OBJECTIVES

- The student will be able to analyze how push-and-pull factors cause immigration.
- The student will be able to interview people to construct an oral history.
- The student will be able to compare and contrast cultural characteristics of two different countries.

STANDARDS

- Common Core CCSS.ELA-LITERACY.CCRA.SL.1: Prepare for and participate effectively in a range of conversations and collaborations with diverse partners, building on others' ideas and expressing their own clearly and persuasively.
- Common Core CCSS.ELA-LITERACY.CCRA.SL.2: Integrate and evaluate information presented in diverse media and formats, including visually, quantitatively, and orally.
- NCSS Standard 1: Culture: Social studies programs should include experiences that provide for the study of culture and cultural diversity.
- NCSS Standard 2: Time, Continuity, and Change: Social studies programs should include experiences that provide for the study of the past and its legacy.
- NCSS Standard 3: People, Places, and Environment: Social studies programs should include experiences that provide for the study of people, places, and environments.
- NCSS Standard 4: Individual Development and Identity: Social studies programs should include experiences that provide for the study of individual development and identity.
- NCSS Standard 5: Individuals, Groups, and Institutions: Social studies programs should include experiences that provide for the study of interactions among individuals, groups, and institutions.

DAILY PLANNER

- The teacher will ask the students to think about and write down what immigration is. Answers will be shared with the class to determine a shared definition of the term: 5 minutes.
- The teacher will read the book *The Lotus Seed* by Sherry Garland: 12 minutes.
- The teacher will ask students questions about the characters in the book to review the story line: 5 minutes.
- Students will work in groups to decide on an immigrant in their lives whom they can interview and to develop interview questions: 15 minutes.
- Student groups will conduct interviews with immigrants (out of class, or possibly before, after, or during class time, depending on availability of equipment and interviewee).
- Students will create a video documentary for the class on the life of their immigrant.

ACTIVATING STRATEGY

Why do people immigrate to the United States? Provide students with time to think about this question, then create a class list of responses.

INSTRUCTION

- The teacher will begin the lesson by asking the students to create their own definition of the term *immigration*.
- Once students have had time to formulate their own definitions, the teacher will call on students to share their definitions with the class, writing down key concepts until the class is able to create a mutually agreed upon definition of the term.
- The teacher will then introduce and read *The Lotus Seed* by Sherry Garland.
- After reading the book, the teacher will ask students what details they can remember from the book. She will write these details on the board. The teacher can ask

questions about the book to elicit more details from the students if necessary (e.g., What country did she come from? Why did she leave?).

- The teacher will ask the students to pretend that this is a true story about a real immigrant. She will ask the students to consider what questions the investigative reporter would have asked in order to find out all the information presented in the book. Questions will include: What country did you come from? What memories do you have of that country? Why did you leave that country? How did you feel about leaving? What surprised you when you came to the U.S.A.? Did you bring anything special with you? Did you have to leave anything behind?
- Once the class has developed a list of interview questions, the teacher will divide the students into groups. Each group will identify one immigrant they know whom they can interview. (If a group cannot think of anyone, the teacher can suggest school or community personnel who may be immigrants.)
- The students will ask the person if they are willing to be interviewed and video recorded. They will then interview their person outside class time and will document the interview using a video camera.
- The following week, the videos will be watched in class. The students can take notes while watching the interviews about the key points.
- After watching the interviews, the teacher can help the students identify common themes. What were the reasons people left their home countries? What were the reasons they came here (push-and-pull factors)? What difficulties did they have when they arrived? How did they overcome these (cultural and linguistic differences)? What customs from their home countries do they still follow (cultural hybridity)? Summarizing all these points will help students see all the issues associated with immigration.

GUIDED & INDEPENDENT PRACTICE

The teacher will model the development of the interview questions and then encourage class members to think of good questions as well.

CLOSURE

The students will create a video documentary for the class on the life of their immigrant. The points brought up in multiple videos will be summarized by the class.

ASSESSMENT/EVALUATION

Students will be formally assessed on how thoroughly their video documentaries answered the questions.

MATERIALS/TECHNOLOGY

- *The Lotus Seed* by Sherry Garland
- Video equipment
- TV and DVD player to show videos in class
- Primary source = immigrant interviews

CROSS-CURRICULAR CONNECTIONS

- Reading the book in class.
- Using language arts skills to interview people.

MEETING INDIVIDUAL NEEDS OF DIVERSE LEARNERS

Since students will be working in groups, ESE and ESOL students can take on roles within the group in which they may feel more comfortable and can rely on the help of their group mates. Multiple intelligences can also be addressed through the choice of roles in the group work.

CHARACTER EDUCATION CONNECTION

Respecting different cultures, relating to the difficulties experienced by other people, learning to work well in groups.

LESSON RESOURCES

If schools/students do not have access to video recording equipment, the lesson can be adapted to use a poster presentation format instead.

LESSON PLAN TWO

Teacher: Brian Furgione
Grade: Sixth Grade
Unit Topic: Civics
Lesson Topic: Developing a Sense of Citizenship

OBJECTIVES (STUDENT FRIENDLY)

- I will be able to examine and evaluate the impact of citizens in my local community.
- I will understand and be able to explain the difference between "duties" and "responsibilities."
- I will understand my role as a citizen and the contributions I can/do make in my community.

STANDARDS

- Common Core CCSS.ELA-LITERACY.CCRA.SL.1: Prepare for and participate effectively in a range of conversations and collaborations with diverse partners, building on others' ideas and expressing their own clearly and persuasively.
- Common Core CCSS.ELA-LITERACY.CCRA.SL.2: Integrate and evaluate information presented in diverse media and formats, including visually, quantitatively, and orally.
- NCSS Standard 2: TIME, CONTINUITY, AND CHANGE: Through the study of the past and its legacy, learners examine the institutions, values, and beliefs of people in the past, acquire skills in historical inquiry and interpretation, and gain an understanding of how important historical events and developments have shaped the modern world. This theme appears in courses in history, as well as in other social studies courses for which knowledge of the past is important.
- NCSS Standard 10: CIVIC IDEALS AND PRACTICES: An understanding of civic ideals and practices is critical to full participation in society and is an essential component of education for citizenship. This theme enables students to learn about the rights and responsibilities of citizens of a democracy, and to appreciate the importance of active citizenship. In schools, the theme typically appears in units or courses dealing with civics, history, political science, cultural anthropology, and fields such as global studies, law-related education, and the humanities.

DAILY PLANNER

~ 90-Minute Lesson

- Opening: Citizens in Action (5 minutes)
- Introduction: Citizens and the Local Community (10 minutes)
- Activities
  - Socratic Seminar Overview (5 minutes)
  - Article Study (15 minutes)
  - Question Generation (5 minutes)
  - Socratic Seminar (30 minutes)
  - Round 1
  - Round 2
  - Round 3
  - Round 4
  - Reflection/Feedback (10 minutes)
- Closing (5 Minutes)

ACTIVATING STRATEGY

- Teacher posts a slide of images of citizens "engaging" in their communities. These images can be positive or negative in nature, as long as they are school appropriate. Above the images, post the following question and instruction for the students:
  - "What is the role of a citizen within their community? Discuss your thoughts with your partner using evidence from the images below."

INSTRUCTION

- Give the students enough time to discuss the activating question with their peers. Using a timer helps facilitate the conversation.
- Once time has expired, randomly select students to stand and share their responses with the rest of the class.
- Following the share out, introduce the topic for the day: "Citizens and the Local Community." Using visuals, display the definitions of *duty* and *responsibility*. Ask students to provide some examples of what these might be for them.
- Once the class has developed a foundation for what it means to be a citizen and the duties and responsibilities of citizens in the local community, present the activity for the day: a Socratic seminar.
- Explain to the students that the Socratic seminar will be driven by their ideas, their questions, and their perspectives.
- Provide students with an article that explores the role of citizens in the community from a local perspective. Have students read through the article, annotating key concepts and ideas relating to the role of citizens in the community. A sample article can be found at the following link, although personalizing the story to the students' local community will help garner buy-in: http://goo.gl/scOGU3.
- Following the study, have students generate open-ended questions relating to the article. These questions will drive the Socratic seminar, so ensure students understand how to generate open-ended questions. Sample stems:
  - How did . . .
  - What do you think . . .
  - Why did this . . .

- Once questions have been generated, have students sit in a large circle, ensuring they can see one another. Begin the seminar by explaining they will be in charge. You will ask a guiding question, but they will be driving the conversation and the dialogue with their questions and prompts. Use a timer to note rounds and redirect when necessary following each round. What is the role of a citizen in the local community? How can citizens carry out their duties and responsibilities in their local community?
    - Note: There are many variations to the Socratic seminar. More detailed instructions on Socratic seminars can be found here: https://goo.gl/7G3lfW. Be sure to familiarize yourself with this strategy prior to implementation.
- Following the seminar, ask students to reflect on the conversation. Provide each student with an index card and instruct them to respond to the following prompt: As a citizen, what contributions can/do I make in my community? What can I do in the future?
- Close out the lesson by collecting all necessary materials. Have students summarize what they have learned and clarify any issues/misconceptions they may have.

GUIDED & INDEPENDENT PRACTICE

Knowing your students' needs will dictate the guidance and independent practice you provide. Opportunities during this lesson include:

- Modeling how to annotate the news article.
- Modeling how to generate questions.
- Conducting a shortened sample round of the Socratic seminar with non-academic questions related to pop culture, current events, food, etc.

Students can also explore news stories through NewsELA (https://newsela.com/) to further their understanding and continue their examination following the lesson.

CLOSURE

- Following the seminar, ask students to reflect on the conversation. Each student will respond to the following prompt: As a citizen, what contributions can/do I make in my community? What can I do in the future?

ASSESSMENT/EVALUATION

- Students will be evaluated on their contributions to the Socratic seminar (informally) and assessed on their reflection during the closing of the lesson (formally).

MATERIALS/TECHNOLOGY

Materials

- Images of engaged citizens
- Current events/news article
- Highlighters
- Index cards

Technology

- Projector
- Desktop/Laptop

CROSS-CURRICULAR CONNECTIONS

- Teachers can collaborate with ELA and science teachers to focus the type of civic activities being evaluated in the news article. Working with a science teacher and conducting a seminar on citizens and the environment could provide links between content areas. Using the lesson as a springboard for a writing prompt in ELA can also push to foster the collaborative nature and engagement found with being a citizen in the local community.

MEETING INDIVIDUAL NEEDS OF DIVERSE LEARNERS

- ELLs – Visual aids are embedded throughout the lesson. The teacher should translate the key vocabulary words into a student's native language, as well as provide a translated copy of the article.
- If articles are pulled from sites like https://newsela.com/, the teacher can scale the lesson based on Lexile level.
- Partnering students with peers can scaffold the learning process and ensure students are held accountable while having someone to support their learning throughout the lesson.

CHARACTER EDUCATION CONNECTION

- Working collaboratively with others.
- Discussing community issues and needs.
- Understanding how citizens contribute to their communities.
- Problem solving and critical thinking.

▶ LOOKING BACK

Effective planning is one of the most important factors in becoming a successful classroom teacher. Planning social studies activities in the elementary school classroom is even more important considering the great number of responsibilities and content areas included in the curriculum, on top of all the pressure to increase test scores on standardized performance assessments. One of the easiest ways to encourage the inclusion of social studies lessons in the elementary classroom is to help teachers see the broad spectrum of topics that social studies addresses and also how the subject can be integrated with other content areas. The lessons provided in this chapter deal with a variety of social studies topics at every elementary grade level. While they are all constructed somewhat differently (narrative form, outline form, etc.), the reader may notice some common elements in the planning process. All lessons need to consider students in the classroom of different ability levels and learning styles. Teachers must always strive to help each and every student be successful in the classroom, and if an activity may prove to be difficult for certain students, consider what modifications or accommodations can be made to support learning. Also, it is imperative that teachers become aware of some internet resources that can help when planning lessons. In the suggested reading section, you will find a list of various websites that contain lesson plans, activity ideas, and valuable resources that can be used/modified to create dynamic learning opportunities. While this list is in no way comprehensive, it will provide educators with a good starting point for finding out more information about the types of lessons that are already available and potentially serve as a catalyst to your own creative lesson ideas!

EXTENSION ACTIVITY

SCENARIO

It is nearing the end of the school year at Yourtown Elementary School (YES), and you are getting excited about the summer break. As the school day comes to a close, you begin cleaning up your classroom, when in walks the principal of YES, Dr. Russell. He greets you with a pleasant smile and congratulates you on a great year of classroom instruction. Dr. Russell continues by informing you that the district superintendent, Dr. Turner, has asked for examples of outstanding lesson plans created by teachers to place on the district website. He explains that these lessons should not only be engaging but also show productive use of school technology, address multiple learning styles, and accommodate the needs of diverse learners. Dr. Russell has personally observed your wonderful and engaging social studies activities and asks you to submit one of your best lessons for this project.

TASK

For this activity, you will need to create and design a dynamic social studies activity (K–6 and topic of choice) that utilizes available technology and is engaging/challenging to all learners. Your lesson plan should have measurable learning objectives, include standards addressed, have multiple forms of assessment, and be detailed enough that other teachers in the district could implement the lesson in their classrooms. All supported resources should be cited and any original materials needed to implement the lesson provided as attachments.

CHECKING FOR UNDERSTANDING

1. Why is effective planning critical to quality classroom instruction and learning?
2. What would you describe as the characteristics of a "good" lesson plan?
3. What are some examples of supplemental resources that could improve lesson plans?
4. What are the lesson plan expectations and guidelines in your local school district?
5. Why is it important to specifically plan for accommodations of diverse learners in your lessons?

▶ **HELPFUL RESOURCES**

Watch this video about teaching historical content in the kindergarten classroom:
www.teachingchannel.org/videos/teaching-kindergarteners-social-studies

Visit this website (Video #5: Leaders, Community, and Citizens) to see an example of a first-grade classroom engaged in a similar activity:

https://www.learner.org/series/social-studies-in-action-a-teaching-practices-library-k-12/leaders-community-and-citizens/

Visit this website (Video #4: China Through Mapping) to see an example of a second-grade classroom engaged in a similar unit on China:

https://www.learner.org/series/social-studies-in-action-a-teaching-practices-library-k-12/china-through-mapping/

Watch this video of a first-grade teacher conducting a similar lesson on student identity, families, and community:

www.teachingchannel.org/videos/first-grade-social-studies

Visit this website (Video #3: Historical Change) to see an example of a first-grade lesson on the evolution of farming techniques:

https://www.learner.org/series/social-studies-in-action-a-teaching-practices-library-k-12/historical-change/

See this video for a third-grade lesson dealing with a similar topic of understanding maps and directions:

www.youtube.com/watch?v=JXYOUZbGVFU

See this video for a fourth-grade lesson dealing with a similar topic of understanding the three branches of government:

www.youtube.com/watch?v=OT6hSVTKNjE

See this video for a third-grade lesson dealing with a similar topic of understanding perimeter:

www.youtube.com/watch?v=qzUKAsjpuzA

Visit this website (Video #16: Explorations in Archeology and History) to see an example of a similar lesson on artifacts:

https://www.learner.org/series/social-studies-in-action-a-teaching-practices-library-k-12/explorations-in-archeology-and-history/

Visit this website (Video #9: Explorers in North America) to see an example of a fifth-grade lesson looking at the theme of exploration and how humans impact the environment:

https://www.learner.org/series/social-studies-in-action-a-teaching-practices-library-k-12/explorers-in-north-america/

Visit this website (Video #12: Using Primary Sources) to see an example of a fifth-grade lesson on primary and secondary sources:

https://www.learner.org/series/social-studies-in-action-a-teaching-practices-library-k-12/using-primary-sources/

View this video about a fifth-grade class engaged in a Civil War Day reenactment:

www.youtube.com/watch?v=LiNSsBlGMLg

View this video on a sixth-grade lesson covering immigration and migration:

www.teachingchannel.org/videos/teaching-human-migration

See this video on a lesson having students explore the concept of democracy and citizenship through art:

www.teachingchannel.org/videos/teaching-democracy-through-art

PBS Teacher Source: The Public Broadcasting Service website contains a teacher-friendly section with over 1,400 lessons and activities in five broad areas, including arts and literature, health and fitness, math, science and technology, and social studies.

Smithsonian Education page: This website contains links to teacher resources (including lesson plans) as well as information about professional development sponsored by the Smithsonian, a calendar of important events, and information about current and future Smithsonian exhibits.

TheGateway.org: This website is a consortium effort to provide educators with quick and easy access to a substantial collection of educational materials found on various federal, state, university, nonprofit, and commercial internet sites.

American Memory Learning Page: This website compiles many lessons and activities relating to the Library of Congress's American Memory collections. It is an excellent place to visit for primary resource documents and photos to supplement social studies lessons.

Teachers.net: Series of free lesson plans to incorporate into social studies instruction for all elementary grade levels. There is also an interactive discussion board by state to help educators stay in touch with the issues most relevant to their classrooms.

Index

Note: Page numbers in *italics* indicate a figure and page numbers in **bold** indicate a table on the corresponding page.

About the Authors

▶ **William B. Russell III** is Professor of Social Science Education at the University of Central Florida, Orlando. He teaches social studies–related courses and serves as the Social Science Education PhD coordinator. Dr. Russell serves as the Director for the International Society for the Social Studies and is the Editor-in-Chief of the preeminent journal in the field of social studies education, *The Journal of Social Studies Research*. His research interests include alternative methods for teaching social studies, pre-service teacher education, and teaching with film. Dr. Russell has published numerous books and peer-reviewed journal articles related to social studies education.

▶ **Stewart Waters** is Associate Professor of Social Science Education in the Department of Theory and Practice in Teacher Education at the University of Tennessee, Knoxville. His research interests include alternative methods for teaching social studies, character education, visual literacy, social studies curriculum, and teaching with film. Dr. Waters is the Conference Coordinator for the International Society for the Social Studies and is the Associate Editor for *The Journal of Social Studies Research*. Dr. Waters has authored numerous books and peer-reviewed journal articles related to social studies education.

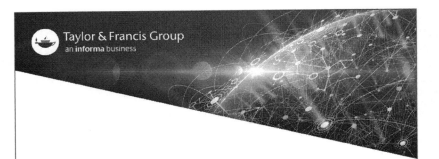

Made in the USA
Middletown, DE
18 January 2022

59053241R00170